Forensic Neuropsychology in Practice

Forensic Neuropsychology in Practice

A guide to assessment and legal processes

Edited by

Susan Young
*Institute of Psychiatry,
King's College London*

Michael Kopelman
*Institute of Psychiatry,
King's College London*

Gisli Gudjonsson
*Institute of Psychiatry,
King's College London*

OXFORD
UNIVERSITY PRESS

OXFORD
UNIVERSITY PRESS

Great Clarendon Street, Oxford OX2 6DP

Oxford University Press is a department of the University of Oxford.
It furthers the University's objective of excellence in research, scholarship,
and education by publishing worldwide in

Oxford New York

Auckland Cape Town Dar es Salaam Hong Kong Karachi
Kuala Lumpur Madrid Melbourne Mexico City Nairobi
New Delhi Shanghai Taipei Toronto

With offices in

Argentina Austria Brazil Chile Czech Republic France Greece
Guatemala Hungary Italy Japan Poland Portugal Singapore
South Korea Switzerland Thailand Turkey Ukraine Vietnam

Oxford is a registered trade mark of Oxford University Press
in the UK and in certain other countries

Published in the United States
by Oxford University Press Inc., New York

© Oxford University Press, 2009

The moral rights of the author have been asserted
Database right Oxford University Press (maker)

First edition published 2009

All rights reserved. No part of this publication may be reproduced,
stored in a retrieval system, or transmitted, in any form or by any means,
without the prior permission in writing of Oxford University Press,
or as expressly permitted by law, or under terms agreed with the appropriate
reprographics rights organization. Enquiries concerning reproduction
outside the scope of the above should be sent to the Rights Department,
Oxford University Press, at the address above

You must not circulate this book in any other binding or cover
and you must impose this same condition on any acquirer

British Library Cataloguing in Publication Data
Data available

Library of Congress Cataloging-in-Publication-Data
Forensic neuropsychology in practice : a guide to assessment and legal processes /
edited by Susan Young, Michael Kopelman, Gisli Gudjonsson.
     p. ; cm.
  Includes bibliographical references and index.
  ISBN 978-0-19-856683-0 (alk. paper)
 1. Forensic neuropsychology. I. Young, Susan, 1957– II. Kopelman, Michael D.
III. Gudjonsson, Gisli H.
   [DNLM: 1. Forensic Psychiatry, 2. Neuropsychology. W 740 F7144 2009]
RA1147.5.F6695 2009
614'.15—dc22
                                                                    2009016314

Typeset by Cepha Imaging Private Ltd., Bangalore, India
Printed in Great Britain
on acid-free paper by the MPG Books Group, Bodmin and King's Lynn

ISBN 978–0–19–856–6830

10 9 8 7 6 5 4 3 2 1

Oxford University Press makes no representation, express or implied, that the drug dosages in
this book are correct. Readers must therefore always check the product information and clinical
procedures with the most up-to-date published product information and data sheets provided by
the manufacturers and the most recent codes of conduct and safety regulations. The authors and the
publishers do not accept responsibility or legal liability for any errors in the text or for the misuse or
misapplication of material in this work. Except where otherwise stated, drug dosages and
recommendations are for the non-pregnant adult who is not breast-feeding.

Foreword

Substantial developments in neuropsychology in the past few years have been fuelled by advances in cognitive neuroscience and continued increases in the sophistication of neuropsychological measurement techniques. A key part of this development in relation to forensic neuropsychology has been a greater understanding of different neurocognitive disorders, providing the basis for integrating such information into clinical practice within a legal setting. This is not just in relation to behavioural and cognitive abnormalities but also a deeper theoretical understanding of neurocognitive *phenomena*. This book reflects these advances across a spectrum of neurological and neuropsychiatric conditions, including, for example, memory disorders, epilepsy, traumatic brain injury, attention deficit hyperactivity disorder (ADHD), and autism. Here, neuropsychology is a necessarily multi-disciplinary endeavour, taking into account, on the one hand, the brain correlates of behaviour and cognitive function, with concurrent psychiatric and neurological issues, and, on the other hand, legal implications within a social and moral framework. The substantial challenge for clinicians working in this field is to ensure that their inferences from neuropsychological observation and data are well grounded in scientific and practical knowledge, and the book highlights the fact that a narrow psychometric approach without theoretical understanding is insufficient. Rather it points us in the right direction, bringing together a number of leading forensic UK-based experts to present a coherent account of specific aspects of this discipline.

The structure of the book is crafted to focus on different clinical disorders, having set the scene by a lucid neurocognitive account of aggression. By considering different conditions in turn, the chapters exploit the interlocking concepts that cross disciplines in this field. The issue of intellectual disability illustrates how cognitive dysfunction may determine reliability of interview or interrogation and considers the factors that might influence capacity to act as a witness within a forensic context; likewise people with ADHD may be especially vulnerable in their interface with criminal justice systems and a careful assessment of their clinical condition may help explain facets of their behaviour in different settings; in autistic spectrum disorder understanding the way a person reacts in a complex social or personal situation may influence the process of legal procedure, taking into account the interface with someone with social disability. The chapters on memory disorder, epilepsy, alcohol and drug misuse, head injury, and malingering underline the importance of diagnostic interpretation though a multi-disciplinary account of fundamental neurocognitive processes, as well as tackling the ubiquitous legal issues concerning understanding responsibility and intent. These chapters stress the need for considered clinical judgement and are illustrated with case studies that provide useful information on how to approach assessment. A final chapter concerns factors to consider when acting as an expertise witness, based on extensive professional practice.

This book is presented by three editors distinguished in forensic psychology and neuropsychiatry. It is successful in distilling knowledge in this field, drawing on a wealth of practical experience, and presented in a manner that will appeal both to those seeking an introduction and to those wishing to increase their understanding of the complex issues underpinning forensic neuropsychology.

Professor Robin G. Morris
King's College Institute of Psychiatry, London

Acknowledgements

This book is a synthesis of expert experience and we are grateful to our contributors for sharing their wealth of knowledge in their respective fields. Together, their contributions have culminated into the development of this unique reference book and practical guide to steer the reader through the challenges and pitfalls that may befall an expert witness walking the paths of the justice process. We would also like to thank Clare Pearse and Sian Roberts for their assistance with editing. Finally, we would like to thank our publishers, in particular Carol Maxwell and Martin Baum, for their support and patience.

Susan Young
Michael Kopelman
Gisli Gudjonsson

Contents

List of contributors *xi*
List of abbreviations for legal references *xiii*
List of abbreviations *xiv*

1 Introduction *1*
Susan Young, Gisli Gudjonsson, and Michael Kopelman

2 The neuropsychology of aggression and violence *7*
Jessica Bramham and Seamus O'Ceallaigh

3 Intellectual disability *53*
Glynis Murphy and Isabel Clare

4 Attention-deficit hyperactivity disorder *81*
Susan Young

5 Autism spectrum conditions *109*
Isabel Clare and Marc Woodbury-Smith

6 Amnesia *135*
Natalie Pyszora, Eli Jaldow, and Michael Kopelman

7 Epilepsy and automatism *165*
Jonathan Bird, Margaret Newson, and Krystyna Dembny

8 Alcohol and drug misuse *193*
Helen Miles and Andrew Johns

9 Traumatic brain injury *223*
Rodger Wood

10 The role of the expert witness and acquired brain injury *247*
Graham Powell

11 Suboptimal effort and malingering *267*
Gisli Gudjonsson and Susan Young

12 Professional issues *301*
Jacqueline Wheatcroft, Gisli Gudjonsson, and Susan Young

13 Conclusion: Themes and issues *331*
Michael Kopelman, Susan Young, and Gisli Gudjonsson

Index *337*

List of contributors

Jonathan Bird
Consultant Neuropsychiatrist,
Department of Neuropsychiatry,
The Burden Centre,
Frenchay Hospital,
Bristol BS16 1JB, UK

Jessica Bramham
University College Dublin,
School of Psychology,
Newman Building,
Belfield,
Dublin 4, Ireland

Isabel Clare
University of Cambridge,
Department of Psychiatry,
Douglas House,
18b Trumpington Road,
Cambridge CB2 2AH, UK

Krystyna Dembny
Department of Neuropsychiatry,
The Burden Centre,
Frenchay Hospital,
Bristol BS16 1JB, UK

Gisli Gudjonsson
Department of Psychology,
Institute of Psychiatry,
De Crespigny Park,
Denmark Hill,
London SE5 8AF, UK

Eli Jaldow
Neuropsychiatry and Memory
Disorders Clinic,
Adamson Centre,
South Wing Block 8,
St Thomas' Hospital,
Westminster Bridge Road,
London SE1 7EH, UK

Andrew Johns
River House,
Bethlem Royal Hospital,
Monks Orchard Road,
Beckenham,
Kent BR3 3BX, UK

Michael Kopelman
Section of Neuropsychiatry,
King's College London,
Institute of Psychiatry,
St Thomas' Hospital,
Westminster Bridge Road,
London SE1 7EH, UK

Helen Miles
Trevor Gibbens Unit,
Kent Forensic Psychiatry Service,
Hermitage Lane,
Maidstone, Kent
ME16 9PH, UK

Glynis Murphy
University of Lancaster,
Institute of Health Research,
Alexandra Square,
Lancaster LA1 4YT, UK

Margaret Newson
Department of Neuropsychology,
The Burden Centre,
Frenchay Hospital,
Bristol BS16 1JB, UK

Seamus O'Ceallaigh
University College Dublin,
School of Psychology,
Newman Building,
Belfield,
Dublin 4, Ireland

Graham Powell
Chartered Clinical Psychologist,
9 Devonshire Place,
London W1G 6HU, UK

Natalie Pyszora
Consultant Forensic Psychiatrist,
Broadmoor Hospital,
Crowthorne,
Berks RG45 7EG, UK

Jacqueline Wheatcroft
Psychology and Social Change
Department,
Manchester Metropolitan University,
Hathersage Road,
Manchester M13 0JA, UK

Rodger Wood
Consultant Clinical
Neuropsychologist,
Swansea University,
Singleton Park,
Swansea SA2 8PP, UK

Marc Woodbury-Smith
c/o Dr Isabel Clare,
University of Cambridge,
Department of Psychiatry,
Douglas House,
18b Trumpington Road,
Cambridge CB2 2AH, UK

Susan Young
Department of Forensic Mental
Health Science,
Institute of Psychiatry,
PO Box 23,
De Crespigny Park,
London SE5 8AF, UK

List of abbreviations for legal references

AC	Appeal Court
All E R	All England Reports
Col L R	Columbia Law Review
Crim L R	Criminal Law Reports
DLR	Dominion Law Reports
EWCA	Court of Appeal of England and Wales
LQR	Law Quarterly Reports
QB	Queen's Bench
RTR	Road Traffic Reports
SCCR	Supreme Court of Canada Reports
UKHL	United Kingdom House of Lords
WLR	Weekly Law Reports

List of abbreviations

ADHD	attention-deficit hyperactivity disorder	GHB	gamma-hydroxybutyrate
ADI-R	Autism Diagnostic Interview – Revised	GSS	Gudjonsson Suggestibility Scale
		HFA	high-functioning autism
ADOS-G	Autism Diagnostic Observation Scale – Generic	HPC	Health Professionals Council
		ICD-10	International Classification of Diseases and Related Health Problems 10th revision
AS	Asperger's syndrome		
ASC	autism spectrum conditions		
AUDIT	Alcohol Use Disorders Identification Test	MacCAT-CA	MacArthur Competence Assessment Tool – Criminal Adjudication
BADDS	Brown Attention Deficit Disorder Scales	MAPPA	Multi-Agency Public Protection Panel Arrangements
BADS	Behavioural Assessment of Dysexecutive Syndrome	MCMI-III	Millon Clinical Multiaxial Inventory – Third
BVS-II	British Picture Vocabulary Scale II	MET	Multiple Errands Test
CARB	Computerized Assessment and Response Bias Test	MMPI-2	Minnesota Multiphasic Personality Inventory – Second Edition
CAST-MR	Competence Assessment for Standing Trial for Defendants with Mental Retardation	MND	malingering of neurocognitive dysfunction
		MRI	magnetic resonance imaging
CPD	continuing professional development	NART-R	National Adult Reading Test – Restandardised
CPR	Civil Procedure Rules	PACE	Police and Criminal Evidence Act
CT	computerized tomography		
DEX	Dysexecutive Questionnaire		
DISCO	Diagnostic Interview for Social and Communication Disorders	PCL-R	Psychopathy Checklist – Revised
		PDS	Paulhus Deception Scales
DSM-IV	*Diagnostic and Statistical Manual of Mental Disorders – Fourth Edition*	PET	positron emission tomography
		PTA	Post-traumatic amnesia
EF	executive functioning	RBMT-3	Rivermead Behavioural Memory Test – Third Edition
FBS	Fake Bad Scale		
FIT-R	Fitness Interview Test – Revised	RMT	Rey 15-Item Test
		SCQ	Social Communication Questionnaire
fMRI	functional magnetic resonance imaging		
		SIMS	Structured Inventory of Malingered Symptomatology
GCS	Gudjonsson Compliance Scale		

SIRS	Structured Interview of Reported Symptoms	VIP	Validity Indicator Profile
SPECT	single proton emission computed tomography	WAIS-III	Wechsler Adult Intelligence Scale – Third Edition
SVT	Symptom Validity Test	WKS	Wernicke–Korsakoff syndrome
ToM	Theory of Mind	WTAR	Wechsler Test of Adult Reading
TOMM	Test of Memory Malingering		

Chapter 1

Introduction

Susan Young, Gisli Gudjonsson, and Michael Kopelman

Clinical neuropsychology is a sub-speciality of clinical psychology. It is comprised of the application of neuropsychological knowledge and skills to the assessment, management, and rehabilitation of people who have impaired nervous system or brain functions due to a range of causes, including congenital, developmental, illness and injury. Forensic psychology, including forensic neuropsychology, can be defined as *'that branch of applied psychology which is concerned with the collection, examination and presentation of evidence for judicial purposes'* (Haward, 1981, p. 21). Within this definition, Haward identifies four key roles for psychologists: clinical, experimental, actuarial, and advisory, which have a range of applications to legal assessments (Gudjonsson & Haward, 1998). As far as forensic neuropsychology is concerned, the key contribution is a clinical role (i.e. an evaluation of the client's neuropsychological functions and other clinical conditions), followed by the advisory role (i.e. giving advice about the strengths and limitations of another expert's evaluation or testimony). During the past decade, the actuarial role has increasingly come to the fore with the recognition that many clients may perform below their actual abilities due to suboptimal effort or malingering.

There is evidence that psychologists are increasingly being asked to prepare reports for legal purposes, and the greatest number of referrals involves personal injury cases (Gudjonsson, 1996, 2007). In compensation cases, the key questions are *'whether a defendant's wrongdoing has caused the plaintiff's brain injury or disability'* (Valciukas, 1995, p. 7), the extent of the injury, its duration and management, and the deleterious impact upon the plaintiff's life. Neuropsychology also has an important contribution to make in criminal cases in relation to both *actus reus* (i.e. commission of the offence) and *mens rea* issues (i.e. the mental state of the defendant at the time of the commission of the offence and the presence or absence of a 'guilty mind'). Here, *'the unique contribution of the neuropsychologist is to render an opinion as to whether the events leading to the defendant's charges can or cannot be explained by well-established facts in neurosciences and clinical neuropsychology*' (Valciukas, 1995, p. 251). Schaapveld (2008) has recently shown the important contribution that neuropsychologists can make to the *mens rea* issues (i.e. the concept of 'intent'), whilst Devonshire (2008) focuses on the neuropsychological aspects of impulsivity and how these can be assessed. Impulsivity is an important concept in many criminal cases and is a key feature in a number of diagnostic disorders, including attention-deficit hyperactivity disorder (ADHD), antisocial personality disorder, and borderline disorder.

Other important contributions of a neuropsychological evaluation are in the areas of competencies. Concepts of legal competency focus on functional abilities, which refer to what *'an individual can do or accomplish, as well as knowledge, understanding, or beliefs that may be necessary for the accomplishment'* (Grisso, 2003, pp. 23–24). Like other legal decisions, these are determined by statute and case law, but here legal codes and practice rely on mental health professionals to assist the courts with their decision-making (Grisso, 2003). In the UK and the USA, the three most common types of legal competencies in criminal cases requiring the services of mental health experts are capacities relating to pleading and standing trial, waiver of rights during custodial interrogation and issues to do with disputed confessions, and criminal responsibility (Grisso, 2003; Gudjonsson, 2007). Heilbronner and Frumkin (2003) have emphasized the need for neuropsychologists and forensic psychologists to work collaboratively on individual cases. Gudjonsson (2006) has similarly advocated that, when appropriate, psychologists and psychiatrists work collaboratively on cases.

In this connection, forensic neuropsychologists are most likely to work closely with forensic psychiatrists and with neuropsychiatrists, and such teamwork, meshing complementary skills, can be enormously rewarding. Forensic psychiatrists have great experience in working with offenders with psychiatric disorders, particularly psychotic conditions and personality problems. Neuropsychiatrists have specialized knowledge of neurological conditions affecting cognition and behaviour. There is much information of value to the forensic neuropsychologist in standard texts, such as *Lishman's Organic Psychiatry*, 4th edition (David et al., 2009), as well as many standard texts in neuropsychology and neuroscience (e.g. Beaumont, 2008; Squire *et al.*, 2008). Indeed, some of the debates and controversies within empirical neuropsychology occasionally spill over into the courtroom. However, these books provide general background texts, whereas the present one focuses specifically on forensic neuropsychology in relation to court and other legal matters.

The neuropsychological evaluation is typically based on multiple sources of information, including comprehensive neuropsychological testing focusing on intellectual, memory, and executive functions, and level of effort (Lezak *et al.*, 2004). The assessment is grounded in neuroscience, but the most difficult part of the assessment is often the interpretation of the neuropsychological evaluation within the legally relevant criteria (Frumkin, 2008).

As editors, we all have different expertise and knowledge, each complementing the other in its span of forensic and clinical psychology and neuropsychiatry. We are frequently consulted by colleagues working within the mental health system, within the prison and probation service, and also within the legal profession for advice about an individual's vulnerabilities and problems. This led us to realize that forensic neuropsychology is often viewed as a mysterious world that has tools and a language of its own. This view is not restricted to that held by individuals outside our respective professions; it is also held by many practitioners working within our professions. Forensic neuropsychology is regarded as a highly specialized area that requires 'special' expertise and training both to administer neuropsychological assessments and to interpret the findings. Yet most clinical psychologists have the core competency to conduct some of these assessments and/or interpret the findings. What they lack is the confidence, practice and expertise.

This book was born from our recognition that what was needed was a practical resource for practitioners and trainees that provided down-to-earth, pragmatic information and guidance. We wished to produce a book to help practitioners grapple with the clinical and neuropsychological problems in the field whilst negotiating the legal labyrinths involved in issues such as competency, fitness to plead and stand trial, mental capacity, and mitigation. From a clinical perspective, this often meant that practitioners were struggling to tease apart the effects of brain damage, depression, and post-traumatic stress disorder, whilst also weighing up the issue of effort and malingering. We aimed to provide a reference book for practitioners—whether this be at the point one suspects there is a particular problem/issue and a need to find out more about how to assess it or whether to help one understand the methodology used by someone else and interpret the findings. Our aim was to 'demystify' forensic neuropsychology in practice, whether this is required by those conducting assessments or those seeking to understand them.

Once we had decided on our aims, the next decision involved us determining what topics to include and how to find an appropriate balance between issues arising in criminal courts and those that occur in civil cases. This was not easy and we have had to be selective. We could not include every topic and so made our decision based on our experience of the issues and topics that are most commonly raised. These topics are not exhaustive, nor are they always mutually exclusive. We 'set the scene' with a chapter that reviews the neuropsychology of aggression, violence, and homicide, followed by three chapters on developmental disorders (learning disability, attention deficit disorder, and autism spectrum conditions). Then we moved on to chapters providing current thinking and practice on 'traditional' problems (e.g. amnesia, epilepsy, alcohol and drug use, and traumatic brain injury). The three final substantive chapters focus on expert testimony, a detailed review of issues and tests related to assessing suboptimal effort and malingering, and on the ethical and professional issues that may arise in relation to the neuropsychological/forensic evaluation.

We have brought together chapters by leading practitioners and clinicians, most of whom are also leaders in related research. The authors were asked to write a synthesis of key knowledge and best practice on their assigned topic, rather than an encyclopaedic review of the literature. Whilst we did not want to be prescriptive to our authors as they are the experts within their own fields, we asked them to adhere to the fundamental practical ethos of the book. We asked that they write in an accessible and understandable way when writing about the psychological/legal issues and gave pragmatic and up-to-date material on the law and incapacity arising out of neuropsychological problems. We asked that they give clear guidelines with regard to specific neurological and neuropsychological conditions and include case studies to illustrate specific problems. It was intended that each chapter would help practitioners recognize a problem, outline the methodology of conducting specific assessments, interpret findings and be aware about the pitfalls that may occur. Each chapter has included information about both criminal and civil aspects, with the balance between these sections varying from chapter to chapter. Thus, the essential value of the book is that we have addressed what really matters to practitioners, disseminated key knowledge about the clinical and legal issues, and drawn conclusions about how such key knowledge might best be applied.

The target readership is for practitioners in clinical and forensic psychology and psychiatry and neuropsychiatry, who are working, or wish to work, in these important areas of forensic consultancy and who need a working knowledge of neuropsychological assessment and legal processes, or an update on key developments. Secondly, we also wanted the book to be of value to clinicians interested in forensic neuropsychology but who need a convenient and authoritative resource for their practical and teaching courses. Thirdly, we hope that the book will be a useful source book and reference volume for lawyers. Forensic neuropsychology is an evolving and developing field. This book breaks new grounds by providing its readers with a thought-provoking and pragmatic guide to practice.

References

Beaumont, J. B. (2008). *Introduction to Neuropsychology*, 2nd edn. New York: The Guildford Press.

David, A., Fleminger, S., Kopelman, M. D., Lovestone, S., and Mellors, J. (2009). *Lishman's Organic Psychiatry*, 4th edn, Oxford: Blackwell Press.

Devonshire, P. (2008). Impulsivity: Multidimensional or unitary concept. *Forensic Update*, **93**:35–41.

Frumkin, I. B. (2008). Psychological evaluation in Miranda waiver and confession cases. In R. Denny and J. Sullivan (eds), *Clinical Neuropsychology in the Criminal Forensic Setting*, pp. 135–175. New York: Guilford Press.

Grisso, T. (2003). *Evaluating competencies: Forensic Assessments and Instruments*, 2nd edn). New York: Kluwer Academic/Plenum Publishers.

Gudjonsson, G. H. (1996). Psychological evidence in Court. Results from the 1995 Survey. *The Psychologist*, **5**:213–217.

Gudjonsson, G. H. (2006). Disputed confessions and miscarriages of justice in Britain: Expert psychological and psychiatric evidence in Court of Appeal. *The Manitoba Law Journal*, **31**:489–521.

Gudjonsson, G. H. (2007). Psychologists as expert witnesses: The 2007 BPS Survey. *Forensic Update*, **92**:23–29.

Gudjonsson, G. H. and Haward, L. R.C (1998). *Forensic Psychology*. London: Batsford.

Haward, L. R.C (1981). *Forensic Psychology: A Guide to Practice*. London: Routledge.

Heilbronner, R., and Frumkin, I. B. (2003). Neuropsychology and forensic psychology: Working collaboratively in criminal cases. *Journal of Forensic Neuropsychology*, **3**:5–12.

Lezak, M. D., Howieson, D. B., and Loring, D. W. (2004). *Neuropsychological Assessment*. Oxford: Oxford University Press.

Schaapveld, P. (2008). The guilty mind: A neuropsychological perspective. *Forensic Update*, **93**:28–34.

Squire, L. R., Albright T., Bloom, F., Gage, F., and Spitzer, N. (eds) (2008) Encyclopedia of Neuroscience. Oxford: Elsevier.

Valciukas, J. A. (1995). *Forensic Neuropsychology: Conceptual Foundations and Clinical Practice*. London: The Haworth Press.

Chapter 2

The neuropsychology of aggression and violence

Jessica Bramham and Seamus O'Ceallaigh

The term aggression encompasses a wide range of hostile, injurious, or destructive behaviours. Violence is often used more narrowly to describe aggressive behaviour that results in physical harm to others, but it may also include destruction of property. The terms aggression and violence have often been used interchangeably to describe a wide range of behaviours, resulting in considerable difficulties when attempting to arrive at precise definitions. Many early studies used broad definitions of violence that are likely to have separable mechanisms and risk factors. However, more recent studies have differentiated between reactive and instrumental aggression (Blair, 2001). Reactive aggression (also referred to as affective or impulsive aggression) occurs when a frustrating or threatening event triggers the aggressive act. The act is carried out without any regard for a potential goal, and is frequently associated with induced anger. In contrast, instrumental aggression is purposeful and directed, with a specific goal in mind. The goal may include increasing one's status within a hierarchy or obtaining the possessions of another. Throughout this chapter, aggression and violence are described together unless more detailed information has been provided about the specific behaviours of interest, although neuropsychological mechanisms for reactive and instrumental versions are considered separately.

The risk of aggression and violence is increased by a range of biological, social, and psychological factors (Raine, 2002). Replicable psychosocial factors have been delineated over the past 50 years, and research into biological risk factors has accelerated during the last 15 years. Although aggressive and violent behaviour can best be understood through the integration of disparate research fields, surprisingly little is known about how different sets of risk factors interact to predispose an individual to aggressive behaviour. The most well-described interactive biosocial effect involves birth complications and developmental difficulties interacting with a harsh early home environment leading to a predisposition to adulthood violence (Dodge, 2000). However, little is known about the mechanisms underlying this interaction (Phelps & McClintock, 1994). A practical barrier to well-integrated research has been the failure of most psychosocial research to take into account biological variables, and vice versa, where psychosocial variables have been seen as covariates or 'nuisance variables' in biological research. If interactive effects are not investigated, non-significant main effect results may lead to the erroneous conclusion that the variables in question are of no aetiological consequence (Raine, 2002). Although the majority of the research presented throughout this chapter is from a biological and neuropsychological perspective, it is important for a forensic neuropsychologist to remain aware of additional psychosocial factors that may also influence an individual's disposition towards aggression and violence, such as exposure to violence in childhood.

There is a wide range of psychiatric and neurological disorders in which aggression and violence may be encountered. This chapter will begin by first describing the disorders associated with aggression and violence and briefly review the relevant neuropsychological literature involving traditional tests, and also emotion recognition and social cognition paradigms. Secondly, explorations of the underpinning neural circuitry of aggression and violence, including structural and functional neuroimaging studies, will be described. The evidence regarding neural circuitry and neuropsychological studies has been assimilated to develop theories to explain reactive and instrumental aggression, and these are reviewed in the second half of the chapter. Finally, issues that a forensic neuropsychologist may need to consider are discussed, including possible instructions from a lawyer, considerations in the courtroom and relevant legal concepts.

Disorders associated with aggression and violence

Aggression and violence can occur in several psychiatric and neurological conditions. These conditions are reviewed in this section with regard to the rates of aggressive and violent behaviour and relevant associated neuropsychological deficits. Antisocial behaviour is a cardinal feature of conduct disorder and antisocial personality disorder, whereas in other conditions such as acquired brain injury, learning disability, and dementia, aggression and violence are exhibited less frequently. It should be borne in mind that these disorders may not be mutually exclusive; for example, an individual with antisocial personality disorder may subsequently sustain a head injury or develop dementia. It is therefore always important for a forensic neuropsychologist to consider both premorbid features and current presentation in their assessment and formulation of a case.

Conduct disorder

Conduct disorder is a disruptive behaviour disorder as defined by the *Diagnostic and Statistical Manual of Mental Disorders—Fourth Edition* (DSM-IV; American Psychiatric Association, 1994). It is diagnosed on the basis of a repetitive and persistent pattern of behaviour that violates the basic rights of others or the rules of society. Such behaviours include aggressive conduct that causes or threatens physical harm to other people or animals, destruction of property, deceitfulness or theft, and serious violations of rules. The onset of conduct disorder can be from the age of 5 or 6 years old, with earlier childhood onset associated with worse outcome than adolescent onset (American Psychiatric Association, 1994). Studies of childhood aggression suggest that aggressive behaviour is relatively stable over time for up to two-thirds of cases (Richman et al., 1982). Furthermore, approximately 50% of children with conduct disorder continue to display antisocial behaviours in adulthood (Webster-Stratton & Dahl, 1995).

Neuropsychological studies of conduct disorder seem to suggest an association between antisocial behaviour and cognitive variables (e.g. Moffitt & Henry, 1989; Gorenstein, 1990). Greater neuropsychological impairment has been associated with earlier onset of delinquency and is predictive of later antisocial behaviours (Moffitt et al., 1994; Raine et al., 2005). The most consistent finding when comparing individuals with conduct disorder with healthy individuals is deficits in verbal abilities (e.g. Linz et al., 1990; Braggio et al., 1993). Aggression may arise because individuals with poor verbal communication skills are less able to use verbal mediation to resolve interpersonal conflicts (Linares-Orama, 2005). In addition, some studies have also identified executive functioning deficits in conduct disorder groups (e.g. Lueger & Gill, 1990), including attentional difficulties (e.g. Hooper & Brown, 1995). These relative deficits occur in the absence of differences in motor, sensory, visual–perceptual or memory functions (Miller, 1988; Moffitt, 1993; Hooper & Brown, 1995; Dery et al., 1999). It has therefore been proposed that specific neuropsychological deficits in verbal abilities and executive functioning are a significant risk factor for conduct disorder.

However, many conduct disorder neuropsychological studies are confounded by the high rates of comorbidity of attention-deficit hyperactivity disorder (ADHD) (Manuzza et al., 1989). ADHD is characterized by hyperactivity and poor response inhibition and attention, and these characteristics may independently be associated with increased risk of antisocial behaviour (Taylor et al., 1996; Bambinski et al., 1999). Furthermore, a diagnosis of ADHD in childhood is among the most important predictors of offending behaviour in adulthood and incarceration (Manuzza et al., 1989; Collins & White, 2002). Chapter 4 discusses the association between ADHD and offending in more detail. It could therefore be argued that the relationship between conduct disorder and aggression and violence is better explained in terms of the third factor of ADHD. However, in a comparison of neuropsychological performance of adolescents with conduct disorder with and without ADHD, the results indicated that the presence of conduct disorder explained differences in comparison with healthy controls on language tasks but not executive functions (Dery et al., 1999). These findings suggest that conduct disorder is most strongly associated with verbal deficits, whereas ADHD adds further executive functioning difficulties such as impulsivity.

Deficits in social communication and cognition have also been identified in children with conduct disorder (Gilmour et al., 2004). They have been shown to exhibit impaired recognition of emotional facial expressions (Blair et al., 2001a). In addition, they have been found to encode fewer social cues (Dodge & Tomlin, 1987) and misinterpret social cues when interacting with peers, particularly in attributing hostile intentions to others' behaviour; for example, they may perceive a neutral situation as having hostile intent (Dodge, 1980; Slaby & Guerra, 1988). Children with conduct disorder also seem to experience deficiencies in social problem-solving skills whereby they generate fewer alternative solutions, seek less information, and anticipate fewer consequences than children without conduct disorder (Renshaw & Asher, 1983; Webster-Stratton & Dahl, 1995). Theory-of-mind deficits have been exhibited by 'hard-to-manage' preschoolers who showed poor prediction or recall of a false belief (Hughes et al., 1998). Such difficulties may lead individuals to interpret behaviour in a literal way and to misunderstand intentions. Given that difficulties with both emotional recognition and theory of mind are characteristics of autistic spectrum disorders, this may explain why there are elevated rates of aggression and violence among this client group (see Chapter 5). However, in a later study of 'hard-to-manage' preschool children, Hughes et al. (2000) found that although mental-state understanding was not significantly correlated with antisocial behaviour, there was a strong association with executive functioning. These findings suggest that aggressive behaviour in young, disruptive children is more likely to be due to a failure of response inhibition than solely to problems in social cognition per se, although the combination of these impairments is likely to increase the risk of aggression and violence further.

Antisocial personality disorder

Antisocial personality disorder is often regarded as a 'grown-up' form of conduct disorder. In order to receive a diagnosis of antisocial personality disorder, it is necessary for the individual to have met the criteria for diagnosis of conduct disorder prior to the age of 15 years (American Psychiatric Association, 1994). Also 25–50% of children with conduct disorder go on to be diagnosed with antisocial personality disorder (Robins & Regier, 1991) and many individuals with the disorder become involved in the criminal justice system. In a sample of prison inmates in the UK, half were shown to meet DSM-IV criteria for antisocial personality disorder (Singleton *et al.*, 1998) and over a third of maximum-security psychiatric hospital inpatients also met the criteria (Coid, 1992).

Violent offenders with antisocial personality disorder have been shown to exhibit deficits in comparison with healthy controls in a wide range of memory and executive functioning tasks including verbal fluency and category fluency tests (e.g. Malloy *et al.*, 1989), qualitative scores on the Porteus Mazes Test (e.g. Porteus, 1945), the Stroop interference test (e.g. Gorenstein, 1982), Part B of the Trail-Making Test (e.g. Hart *et al.*, 1990), and perseverative error scores on the Wisconsin Card Sorting Test (e.g. Sutker *et al.*, 1983). These findings have been reviewed by Moffitt & Henry (1989) and Dolan (1994). In a meta-analysis of neuropsychological studies examining the relationship between antisocial behaviour and executive functioning, it was found that antisocial groups performed 0.62 standard deviations (i.e. a medium to large effect size; Cohen, 1988) worse on executive functioning tests than normal controls (Morgan & Lilienfeld, 2000). This link between poor executive functioning and aggressive or violent behaviour has been developed to provide an explanation for reactive aggression in terms of poor inhibitory control and problem-solving abilities.

Psychopathy

Psychopathy is a form of antisocial personality disorder characterized by a constellation of personality traits that includes features such as a lack of remorse or sincerity, dishonesty, and impoverished affective reactions (Cleckley, 1941/1988; Hare, 1991). It is often assessed using diagnostic tools such as the Psychopathy Checklist—Revised (PCL-R; Hare, 1991), which includes a greater number of emotional symptoms than antisocial personality disorder, where the emphasis is on behavioural characteristics. It is a rarer diagnosis than antisocial personality disorder and is estimated to include 20% of prisoners with antisocial personality disorder (Hare, 1998). Consistent with antisocial personality disorder, individuals with psychopathy display behaviour that can be interpreted as reactive aggression, but additionally they are more likely to exhibit instrumental aggression in the absence of a heightened emotional state (Cornell *et al.*, 1996).

When comparing criminals with psychopathy with non-psychopathic criminals (as classified by the PCL-R), several studies have not replicated the findings of standard executive functioning deficits that have been reported in 'general' criminal populations (Hare, 1984; Hoffman *et al.*, 1987; Hart *et al.*, 1990; LaPierre *et al.*, 1995). The neuropsychological deficits associated with criminals with psychopathy (compared with non-psychopathic criminals) seem to be related to ventromedial prefrontal cortex functions, which are assessed by visual go/no-go tasks (LaPierre *et al.*, 1995; Dinn & Harris, 2000), rather than dorsolateral prefrontal cortex functions, which are assessed using traditional 'executive function' tests (Smith & Jonides, 1999). Individuals with psychopathy have also been shown to exhibit impairments on tasks specifically associated with orbitofrontal cortex functioning such as response reversal and related extinction tasks (Blair *et al.*, 2001b; Budhani & Blair, 2005; Budhani *et al.*, 2006), and olfactory identification (LaPierre *et al.*, 1995). These findings suggest a specific role of the orbitofrontal cortex and ventromedial prefrontal cortex in psychopathy.

However, individuals with psychopathy also show limitations on stimulus-reinforcement association learning tasks (Lykken, 1957; Newman & Kosson, 1986; Blair *et al.*, 2004) and further deficits have been shown with regard to emotional processing. For example, children with psychopathic tendencies have been shown to be impaired in their ability to recognize emotional expressions (Blair *et al.*, 2001b). Consistent with this finding, people with psychopathic tendencies also exhibit reduced amygdala responses to emotional expressions (Gordon *et al.*, 2004) and reduced autonomic responses (Blair *et al.*, 1997). This evidence may be interpreted to infer that amygdala dysfunction may additionally be associated with psychopathy. The evidence regarding the two core impairments in psychopathy relating to ventrolateral prefrontal cortex and amygdala dysfunction has been developed and assimilated by Blair and colleagues to provide explanations of both reactive and instrumental aggression, respectively. These theories are described later in this chapter.

Acquired brain injury

Agitated behaviour and aggression are common problems in the traumatic brain injury population. There are several DSM-IV subclassifications of 'personality change secondary to a general medical condition', which attempt to distinguish between the types of behaviour displayed following an acquired brain injury, which may include aggression or violence. The characteristics of 'aggressive type' are self-explanatory. 'Disinhibited type' includes disinhibition and sexual indiscretion, but can include violence resulting from situations where disinhibited behaviour is thwarted or in the context of frustration.

'Labile type' involves mainly affective lability, but can include verbally aggressive outbursts without threatening or violent behaviour.

During the acute recovery period, agitated behaviour can occur in 35–96% of individuals (Levin & Grossman, 1978; Rao *et al.*, 1985) but this generally resolves before the end of post-traumatic amnesia (Van der Naalt *et al.*, 1999). However, more persistent aggressive behaviour can occur in approximately 34–70% of individuals (Tateno *et al.*, 2003) and this may continue even up to 60 months post-injury (Baguley *et al.*, 2006). It also seems that traumatic brain injury places individuals at increased risk of incarceration. A study of the prevalence of traumatic brain injury in a US county jail showed that 87% of a randomly selected group of 69 inmates reported a traumatic brain injury in their lifetime and 36.2% reported a traumatic brain injury in the previous year (Slaughter *et al.*, 2003). Although these inmates may also have committed non-violent crimes, the group who had experienced a recent traumatic injury reported greater anger and aggression scores on a brief anger and aggression inventory. This finding suggests that reactive aggression is more likely in traumatic brain injury than instrumental aggression.

Aggression following traumatic brain injury can be poorly directed with little evidence of a trigger and following minimal provocation (Wood & Liossi, 2006). However, there is limited evidence for the efficacy of psychopharmacological interventions to treat agitation and aggression (Fleminger *et al.*, 2006). Possible environmental factors that may lead to aggression and violence in traumatic brain injury include too much stimulation, such as overcrowding or excessive noise, restrictions such as locked doors, lack of privacy, loss of independence, and difficulty with interpersonal interactions (Pryor, 2004). Depression has also been found to be strongly associated with aggressive behaviour (Baguley *et al.*, 2006).

The relationship between traumatic brain injury and aggression and violence is complicated by premorbid risk factors. Aggression is more likely to occur within the traumatic brain injury population in individuals who have a premorbid psychiatric history, particularly of substance misuse (Dunlop *et al.*, 1991), a history of impulsive aggression (Greve, *et al.*, 2001) and also a history of previous arrests (Kreutzer *et al.*, 1995). It is therefore difficult to determine whether aggression in the context of a brain injury is a continuation or exacerbation of premorbid characteristics rather than an acquired behaviour directly attributable to the injury. Nevertheless, individuals who sustain more than one traumatic brain injury have been shown to develop increasing irritability following each subsequent injury (Carlsson *et al.*, 1987). This provides further evidence in favour of a more direct relationship between traumatic brain injury and aggression.

Aggression seems to be most likely to occur in traumatic brain injury following damage to prefrontal structures (Grafman et al., 1996). However, there is very limited literature specifically examining the neuropsychological performance of individuals displaying aggressive behaviour following brain injury. Greve et al. (2001) found no difference between the neuropsychological profiles of aggressive and non-aggressive traumatic brain injury groups from a residential setting. In a large prospective traumatic brain injury cohort study covering multiple cognitive domains including executive functioning, Wood & Liossi (2006) found that only verbal memory and visuospatial abilities differentiated aggressive individuals from non-aggressive individuals. They also found that the aggressive group left school earlier, were younger, had lower premorbid socioeconomic status, and were more likely to be male. These results suggest that several factors may influence an individual with a traumatic brain injury to exhibit aggressive behaviour and that there is likely to be an interaction between both pre- and post-injury neuropsychological and psychosocial variables.

Prefrontal cortex damage

The prefrontal cortex is particularly likely to be involved in the pathogenesis of aggressive and violent behaviour due to its function in controlling, planning, and regulating behaviour as well as understanding and predicting its future consequences (Kolb & Whishaw, 1996). Focal prefrontal cortex lesions have been associated with increased aggressive and violent behaviour (Meyers et al., 1992; Tranel, 1994; Blair & Cipolotti, 2000) and earlier onset of damage may lead to more severe antisocial behaviour (Anderson et al., 1999). Further evidence supporting the link between the prefrontal cortex and aggression includes studies indicating elevated rates of aggression in many conditions associated with frontal lobe pathology including traumatic brain injury (Grafman et al., 1996), schizophrenia, ADHD (Pennington & Ozonoff, 1996), and frontotemporal dementia (Stip, 1995; Miller et al., 1997). Impairments of prefrontal cortex functions as measured by executive functioning neuropsychological tests have been described specifically among conduct-disordered and antisocial personality disordered offenders (as reviewed above), as well as death row inmates (Lewis et al., 1986), forensic psychiatric inpatients (Martell, 1992) and other individuals with a history of violence (Brower & Price, 2001). Although a review of neuropsychological studies examining frontal lobe dysfunction and antisocial behaviour performed in 1989 (Kandel & Freed, 1989) concluded that there was only a weak association between violent behaviour and frontal lobe dysfunction, an updated review in 2001 found greater evidence for a relationship between focal prefrontal cortex damage and an impulsive subtype of aggressive behaviour or reactive aggression (Brower & Price, 2001).

In particular, damage to the orbitofrontal cortex has been associated with increased antisocial behaviour, including a disregard for the feelings of others, tactlessness, and poor impulse control, in the absence of other cognitive changes detectable with standard neuropsychological tests. This phenomenon has become known as 'pseudopsychopathy' (Blumer & Benson, 1975) or 'acquired sociopathy' (Meyers *et al.*, 1992; Tranel, 1994; Blair & Cipolotti, 2000). Evidence stems back as far as the first account of damage to the orbitofrontal and ventromedial frontal lobes, the infamous case of Phineas Gage, who became irritable, short-tempered and obnoxious following his injury (Harlow, 1848; Damasio *et al.*, 1994). Other cases of acquired aggressive behaviour have been described in the context of left unilateral orbitofrontal cortex damage (Meyers *et al.*, 1992) and bilateral orbitofrontal lesions (Blair & Cipolotti, 2000).

The orbitofrontal cortex, particularly its most posterior and medial regions, has also been implicated in regulation of autonomic processes (Critchley, 2005). Damage to this region can affect emotion expression recognition (Hornak *et al.*, 1996, 2003) and this ability has been shown to correlate with inappropriate social behaviour. Another deficit identified following orbitofrontal cortex damage is impaired extinction and reversal learning (Rolls *et al.*, 1994; Hornak *et al.*, 2004). It was found that performance on reversal and extinction tests was also strongly related to behaviour such as disinhibition, misinterpretation of the moods of others, unconcern for their condition, and lack of initiative as measured by an informant-reported questionnaire.

Given the involvement of the orbitofrontal cortex in many aspects of behaviour and emotional regulation, several explanations have evolved that attempt to explain its function in the mediation of aggressive behaviour. These include the reversal learning theory, which proposes a deficit in the ability to respond appropriately to social reinforcers and adapt to changing contingencies (Rolls *et al.*, 1994), and the somatic marker hypothesis, which suggests that such behaviour arises due to the inability to use emotions in decision-making (Damasio *et al.*, 1990; Damasio, 1996). These theories are discussed later in the chapter.

Whilst there are many similarities between the behaviour of individuals with orbitofrontal or ventromedial prefrontal cortex damage and individuals with psychopathy, there are also some differences. In a study comparing a single case of acquired orbitofrontal damage (CL) with a group of developmental psychopaths, CL exhibited difficulties on facial expression recognition and inappropriate social behaviour recognition tasks, but not on tasks assessing stimulus-reinforcement associations (Mitchell *et al.*, 2006a). In contrast, the developmental psychopaths had difficulty on tasks assessing vocal and facial emotion expressions and also poor stimulus-reinforcement association learning. Blair (2003) argues that the difference between acquired psychopathy and developmental psychopathy is additional dysfunction of the amygdala, which leads not only to emotion recognition deficits but also to an inability to form appropriate stimulus-reinforcement relationships that can guide moral behaviour. This difference is also suggested to explain why psychopathy acquired through orbitofrontal cortex damage leads to reactive aggression, whereas developmental psychopaths additionally display elevated levels of instrumental aggression (Blair, 2004). This hypothesis is discussed later in the chapter.

Learning disability

Aggressive and violent behaviour is more common in the learning disabled population than the non-learning disabled population (e.g. Emerson, 1995). Rates of aggressive behaviour have been reported ranging between 36 and 50% in community samples from the learning disabled population (Harris, 1993; Emerson & Bromley, 1995). Physical aggression is more likely to be displayed by males, younger individuals, people with more severe learning disabilities, and people in institutional settings (Tyrer *et al.*, 2006). Typical behaviours include punching, slapping, kicking, pinching, pulling hair, and biting. They are often referred to as 'challenging behaviours' and could constitute a criminal offence, although many people with learning disabilities are never reported to the police (Clare & Murphy, 1998). Analysis of behaviour often reveals that aggressive behaviour serves a function such as communication in the context of social skills deficits (Duncan *et al.*, 1999), facilitation of escape, or avoidance of aversive situations. For example, an aggressive outburst may be a maladaptive means of communicating fear or discomfort. Aggressive men with mild learning disabilities are more likely to generate an aggressive solution to anticipated problems (Fuchs & Benson, 1995). Many interventions that aim to address aggressive behaviour are focused on problem-solving techniques and the establishment of more appropriate ways of acting or communicating in situations that evoke aggression (Emerson *et al.*, 1998).

Whilst there is a dearth of literature regarding neuropsychological functioning and aggression in learning disabilities, studies of aggressive versus non-aggressive learning disabled individuals have shown relative deficits in detection of facial emotional expression recognition. Walz & Benson (1996) found that an aggressive group were more likely to misidentify faces as angry or sad. Matheson & Jahoda (2005) showed that an aggressive group had greater difficulty in labelling emotions in contextually rich photographs and cartoons, with the most likely misinterpretation being of anger. These results suggest that aggressive individuals with a learning disability may show specific deficits similar to those shown by aggressive individuals from the non-learning disabled population. Therefore, it may also be possible to apply similar neuropsychological theories in order to explain aspects of their aggressive behaviour.

Dementia

Aggressive behaviour displayed by people with dementia is classified as one of its behavioural and psychological symptoms (Turner, 2005). It is more common among people with dementia than among older people without dementia (Chou *et al.*, 1996; Wystanski, 2000). However, estimating the rates of aggressive behaviour is difficult as it is often not clearly defined and is likely to be under-reported by family members and care staff, even though aggression against family members is a very common reason for someone with dementia to enter residential care (Gates *et al.*, 1999). In a residential care sample, aggression has been reported in up to 86% of individuals with dementia (Ballard *et al.*, 2001), ranging from low-impact aggression to homicide (Hindley & Gordon, 2000).

Antisocial and aggressive behaviour is more prominent in frontotemporal dementias than other dementing illnesses (Miller *et al.*, 1997; Mendez *et al.*, 2005). A study of individuals with frontotemporal dementia who had sociopathic traits showed that they exhibited relative impairment on motor inhibition tasks compared with a comparison group (Mendez *et al.*, 2005). In addition, these individuals were aware that their antisocial behaviour was wrong, but they claimed they could not prevent themselves from acting on impulse. A matched sample of individuals with Alzheimer's disease exhibited significantly lower levels of sociopathic behaviour (Mendez *et al.*, 2005). However, another study did identify a relationship between impairments on executive functioning tasks and severity and frequency of agitated and aggressive behaviour in a sample of individuals with Alzheimer's disease (Engelborghs *et al.*, 2006).

It possible that the mechanisms that underpin aggressive behaviour in other neuropsychological disorders involving the prefrontal cortex are also present in dementia. However, several other factors are also important to consider for this client group, as links between aggressive behaviour and other psychological symptoms of dementia have also been identified, including delusional thinking (Gormley *et al.*, 1998; Eustace *et al.*, 2001) and depression (Lyketsos *et al.*, 1999; Talerico *et al.*, 2002). As with all later-onset disorders associated with aggression, premorbid factors must also be taken into account. For example, O'Leary *et al.* (2005) showed that people with dementia who had conduct disorder in childhood were more likely to be aggressive towards their partners. Nevertheless, other studies have not shown a link between premorbid personality features and aggressive behaviour in dementia (Kolanowski & Garr, 1999; Low et al., 2002). Finally, aggressive behaviour in dementia could be construed as a way of communicating a need or a response to a perceived threat (Stokes, 2000). Consistent with this view is the finding that aggressive behaviour often occurs when people with dementia are receiving intimate care, which may be misinterpreted as a personal violation (Keene et al., 1999). Interaction style of carers has also been shown to be linked to the display of aggression (Duxbury, 2000), and it is likely that in some circumstances aggressive behaviour is reinforced, such as gaining attention when screaming or threatening others. Therefore, when considering aggression and violence in individuals with dementia, it is particularly important for a forensic neuropsychologist to look beyond their test results when interpreting behaviour.

Epilepsy

Aggression in the context of epilepsy is usually reactive or defensive, as it occurs in the context of high emotional arousal, anger, or fear (Van Elst et al., 2000). It may occur during a seizure (ictal aggression) or immediately following a seizure (postictal aggression), but more commonly occurs in between seizures (interictal aggression) (Devinsky et al., 1994).

Ictal violence is relatively rare but has been raised in public awareness by the use of epileptic automatisms as a defence in violent crimes (Marsh & Krauss, 2000). In a large sample of individuals with epilepsy, fewer than 1% displayed aggressive or violent behaviour during seizures. However, an interictal syndrome of aggression has been shown to be more likely in individuals with temporal lobe epilepsy, and has become known as episodic dyscontrol or intermittent explosive disorder as classified by DSM-IV (Stone et al., 1986; Van Elst et al., 2000). Episodic dyscontrol is behaviour out of proportion to the stressor and is in the context of high arousal. It was thought to be associated with amygdala pathology (Fenwick, 1986; Trimble et al., 1996), but a more recent study showed that only 20% of an aggressive temporal lobe epilepsy group had severe amygdala atrophy (Van Elst et al., 2000). Other aggressive temporal lobe epilepsy participants had more distributed bilateral or left-hemisphere brain pathology, particularly in the left temporal lobes. The involvement of temporal lobe structures in aggression and violence is discussed in more detail during the neuroimaging section of this chapter.

Postictal aggressive or violent behaviour may occur when an individual may be experiencing confusion, depression, or psychotic symptoms. These can affect up to 10% of individuals with epilepsy (Lancman, 1999). Postictal violence can be relatively stereotyped and may be more likely to occur after a cluster of seizures (Gerard et al., 1998). In contrast, interictal violence seems to be more associated with psychopathology and learning disability than with epileptiform activity or other seizure variables (Mendez et al., 1993). There is a greater prevalence of epilepsy among prisoners but no greater rates of violent crimes than among individuals without epilepsy (Treiman, 1986). In a sample of offenders with epilepsy, almost half had a head trauma and hence may have had underlying prefrontal cortex damage (Whitman et al., 1984). This could indicate that underlying neuropathology, rather than epileptiform phenomena, makes a more significant contribution to aggressive behaviour. Furthermore, individuals with epilepsy are more likely to exhibit cognitive impairments, including lower general intellectual functioning and executive functioning deficits (e.g. Elger et al., 2004), which may be specifically related to the display of aggression and violence via mechanisms described later in this chapter.

Schizophrenia

Several neuropsychological investigations comparing violent and non-violent individuals with schizophrenia have been conducted, but the results are inconclusive, with evidence of worsened, improved, and unchanged performance in the group (Naudts & Hodgins, 2006). Three studies have linked violence in schizophrenia to neuropsychological deficits. One study found impaired performance on visual task completion and visual retention and reduced-performance IQ in a violent schizophrenia group (Krakowski et al., 1999). However, the individuals with schizophrenia in the study had significantly lower full-scale IQ scores than in most other schizophrenia studies, which makes the results difficult to interpret. Another study examining violent and non-violent patients in a secure hospital found that the violent group made significantly more errors during the Wisconsin Card Sorting Task and the Stroop test (Barkataki et al., 2005) and a further study showed neuropsychological impairment on additional tasks assessing executive functions (Rasmussen et al., 1995). However, the latter study also showed that the non-aggressive group had significantly slower reaction times (i.e. worse performance) than the aggressive group on several tasks.

Two further studies have reported improved neuropsychological task performance in individuals with schizophrenia who had a history of violence (LaPierre et al., 1995; Roy et al., 1987). In particular, one study examining violence in schizophrenia patients with and without comorbid antisocial personality disorder found a significant positive correlation between the number of assaults causing injury to victims and performance on executive function tasks (LaPierre et al., 1995). In addition, a study of violence in schizophrenia patients judged to be treatment resistant showed that the violent group had significantly better scores on WAIS performance subtests, including visuoperception and visuomotor coordination, and coordination (Roy et al., 1987). Three other investigations found no differences between violent and non-violent groups of schizophrenia patients (Krakowski et al., 1997; Wong et al., 1997; Lafayette et al., 2003). In a study comparing a persistently violent schizophrenia group with a transiently violent group on an inpatient unit, no differences were found between groups on verbal or performance IQ (Krakowski et al., 1997). When schizophrenia outpatients were divided into those who had committed a violent offence, those who had committed a non-violent offence, and those who had not committed an offence, no difference was found between groups with regard to full-scale IQ or other neuropsychological measures (Lafayette et al., 2003). A study comparing mentally disordered offenders who had committed violent offences with those who had committed non-violent offences also found no differences between groups on full-scale IQ scores (Wong et al., 1997). Barkataki et al. (2005) reported that, whilst cognitive impairment seems to be more associated with schizophrenia than violence, there is evidence that a combination of schizophrenia and violent behaviour is related to greater cognitive deficits than antisocial personality disorder alone.

Substance misuse

The most commonly used drug that is associated with aggression and violence is alcohol. It is associated with 60–70% of homicides, 70% of stabbings and beatings, and 50% of domestic assaults (Touhig, 1998). However, there is also a relationship between violence and several illicit drugs including cocaine, crack, amphetamines, anabolic androgen steroids, benzodiazepines, and cannabis (Snowden, 2001). Aggression and violence may occur in the context of acute intoxication, withdrawal, and/or dependence (Snowden, 2001). Alcohol may be more likely to be associated with reactive aggression. In contrast, illicit drug use may be more likely to be associated with instrumental aggression, for example, through robbery and theft, in order to support an expensive habit.

Substance misuse is a factor that is of relevance in all of the disorders described above and may be a confounding variable for many studies of other disorders. For example, on an adult acute psychiatric ward over a period of 9 months, 68% of individuals exhibiting aggressive behaviour had a history of substance misuse (El-Badri & Mellsop, 2006). Substance misuse could potentially contribute to the relationship between aggression and the different disorders as a predisposing factor, a catalyst, or a causal agent. It may also interact with and exacerbate an existing disorder and its treatment, for example in psychosis or epilepsy.

The neuropsychological mechanisms proposed to mediate the relationship between substance use and violence is a disruption of the executive functioning system. This may lead to impaired response inhibition, in addition to poor planning and problem solving and information processing (Bushman & Cooper, 1990). In particular, alcohol seems to impair judgement and lead to individuals taking greater risks than usual (MacDonald *et al.*, 1996). Also, substances may affect normal processing of social and emotional cues. Following excessive alcohol consumption, an individual is much more likely to view an accidental event as a purposeful one, and therefore to act more aggressively. In addition, in healthy individuals, alcohol and diazepam have been shown to induce impairment in the ability to process angry facial expressions (Borrill *et al.*, 1987; Blair & Curran, 1999). Theories explaining aggression and violence in terms of poor inhibitory control and emotional processing deficits described later may therefore also be relevant in cases where an individual has misused substances.

Neural circuitry of aggression and violence

The neural circuitry involved in reactive aggression is common to humans and other mammalian species (Panksepp, 1998; Gregg & Siegel, 2001). The circuit runs downward from the medial area of the amygdala, largely via the stria terminalis to the medial hypothalamus, and from there to the dorsal half of the periaqueductal grey matter (Blair, 2004). The system is organized in a hierarchical manner: aggression evoked from the amygdala is dependent on an intact medial hypothalamus and periaqueductal grey matter, but aggression evoked from the periaqueductal grey matter is not dependent on an intact amygdala (Panksepp, 1998; Gregg & Siegel, 2001). The system mediates the animal's response to threat (Blair, 2004). At low levels of stimulation associated with a distant threat, a freeze response is elicited. At higher levels of threat, from a closer threat, an escape attempt is elicited. As the threat closes in and escape is no longer possible, reactive aggression is more likely to be exhibited (Blanchard *et al.*, 1977).

Aggression responses are modulated by the amygdala and the orbitofrontal cortex via their projections to the medial hypothalamus and midbrain periaqueductal grey matter (Gregg & Siegel, 2001). The amygdala responds to reinforcing and aversive stimuli (Everitt *et al.*, 2000). The amygdala may thus upgrade (as a response to an aversive stimulus) or downgrade (as a response to reinforcement) the responsiveness of the subcortical threat-response systems. This is suggested by the startle response literature (Blair, 2004). The startle response is mediated by the subcortical threat-response systems, and can be modulated by the presence of visual or auditory primes occurring shortly before the startle stimulus. An aversive visual threat prime augments the magnitude of the startle reflex relative to neutral primes, whereas appetitive visual primes reduce the magnitude of the startle reflex (Lang *et al.*, 1990). This modulation of the subcortical response systems is specifically mediated by the amygdala (Campeau & Davis, 1995; Angrilli *et al.*, 1996; Davis & Whalen, 2001; Funayama *et al.*, 2001).

Amygdala lesions may reduce the likelihood of reactive aggression in threatening circumstances by reducing the individual's sensitivity to learned threat. In these circumstances, learned threats would not activate the amygdala appropriately, which in turn would not activate the subcortical systems that mediate aggression (Blair, 2004). Indeed, bilateral amygdalectomies have been reported to decrease aggressive behaviour in 70–76% of cases (Ramamurthi, 1988). However, amygdala lesions can also increase the probability of reactive aggression in non-threatening situations if appetitive stimuli in the environment do not suppress reactive aggression through the amygdala correctly (Blair, 2004). Consistent with this proposition, the literature suggests that amygdala lesions can also increase the likelihood of reactive aggression. For example, very severe amygdala atrophy has been found in a subgroup of aggressive patients with temporal lobe epilepsy (Van Elst *et al.*, 2000). Moreover, unilateral damage to the central nucleus of the amygdala in cats increases the expression of reactive aggression (Zagrodzka *et al.*, 1998). These results clearly indicate a possible role of the amygdala both in reducing sensitivity to threat and in increasing the likelihood of reactive aggression.

The prefrontal cortex is also involved in the modulation of the subcortical circuit, which mediates reactive aggression. It has been suggested that the orbitofrontal cortex exerts inhibitory control over the amygdala by providing top-down control of the responsiveness and expression of negative emotion via the amygdala (Quirk & Beer, 2006). Orbitofrontal lesions have been found to increase aggression in male rats (de Bruin *et al.*, 1983) and rhesus monkeys (Machado & Bachevalier, 2006). However, given the relative underdevelopment of this brain region in other mammalian species, most evidence is derived from human lesion studies as described earlier (e.g. Grafman *et al.*, 1996; Anderson *et al.*, 1999). Furthermore, several functional neuroimaging studies have reported reduced frontal functioning in individuals who display reactive aggression (Volkow *et al.*, 1995; Amen *et al.*, 1996). The main findings of neuroimaging studies of aggression and violence are reviewed in the following section.

Neuroimaging of aggression and violence

Neuroimaging studies provide information on brain structure and function. A structural brain lesion may not be associated with obvious abnormality of function, and functional deficits may occur in the absence of structural abnormality. Refinement of brain imaging techniques over time has yielded much-improved resolution and sensitivity, thereby reducing the likelihood of type two errors. Earlier studies of brain structure in violence used computerized tomography (CT), and more recent studies have used magnetic resonance imaging (MRI), which allows greater resolution without the need for ionizing radiation. Functional neuroimaging techniques include single proton emission computed tomography (SPECT), positron emission tomography (PET), and functional magnetic resonance imaging (fMRI).

Structural neuroimaging

Many structural imaging studies using CT scans have not identified any brain abnormalities in violent and aggressive offenders in comparison with non-aggressive offenders. For example, a CT study that compared 18 murderers, 21 individuals who had assaulted others, and 16 who had caused damaged to property reported no significant differences among the groups (Langevin *et al.*, 1987). Another CT study of 31 individuals diagnosed with temporal lobe epilepsy compared 14 aggressive individuals with those who did not have a significant history of aggression. There were no significant differences between the groups (Herzberg & Fenwick, 1988). However, these null results may be attributable to the lack of sensitivity of CT in detecting subtle abnormalities.

Later studies used MRI scans and found structural differences between aggressive and non-aggressive groups, particularly within the temporal lobes, but also in the frontal lobes. Tonkonogy (1991) used both CT and MRI to assess 87 individuals referred for neuropsychiatric examination due to alcohol abuse, cerebrovascular accidents, or head injury. Twenty-three of the assessed individuals had evidence of structural brain abnormality. Fourteen of these individuals had what was termed 'frequent episodes of violent behaviour' and were significantly more likely to have lesions in the anterior inferior area of the temporal lobe. Five of the individuals had lesions in this area, and four of these were lateralized to the right hemisphere. The authors speculated that violence may result from unilateral tissue loss in the amygdala–hippocampal region of the temporal lobe.

MRI scans have also been used to compare the brain structures of aggressive versus non-aggressive individuals within disorders associated with aggression such as schizophrenia, antisocial personality disorder, and epilepsy. A study comparing 20 repetitive and 19 non-repetitive violent offenders with schizophrenia reported that asymmetric gyral patterns in the temporoparietal region were common in the repetitive group and absent in the non-repetitive group (Wong *et al.*, 1997). An MRI study (Barkataki *et al.*, 2005) of antisocial personality disorder, and of schizophrenia patients with and without a history of violence, reported reduced temporal lobe volume in the antisocial personality disorder group and the violent schizophrenia group. The authors interpreted this finding as evidence in support of the role of the temporal lobe region in mediating violent behaviour. However, in a sample of violent and non-violent individuals with known temporal lobe disruption through temporal lobe epilepsy, those with a history of aggression had reduced grey matter volume, which was most marked in the left frontal lobe (Woermann et al., 2000). This finding is suggestive of additional frontal lobe involvement in aggressive behaviour. This possibility has been explored further using functional scans and paradigms designed to activate the prefrontal cortex.

Functional neuroimaging

Many of the functional imaging studies of aggression have involved small samples, and variations in methodology make comparisons difficult. Some researchers have scanned patients 'at rest' when it is not possible to control individual brain activity during the scan. Other studies have used cognitive tasks to probe brain regions theoretically involved in the modulation of aggression.

The relatively low spatial resolution of SPECT requires relatively large samples, which only a few studies have achieved. One study compared brain perfusion in 40 individuals who had been violent in the 6 months before the scan with 40 healthy individuals (Amen et al., 1996). The aggressive group showed relatively reduced activity in the prefrontal cortex, but increased activity in the anteromedial portions of the frontal lobes and increased activity in the left basal ganglia. Another study used SPECT scans of individuals subsequently convicted of violent offences and found significant reductions in blood flow in the right angular gyrus, the right medial temporal gyrus, bilaterally in the hippocampus, and in the left white frontal matter (Soderstrom et al., 2000). Blood flow was significantly increased in the parietal association cortex bilaterally. The abnormalities were present in the whole group of individuals accused of violent offences, irrespective of mental health diagnosis, substance use, or medication status. It is also significant to note that there was no corresponding damage on MRI, which suggests that functional scanning paradigms may be more sensitive to the brain changes associated with aggression and violence.

PET scanning is another method of assessing brain metabolism that has been able to detect differences between aggressive and non-aggressive groups. Volkow et al. (1995) studied individuals with a history of repetitive violence and healthy individuals, and found that, when at rest, the aggressive individuals had significantly lower relative metabolic values in their medial temporal and prefrontal cortex. This method has also been used to measure blood flow during performance of neuropsychological tasks. When performing a continuous performance task in a PET scan, a group of murderers who had pleaded not guilty by reason of insanity showed evidence of reduced blood flow in the prefrontal cortex (Raine *et al.*, 1994, 1997). A later study demonstrated that reduced prefrontal cortex blood flow was only present in individuals who had used reactive aggression, and was not exhibited by those who used instrumental aggression (Raine *et al.*, 1998).

The existing functional neuroimaging literature of aggression has tended to ignore the separable regions of the prefrontal cortex. One of the few studies to report on dissociable areas of the prefrontal cortex scanned individuals with personality disorder who engaged in reactive aggression and found that they exhibited reduced resting blood flow in the lateral orbitofrontal cortex (Goyer *et al.*, 1994). However, fMRI paradigms may allow further discrimination of activity in discrete regions within the prefrontal cortex using relevant stimuli. Coccaro *et al.* (2007) used visual presentation of emotional faces as probes during fMRI to compare brain activation in ten individuals with reactive aggression to ten healthy individuals. The reactive aggression group showed relatively exaggerated activation of the amygdala and relatively reduced activation of the orbitofrontal cortex to angry faces. The authors interpreted this as evidence of a link between aggression and dysfunction in the frontal-limbic network, again involving the amygdala and orbitofrontal cortex.

To summarize, there are a number of limitations to functional neuroimaging studies of aggression and the results should be interpreted cautiously. Earlier 'at rest' studies had no control over what the individuals were doing at the time of the scan and many of the studies had very small sample sizes. Nevertheless, most studies support structural CT and MRI data indicating that temporal and frontal regions are involved in some forms of aggressive behaviour. Several studies have indicated that aggressive individuals have reduced activity in the prefrontal cortex (Goyer *et al.*, 1994; Raine *et al.*, 1998; Coccaro *et al.*, 2007) and techniques that can identify subregions of the prefrontal cortex have specifically reported reduced orbitofrontal activation in reactive aggression (Goyer *et al.*, 1994; Coccaro *et al.*, 2007), coupled with exaggerated activation of the amygdala (Coccaro *et al.*, 2007). These findings are consistent with the neuropsychological and animal literature, and have been integrated within neuropsychological theories to explain violence and aggression.

Neuropsychological explanations for aggression and violence

Blair (2001) suggested there may be different explanations for aggressive or violent behaviour according to whether aggression is reactive, i.e. is elicited in response to frustration or threat, or whether it is instrumental aggression. These two forms of aggression may be subserved by different neural circuitry and consequently different neuropsychological mechanisms.

Reactive aggression

Theories that explain reactive aggression are generally based on a previous understanding of the functions of the prefrontal cortex. The first and most general explanation is in terms of poor inhibitory control and other executive functioning deficits (e.g. Barratt et al., 1997). However, more recently, improved understanding of the role of the ventromedial and orbitofrontal prefrontal cortex regions in affective processes has led to models that can explain aggressive behaviour in terms of deficient emotion recognition and response reversal learning (e.g. Rolls et al., 1994; Blair, 2001) or lack of a 'somatic marker' system (e.g. Damasio, 1994).

Inhibitory control theories

Impulsivity may be regarded as a core dimension of human personality (Eysenck & Eysenck, 1975). However, pathological impulsivity has been associated with several neurological and psychiatric conditions such as traumatic brain injury, ADHD, borderline personality disorder, and antisocial personality disorder. These are all disorders where there is an increased likelihood of aggression and violence (Stein et al., 1993).

Reactive or hostile aggression arises in the context of anger or heightened emotion. This is likely to be adaptive in situations where an individual, their offspring, or their environment is threatened. Nevertheless, despite this being an evolutionarily adaptive behaviour, in today's society there are very few situations that warrant a full 'fight' response. Therefore, humans as a species have evolved to be able to regulate or suppress reactive aggression in the context of anger. Response inhibition mechanisms for this purpose are proposed to be located in the prefrontal cortex, particularly the right inferior region (Rubia et al., 2003; Boecker et al., 2007; Chikazoe et al., 2007). However damage to the systems that facilitate suppression may lead to an inability to inhibit aggressive impulses (Barratt, 1994; Barratt et al., 1997).

Two types of inhibitory control have been described by Nigg (2000) in the context of disruptive behaviour problems in childhood—executive inhibition and motivational or reactive inhibition. Executive inhibition involves a deliberate or effortful suppression of a response in order to achieve long-term goals, and does not involve anxiety activation. Motivational or reactive inhibition is an unconscious suppression of a response relating to novel or fear-related stimuli (c.f. Gray, 1982—behavioural inhibition system). A well-adjusted individual will use a balance of these two interrelated inhibition systems to control aggressive or violent behaviour. However, the systems can break down to form different patterns of disinhibition. Nigg (2003) suggests that ADHD is characterized by disruption of the executive control systems, with secondary breakdown in reactive inhibition. In contrast, it is proposed that aggressive conduct disorder represents primary failure of reactive or motivational control processes and secondary breakdown in executive control. This distinction may potentially be extended to adulthood disorders whereby aggression and violence in antisocial personality disorder and acquired prefrontal cortex injury may be related to primary executive inhibition deficits, whereas psychopathy can be explained in terms of a reactive inhibition impairment, for example through lack of fear of punishment (Lykken, 1957).

The main strength of an inhibitory model is that it does not argue for one process acting in isolation to cause aggressive behaviour, but assumes a relationship between different regulatory systems. This fits with neuropsychological literature, which shows mixed results with regard to the presence of response inhibition deficits in the context of aggression and violence (e.g. Gorenstein, 1982; LaPierre *et al.*, 1995). However, inhibitory models seem to suffer from a lack of specificity with regard to neural underpinnings and the processes through which inhibitory control could be achieved. Blair (2001) suggests that impulsivity models could be considered as re-descriptions of the literature rather than theories from which hypotheses may be formulated and tested.

Reversal learning theories

Reversal learning theories explain inappropriate social behaviour in terms of the combination of two main functions of the orbitofrontal cortex—facial emotion expression recognition and reversal learning.

Facial and auditory emotional expressions act as reinforcing signals for shaping social and emotional behaviour (Rolls, 1999). For example, angry expressions may limit or restrain behaviour in situations where social rules have been broken (Blair, 2001). Difficulties in identifying facial and vocal emotional expressions have been shown by individuals with ventral frontal lobe damage, and also more specifically damage to the orbitofrontal cortex and medial prefrontal cortex (Hornak *et al.*, 1996, 2003). Furthermore, impaired performance in emotional recognition tasks has been shown to be correlated with inappropriate social behaviour as rated by informants. It is therefore possible that the inability to detect such social cues can potentially lead to aggression and violence through misreading another's emotions. For example, an individual may misinterpret a neutral face as angry and therefore respond by squaring up for a fight. Alternatively, the individual may recognize that another person is angry and persist in behaving in a threatening manner.

A further related difficulty exhibited by individuals with damage to the orbitofrontal cortex is in reversal learning. Lesions to the orbitofrontal cortex in non-human primates have been found to lead to impaired extinction and reversal learning (Rolls, 1995). In a visual discrimination task, monkeys were able to learn that one stimulus was associated with reward and another stimulus was associated either with no reward or with punishment. However, when the contingencies reversed, they were unable to reverse their choices accordingly. When the reinforcement was terminated, their responses did not extinguish; hence, they had failed to break the association between the stimulus and primary reinforcer.

Using a similar reversal learning paradigm involving choosing stimuli associated with monetary rewards and punishment, the same deficit has been shown for humans with both diffuse and circumscribed lesions involving the orbitofrontal cortex (Rolls *et al.*, 1994; Hornak *et al.*, 2004). Rolls (1996) argues that many of the difficulties exhibited by individuals with prefrontal cortex damage may stem from this impairment, such as perseverative behaviour despite social cues indicating that it is ill-advised. In particular, failure to alter behaviour when reinforcement contingencies change may lead to circumstantially inappropriate behaviour including aggression and violence when a threat has been misinterpreted or has dissipated. Performance in reversal and extinction tests was shown to be strongly correlated with inappropriate social behaviour including disinhibition, misinterpretation of the moods of others, and unconcern for their condition (Rolls, 1999; Hornak *et al.*, 2004). These findings support the argument that antisocial behaviour is mediated by the inability to recognize and respond to social cues in the context of changing contingencies (e.g. Rolls, 1999). Consistent with this suggestion is the finding that individuals with psychopathy also show impaired reversal learning (Mitchell *et al.*, 2002). However, the pattern of responding was not in keeping with Rolls' prediction of perseveration when contingencies had reversed. Reversal learning task failure in psychopathy was more attributable to a failure to avoid returning to the punished response.

In addition, Blair & Cipolotti's (2000) single case finding is contrary to the notion that the combination of both impaired reversal learning and poor emotion expression recognition following orbitofrontal cortex damage leads to inappropriate social behaviour. They reported a patient, JS, who had disturbed aggressive behaviour following frontal lobe damage involving the bilateral orbitofrontal regions and some of the left temporal lobe including the amygdala. JS was deficient in his recognition of happiness, anger, disgust, and sadness, but not surprise or fearfulness, in comparison with a psychopathic inmate population. He was also significantly impaired at recognizing anger and disgust but not the other four emotional expressions, in comparison with an individual with dysexecutive syndrome but without acquired sociopathy. However, in contrast to previous studies (e.g. Rolls *et al.*, 1994), JS was able to reverse responses to stimuli that had previously been associated with reward adequately when they subsequently became associated with punishment. In addition, it has been shown that boys with psychopathic tendencies are unimpaired on a response reversal task (Blair *et al.*, 2001b).

Preservation of reversal learning in the context of impaired emotion recognition is suggestive of a dissociation of these two functions. Blair and Cipolotti (2000) proposed an alternative reversal learning hypothesis to explain the disturbed aggressive behaviour exhibited by JS in terms of a second social response reversal system that modulates behaviour when encountering negative social cues. They suggested that his behaviour arose through dysfunction of a system that is responsible for extinguishing on-going behaviour and reversing the current response following perception of another individual's angry expression. Such a system is proposed to be activated by current angry expressions or representations of situations that have previously been associated with another's actual or anticipated angry response. This facilitates judgement of appropriate behaviour according to the other individual's reactions. Conversely, disruption of this system may lead to aggressive and violent behaviour.

Somatic marker hypothesis

The somatic marker hypothesis was developed following exploration of the role of the ventral and medial aspects of the prefrontal cortex, particularly with regard to autonomic functioning (Damasio, 1994). The central tenet is that 'somatic markers' influence responses to stimuli, both consciously and non-consciously. Somatic markers are changes in body state including musculoskeletal and visceral alterations associated with emotional states. Such somatic states are evoked by situations, due to their previous link with reward or punishment, in order to signal the potential outcome on subsequent presentations of the stimulus. The somatic signals guide decision-making such that a non-cognitive 'hunch' about an outcome may act either as an alarm or as an incentive to bias judgement. This facilitates efficient decision-making in the face of uncertainty, particularly in complex social situations with several response options including aggression or violence.

The absence of somatic markers renders a person incapable of discriminating between several potential outcomes by exploiting the guidance of previous experience. This is conjectured to lead to the random and impulsive decision-making exhibited by individuals with ventromedial prefrontal cortex damage, which may be aggressive or violent in nature. For example, the option of hitting someone may previously have been associated with punishment, and therefore somatic markers would guide a healthy individual away from this option. However, someone who was unable to generate somatic markers would not benefit from this previous association and hence would be more likely to go ahead and strike someone (Blair, 2001).

Experiments with patients who have bilateral ventromedial damage support the prediction that they are no longer able to generate somatic responses to emotionally charged stimuli. Skin conductance responses were measured on presentation of neutral stimuli (e.g. landscape) and emotional stimuli (e.g. mutilated body). In contrast to normal and non-frontal lobe brain-damaged controls, patients with ventromedial damage failed to produce standard skin conductance responses to emotional stimuli in comparison with neutral stimuli (Damasio et al., 1990; Tranel & Damasio 1994).

Further evidence comes from a study using a task that attempts to simulate a real-life situation, called the Iowa gambling task (Bechara et al., 1994). This involves decision-making with uncertain premises and outcome, through a regimen of monetary reward and punishment. Subjects have to forego immediate monetary reward in order to achieve increased long-term delayed reward. It is not possible to calculate the exact net gains or losses for each deck so subjects have to develop a sense of which decks are the most profitable. Individuals with ventromedial damage were significantly impaired on this task, choosing decks that offered high immediate reward but lost large amounts of money in the long term (Bechara et al., 1994). Boys with psychopathic tendencies were also found to be impaired in this task (Blair et al., 2001b).

When skin conductance was measured during performance of the task, Bechara et al. (1996) found that normal subjects showed a high-amplitude anticipatory skin conductance response prior to choosing the bad decks but not before selecting the good decks. This occurred in advance of self-reported understanding of the task, thus suggesting that this is an automatic process that operates entirely at a non-conscious level, although it can be made available to awareness (Damasio, 1999). This anticipatory effect was not shown in patients with ventromedial damage, although they did show normal skin conductance responses to reward and punishment following their choice (Bechara et al., 2000). Damasio interprets this as suggesting that the autonomic response is normally triggered from the ventromedial region as a very early alarm signal that biases further evaluation of factual knowledge regarding the situation (Damasio, 1999).

However, contrary to this model is the finding that Blair & Cipolotti's (2000) case with acquired sociopathy was able to perform the Iowa gambling task, despite having orbitofrontal cortex damage. Nevertheless, like Damasio's patients, he failed to generate autonomic responses to negative visual stimuli including sad and angry emotional expressions in comparison with neutral faces, and threatening objects such as weapons in comparison with neutral objects such as household items. This pattern of deficits is not in keeping with the somatic marker hypothesis, which would suggest a relationship between autonomic responding and performance on the gambling task.

Further criticism of the somatic marker hypothesis is that it is not efficient in eliciting autonomic responses each time a decision is made. Rolls (1995) suggests that a more efficient neural route is the direct pathway from the orbitofrontal cortex and amygdala to the basal ganglia in order to produce behavioural responses to learned stimuli. Rolls (1996) interprets the skin conductance research findings as consistent with the notion that learned reinforcers elicit autonomic responses as by-products through stimulus-reinforcement learning. The role of stimulus-reinforcement learning and a lack of autonomic responsivity in aggression is explored further by Blair (2004) with regard to instrumental aggression.

Instrumental aggression

Neuropsychological mechanisms that have been proposed to explain instrumental aggression include insensitivity to punishment and also a reduced sensitivity to others, or lack of empathy. These hypotheses individually account for some but not all of the available evidence about instrumental aggression in psychopathy. However the integrated emotions systems model (Blair, 2006) combines both approaches and also draws from the reactive aggression literature to provide the most comprehensive explanation.

Insensitivity to punishment

Theories of stimulus reinforcement can be applied to facilitate understanding of instrumental aggressive behaviours. An inability to form and use stimulus reinforcement means that an individual will not associate fear with an action that previously led to punishment. Given that morals are alleged to develop through the use of punishment (Eysenck & Gudjonsson, 1989), this means that, without this ability, an individual will not become frightened by punishment and this will not inhibit future attempts to re-engage in the punished action such as an act of aggression.

In particular, Blair (2004) argues that the mechanism underpinning instrumental aggression in psychopathy is impairment of the formation and use of stimulus-reinforcement associations due to amygdala dysfunction. Evidence in favour of this stance includes the finding that individuals with psychopathy have been shown to have reduced amygdala volume (Tiihonen *et al.*, 2000), are impaired in aversive conditioning (e.g. Lykken, 1957; Flor *et al.*, 2002), and also exhibit reduced amygdala activation during the aversive conditioning process (Veit *et al.*, 2002; Birbaumer *et al.*, 2005). Furthermore, individuals with psychopathy have been shown to exhibit impairments in passive avoidance learning (Lykken, 1957; Newman & Kosson, 1986; Blair *et al.*, 2004).

It has previously been suggested that the limitations in stimulus reinforcements exhibited by psychopaths extends only to stimulus-punishment associations but not to stimulus-reward associations. This is supported by research showing that, in psychopathy, following the presentation of positive visual primes, individuals show appropriate suppression of the startle reflex, but, in contrast, following the presentation of negative visual primes, there is reduced intensification of the startle reflex (Patrick *et al.*, 1993; Levenston *et al.*, 2000; Herpertz *et al.*, 2001; Pastor *et al.*, 2003). However, Blair and colleagues have argued more recently that stimulus-reward associations are also affected in the disorder, albeit to a lesser extent. They have found that individuals with psychopathy show disadvantages on both positive and negative lexical decision-making priming tasks (Verona *et al.*, 2004) and emotional attention paradigms (Mitchell *et al.*, 2006b). Whilst impairments were found in processing both positive and negative material, this was most pronounced for negative material, including facial expressions. This specific deficit may also be interpreted as indicating a lack of empathy.

Impaired empathy

A lack of empathy and diminished capacity for remorse are characteristics of psychopathy and may be related to instrumental violence displayed by this group. Empathy has been broadly divided into two components—cognitive empathy and emotional empathy (Restak, 1984). Cognitive empathy is the ability to take the perspective of another person whereas emotional empathy is the ability to appreciate another's emotional state and experience an emotional change in response.

There is little evidence to suggest that cognitive empathy is affected in conditions associated with aggression. Individuals with psychopathy do not exhibit deficits in the theory-of-mind reasoning or cognitive empathy (Richell *et al.*, 2003) and whilst some studies of children with aggressive behaviour showed some theory-of-mind impairments (Hughes *et al.*, 1998), this has not been replicated by several other studies using different measures (Happé & Frith, 1996; Hughes *et al.*, 2000; Sutton *et al.*, 2001). In contrast, emotional empathy seems to be dissociated from cognitive empathy and may be differentially affected in individuals with psychopathy.

People with psychopathic tendencies have difficulties recognizing the emotion of sadness, particularly in childhood (Blair *et al.*, 2001a; Stevens *et al.*, 2001).

However, they have more reliable deficits in recognition of fear in both facial and vocal emotion recognition tasks (Blair *et al.*, 2001a, 2005). In contrast, they do not have difficulty in recognizing other emotions states, which suggests that this deficit is very specific. Sad and fearful expressions can be regarded as aversive unconditioned stimuli, and an appropriate response to these stimuli is necessary for adaptive social behaviour (Blair, 1995). Therefore, if individuals with psychopathic tendencies have difficulty recognizing and responding to these aversive emotional expressions, they are unlikely to inhibit aggressive behaviour when faced with such responses. This proposal is known as the violence inhibition mechanism model (Blair, 1995; Blair *et al.*, 1997).

The violence inhibition mechanism model was developed to explain the role of empathy in moral socialization. Distress cues from other humans are aversive stimuli and lead to increased autonomic activity, attention, and activation of the brainstem threat-response system. For a normally developing child, such distress cues in others become paired with the act that caused the distress through classical conditioning. Therefore, a child will learn that a person being hit is aversive because it has been paired with the person exhibiting distress. This type of learning forms part of the normal socialization process. However, disruption to the violence inhibition mechanism system in psychopathy may arise if the individual does not find the distress cue aversive and it does not become established as a conditioned stimulus paired with antisocial actions. This means that the use of instrumental aggression or violence is more in order for an individual with psychopathy to achieve their goals (Blair, 1995, 2004).

Evidence to support this model relates to the well-established involvement of the amygdala in processing sad and fearful expressions (e.g. Morris *et al.*, 1996; Phillips *et al.*, 1998) and the finding that amygdala functioning seems to be deficient in individuals with psychopathic tendencies. They show reduced amygdala responses to emotional expressions (Gordon *et al.*, 2004) and also show reduced autonomic responses to these expressions (Aniskiewicz, 1979; Blair *et al.*, 1997). Therefore, in the absence of the ability to respond emotionally to another person's distressed expression, an individual is more likely not to inhibit an aggressive behaviour that induces fear in another person.

Integrated emotions systems model

The integrated emotions systems model (Blair, 2006) provides a neurocognitive model of emotional functioning that can be applied to explain both reactive and instrumental aggression in psychopathy in terms of dysfunction of the ventrolateral prefrontal cortex and amygdala. The model posits that the ventrolateral prefrontal cortex is involved in the modulation of reactive aggression, particularly through difficulties in response reversal following contingency change. Inability to alter stimulus-response associations following a change in contingency may evoke frustration as the individual is left not receiving a reward when they are expecting one. This frustration leads to a heightened risk of reactive aggression in psychopathy (Blair, 2004).

However, the amygdala is proposed to play a primary role in the dysfunctional behaviour in instrumental aggression through difficulties in the formation and use of stimulus-reinforcement associations as described above. Blair (2004) additionally suggests that the amygdala interacts with the temporal cortex to allow enhancement of attention for emotional stimuli. Impairments of this process lead to a reduced effect of emotion on attentional processes. For example, on a lexical decision task where emotional words are normally recognized more quickly as words than neutral words, this discrepancy in favour of emotion words is less pronounced for individuals with psychopathy (Day & Wong, 1996; Lorenz & Newman, 2002). In addition, individuals with psychopathy are less distracted by emotional stimuli in an emotional interruption task (Mitchell *et al.*, 2006b). These results suggest that if individuals with psychopathy do not differentially attend to emotional stimuli above neutral stimuli, they are less likely to recognize and hence develop conditioned responses to aversive cues.

Whilst many of the deficits attributed to amygdala dysfunction could be regarded as having additional orbitofrontal cortex involvement, Blair (2004) argues that they are unlikely to be due to orbitofrontal cortex impairment, as lesions to this region do not impair aversive conditioning (Quirk *et al.*, 2000) or passive avoidance (Schoenbaum *et al.*, 2002). However, Blair (2004) suggests that, in developmental psychopathy, reduced input to the orbitofrontal cortex from the amygdala may over time affect its responsivity. This explanation would account for why both reactive and instrumental aggression are prominent in psychopathy (Cornell *et al.*, 1996) whereas only reactive aggression tends to be exhibited by individuals following acquired brain lesions involving the prefrontal cortex (Anderson *et al.*, 1999; Blair, 2004).

Issues for a forensic neuropsychologist

A forensic neuropsychologist may be instructed to provide an expert opinion about a defendant in cases involving aggression and violence. In criminal cases, the most likely reason for a neuropsychological assessment is to establish whether the defendant is suffering from a neurological or psychiatric condition associated with aggression, such as those described at the beginning of the chapter, and/or to evaluate the extent to which neuropsychological deficits impact on the defendant's ability to engage in the court process and/or constitute mitigating factors. The high rates of violent and aggressive behaviour following traumatic brain injury and also the high prevalence of traumatic brain injury among incarcerated inmates (Slaughter *et al.*, 2003) indicate that it is important for a forensic neuropsychologist to clearly explore the possibility of head injury and other acquired brain injury aetiologies with a defendant. It is also important to remember that conditions may not be mutually exclusive; for example, an individual with a traumatic brain injury may also suffer from dementia or epilepsy.

Identification of neuropsychological deficits has several implications for legal proceedings and therefore, particularly in homicide cases, a defence team may be keen to conduct multiple investigations to establish the presence of a relevant disorder. It is helpful to gain clear instructions regarding the rationale for an assessment before accepting a case, rather than undertaking a general neuropsychological 'fishing trip'. It is important for a forensic neuropsychologist to determine whether previous assessments have been administered and also to bear in mind the possibility of underperformance, given that it may be in a defendant's interests to exhibit cognitive deficits. This issue is dealt with in more detail in Chapter 11.

There are several reasons why neuropsychological impairments are relevant in cases of aggression and violence. Firstly, the neuropsychological deficits may affect the defendant's fitness to plead. The second consideration is to determine whether they constitute mitigating factors. This may allow their defence team to introduce a defence of diminished responsibility in a homicide case. The usual practice is for an individual to be tried for murder, but the judge or defence team may introduce manslaughter as an alternative indictment. In this case, the jury will be instructed to determine whether the individual is guilty or not guilty of murder, and if they decide not guilty, they then need to consider whether the individual is guilty or not guilty of manslaughter. Manslaughter can be voluntary or involuntary, whereby the accused did not intend to cause death but caused it through recklessness or criminal negligence. Voluntary manslaughter is when a killing is intentional but the accused has a mitigatory defence such as provocation or diminished responsibility.

In a provocation defence, it has to be shown that the provoking act was such that a 'reasonable man' would have responded as the defendant did under the same circumstances. Furthermore, it has to be demonstrated that the killing was the result of a sudden and temporary loss of self-control, i.e. that it was reactive aggression rather than premeditated or instrumental aggression. Thus, the forensic neuropsychologist may be asked for an opinion regarding whether an aggressive act was reactive or instrumental.

To argue a case of diminished responsibility, the defendant must prove that their mind was impaired by an abnormality at the time of the killing. The phrase 'abnormality of mind' is defined as a state of mind that is so different from an ordinary person that a reasonable man would find it abnormal.

Neuropsychological impairments, particularly in the context of a recognized neurological or psychiatric disorder, may therefore be relevant for a diminished responsibility defence. However, states of mind that might be experienced by the reasonable man (such as hatred, rage, jealousy, or a state of mind induced by alcohol or drugs) are not classed as being an abnormality of mind. The majority of aggressive and violent offences occur in the context of alcohol use, the implications of which are addressed in Chapter 8. It is therefore important for a forensic neuropsychologist to establish whether a defendant was intoxicated or under the influence of drugs at the time of a crime, but also address the possibility that this may have exacerbated pre-existing neuropsychological deficits associated with aggression and violence.

In cases where neuropsychological impairments are used as a defence, a forensic neuropsychologist should make the court aware that it is difficult to infer a direct causal relationship between neuropsychological deficits and an aggressive offence. For example, from the literature it is difficult to conclude firmly that a particular pathology has a causal relationship with violence, as most studies do not account for the possibility of higher premorbid levels of violence in many of these patient groups, e.g. aggressive and violent criminal behaviour only occurs in a minority of individuals with frontal lobe injuries. In a study of Finnish World War II veterans, fewer than 5% of individuals with frontal lobe damage had a criminal conviction, with only one relating to a violence offence (Virkkunen *et al.*, 1976). It has been suggested that the increased risk of violence associated with focal frontal lobe injury is only 10% above the base rate of a given population (Brower & Price, 2001). Nevertheless, it may be possible to comment on whether the presence of impairment increased the likelihood of an offence occurring, given the particular presenting disorder and the circumstances. For example, in individuals with a previous risk of aggression, the presence of executive functioning deficits may be relevant when assessing the future likelihood of similar behaviour.

Finally, whilst the majority of expert witness opinion requests in cases of aggression and violence are likely to be concerning a defendant's cognitive functioning, a neuropsychology assessment may also be requested in other circumstances. For example, it may be necessary to determine whether the victim of aggression or violence is a reliable witness, particularly following a head injury and/or where a victim has been subjected to sustained physical abuse. Another potential medico-legal issue addressed by forensic neuropsychologists is aggression in the context of a traumatic brain injury, which may lead to alienation from the family, loss of employment, and other adverse social outcomes (Kim, 2002). A neuropsychologist may therefore be required to comment on these factors in personal injury proceedings. Therefore, whilst a forensic neuropsychologist is more likely to be involved in criminal prosecution cases where there are issues of violence and aggression, they may also be involved in civil court proceedings (see Chapter 9).

Conclusions

Neuropsychological impairments have been associated with aggressive or violent behaviours in the context of a range of psychiatric and neurological conditions. Three brain regions—the dorsolateral prefrontal cortex, the orbitofrontal/ventrolateral prefrontal cortex, and the amygdala—seem to be differentially affected in several of these disorders, and each region may play a different role with regard to the display of reactive and instrumental aggression.

Dorsolateral prefrontal cortex dysfunction is associated with developmental behavioural disorders including conduct disorder, attention deficit disorder, and subsequently antisocial personality disorder. These groups are likely also to have experienced comorbid educational and social disadvantages, which may additionally influence aggressive behaviour through social learning processes (e.g. Bandura & Ribes-Inesta, 1976) and poor verbal communication skills (Brower & Price, 2001). However, it seems that executive functioning deficits may increase the risk of reactive aggression through poor inhibitory control of impulses. Furthermore, if an individual presents with a constellation of executive functioning difficulties, they will not only have difficulty in inhibiting an aggressive response, they will also have problems with planning or problem-solving regarding an alternative non-aggressive solution and objectively reasoning through the future consequences of these options before acting.

Disruption of orbitofrontal/ventrolateral cortex functioning is likely to occur in the context of acquired brain injuries but also may be relevant in psychopathy. Here, aggressive behaviour is associated with poor social judgement and an inability to respond appropriately to social cues such as angry faces. Problems with reversal learning following contingency changes may lead to frustration and reactive aggression, particularly when an individual is expecting a reward and it is not received.

Amygdala dysfunction has been specifically identified as playing a role in developmental psychopathy, although it may also have importance in certain epilepsy conditions such as temporal lobe epilepsy. In psychopathy, amygdala dysfunction is associated with insensitivity to punishment and insensitivity to the emotional responses of others. This means that individuals do not undergo normal socialization through classical conditioning of aversion to another person's distress, nor are they able to recognize or respond to distress cues. This leads to increased instrumental aggression or violence, as this is not deterred by the experience of aversive reinforcement through harm to others.

A forensic neuropsychologist may be involved as an expert witness in cases involving aggression and violence in order to assess the relevance and impact of neuropsychological impairments and associated conditions. In homicide cases, evidence of neuropsychological impairments may be used to form a defence of provocation or diminished responsibility. Whilst it is difficult to infer a direct causal relationship between aggression and neuropsychological functions, it may be possible to provide an opinion regarding whether the presence of impairment increased the likelihood of aggression and violence, given the particular presenting deficits and possible neuropsychological mechanisms.

Forensic neuropsychologists have knowledge about the neuropsychological profiles of psychiatric and neurological conditions associated with aggression and violence. They have an understanding of the neurological underpinnings of these conditions and an ability to apply neuropsychological models to provide detailed case formulations. These factors, together with their experience of the legal process and/or of forensic settings, place them in a strong position to provide a valuable opinion as an expert witness in court proceedings.

References

Amen, D. G., Stubblefield, M., Carmicheal, B., and Thisted, R. (1996). Brain SPECT findings and aggressiveness. *Annals of Clinical Psychiatry*, **8**:129–137.

American Psychiatric Association (1994). *Diagnostic and Statistical Manual of Mental Disorders*, 4th edn. Washington, DC: American Psychiatric Association.

Anderson, S. W., Bechara, A., Damasio, H., Tranel, D., and Damasio, A. R. (1999). Impairment of social and moral behavior related to early damage in human prefrontal cortex. *Nature Neuroscience*, **2**:1032–1037.

Angrilli, A., Mauri, A., Palomba D., et al. (1996). Startle reflex and emotion modulation impairment after a right amygdala lesion. *Brain*, **119**:1991–2000.

Aniskiewicz, A. S. (1979). Autonomic components of vicarious conditioning and psychopathy. *Journal of Clinical Psychology*, **35**:60–67.

Baguley, I. J., Cooper, J., and Felmingham, K. (2006). Aggressive behavior following traumatic brain injury: how common is common? *Journal of Head Trauma Rehabilitation*, **21**:45–56.

Ballard, C. G., Margallo-Lana, M., Fossey J., et al. (2001). A one-year follow-up study of behavioral and psychological symptoms in dementia among people in care environments. *Journal of Clinical Psychiatry*, **62**:631–636.

Bambinski, L. M., Hartsough, C. S., and Lambert, N. M. (1999). Childhood conduct problems, hyperactivity-impulsivity, and inattention as predictors of adult criminal activity. *Journal of Child Psychology and Psychiatry*, **40**:347–355.

Bandura, A. and Ribes-Inesta, E. (1976). *Analysis of Delinquency and Aggression*. New Jersey: Lawrence Erlbaum Associates.

Barkataki, I., Kumari, V., Das, M., et al. (2005). A neuropsychological investigation into violence and mental illness. *Schizophrenia Research*, **74**:1–13.

Barratt, E. S. (1994). Impulsiveness and aggression. In: J. Monahan and H. J. Steadman (eds), *Violence and Mental Disorder: Developments in Risk Assessment*, pp. 61–79. Washington, DC: University of Chicago Press.

Barratt, E. S., Stanford, M. S., Kent, T. A., and Felthous, A. (1997). Neuropsychological and cognitive psychophysiological substrates of impulsive aggression. *Biological Psychiatry*, **41**:1045–1061.

Bechara, A., Damasio, A. R., Damasio, H., and Anderson, S. W. (1994). Insensitivity to future consequences following damage to human prefrontal cortex. *Cognition*, **50**:7–15.

Bechara, A., Tranel, D., Damasio, H., and Damasio, A. R. (1996). Failure to respond autonomically to anticipated future outcomes following damage to prefrontal cortex. *Cerebral Cortex*, **6**:215–25.

Bechara, A., Damasio, H., and Damasio, A. R. (2000). Emotion, decision-making and the orbitofrontal cortex. *Cerebral Cortex*, **10**:295–307.

Birbaumer, N., Veit, R., Lotze, M., et al. (2005). Deficient fear conditioning in psychopathy: A functional magnetic resonance imaging study. *Archives of General Psychiatry*, **62**:799–805.

Blair, R. J. R. (1995). A cognitive developmental approach to morality: Investigating the psychopath. *Cognition*, **57**:1–29.

Blair, R. J. R. (2001). Neuro-cognitive models of aggression, the antisocial personality disorders, and psychopathy. *Journal of Neurology, Neurosurgery and Psychiatry*, **71**:727–731.

Blair, R. J. R. (2003). A neurocognitive model of the psychopathic individual. In: M. A. Ron and T. W. Robbins (eds), *Disorders of Brain and Mind 2*, pp. 200–420. Cambridge: Cambridge University Press.

Blair, R. J. R. (2004). The roles of orbital frontal cortex in the modulation of antisocial behavior. *Brain and Cognition*, **55**:198–208.

Blair, R. J. R. (2006). The emergence of psychopathy: Implications for the neuropsychological approach to developmental disorders. *Cognition*, **101**:414–442.

Blair, R. J. R. and Cipolotti, L. (2000). Impaired social response reversal. A case of neural responses to facial expressions of sadness and anger. *Brain*, **122**:883–93.

Blair, R. J. R. and Curran, H. V. (1999). Selective impairment in the recognition of anger induced by diazepam. *Psychopharmacology*, **147**:335–338.

Blair, R. J. R., Jones, L., Clark, F., and Smith, M. (1997). The psychopathic individual: A lack of responsiveness to distress cues? *Psychophysiology*, **34**:192–198.

Blair, R. J. R., Colledge, E., Murray, L., and Mitchell, D. G. (2001a). A selective impairment in the processing of sad and fearful expressions in children with psychopathic tendencies. *Journal of Abnormal Child Psychology*, **29**:491–498.

Blair, R. J. R., Colledge, E., and Mitchell, D. G. (2001b). Somatic markers and response reversal: Is there orbitofrontal cortex dysfunction in boys with psychopathic tendencies? *Journal of Abnormal Child Psychology*, **29**:499–511.

Blair, R. J. R., Mitchell, D. G. V., Leonard, A., Budhani, S., Peschardt, K. S., and Newman, C. (2004). Passive avoidance learning in individuals with psychopathy: modulation by reward but not by punishment. *Personality and Individual Differences*, **37**:1179–1192.

Blair, R. J. R., Budhani, S., Colledge, E., and Scott, S. (2005). Deafness to fear in boys with psychopathic tendencies. *Journal of Child Psychology and Psychiatry*, **46**:327–336.

Blanchard, R. J., Blanchard, C. D., Takahashi, T., and Kelley, M. J. (1977). Attack and defensive behaviour in the albino rat. *Animal Behaviour*, **25**:622–34.

Blumer, D. and Benson, D. F. (1975) Personality changes with frontal lobe lesions. In: D. F. Benson and D. Blumer (eds), *Psychiatric Aspects of Neurological Disease*, pp. 151–170. New York: Grune & Stratton.

Boecker, M., Buecheler, M. M., Schroeter, M. L., and Gauggel, S. (2007). Prefrontal brain activation during stop-signal response inhibition: an event-related functional near-infrared spectroscopy study. *Behaviour Brain Research*, **176**:259–266.

Borrill, J. A., Rosen, B. K., and Summerfield, A. B. (1987). The influence of alcohol on judgement of facial expression of emotion. *British Journal of Medical Psychology*, **60**:71–77.

Braggio, J. T., Pishkin, V., Gameros, T. A., and Brooks, D. L. (1993). Academic achievement in substance-abusing and conduct-disordered adolescents. *Journal of Clinical Psychology*, **49**:282–291.

Brower, M. C. and Price, B. H. (2001). Neuropsychiatry of frontal lobe dysfunction in violent and criminal behaviour: A critical review. *Journal of Neurology, Neurosurgery and Psychiatry*, **71**:720–726.

Budhani, S. and Blair, R. J. R. (2005). Response reversal and children with psychopathic tendencies: Success is a function of salience of contingency change. *Journal of Child Psychology and Psychiatry*, **46**:972–981.

Budhani, S., Richell, R. A., and Blair, R. J. (2006). Impaired reversal but intact acquisition: probabilistic response reversal deficits in adult individuals with psychopathy. *Journal of Abnormal Psychology*, 115(3), 552–558.

Bushman, B. J. and Cooper, H. M. (1990). Effects of alcohol on human aggression: An integrative research review. *Psychological Bulletin*, **107**:341–354.

Campeau, S. and Davis, M. (1995). Involvement of subcortical and cortical afferents to the lateral nucleus of the amygdala in fear conditioning measured with fear-potentiated startle in rats trained concurrently with auditory and visual conditioned stimuli. *Journal of Neuroscience*, **15**:2312–2327.

Carlsson, G. S., Svardsudd, K., and Welin, L. (1987). Long-term effects of head injuries sustained during life in three male populations. *Journal of Neurosurgery*, **67**:197–205.

Chikazoe, J., Konishi, S., Asari, T., Jimura, K., and Miyashita, Y. (2007). Activation of right inferior frontal gyrus during response inhibition across response modalities. *Journal of Cognitive Neuroscience*, **19**:69–80.

Chou, K. R., Kaas, M. J., and Richie, M. F. (1996). Assaultive behavior in geriatric patients. *Journal of Gerontological Nursing*, **22**:30–38.

Clare, I. C. H. and Murphy, G. H. (1998). Working with offenders or alleged offenders with intellectual disabilities. In: E. Emerson, C. Hatton, J. Bromley, and A. Caine (eds), *Clinical Psychology and People with Intellectual Disabilities*, pp. 154–176. Chichester, UK: Wiley.

Cleckley, H. (1941/1988). *The Mask of Sanity* (5th edn). St Louis: Mosby Co.

Coccaro, E. F., McCloskey, M. S., Fitzgerald, D. A., and Phan, K. L. (2007). Amygdala and orbitofrontal reactivity to social threat in individuals with impulsive aggression. *Biological Psychiatry*, **62**:168–178.

Cohen, J. (1988). *Statistical power analysis for the behavioral sciences*. Hillsdale, NJ: Lawrence Erlbaum Associates.

Coid, J. W. (1992). DSM-III diagnosis in criminal psychopaths: A way forward. *Criminal and Mental Health*, **2**:78–94.

Collins, P. and White, T. (2002). Forensic implications of attention deficit hyperactivity disorder (ADHD) in adulthood. *Journal of Forensic Psychiatry*, **13**:263–284.

Cornell, D. G., Warren, J., Hawk, G., Stafford, E., Oram, G., and Pine, D. (1996). Psychopathy in instrumental and reactive violent offenders. *Journal of Consulting and Clinical Psychology*, **64**:783–790.

Critchley, H. D. (2005). Neural mechanisms of autonomic, affective, and cognitive integration. *Journal of Comparative Neurology*, **493**:154–166.

Damasio, A. R. (1994). *Descartes' Error: Emotion, Reason, and the Human Brain.* New York: Putnam.

Damasio, A. R. (1996). The somatic marker hypothesis and the possible functions of the prefrontal cortex. *Philosophical Translations of the Royal Society of London B*, **351**:1413–1420.

Damasio, A. R. (1999). *The feeling of what happens: Body and emotion in the making of consciousness.* San Diego, CA: Harcourt.

Damasio, A. R., Tranel, D., and Damasio H. (1990). Individuals with sociopathic behaviour caused by frontal damage fail to respond autonomically to social stimuli. *Behavioural Brain Research*, **41**:81–94.

Damasio, H., Grabowski, T., Frank, R., Galaburda, A. M., and Damasio, A. R. (1994). The return of Phineas Gage: Clues about the brain from the skull of a famous patient. *Science*, **264(5162)**, 1102–1105.

Davis, M. and Whalen, P. J. (2001). The amygdala: Vigilance and emotion. *Molecular Psychiatry*, **6**:13–34.

Day, R. and Wong, S. (1996). Anomalous perceptual asymmetries for negative emotional stimuli in the psychopath. *Journal of Abnormal Psychology*, **105**:648–652.

de Bruin, J. P., van Oyen, H. G., and van de Poll, N. (1983). Behavioural changes following lesions of the orbital prefrontal cortex in male rats. *Behavioural Brain Research*, **10(2–3)**, 209–232.

Dery, M., Toupin, J., Pauze, R., Mercier, H., and Fortin, L. (1999). Neuropsychological characteristics of adolescents with conduct disorder: Association with attention-deficit-hyperactivity and aggression. *Journal of Abnormal Child Psychology*, **27**:225–236.

Devinsky, O., Ronsaville, D., Cox, C., Witt, E., Fedio, P., and Theodore, W. H. (1994). Interictal aggression in epilepsy: The Buss-Durkee Hostility Inventory. *Epilepsia*, **35**:585–590.

Dinn, W. M. and Harris, C. L. (2000). Neurocognitive function in antisocial personality disorder. *Psychiatry Research*, **97**:173–190.

Dodge, K. A. (1980). Social cognition and children's aggressive behavior. *Child Development*, **51**:162–170.

Dodge, K. (2000). Conduct disorder. In: A. J. Sameroff, M. Lewis, and S. M. Miller (eds), *Handbook of Developmental Psychopathology*, 2nd edn, pp. 447–463. New York: Kluwer Academic/Plenum Publishers.

Dodge, K. and Tomlin, A. (1987). Utilization of self-schemas as a mechanism of interpretational bias in aggressive children. *Social Cognition*, **5**:280–300.

Dolan, M. C. (1994). Psychopathy—a neurobiological perspective. *British Journal of Psychiatry*, **165**:151–159.

Duncan, D., Matson, J. L., Bamburg, J. W., Cherry, K. E., and Buckley, T. (1999). The relationship of self-injurious behaviour and aggression to social skills in persons with severe and profound learning disability. *Research in Developmental Disabilities*, **20**:441–448.

Dunlop, T. W., Udvarhelyi, G. B., Stedem, A. F., *et al.* (1991). Comparison of patients with and without emotional/behavioral deterioration during the first year after traumatic brain injury. *Journal of Neuropsychiatry and Clinical Neuroscience*, **3**:150–156.

Duxbury, J. (2000). An evaluation of staff and patient views of and strategies employed to manage inpatient aggression and violence on one mental health unit: A pleuralistic design. *Psychiatric Bulletin*, **30**:166–168.

El-Badri, S. M. and Mellsop, G. (2006). Aggressive behaviour in an acute general adult psychiatric unit. *Psychiatric Bulletin*, **30**:166–168.

Elger, C. E., Helmstaedter, C., and Kurthen, M. (2004). Chronic epilepsy and cognition. *Lancet Neurology*, **3**:663–672.

Emerson, E. (1995). *Challenging Behaviour: Analysis and Intervention in People with Learning Difficulties*. Cambridge: Cambridge University Press.

Emerson, E. and Bromley, J. (1995). The form and function of challenging behaviours. *Journal of Intellectual Disability Research*, **39**:388–398.

Emerson, E., Caine, A., Bromley, J., and Hatton, C. (1998). Introduction. In: E. Emerson, C. Hatton, J. Bromley, and A. Caine (eds), *Clinical Psychology and People with Intellectual Disabilities*, p. 16. Chichester, UK: Wiley.

Engelborghs, S., Maertens, K., Marien P., *et al.* (2006). Behavioural and neuropsychological correlates of frontal lobe features in dementia. *Psychological Medicine*, **36**:1173–1182.

Eustace, A., Kidd, N., Greene E., *et al.* (2001). Verbal aggression in Alzheimer's disease: Clinical, functional and neuropsychological correlates. *International Journal of Geriatric Psychiatry*, **16**:858–861.

Everitt, B. J., Cardinal, R. N., Parkinson, J. A., and Robbins, T. W. (2000). Appetitive behavior: Impact of amygdala-dependent mechanisms of emotional learning. *Annual New York Academy of Sciences*, **985**:233–250.

Eysenck, H. J. and Eysenck, S. B. G. (1975). *Manual of the Eysenck Personality Questionnaire*. London: Hodder & Stoughton.

Eysenck, H. J. and Gudjonsson, G. H. (1989). *The Causes and Cures of Criminality*. London: Plenum Press.

Fenwick, P. B. (1986). Aggression and epilepsy. In: M. R. Trimble and T. Bolwig (eds), *Epilepsy and Psychiatry*, pp. 31–60. Chichester, UK: John Wiley.

Fleminger, S., Greenwood, R. J., and Oliver, D. L. (2006). Pharmacological management for agitation and aggression in people with acquired brain injury. *Cochrane Database Systematic Review*, **18**, CD003299.

Flor, H., Birbaumer, N., Hermann, C., Ziegler, S., and Patrick, C. J. (2002). Aversive Pavlovian conditioning in psychopaths: Peripheral and central correlates. *Psychophysiology*, **39**:505–518.

Fuchs, C. and Benson, B. A. (1995). Social information processing by aggressive and nonaggressive men with mental retardation. *American Journal of Mental Retardation*, **100**:244–252.

Funayama, E. S., Grillon, C., Davis, M., and Phelps, E. A. (2001). A double dissociation in the affective modulation of startle in humans: Effects of unilateral temporal lobectomy. *Journal of Cognitive Neuroscience*, **13**:721–729.

Gates, D. M., Fitzwater, E., and Meyer, U. (1999). Violence against caregivers in nursing homes. Expected, tolerated, and accepted. *Journal of Gerontological Nursing*, **25**:12–22.

Gerard, M. E., Spitz, M. C., Towbin, J. A., and Shantz, D. (1998). Subacute postictal aggression. *Neurology*, **50**:384–388.

Gilmour, J., Hill, B., Place, M., and Skuse, D. H. (2004). Social communication deficits in conduct disorder: A clinical and community survey. *Journal of Child Psychology and Psychiatry*, **45**:967–978.

Gordon, H. L., Baird, A. A., and End, A. (2004). Functional differences among those high and low on a trait measure of psychopathy. *Biological Psychiatry*, **56**:516–521.

Gorenstein, E. E. (1982). Frontal lobe functions in psychopaths. *Journal of Abnormal Psychology*, **91**:368–379.

Gorenstein, E. (1990). Neuropsychology of juvenile delinquency. *Forensic Reports*, **3**:15–48.

Gormley, N., Rizwan, M. R., and Lovestone, S. (1998). Clinical predictors of aggressive behaviour in Alzheimer's disease. *International Journal of Geriatric Psychiatry*, **13**:109–115.

Goyer, P. F., Andreason, P. J., Semple, W. E., *et al.* (1994). Positron-emission tomography and personality disorders. *Neuropsychopharmacology*, **10**:21–28.

Grafman, J., Schwab, K., Warden, D., Pridgen, A., Brown, H. R., and Salazar, A. M. (1996). Frontal lobe injuries, violence, and aggression: A report of the Vietnam Head Injury Study. *Neurology*, **46**:1231–1238.

Gray, J. A. (1982). *The Neuropsychology of Anxiety: An Enquiry into the Functions of the Septo-hippocampal System*. New York: Oxford University Press.

Gregg, T. R. and Siegel, A. (2001). Brain structures and neurotransmitters regulating aggression in cats: Implications for human aggression. *Progress in Neuro-psychopharmacological and Biological Psychiatry*, **25**:91–140.

Greve, K. W., Sherwin, E., Stanford, M. S., Mathias, C., Love, J., and Ramzinski, P. (2001). Personality and neurocognitive correlates of impulsive aggression in long-term survivors of severe traumatic brain injury. *Brain Injury*, **15**:255–262.

Happé, F. and Frith, U. (1996). Theory of mind and social impairment in children with conduct disorder. *British Journal of Developmental Psychology*, **14**:385–398.

Hare, R. D. (1984). Performance of psychopaths on cognitive tasks related to frontal lobe function. *Journal of Abnormal Psychology*, **93**:133–140.

Hare, R. D. (1991). *The Hare Psychopathy Checklist—Revised*. Toronto, ON: Multi-Health Systems.

Hare, R. D. (1998). Psychopathy, affect and behaviour. In: D. Cooke, A. Forth, and R. Hare (eds), *Psychopathy: Theory, Research and Implications for Society*, pp. 105–139. Dordrecht: Kluwer.

Harlow, J. M. (1848). Passage of an iron rod through the head. *Boston Medical Surgery Journal*, **39**:389–893.

Harris, P. (1993). The nature and extent of aggressive behaviour amongst people with learning difficulties (mental handicap) in a single health district. *Journal of Intellectual Disability Research*, **37**:221–242.

Hart, S. D., Forth, A. E., and Hare, R. D. (1990). Performance of criminal psychopaths on selected neuropsychological tests. *Journal of Abnormal Psychology*, **99**:374–379.

Herpertz, S. C., Werth, U., Lukas G., et al. (2001). Emotion in criminal offenders with psychopathy and borderline personality disorder. *Archives of General Psychiatry*, **58**:737–745.

Herzberg, I. L. and Fenwick, P. B. C. (1988). The aetiology of aggression in temporal lobe epilepsy. *British Journal of Psychiatry*, **153**:50–55.

Hindley, N. and Gordon, H. (2000). The elderly, dementia, aggression and risk assessment. *International Journal of Geriatric Psychiatry*, **15**:254–259.

Hoffman, J. J., Hall, R. W., and Bartsch, T. W. (1987). On the relative importance of 'psychopathic' personality and alcoholism on neuropsychological measures of frontal lobe dysfunction. *Journal of Abnormal Psychology*, **96**:158–160.

Hooper, S. R. and Brown, T. T. (1995). Neuropsychological functioning of children and adolescents with conduct disorder and aggressive-assaultive features. *Archives of Clinical Neuropsychology*, **10**:343–344.

Hornak, J., Rolls, E. T., and Wade, D. (1996). Face and voice expression identification in patients with emotional and behavioural changes following ventral frontal lobe damage. *Neuropsychologia*, **34**:247–261.

Hornak, J., Bramham, J., Rolls, E. T., et al. (2003). Changes in emotion after circumscribed surgical lesions of the orbitofrontal and cingulate cortices. *Brain*, **126**:1691–1712.

Hornak, J., O'Doherty, J., Bramham, J., et al. (2004). Reward-related reversal learning after surgical excisions in orbito-frontal or dorsolateral prefrontal cortex in humans. *Journal of Cognitive Neuroscience*, **16**:463–78.

Hughes, C., Dunn, J., and White, A. (1998). Trick or treat?: Uneven understanding of mind and emotion and executive dysfunction in 'hard-to-manage' preschoolers. *Journal of Child Psychology and Psychiatry*, **39**:981–994.

Hughes, C., White, A., Sharpen, J., and Dunn, J. (2000). Antisocial, angry, and unsympathetic: 'hard-to-manage' preschoolers' peer problems and possible cognitive influences. *Journal of Child Psychology and Psychiatry*, **41**:169–179.

Kandel, E. and Freed, D. (1989). Frontal-lobe dysfunction and antisocial behavior: A review. *Journal of Clinical Psychology*, **45**:404–413.

Keene, J., Hope, T., Fairburn, C. G., Jacoby, R., Gedling, K., and Ware, C. J. (1999). Natural history of aggressive behaviour in dementia. *International Journal of Geriatric Psychiatry*, **14**:541–548.

Kim, E. (2002). Agitation, aggression, and disinhibition syndromes after traumatic brain injury. *Neurorehabilitation*, **17**:297–310.

Kolanowski, A. M. and Garr, M. (1999). The relation of premorbid factors to aggressive physical behavior in dementia. *Journal of Neuroscience Nursing*, **31**:278–284.

Kolb, B. and Whishaw, I. Q. (1996). *The Frontal Lobes: Fundamentals of Human Neuropsychology*, 4th edn, pp. 329–330. New York: WH Freeman & Co.

Krakowski, M., Czobor, P., Libiger, J., Kunz, M., Papezova, H., and Parker, B. B. (1997). Violence in schizophrenic patients: The role of positive psychotic symptoms and frontal lobe impairment. *American Journal of Forensic Psychiatry*, **18**:39–50.

Krakowski, M. I., Convit, A., Jaeger, J., Lin, S., and Volavka, J. (1999). Neurological impairment in violent schizophrenic inpatients. *American Journal of Psychiatry*, **146**:849–853.

Kreutzer, J. S., Marwitz, J. H., and Witol, A. D. (1995). Interrelationships between crime, substance abuse, and aggressive behaviours among persons with traumatic brain injury. *Brain Injury*, **9**:757–768.

Lafayette, J. M., Frankle, W. G., Pollock, A., Dyer, K., and Goff, D. C. (2003). Clinical characteristics, cognitive functioning and criminal histories of outpatients with schizophrenia. *Psychiatric Services*, **54**:1635–1640.

Lancman, M. (1999). Psychosis and peri-ictal confusional states. *Neurology*, **53** (Suppl. 2), S33–S38.

Lang, P. J., Bradley, M. M., and Cuthbert, B. N. (1990). Emotion, attention, and the startle reflex. *Psychological Review*, **97**:377–395.

Langevin, R., Ben-Aron, M., Wortzman, G., Dickey, R., and Handy, L. (1987). Brain damage, diagnosis, and substance abuse among violent offenders. *Behavioural Sciences and the Law*, **5**:77–94.

LaPierre, D., Braun, C. M. J., and Hodgins, S. (1995). Ventral frontal deficits in psychopathy: Neuropsychological test findings. *Neuropsychologia*, **33**:139–151.

Levenston, G. K., Patrick, C. J., Bradley, M. M., and Lang, P. J. (2000). The psychopath as observer: Emotion and attention in picture processing. *Journal of Abnormal Psychology*, **109**:373–386.

Levin, H. S. and Grossman, R. G. (1978). Behavioral sequelae of closed head injury. A quantitative study. *Archives of Neurology*, **35**:720–727.

Lewis, D. O., Pincus, J. H., Feldman, M., Jackson, L., and Bard, B. (1986). Psychiatric, neurological, and psychoeducational characteristics of 15 death row inmates in the United States. *American Journal of Psychiatry*, **143**:838–845.

Linares-Orama, N. (2005). Language-learning disorders and youth incarceration. *Journal of Communication Disorders*, **38**:311–319.

Linz, T. D., Hooper, S. R., Hynd, G. W., Isaac, W., and Gibson, L. J. (1990). Frontal lobe functioning in conduct disordered juveniles: Preliminary findings. *Archives of Clinical Neuropsychology*, **5**:411–416.

Lorenz, A. R. and Newman, J. P. (2002). Deficient response modulation and emotion processing in low-anxious caucasian psychopathic offenders: Results from a lexical decision task. *Emotion*, **2**:91–104.

Low, L. F., Brodaty, H., and Draper, B. (2002). A study of premorbid personality and behavioural and psychological impairments in dementia in nursing home residents. *International Journal of Geriatric Psychiatry*, **17**:779–783.

Lueger, R. J. and Gill, K. J. (1990). Frontal-lobe cognitive dysfunction in conduct disorder adolescents. *Journal of Clinical Psychology*, **46**:696–706.

Lyketsos, C. G., Steele, C., Galik, E., *et al.* (1999). Physical aggression in dementia patients and its relationship to depression. *American Journal of Psychiatry*, **156**:66–71.

Lykken, D. T. (1957). A study of anxiety in the sociopathic personality. *Journal of Abnormal and Social Psychology*, **55**:6–10.

MacDonald, T. K., Zanna, M. P., and Fong, G. T. (1996). When common sense goes out the window. *Personality and Social Psychology Bulletin*, **22**:763–775.

Machado, C. J. and Bachevalier, J. (2006). The impact of selective amygdala, orbital frontal cortex, or hippocampal formation lesions on established social relationships in rhesus monkeys. *Behavioural Neuroscience*, **120**:781–786

Malloy, P., Noel, N., Rogers, S., Longabaugh, R., and Beattie, M. (1989). Risk factors for neuropsychological impairments in alcoholics: Antisocial personality, age, years of drinking and gender. *Journal of Studies on Alcohol*, **50**:422–426.

Manuzza, S., Klein, R., Konig, P., and Giampino, T. (1989). Hyperactive boys almost grown up: IV. Criminality and its relationship to psychiatric status. *Archives of General Psychiatry*, **46**:1073–1079.

Marsh, L. and Krauss, D. L. (2000). Aggression and violence in patients with epilepsy. *Epilepsy and Behavior*, **1**:160–168.

Martell, D. A. (1992). Estimating the prevalence of organic brain dysfunction in maximum-security forensic psychiatric patients. *Journal of Forensic Science*, **37**:878–893.

Matheson, E. and Jahoda, A. (2005). Emotional understanding in aggressive and nonaggressive individuals with mild or moderate mental retardation. *American Journal of Mental Retardation*, **110**:57–67.

Mendez, M. F., Doss, R. C., and Taylor, J. L. (1993). Interictal violence in epilepsy. Relationship to behavior and seizure variables. *Journal of Nervous and Mental Disorders*, **181**:566–569.

Mendez, M. F., Chen, A. K., Shapira, J. S., and Miller, B. L. (2005). Acquired sociopathy and frontotemporal dementia. *Dementia and Geriatric Cognitive Disorders*, **20(2–3)**, 99–104.

Meyers, C. A., Berman, S. A., Scheibel, R. S., and Hayman, A. (1992). Case report: Acquired antisocial personality disorders associated with unilateral left orbital frontal lobe damage. *Journal of Psychiatry Neuroscience*, **17**:121–125.

Miller, L. (1988). Neuropsychological perspectives on delinquency. *Behavioral Sciences and the Law*, **6**:409–428.

Miller, B. L., Darby, A., Benson, D. F., Cummings, J. L., and Miller, M. H. (1997). Aggressive, socially disruptive and antisocial behaviour associated with fronto-temporal dementia. *British Journal of Psychiatry*, **170**:150–154.

Mitchell, D. G. V., Colledge, E., Leonard, A., and Blair, R. J. R. (2002). Risky decisions and response reversal: Is there evidence of orbitofrontal cortex dysfunction in psychopathic individuals? *Neuropsychologia*, **40**:2013–2022.

Mitchell, D. G., Avny, S. B., and Blair, R. J. (2006a). Divergent patterns of aggressive and neurocognitive characteristics in acquired versus developmental psychopathy. *Neurocase*, **12**:164–178.

Mitchell, D. G. V., Richell, R. A., Leonard, A., and Blair, R. J. R. (2006b). Emotion at the expense of cognition: Psychopathic individuals outperform controls on an operant response task. *Journal of Abnormal Psychology*, **115**:559–566.

Moffitt, T. E. (1993). Adolescence-limited and life-course-persistent antisocial behavior: A developmental taxonomy. *Psychological Review*, **100**:647–701.

Moffitt, T. E. and Henry, B. (1989). Neuropsychological assessment of executive function in self-reported delinquents. *Developmental Psychopathology*, **1**:105–118.

Moffitt, T. E., Lynam, D. R., and Sylva, P. A. (1994). Neuropsychological tests predicting persistent male delinquency. *Criminology*, **32**:277–300.

Morgan, A. B. and Lilienfeld, S. O. (2000). A meta-analytic review of the relation between antisocial behavior and neuropsychological measures of executive function. *Clinical Psychology Review*, **20**:113–136.

Morris, J. S., Frith, C. D., Perrett, D. I., *et al.* (1996). A differential response in the human amygdala to fearful and happy facial expressions. *Nature*, **383**:812–815.

Naudts, K. and Hodgins, S. (2006). Schizophrenia and violence: A search for neurobiological correlates. *Current Opinion in Psychiatry*, **19**:533–538.

Newman, J. P. and Kosson, D. S. (1986). Passive avoidance learning in psychopathic and nonpsychopathic offenders. *Journal of Abnormal Psychology*, **95**:252–256.

Nigg, J. T. (2000). On inhibition/disinhibition in developmental psychopathology: Views from cognitive and personality psychology and a working inhibition taxonomy. *Psychological Bulletin*, **126**:200–246.

Nigg, J. T. (2003). Response inhibition and disruptive behaviors. Toward a multiprocess conception of etiological heterogeneity for ADHD combined type and conduct disorder early-onset type. *Annals of New York Academy of Science*, **1008**:170–182.

O'Leary, D., Jyringi, D., and Sedler, M. (2005). Childhood conduct problems, stages of Alzheimer's disease, and physical aggression against caregivers. *International Journal of Geriatric Psychiatry*, **20**:401–405.

Panksepp, J. (1998). *Affective Neuroscience: The foundations of Human and Animal Emotions*. New York: Oxford University Press.

Pastor, M. C., Molto, J., Vila, J., and Lang, P. J. (2003). Startle reflex modulation, affective ratings and autonomic reactivity in incarcerated Spanish psychopaths. *Psychophysiology*, **40**:934–938.

Patrick, C. J., Bradley, M. M., and Lang, P. J. (1993). Emotion in the criminal psychopath: Startle reflex modulation. *Journal of Abnormal Psychology*, **102**:82–92.

Pennington, B. F. and Ozonoff, S. (1996). Executive functions and developmental psychopathology. *Journal of Child Psychology and Psychiatry*, **37**:51–87.

Phelps, L. and McClintock, K. (1994). Papa and peers: A biosocial approach to conduct disorder. *Journal of Psychopathology and Behavioral Assessment*, **16**:53–67.

Phillips, M. L., Young, A. W., Scott, S. K., *et al.* (1998). Neural responses to facial and vocal expressions of fear and disgust. *Proceedings of the Royal Society of London B, Biological Sciences*, **265**:1809–1817.

Porteus, S. D. (1945). Q scores, temperament and delinquency. *Journal of Social Psychology*, **21**:81–103.

Pryor, J. (2004). What environmental factors irritate people with acquired brain injury? *Disability Rehabilitation*, **26**:974–980.

Quirk, G. J. and Beer, J. S. (2006). Prefrontal involvement in the regulation of emotion: Convergence of rat and human studies. *Current Opinion in Neurobiology*, **16**:723–727.

Quirk, G. J., Russo, G. K., Barron, J. L., and Lebron, K. (2000). The role of ventromedial prefrontal cortex in the recovery of extinguished fear. *Journal of Neuroscience*, **20**:6225–6231.

Raine, A. (2002). Biosocial studies of antisocial and violent behavior in children and adults: A review. *Journal of Abnormal Child Psychology*, **30**:311–326.

Raine, A., Buchsbaum, M. S., Stanley, J., Lottenberg, S., Abel, L., and Stoddard, J. (1994). Selective reductions in prefrontal glucose metabolism in murderers. *Biological Psychiatry*, **36**:365–373.

Raine, A., Buchsbaum, M., and LaCasse, L. (1997). Brain abnormalities in murderers indicated by positron electron tomography. *Biological Psychiatry*, **42**:495–508.

Raine, A., Meloy, J. R., Bihrle, S., Stoddard, J., LaCasse, L., and Buchsbaum, M. S. (1998). Reduced prefrontal and increased subcortical brain functioning assessed in positron emission tomography in predatory and affective murders. *Biological Sciences and the Law*, **16**:319–332.

Raine, A., Moffitt, T. E., Caspi, A., Loeber, R., Stouthamer-Loeber, M., and Lynam, D. (2005). Neurocognitive impairments in boys on the life-course persistent antisocial path. *Journal of Abnormal Psychology*, **114**:38–49.

Ramamurthi, B. (1988). Stereotactic operation in behaviour disorders. Amygdalotomy and hypothalamotomy. *Acta Neurochirurgica Supplement*, **44**:152–157.

Rao, N., Jellinek, H. M., and Woolston, D. C. (1985). Agitation in closed head injury: Haloperidol effects on rehabilitation outcome. *Archives of Physical Medicine Rehabilitation*, **66**:30–34.

Rasmussen, K., Levander, S., and Sletvold, H. (1995). Aggressive and non-aggressive schizophrenics: Symptom profile and neuropsychological differences. *Psychology, Crime and Law*, **2**:119–129.

Renshaw, P. D. and Asher, S. R. (1983). Children's goals and strategies for social interaction. *Merrill-Palmer Quarterly*, **29**:353–374.

Restak, R. M. (1984). Possible neurophysiological correlates of empathy. In: M. Lichtenberg, M. Bornstein, and D. Silver (eds), *Empathy I*, pp. 63–73. Hillsdale, NJ: Lawrence Erlbaum Associates.

Richell, R. A., Mitchell, D. G., Newman, C., Leonard, A., Baron-Cohen, S., and Blair, R. J. (2003). Theory of mind and psychopathy: Can psychopathic individuals read the 'language of the eyes'? *Neuropsychologia*, **41**:523–526.

Richman, N., Stevenson, J., and Graham, P. J. (1982). *Pre-school to School: A Behavioural Study*. London: Academic Press.

Robins, L. N. and Regier, D. A. (1991). *Psychiatric disorders in America*. New York: The Free Press.

Rolls, E. T. (1995). A theory of emotion and consciousness, and its application to understanding the neural basis of emotion. In: M. S. Gazzaniga (eds), *The Cognitive Neurosciences*, pp. 1091–106. Cambridge, MA: MIT Press.

Rolls, E. T. (1996). The orbitofrontal frontal cortex. *Philosophical Transactions of the Royal Society of London B*, **351**:1433–1444.

Rolls, E. T. (1999). *The Brain and Emotion*. Oxford: Oxford University Press.

Rolls, E. T., Hornak, J., Wade, D., and McGrath, J. (1994). Emotion-related learning in patients with social and emotional changes associated with frontal lobe damage. *Journal of Neurology, Neurosurgery and Psychiatry*, **57**:1518–24.

Roy, S., Herrera, J., Parent, M., and Costa, J. (1987). Violent and non-violent schizophrenic patients: Clinical and developmental characteristics. *Psychological Reports*, **61**:855–861.

Rubia, K., Smith, A. B., Brammer, M. J., and Taylor, E. (2003). Right inferior profrontal cortex mediates response inhibition while mesial prefrontal cortex is responsible for error detection. *Neuroimage*, **20**:351–358.

Schoenbaum, G., Nugent, S. L., Saddoris, M. P., and Setlow, B. (2002). Orbitofrontal lesions in rats impair reversal but not aquisition of go, no-go discriminations. *Neuroreport*, **13**:885–890.

Singleton, N., Meltzer, M., and Gatward, R. (1998). *Psychiatric Morbidity Among Prisoners in England and Wales*. London, Government Statistical Service: The Stationary Office.

Slaby, R. G. and Guerra, N. G. (1988). Cognitive mediators of aggression in adolescent offenders: I. Assessment. *Developmental Psychology*, **24**:580–588.

Slaughter, B., Fann, J. R., and Ehde, D. (2003). Traumatic brain injury in a county jail population: Prevalence, neuropsychological functioning and psychiatric disorders. *Brain Injury*, **17**:731–741.

Smith, E. E. and Jonides, J. (1999). Storage and executive processes in the frontal lobes. *Science*, **283**:1657–1661.

Snowden, P. (2001). Substance misuse and violence: The scope and limitations of forensic psychiatry's role. *Advances in Psychiatric Treatment*, **7**:189–197.

Soderstrom, H., Tullberg, M., Wikkelso, C., Ekholm, S., and Forman, A. (2000). Reduced regional cerebral blood flow in non-psychotic violent offenders. *Psychiatry Research*, **98**:29–41.

Stein, D. J., Hollander, E., and Liebowitz, M. R. (1993). Neurobiology of impulsivity and impulse control disorders. *Journal of Neuropsychiatry and Clinical Neuroscience*, **5**:9–17.

Stevens, D., Charman, T., and Blair, R. J. (2001). Recognition of emotion in facial expressions and vocal tones in children with psychopathic tendencies. *Journal of Genetic Psychology*, **162**:201–211.

Stip, E. (1995). Compulsive disorder and acquired antisocial behavior in frontal lobe dementia. *Journal of Neuropsychiatry and Clinical Neuroscience*, **7**:116.

Stokes, G. (2000). *Challenging Behaviour in Dementia*. Bicester: Speechmark.

Stone, J. L., McDaniel, K. D., Hughes, J. R., and Hermann, B. P. (1986). Episodic dyscontrol disorder and paroxysmal EEG abnormalities: Successful treatment with carbamazepine. *Biological Psychiatry*, **21**:208–212.

Sutker, P. B., Moan, C. E., and Allain, A. N. (1983). Assessment of cognitive control in psychopathic and normal prisoners. *Journal of Behavioral Assessment*, **5**:275–287.

Sutton, J., Smith, P. K., and Swettenham, J. (2001). It's easy, it works, and it makes me feel good. *Social Development*, **10**:74–78.

Talerico, K. A., Evans, L. K., and Strumpf, N. E. (2002). Mental health correlates of aggression in nursing home residents with dementia. *Gerontologist*, **42**:169–177.

Tateno, A., Jorge, R. E., and Robinson, R. G. (2003). Clinical correlates of aggressive behavior after traumatic brain injury. *Journal of Neuropsychiatry and Clinical Neuroscience*, **15**:155–160.

Taylor, E., Chadwick, O., Heptinstall, E., and Danckaerts, M. (1996). Hyperactivity and conduct problems as risk factors for adolescent development. *Journal of the American Academy of Child and Adolescent Psychiatry*, **35**:1213–1226.

Tiihonen, J., Hodgins, S., Vaurio O., et al. (2000). Amygdaloid volume loss in psychopathy. *Society for Neuroscience Abstracts*, 2017.

Tonkonogy, J. M. (1991). Violence and temporal lesion: Head CT and MRI data. *Journal of Neuropsychiatry and Clinical Neuroscience*, **3**:189–196.

Touhig, D. (1998). A British All-Party Committee view on alcohol and violence. *Alcohol and Alcoholism*, **33**:89–91.

Tranel, D. (1994). 'Acquired sociopathy': The development of sociopathic behavior following focal brain damage. *Progress in Experimental Personality and Psychopathology Research*, **17**:285–311.

Tranel, D. and Damasio, H. (1994). Neuroanatomical correlates of electrodermal skin conductance responses. *Psychophysiology*, **31**:427–438.

Treiman, D. M. (1986). Epilepsy and violence: Medical and legal issues. *Epilepsia*, **27**, S77–S104.

Trimble, M. R., Ring, H. A., and Schmitz, B. (1996). Neuropsychiatric aspects of epilepsy. In: B. S. Fogel, R. B. Schiffer, and S. M. Rao (eds), *Neuropsychiatry*, pp. 771–803. Baltimore: Williams & Wilkins.

Turner, S. (2005). Behavioural symptoms of dementia in residential settings: A selective review of non-pharmacological interventions. *Aging Mental Health*, **9**:93–104.

Tyrer, F., McGrother, C. W., Thorp, C. F., et al. (2006). Physical aggression towards others in adults with learning disabilities: Prevalence and associated factors. *Journal of Intellectual Disability Research*, **50**:295–304.

Van der Naalt, J., van Zomeren, A. H., Sluiter, W. J., and Minderhoud, J. M. (1999). One year outcome in mild to moderate head injury: The predictive value of acute injury characteristics related to complaints and return to work. *Journal of Neurology, Neurosurgery and Psychiatry*, **66**:207–213.

Van Elst, L. T., Woermann, F. G., Lemieux, L., Thompson, P. J., and Trimble, M. R. (2000). Affective aggression in patients with temporal lobe epilepsy: A quantitative MRI study of the amygdala. *Brain*, **123**:234–243.

Veit, R., Flor, H., Erb M., et al. (2002). Brain circuits involved in emotional learning in antisocial behavior and social phobia in humans. *Neuroscience Letters*, **328**:233–236.

Verona, E., Patrick, C. J., Curtin, J. J., Bradley, M. M., and Lang, P. J. (2004). Psychopathy and physiological response to emotionally evocative sounds. *Journal of Abnormal Psychology*, **113**:99–108.

Virkkunen, M., Nuutila, A., and Huusko, S. (1976). Effect of brain injury on social adaptability. Longitudinal study on frequency of criminality. *Acta Psychiatrica Scandinavia*, **53**:168–172.

Volkow, N. D., Tancredi, L. R., Grant, C., et al. (1995). Brain glucose metabolism in violent psychiatric patients: A preliminary study. *Psychiatry Research*, **61**:243–253.

Walz, N. C. and Benson, B. A. (1996). Labeling and discrimination of facial expressions by aggressive and nonaggressive men with mental retardation. *American Journal of Mental Retardation*, **101**:282–291.

Webster-Stratton, C., and Dahl, R. (1995). Conduct disorder. In: M. Herson and R. T. Ammerman (eds), *Advanced Abnormal Child Psychology*, pp. 333–335. Hillsdale, NJ: Lawrence Erlbaum Associates.

Whitman, S., Coleman, T. E., Patmon, C., Desai, B. T., Cohen, R., and King, L. N. (1984). Epilepsy in prison: Elevated prevalence and no relationship to violence. *Neurology*, **34**:775–782.

Woermann, F. G., van Elst, L. T., Koepp, M. J., Free, S. L., Thompson, P. J., and Trimble, M. R. (2000). Reduction of frontal neocortical grey matter associated with affective aggression in patients with temporal lobe epilepsy: An objective voxel by voxel analysis of automatically segmented MRI. *Journal of Neurology, Neurosurgery and Psychiatry*, **68**:168–169.

Wong, M., Fenwick, P., Fenton, G., Lumsden, J., Maisey, M., and Stevens, J. (1997). Repetitive and non-repetitive violent offending behaviour in male patients in a maximum security mental hospital—clinical and neuroimaging findings. *Medicine, Science and Law*, **37**:150–160.

Wood, R. L. and Liossi, C. (2006). Neuropsychological and neurobehavioral correlates of aggression following traumatic brain injury. *Journal of Neuropsychiatry and Clinical Neuroscience*, **18**:333–341.

Wystanski, M. (2000). Assaultive behaviour in psychiatrically hospitalized elderly: A response to psychosocial stimulation and changes in pharmacotherapy. *International Journal of Geriatric Psychiatry*, **15**:582–585.

Zagrodzka, J., Hedberg, C. E., Mann, G. L., and Morrison, A. R. (1998). Contrasting expressions of aggressive behavior released by lesions of the central nucleus of the amygdala during wakefulness and rapid eye movement sleep without atonia in cats. *Behavioral Neuroscience*, **112**:589–602.

Chapter 3

Intellectual disability

Glynis Murphy and Isabel Clare

People with intellectual disabilities (i.e. men and women with significant impairments of intellectual functioning [usually defined as a full-scale IQ <70] and significant impairments of adaptive behaviours, of childhood onset) are likely to have a number of vulnerabilities, which means that they are at increased risk of being disadvantaged when they come into contact with the civil or criminal justice system.

In this chapter, we review the vulnerabilities of people with intellectual disabilities. Very little systematic information is available about the experiences of this group of men and women in the civil justice system (for example, during cases involving challenges to their capacity to parent; see Murphy & Clare, 2003, for further details). We have focused, therefore, on the criminal justice system, but it should be noted that many of the same issues are relevant to the civil justice system. For clarity, we consider people with intellectual disabilities first as witnesses for the police and in court, and then as suspects/defendants. Many of the issues are relevant to both situations and we have indicated this where necessary, without repeating information.

Acting as a witness

Likelihood of acting as a witness

It is now well established that people with intellectual disabilities are likely to be the victims of various kinds of crime and abuse (for review, see Murphy, 2007), including what are increasingly recognized as 'hate crimes'.

Whilst awareness of the issue of victimization of people with intellectual disabilities has grown, it still seems to be the case in England and Wales that, as in many Western countries (Luckasson, 1992), few alleged offences are investigated by the police, let alone prosecuted. For example, in surveys carried out in the UK, it was found that fewer than one-third of cases of alleged sexual abuse involving people with intellectual disabilities were investigated by the police (see Murphy, 2007, for further details). Similarly, whilst 90% of adults with intellectual disabilities interviewed in a large survey (Mencap, 1999) reported that they had been victims of what was referred to as 'bullying' (a term including physical assaults requiring treatment in hospital), fewer than one in five of the incidents (17%) had been reported to the police. Studies with higher reporting and prosecution rates have usually involved a biased sample, such as very high profile or serious cases.

Even when alleged crimes are reported, it has been found that the police do not always investigate them vigorously. This may, in part, reflect a belief that men and women with intellectual disabilities are unable to give evidence in court. This is a misunderstanding of the law in England and Wales, the USA, and elsewhere. For England and Wales, it is clear from the Youth Justice and Criminal Evidence Act 1999 s. 53(1) that the starting point is that witnesses, of any age, are competent (or have 'capacity') at all stages in criminal proceedings; they do not have to prove their competence. The police may also be concerned, as are many carers, about the possibility of victims being further traumatized by appearing at court. However, such a view is by no means always shared by men and women with intellectual disabilities who have been through the process of acting as witnesses (see, for example, 'Michael' & Pathak, 2007).

Vulnerabilities of witnesses with intellectual difficulties

There are a number of factors that may compromise the accuracy (known legally as reliability) and completeness of accounts from witnesses with intellectual disabilities (Murphy & Clare, 2006), some of which also affect their ability to cope with police detention and interviewing when they are suspects (see section on Assessing suspects or defendants below). Whilst men and women with intellectual disabilities are a heterogeneous population, and any generalizations need to be treated with caution, there is evidence suggesting that, compared with the general population, they are at greater risk of impairments of visual and verbal memory and executive functioning, have more limited understanding of and ability to use verbal language, and other cognitive problems. They are also at increased risk of additional difficulties, such as epilepsy, autism spectrum conditions, and/or mental health problems, and, moreover, are often socially disadvantaged (Murphy & Clare, 2003). In the context of acting as a witness, the vulnerabilities of people with learning disabilities are reflected primarily in providing eyewitness evidence, in problems in interviews, and in making sense of legal proceedings.

Sometimes eyewitness identification may be the main, or even the only, evidence regarding a particular crime. So, in the prosecution of crimes against people with intellectual disabilities, the ability to act as an eyewitness is an important issue. Surprisingly little research has been carried out with adults.

Ericson & Isaacs (2003), however, using a mock line-up procedure, found that men and women with intellectual disabilities made as many correct identifications as their counterparts without disabilities but more incorrect identifications and fewer 'no selection' responses. Their explanation draws on Malpass & Devine's (1984) proposal that eyewitness identification reflects both information about the appearance of the alleged offender (relying on witnesses' memories) and the circumstances (lighting, timing, physical position, and so on) under which the event was witnessed, and the social value of choosing (which may be heavily influenced by the desire for social approval). Ericson & Isaacs (2003) argued that the participants with intellectual disabilities had memories of the appearance of the 'offender' that were as good as those of their general population counterparts but they were more influenced by the social value of making an identification. The implication of this argument, which is supported by the other studies with both adults and children (Milne *et al.*, 1999; Gudjonsson & Henry, 2003) with intellectual disabilities, is that it is very important that eyewitness and other interviews are carried out carefully.

It is now well established that interviewing people with intellectual disabilities can be challenging. As a group, they tend to show higher degrees of acquiescence (i.e. saying 'yes' to questions requiring a yes/no answer, regardless of their content) and a greater tendency to confabulate (i.e. to distort or fabricate information to 'fill in' gaps in their memories) than those without disabilities (Clare & Gudjonsson, 1993; Finlay & Lyons, 2002). They are also more likely to be compliant, i.e. to say or do what they believe is wanted, regardless of their own views. In addition, it seems that, overall, both children and adults with intellectual disabilities are more suggestible than people without disabilities (Clare and Gudjonsson, 1993; Cardone & Dent, 1996; Everington & Fulero, 1999; Henry & Gudjonsson, 1999; Milne *et al.*, 1999; Milne *et al.*, 2002; Gudjonsson & Henry, 2003). Some studies, such as that of Everington & Fulero (1999) have found that people with intellectual disabilities are more vulnerable both to 'yield', i.e. to being misled by leading questions, and to 'shift', i.e. to changing their responses following interrogative pressure; others, however, have found differences in yield but not in shift (Clare & Gudjonsson, 1993; Milne *et al.*, 2002).

There has been a suggestion that this increased suggestibility of people with intellectual disabilities simply reflects measurement artefacts. For example, Beail (2002) has argued that the Gudjonsson Suggestibility Scale (GSS) (Gudjonsson, 1997), which is the most widely used measure of suggestibility, relies on semantic memory for a story. As the memories of men and women with intellectual disabilities are usually more limited, they are automatically disadvantaged. However, it seems that, whilst taking account of the poorer recall for the story in the GSS reduces the differences between groups of people with and without disabilities, it does not eliminate them entirely (Gudjonsson & Henry, 2003). Beail (2002) also argued that, in real life, witness testimony reflects episodic and autobiographical memory, which may be better than semantic memory in people with intellectual disabilities. Nevertheless, when a videotaped incident, rather than a story, has been used, people with intellectual disabilities are still more suggestible than their general population counterparts (Milne et al., 2002). Moreover, the GSS is a good predictor of suggestibility in responding to questions about real-life events (Henry & Gudjonsson, 2003).

Nonetheless, people with intellectual disabilities vary in the extent to which they are acquiescent, suggestible, or compliant; some men and women are no more susceptible than those without disabilities. Nor do people with intellectual disabilities necessarily confabulate more. In any case, their problems seem to be no greater than those of many children who are accepted as witnesses. Often, the style of questioning can be adjusted to minimize the problems. For example, free recall can be encouraged because, when asked simply to 'tell what happened', people with intellectual disabilities make no more errors than others, although their accounts may be less full (Perlman et al., 1994). Provided questions are phrased simply, are open rather than closed, are not leading, and it is stated clearly that it is acceptable to say 'I don't know' as a response, many people with intellectual disabilities are as reliable as other witnesses (Perlman et al., 1994). Milne et al. (1999) suggested that a cognitive interview approach, in which the questioning becomes increasingly focused, produces the best evidence.

Being a witness in court, rather than simply giving a statement to the police, involves not just being able to give an account of events when questioned, including, potentially, an eyewitness account, but also being able to understand and cope with complex legal proceedings. People with intellectual disabilities often find the language used in court very difficult to understand. Ericson & Perlman (2001), in Canada, compared the understanding of 34 common legal words (including the words judge, lawyer, defendant, arrest, allegation, charge, prosecute, suspect, testimony, innocent, guilty, and jail) among men and women with intellectual disabilities and their counterparts in the general population. With the exception of 'police officer', which was understood equally well by both groups, the participants with intellectual disabilities had a more limited understanding of all the words. 'Allegation' and 'prosecute' were among the most difficult for them, but they also had problems with 'accused', 'trial', 'adjourn', 'charges', 'defendant', 'suspect', 'victim', 'evidence', and 'guilty' (as Smith, 1993, also found for suspects with intellectual disabilities). However, there was considerable variability among the group with disabilities; one person was only able to define one term whilst another could define 32 of the 34.

Once people with intellectual disabilities are giving evidence in court, especially if they find legal terminology confusing, it is easy for lawyers to make them appear unreliable as witnesses, particularly during cross-examination. Kebbell *et al.* (2004) compared the transcripts of 16 trials in England and Wales involving witnesses with intellectual disabilities and 16 trials in which none of the witnesses were men or women with disabilities. For both groups, they found that lawyers asked significantly more yes/no, leading, negative, and multiple questions during cross-examination. The kinds of questions asked of witnesses with and without disabilities differed little (with slightly fewer leading questions and slightly more repeated questions for witnesses with disabilities), so it seemed that lawyers did not adjust their questioning style to take account of the needs of witnesses. Not surprisingly, witnesses with intellectual disabilities were significantly more likely to be affected by leading questions, especially during cross-examination, than their general population counterparts.

In England and Wales, judges are allowed to interrupt court proceedings to ensure a fair trial (Pattenden, 1990). O'Kelly *et al.* (2003) compared the number of times in which judges intervened in 16 trials involving witnesses with intellectual disabilities, and the same number in which none of the witnesses had disabilities. The transcripts were used to categorize judges' interventions into three classes (with witnesses, with lawyers, and with juries) and subsequently into 18 subcategories (see O'Kelly *et al.*, for details). No significant differences were found in either the broad classes or the subcategories. These findings suggest that judges are probably not sensitive to the vulnerabilities of witnesses with intellectual disabilities.

Support for witnesses with intellectual disabilities

Until recently, in England and Wales, as in many other countries (Dinerstein & Buescher, 1999), there was no special provision to help people with intellectual disabilities to give evidence in court. Their ability to give evidence was determined by the judge (or magistrates, in Magistrates' Courts) in relation to whether they were able to understand the nature and the special responsibility of the oath (the obligation to tell the truth in court) and to give a rational verbal account of what happened (or what had been seen). The judge (in a

Crown Court) was not, however, obliged to decide whether the witness was reliable. In England and Wales, this has always been for the jury to decide. Similar abilities were required in the USA (see Herr, 1999).

However, Gudjonsson *et al.* (2000) showed that these strict rules prevented some people with intellectual disabilities from giving evidence in court: potential witnesses in a case of alleged physical and sexual abuse were assessed for their understanding of the oath, for acquiescence and suggestibility (using the GSS), and for their ability to be interviewed by the police (a clinical judgement), as well as for their degree of intellectual disability. Seventeen of the 49 men and women assessed were judged to be able to give sufficiently coherent accounts to be interviewed by the police. As Gudjonsson *et al.* (2000) point out, whilst case law provides criteria for competence to be a witness in court, there are no such criteria for being interviewed by the police. The police will be concerned not only with interviewing people who could be witnesses in court but also with gathering any evidence that will further their investigation. However, whilst all of those with IQs >60 understood the oath, only one-third of those with IQs between 50 and 59 understood it, and none of those with IQs below 50. This means that many potential witnesses would have been prevented from gaining access to justice.

In England and Wales in the late 1990s, there were mounting concerns about the difficulties for witnesses in police stations and at court, leading to pressure for better training for the police (VOICE UK, 1998; see also Bailey & Barr, 2000), and others involved in the criminal justice system, and calls for new legislation to increase the likelihood of trial and conviction for those guilty of crimes against people with intellectual disabilities.

In England and Wales, the Youth Justice and Criminal Evidence Act 1999 s. 53(3) introduced new criteria for capacity to act as a witness, so that now a person is considered competent if he or she is able to:

1. Understand questions put to him or her
2. Give answers to these questions that can be understood.

If a potential witness's capacity is challenged, and he or she is a person with an intellectual disability, the court can be assisted, for example by a report from a psychologist, in determining competence (Ormerod & Roberts, 2006). In addition, new rules of evidence have been provided for 'vulnerable witnesses' (young people under the age of 17, and anyone older with a disability or impairment that is likely to affect their evidence) or 'intimidated witnesses' (anyone experiencing fear or distress). Alleged victims of sexual offences are also automatically made eligible, unless they have requested otherwise.

Under this Act, which has been implemented bit by bit, vulnerable witnesses have been allowed 'special measures' according to their needs (Cooke & Davies, 2001). These have included:

- the removal of wigs and gowns by the judge and barristers
- the use of screens to protect the victim from seeing the perpetrator
- exclusion of the public from court
- giving unsworn evidence rather than taking the oath
- giving videotaped evidence in chief
- cross-examination by video
- the use of an intermediary, to assist the witness to understand questions and communicate answers in the court
- communication aids, such as signs, symbol boards, and electronic aids.

The Home Office has published guidance on the implementation of these special measures, including material to help in identifying and, in particular, interviewing vulnerable witnesses (Home Office, 2002). Access to these 'special measures' has to be determined in a pre-trial hearing (Magistrates' Court) or Plea and Directions Hearing (Crown Court) and it is recommended that all vulnerable witnesses be assessed prior to these hearings to determine their needs. Clearly, such assessments need to be completed as early as possible after an alleged crime in order to influence the way the police conduct their interview of the witness.

An early evaluation of the impact of the new legislation (Hamlyn *et al.*, 2004) has suggested that vulnerable witnesses (by no means all of these were people with intellectual disabilities) felt somewhat less intimidated, more satisfied with the criminal justice system, and less anxious in court than before. However, the number of people who have used special measures such as communication aids and intermediaries remains unclear. Certainly, the experience from Australia, where these and some other special measures have been available to witnesses for some time, is that they are not often used (Balandin, 2000; Davis, 2000).

Some experts have argued that good-quality evidence is best achieved through an approach that focuses on both changes in the civil or criminal justice systems and on the witness (Monaghan & Pathak, 2000). Arguably, 'special measures' are largely ways to alter the physical environment, and these alterations may be far less important than those that enhance the witness's skills and confidence. In north-west England, the 'Liverpool Model of Witness Support, Preparation and Profiling' has been developed to promote equal access to justice for individuals with intellectual disabilities and other 'vulnerable' witnesses. Without engaging in any discussion of the evidence, a detailed 'package' is provided, focusing on both the needs of the individual witness and the changes that are required in the justice system to enable that individual's needs to be met. The use of one or more 'special measures' may be recommended, as may 'additional measures to assist'. The effectiveness of this model has led to it being approved by the Crown Prosecution Service for adoption throughout England and Wales ('Michael' & Pathak, 2007).

Assessing the ability to act as a witness

Assessments of witnesses with intellectual disabilities will need to include standardized psychometric assessments to evaluate the person's:

- cognitive skills; for example, using the appropriate version of the Wechsler Adult Intelligence Scale—Third Edition (WAIS-III^{UK}; Wechsler, 1999)
- language skills; for example, with the British Picture Vocabulary Scale II (BPVS-II; Dunn *et al.*, 1997)
- memory functioning; for example, with the Rivermead Behavioural Memory Test—Third Edition (RBMT-3; Wilson *et al.*, 2007).

Some more specific assessments may also be needed, depending on the nature of the alleged offence. For example, it may be helpful to establish (using a set of pictures such as those provided by McCarthy & Thompson, 2007) what words the person uses for particular parts of the body, or whether they have the capacity to consent to sexual relationships (Murphy & O'Callaghan, 2004). Various other kinds of information may be needed to enable the police and those who know the witness to provide appropriate support.

If the person needs to appear in court, additional assessments may be needed (see Gudjonsson *et al.*, 2000). These may include the following:

- Understanding of the oath or affirmation (see Gudjonsson et al., 2000).
- Suggestibility; for example, using the GSS (Gudjonsson, 1997).
- Acquiescence (the most commonly used test, by Winkler et al. (1982), is probably too complex; a preferable test is that of Gudjonsson et al., 2000).
- Confabulation, comprising distortions and fabrications (scored from the GSS; Gudjonsson, 1997).
- Compliance, using the Gudjonsson Compliance Scale (GCS; Gudjonsson, 1997). The material is complex for people who are significantly intellectually disadvantaged so, for men and women with intellectual disabilities, Form E, the informant version, should be used. If the informant has not known the individual in childhood, items 1 and 5 cannot be completed; instead, the score must be pro rated from the remaining 18 items.

- Understanding of the court process and legal terminology (adapted from Ericson & Perlman, 2001).

Depending on the particular jurisdiction, potential witnesses should also be assessed as to whether 'special' or any other 'additional' measures may be helpful. In England and Wales, psychologists should consider at least the following questions:

- How anxious would the person be in a 'normal' courtroom? (Does he or she need the courtroom to be cleared? What about wigs and gowns? Should he or she give evidence by video?)
- What are the possible effects of seeing the alleged perpetrator? (Does he or she need screens?)
- What are the communication skills of the witness? (Will he or she need to take communication aids into the courtroom? Will he or she need an intermediary? How should lawyers best communicate with the witness?)

Again, information is also needed to help establish the kind of support that may be required. Most courts now have witness support schemes that will assist, and there are also a number of books, including 'books without words', which explain the court process and show it in pictures (see, for example, Hollins *et al.*, 2007) to help vulnerable witnesses understand what going to court may be like.

It is important to note that, during assessments and interviews of this kind, whether for the police or for the court, the witness should not be asked anything about the actual circumstances of the alleged crime. This can be difficult, as vulnerable witnesses with intellectual disabilities are very often also the alleged victims and they may wish to talk about their experiences. However, if the alleged offence is discussed, it is likely to be argued in court that the witness was coached and the case will not proceed. It is, nevertheless, perfectly acceptable for him or her to be assisted to understand what happens during police interviewing and the court process, to visit the court before the trial, and to be taught how to deal with lawyers through role play, so that he or she feels confident that it is acceptable to say 'I don't know' or 'Please explain'.

Acting as a suspect or defendant

Likelihood of contact with the criminal justice system

It is now recognized that, whilst many suspects (Gudjonsson *et al.*, 1993), and therefore many defendants and convicted offenders, are intellectually disadvantaged, people who meet the criteria for an intellectual disability are not over-represented in the criminal justice system (see Murphy & Mason, 2007, for a review of this issue). Probably the best guide to the numbers of people with intellectual disabilities in contact with the criminal justice system comes from community-based studies focusing on people receiving intellectual disabilities services in particular geographical areas. In the largest and best of these studies, McBrien *et al.* (2003) examined contacts with the criminal justice system among all 1326 adults known to intellectual disabilities services within a city with a general population of almost 200 000. It was found that:

- 0.8% of the 1326 were currently in prison
- 3% had a conviction of some kind (current or past)
- a further 7% had had contact with the criminal justice system as a suspect but did not have a criminal conviction
- an additional 17% engaged in challenging behaviour that was 'risky' in the sense that it could have been interpreted as offending.

Vulnerabilities at the police station and at court

As suspects, people with intellectual disabilities are likely to be disadvantaged in a number of different ways (see section on Vulnerabilities of witnesses with intellectual disabilities, above; and Gudjonsson, 2003, for a thorough review and discussion). In the context of being accused of committing a crime, these vulnerabilities are likely to manifest in three main ways: limited understanding of the caution and legal rights during detention and interviewing by the police; poor decision-making both at the police station and in court; and difficulties in dealing with court procedures.

In England and Wales, the police are required to 'caution' individuals when they arrest them and at other stages during detention and interviewing. The current caution (since 1994) is as follows:

> You do not have to say anything, but it may harm your defence if you do not mention when questioned something which you later rely on in court. Anything you do say may be given in evidence.

It is now well established that this caution is too complex both for the general population to comprehend under experimental conditions (Clare *et al.*, 1998; Fenner *et al.*, 2002) and for 'ordinary' suspects in police detention (Fenner *et al.*, 2002). In addition to the caution, suspects in police detention are also given advice about their legal rights (such as the right to free legal advice), both orally and in writing. Studies in England and Wales, and in other jurisdictions that provide similar safeguards to suspects, for example the USA (following *Miranda v Arizona* [1966]; see Gudjonsson, 2003), Canada, and Scotland, suggest the following:

- Material about the caution and legal rights is poorly understood, even by the general population (Gudjonsson, 1991; Clare *et al.*, 1998; Fenner *et al.*, 2002), with many people misunderstanding the meaning of words such as 'caution' and 'right' (Grisso, 1981; and see section on Vulnerabilities of witnesses with intellectual disabilities, above), which have common non-legal meanings and usage (Rock, 1999).

- Understanding of information about legal rights is related to intellectual ability, so that the least able are the most disadvantaged (Scotland: Cooke & Philip, 1998; Canada: Olley & Ogloff, 1993; USA: Grisso, 1981). It is unlikely that the material can be understood fully by people with intellectual disabilities, even under ideal conditions (Fulero and Everington, 1995; Everington & Fulero, 1999; Clare, 2003).

- Understanding of the caution and legal rights is not related to self-reported confidence (Cooke & Philip, 1998; Fenner *et al.*, 2002) or experience of the criminal justice system (Grisso, 1981; Fenner *et al.*, 2002), and, contrary to popular belief, there is no evidence that the experience of police detention 'focuses the mind' and improves understanding (Fenner *et al.*, 2002).

During a police interview, people with intellectual disabilities may be able to give an accurate account of an event (Perlman *et al.*, 1994) but their vulnerabilities (see above, under Witnesses) may lead, in the worst cases, to false confessions (Gudjonsson, 2003; Fulero & Everington, 2004). Such confessions are not always made inadvertently: some men and women do not appreciate the consequences of their decisions and think that if they make a false confession, even to a serious crime, they will be allowed to return home from police detention, setting things right later in court (Clare & Gudjonsson, 1995). This belief that others will somehow know that they are innocent has been referred to as the 'illusion of transparency' (Gudjonsson, 2003; Kassin & Norwick, 2004).

In England and Wales, following some notorious miscarriages of justice during the second part of the last century (see Gudjonsson, 2003), the police appear to have made more stringent efforts to ensure that men and women with intellectual disabilities are identified when they are suspected of more serious offences, so that they can be provided with the safeguards to which they are entitled. However, they may be less concerned when the alleged offence is minor, and when a suspect who admits to a crime is not going to be charged (instead, for example, being given a formal 'caution' by a senior police officer). It is difficult for suspects, who normally wish to leave police custody as quickly as possible, to appreciate that making an admission in these circumstances may have future adverse consequences (for example, it can be taken into account in sentencing following a conviction by a court).

Safeguards in the criminal justice system

Safeguards at the police station

In England and Wales, and elsewhere, there are a number of provisions that are intended to protect designated groups of 'vulnerable' men and women, including men and women with intellectual disabilities, from wrongful conviction. In England and Wales, suspects may not be detained or interviewed if they are not 'fit' (see Gudjonsson, 2003, pp. 270–272, for an account of recent developments with regard to fitness for interview), and, since the introduction of the Police and Criminal Evidence Act 1984 (PACE), all police interviews have to be audiotaped. In addition, there is a requirement that an independent person who is not a solicitor, an 'appropriate adult', is present during interviewing and other formal procedures. Similar provision now exists in Scotland and is also in place in Australia (Baroff et al., 2004).

Fitness to be detained and/or interviewed is normally judged by a medical practitioner on the basis of an examination of the suspect, based on three broad criteria (Gudjonsson, 1995; Gudjonsson & Grisso, 2008): (i) whether the person understands the police caution; (ii) whether he or she has an understanding of the time and place of the interview and the relevant people and their roles; and (iii) whether his or her answers are likely to be misinterpreted by the court; for example, due to an inability to perceive the consequences of his or her statements. It should be noted, however, that suspects are often advised by their legal representatives to take part in police interviews, provided that they appear able and willing to respond 'no comment' to questions and/or make a prepared statement.

In England and Wales, the most commonly used safeguard for 'vulnerable' suspects, including suspects with intellectual disabilities, in police detention is the presence of an 'appropriate adult' to support and assist them. Unfortunately, the guidance that accompanies PACE (Home Office, 2005) is poorly worded and there continue to be widely different views about the role of the appropriate adult among police officers, lawyers, and advocacy groups (see Palmer & Hart, 1996, for more detailed discussion), which have not been clarified by the limited case law. In practice, this means that many appropriate adults, who may be family members, support workers, health or social care practitioners, or others, are often uncertain about their responsibilities (c.f. Scotland, where more detailed guidance is available; Scottish Office, 1998). Mostly, they are passive, at least during interviews (Medford *et al.*, 2003), although 'lay' appropriate adults (such as family members) are more likely than 'professionals' (such as social workers) to adopt the role of the investigating officer. Nevertheless, their sheer presence has an impact (Medford *et al.*, 2003), as it appears to increase the likelihood that the suspect will have legal representation and that this representative will take on a more active role. In addition, it seems that less pressure will be exerted on the suspect by the police during the interview. These findings suggest that, whilst there has been some progress at ground level, for example in setting up volunteer schemes to provide appropriate adults and clarify 'good practice' for them (see the website of the National Appropriate Adult Network, http://www.appropriateadult.org.uk/), more needs to be done to improve the effectiveness of this safeguard. The impact of any changes made as a result of the current review of PACE (Home Office, 2007) remains to be seen.

Of course, issues relating to appropriate adults only arise when suspects are identified by the police as being 'vulnerable'. In a number of police forces in England and Wales, formal screening of all suspects is now carried out, suggesting some progress. Nevertheless, all of the available studies suggest that the proportion of adult suspects identified as 'vulnerable' by the police remains far lower than 'best estimates' by clinicians suggest (Gudjonsson *et al.*, 1993; Gudjonsson, 2003).

Safeguards following charging

In England and Wales (following Home Office Circular 66/90), as in the USA and many other countries, there are other safeguards for people with intellectual disabilities once they have been charged with a criminal offence to prevent them from being remanded in, or sentenced to, prison when their behaviour might be more appropriately dealt with by treatment and/or support. This can take place, if the necessary criteria are fulfilled, in a psychiatric hospital under mental health legislation (in England and Wales, at present, the Mental Health Act 1983 provides the relevant statutory framework), but in many countries, a range of community-based options combining elements of both criminal justice and health/social care is also available, both before trial (such as bail with conditions relating to residence or treatment) or following conviction (for example, Probation Orders with a condition of treatment; Laski, 1992; James, 1996). No systematic information is available about the extent to which these options are used for men and women with intellectual disabilities, but anecdotal evidence from England and Wales suggests that, even within a single jurisdiction, there is widespread variation according to geographical location.

Fitness to plead

There are also safeguards for men and women whose right to a fair trial may be compromised because they are 'unfit to plead' (England and Wales), 'not competent' (USA) or (Scotland), 'insane in bar of trial' or its equivalent (Rasch, 1990; Bonnie, 1992; Grisso, 2003, pp. 69–148; Murphy & Clare, 2003; Baroff *et al.*, 2004). These procedures are intended to enable trial proceedings to be postponed whilst defendants receive (normally as inpatients) treatment to enable them to gain, or regain, capacity to return to court. In England and Wales, under the Domestic Violence, Crime and Victims Act 2004, which amends previous legislation, issues relating to 'fitness to plead' may be put forward by the defence, the prosecution, or the court. If presented by the defence, the onus of proof lies with the defence and is discharged if the court is satisfied on the balance of probabilities that the accused is 'unfit'. In contrast, if the allegation is made by the prosecution and disputed by the defence, the burden lies upon the prosecution and the standard of proof is beyond reasonable doubt (*R v Robertson* [1968] 1 WLR 1767). There is no clear authority as to the burden or standard of proof when the issue is raised by the court.

Longstanding concerns in England and Wales about the functioning of the 'fitness to plead' safeguard were highlighted at the end of the last century, when Grubin (1991a, b) conducted a survey of the 286 men and women detained in hospital under the relevant legislation (Criminal Procedure (Insanity Act) 1964). Worryingly, a number remained there indefinitely, because they were never judged to be sufficiently 'fit' to be tried in court; almost half of them were people with intellectual disabilities. The detention of men and women whose guilt had never been established in court raised serious human rights issues. Subsequently, the law was amended (first, by the Criminal Procedure (Insanity and Fitness to Plead) Act 1991 and, more recently, by the Domestic Violence, Crime and Victims Act 2004) so that a 'trial of the facts' could take place. If there is not sufficient evidence to establish that the defendant was the person responsible for the alleged offence, he or she can be acquitted; otherwise, a range of options is available (see below).

In contrast to England and Wales, where 'fitness to plead' is rarely considered (Mackay & Kearns, 2000), in the USA and Canada 'competence' hearings often take place. For example, Steadman *et al.* (1982) estimated that, in the early 1980s, there were around 25 000 hearings a year in the USA; there is no reason to think the number has decreased (Grisso, 2003). Despite the differences in numbers between different jurisdictions, however, there have been similar concerns about the fate of those who have been found 'incompetent'. For example, McGarry *et al.* (1968) reported that, in the USA, more 'incompetent' people left hospital through dying than through returning to court. Subsequently, following the case of *Jackson v Indiana* (1972) 406 US 715, the USA Supreme Court ruled that 'incompetent' defendants could not be detained in hospital if there was no reasonable possibility that they could be treated and returned to court. The state has to set them free, with the charges against them dropped, or admit them to a psychiatric hospital using civil procedures. This ruling has had a tremendous impact on the average duration of treatment for incompetent defendants with a mental illness (Steadman *et al.*, 1982). However, its impact on people with intellectual disabilities who are subject to 'incompetence' hearings is uncertain. In any case (and in contrast to a 'trial of the facts'), it does not address issues relating to the individual's responsibility for the alleged offence.

The criteria for 'fitness to plead' or its equivalent are broadly similar in England and Wales, Scotland, the USA, Canada and Australia (Grisso, 2003; Baroff *et al.*, 2004). In England and Wales, the criteria (based on *R v Pritchard* (1836) 7 C&P 303) relate to:

- understanding of the charge
- understanding the meaning of entering a plea of guilty or not guilty and its consequences
- ability to instruct solicitors and other legal representatives
- understanding of the details of the evidence
- ability to follow the proceedings so as to make a proper defence, for example by challenging a juror (James *et al.*, 2001; Lawson *et al.*, 2005).

Legally, the person need only lack capacity for one of the criteria for a finding of unfitness to be made (Richardson, 1993, cited in James *et al.*, 2001).

In practice, assessments to contribute to decisions about 'fitness to plead' are normally carried out through an interview with a clinician (depending on the jurisdiction and the circumstances, a psychiatrist, rather than a psychologist, may be required), focusing on establishing the person's capacity in relation to each of the criteria (see also 'Mr B' in Chapter 5 of this volume). In the USA, a number of standardized measures have been developed (Grisso, 2003, pp. 89–139), including at least two that are highly sophisticated: the MacArthur Competence Assessment Tool—Criminal Adjudication (MacCAT-CA; Poythress *et al.*, 1999) and the Fitness Interview Test—Revised (FIT-R; Roesch *et al.*, 2006). Only two measures have been designed specifically for people with intellectual disabilities, both of which are North American. One is a brief screening test (Smith & Hudson, 1995); the other is a more thorough assessment, the Competence Assessment for Standing Trial for Defendants with Mental Retardation (CAST-MR; Everington & Luckasson, 1992), but this needs further development (Grisso, 2003).

Defendants who are found 'unfit to plead' are sometimes also judged by courts to lack 'criminal responsibility', which relates to the person's mental state at the time of the offence. 'Fitness to plead' and 'criminal responsibility' are often confused (Johnson et al., 1990), but they are not the same.

Criminal responsibility

Not all illegal behaviour is a criminal offence. As well as the *actus reus* (an unlawful act), the courts normally have to establish some motivation; in criminal offences, the most important of these is *mens rea* (intent to commit the act or to have foreseen its consequences). Where an individual is judged to have lacked *mens rea*, he or she lacks criminal responsibility and is therefore 'not guilty by reason of insanity'.

Different legal standards for criminal responsibility are used in different jurisdictions and in different states within single jurisdictions. In England and Wales, it is judged by the House of Lords' ruling in *R v M'Naghten* [1843] UKHL J16 (19th June). According to this standard, a defence of 'not guilty by reason of insanity' is established when it is proved that, at the time of committing the offence, the mental 'disease or defect' (Borum, 2003, p. 196) of the accused was such that he or she did not know the nature or quality of his or her act or did not know that it was (legally) wrong. Some of the States of the USA also use this standard, but in others it is supplemented with an 'irresistible impulse' test, allowing courts to consider difficulties that may have compromised the defendant's ability to control his or her actions (using the American Law Institute (1962) standard).

It is unusual for the issue of criminal responsibility to be raised in any Western jurisdiction, particularly for people with intellectual disabilities. This seems surprising, given that it is not unusual for courts still to use concepts of 'mental age'.

In England and Wales, children under the age of 10 years are regarded as incapable of having *mens rea* and cannot, therefore, be convicted of a criminal offence (although other action can be taken), whilst at age 14, the law treats young people as fully responsible, in the same way as adults. Between the ages of 10 and 14 years, a conviction is possible if the prosecution shows that the person knew that what he or she was doing was wrong. In everyday practice, suspects or defendants with severe or profound intellectual disabilities rarely have contact with the criminal justice system, although it is not clear whether this reflects concerns about *mens rea* or fitness to plead. Similar issues of intent may also be relevant for some people with mild intellectual disabilities, particularly if the broader USA standard of criminal responsibility is used. The courts, however, have been very reluctant to accept expert evidence in such cases unless it is argued that defendant's mental state was abnormal at the time of his or her behaviour (see Ormerod & Roberts, 2006).

Very little information is available in the professional or scientific literature about evaluations of criminal responsibility and what is known is based on self-report, or reports by mental health practitioners; in contrast to 'fitness to plead', very few measures have been developed to assist in evaluations. In any case, developments in neuroscience mean that this is a rapidly changing area (see, for example, the recently announced MacArthur Law and Neuroscience Project: http://www.macfound.org).

Nevertheless, there is some consensus among experienced forensic psychologists and psychiatrists about the information that should be available in a competent report (Borum & Grisso, 1996; see also Borum, 2003, pp. 202–203) to assist decision-makers.

In England and Wales, following the introduction of the Domestic Violence, Crime and Victims Act 2004, a court's finding that a defendant carried out the act with which he or she is charged but is 'unfit to plead' or 'not guilty by reason of insanity' leads to three options (under s. 5 (2)):

1. An order for absolute discharge.
2. A supervision order (with the supervision carried out by social services or probation, and with the possibility of conditions about place of residence, treatment, and so on).
3. A hospital order under the Mental Health Act 2007 (with or without a Restriction Order).

In the USA, there seems to be less flexibility: defendants who meet the criteria are likely to be detained in a psychiatric hospital under a civil commitment order.

The effectiveness of these and other safeguards provided for suspects and defendants with intellectual disabilities is unknown, at least in England and Wales and other parts of the UK. However, it seems that the provisions are not always effective, at least at a sufficiently early stage. In a recent case (*R v Cash* [2004] EWCA Cr 666), for example, a man went through the whole criminal justice process without his intellectual disability being recognized by the police, or the duty solicitor present during his police interview, or his legal advisors during court proceedings, or the court itself during his trial. It was only almost 4 years later, when it became apparent that Mr Cash was unable to cope with imprisonment, that his vulnerabilities came to light and his conviction was quashed by the Court of Appeal.

Assessing suspects or defendants

The assessment of suspects or defendants is similar to that of witnesses (see section on Vulnerabilities of witnesses with intellectual disabilities, above) in that both normally involve evaluations of:

- a person's psychological resources (intellectual functioning, suggestibility, anxiety, and so on) that are directly relevant to a particular legal context (for example, acting as a suspect during police detention and interviewing; criminal responsibility)
- the specific situation within the particular legal context in which this person has to, or had to, use these resources (for example, a brief interview with support from a legal advisor and an appropriate adult versus a series of prolonged interviews with no support)
- the extent to which this person's psychological resources met, or are likely to meet, the demands of the specific situation.

Many contexts within the criminal justice system require similar psychological resources (for example, the ability to withstand interrogative pressure), so some of the measures are likely to be the same (see section on Vulnerabilities of witnesses with intellectual disabilities above); others, however, will be very different (for example, an assessment of fitness to plead). An illustration of the way in which forensic neuropsychology might contribute to the assessment of a suspect is provided in the case study below.

Case Study

Mr C (a real person, whose details have been changed in some ways to protect his anonymity) had been charged with three counts of burglary, allegedly committed with another, older, man. He admitted the offences during the second of two police interviews, carried out on the same day without a legal advisor or an appropriate adult. When he returned home on bail, Mr C retracted his confession, which was the only evidence against him. His solicitor asked for a report regarding his psychological vulnerabilities and their possible impact.

Mr C was from a travelling background and lived with his parents and some other family members on an established local site. It was known, from his former head teacher, that he had attended a school for pupils with special educational needs from an early age. He was bullied there because of his background and on one occasion was injured so severely that he required treatment in hospital.

Mr C had been unemployed since leaving school. He had one adult conviction, for an offence of theft and handling stolen property. He received a 12-month Probation Order for this offence, which took place after the alleged burglaries but involved the same older man. Since being placed on probation, Mr C had not had any contact with the police or this man. Mr C was not known to, and had never received any support from, specialist health or social services for people with intellectual disabilities.

A summary of the assessments carried out with Mr C is given in Table 3.1.

Table 3.1 Summary of assessments carried out with Mr C

Area of assessment	Test used
Intellectual ability—to establish whether he fulfilled the criteria for an intellectual disability	WAIS-III^{UK} (Wechsler, 1999)
Adaptive functioning—completed during an interview with Mr C's mother (with some items checked during interview with Mr C himself) to establish whether he met the criteria for intellectual disability	Adaptive Behavior Scale—Residential and Community Version, 2nd edn (Nihira et al., 1993), which has standard scores with a mean of 10 and a standard deviation of 3 (although this is not as good a measure as the Vineland II (Vineland Adaptive Behavior Scales, 2nd edn; Sparrow et al., 2005), which includes normative data from the 'general population')
Literacy and other cognitive skills—using 'quick and dirty' tests to assist in establishing whether Mr C's putative vulnerabilities could have been identified by the police	Schonell Graded Word Reading Test (Schonell & Goodacre, 1974); informal tests of writing (his own name and simple sentences) and everyday knowledge (date of birth, days of the week, months of the year, etc.)
Suggestibility—assessment of suggestibility and confabulation	Gudjonsson Suggestibility Scale, Form 2 (GSS 2; Gudjonsson, 1997)
Acquiescence	Gudjonsson et al. (2000a)
Compliance	Gudjonsson Compliance Scale Form D (Gudjonsson, 1997) with Mr C; 18 items of Form E completed by his Probation Officer
Understanding of the caution	Mr C asked to explain the caution in his own words
Self-reported account of alleged offences, police interviews, relationship with the other suspect, decision-making around confession and retraction, aspirations and plans for the future	Interview with Mr C
Reconstruction, as far as possible, of police interview	Listening to copies of audiotapes of police interviews, focusing particularly on any evidence of leading questioning or other kinds of interrogative pressure
Advice for the court if Mr C was found guilty that would provide him with treatment and support and meet the needs of public protection	Interview with Probation Officer and phone calls to the local community team for people with learning disabilities to identify available resources

- Mr C fulfilled the criteria for an intellectual disability. He had a history of developmental delay; his overall intellectual ability, as well as his verbal and performance scores, fell at the upper end of the intellectual disability range; and his social functioning was also significantly impaired.

- Mr C's other intellectual skills were also impaired. His score on the test of reading indicated that he could not read material of any complexity. With hesitation, he could print his own name, but he found difficulty in writing even simple sentences, and his knowledge of the date, the days of the week, and so on was very limited.

- In addition, Mr C had a poor memory for verbal material but he did not have any abnormal tendency to 'fill in the gaps' by fabricating or distorting information. As expected from his low score on the test of acquiescence, he was not (mis)led by leading questions when they were first presented. However, consistent with his history of being bullied, which is often associated with low self-esteem in later life (Hawker & Boulton, 2000), Mr C was unusually suggestible in terms of shifting his answers following negative feedback. Following negative feedback about his initial responses, he changed almost all of them. Similarly, he was unusually compliant.

- The police interviews proceeded very rapidly, and as was noted by the interviewing officers, Mr C appeared to have had some difficulties in providing a detailed account (one of the officers said 'You're not all there, are you?'). However, whilst Mr C appeared anxious, the audiotapes did not suggest that his admissions reflected any type of pressure, and they appeared to be spontaneous. He was able to deny some of the offences about which he was questioned.

- Mr C admitted during the psychological assessment that he took part in the alleged offences, but he claimed that he was only a 'lookout'. He said he did not benefit financially, giving his co-suspect his share of the money. Whilst he claimed he was frightened of this man, he appeared to have remained in contact until his father intervened. Such a lack of assertiveness was consistent with his unusually high level of compliance.

- Mr C was not able to explain why he did not seek legal advice, particularly after the first police interview, when he said he felt very frightened. He said he retracted his confession because of his parents' reaction when he told them about it.

- The alleged offences took place in the absence of a framework of structure and supervision for Mr C. Since he received his Probation Order, he did not seem to have committed any further offences or have had any contact with the other suspect. He had an opportunity, through his Probation Officer, to undertake regular part-time paid employment that fitted well with his skills and aspirations.

The following opinions and recommendations were formed:

- Mr C fulfilled the criteria for a 'mental handicap' (in modern terminology, an intellectual disability) under s. 77(3) of PACE.

- Mr C also had a number of other long-standing psychological vulnerabilities, as a result of which he had limited resources to enable him to withstand pressure from those whom he perceived as powerful or intimidating.

- The relationship between Mr C's vulnerabilities and (i) the offences with which he was charged, and (ii) his responses to the police interviews, was uncertain. Nevertheless, an 'appropriate adult' should have been present during his detention at the police station.

Clues as to Mr C's need for this support were available during the 'booking in' process and during the interviews, but they were not acted on by the police.

- Mr C did not receive any support when he left school. This only became available when he was placed on a Probation Order. From his own account, and that of his Probation Officer, he avoided further offending, obtained paid employment, and terminated his contact with the other suspect. This suggested that he was benefiting from the structured framework that was now available to him.

- Given his intellectual disability and psychological vulnerabilities, it was likely that Mr C would continue to need support and practical assistance for a sustained period. With Mr C's consent, a referral to his local specialist community disabilities (intellectual disabilities) team was made, initially for liaison with his Probation Officer.

After receiving this report, the Crown Prosecution Service decided that, in the overall circumstances of the case, it would not proceed. This meant that Mr C did not have to appear in court. The community learning disabilities team judged that he would be eligible for specialist health care support (for example, to address his lack of assertiveness), but he did not meet the criteria for accessing social care because his needs were not considered 'critical' or 'substantial'. Consequently, there was no provision to maintain and develop the progress he had made during his Probation Order. Unfortunately, as is so often the case for men and women with mild intellectual disabilities, his needs for social support and care were only met when he offended.

Conclusions

Forensic neuropsychology involving the heterogeneous group of people with intellectual disabilities is a developing area; up to now, it has focused primarily on the vulnerability of this group of suspects and defendants within the criminal justice system. It is likely, however, that as a functional approach, long championed by clinicians and researchers (Grisso, 1986, 2003; Gudjonsson, 1992, 2003; Murphy & Clare, 1995, 2003), becomes more widely used, a broader range of forensic topics will begin to be addressed. This will require the development of more sophisticated and naturalistic assessment methods of individuals and of different forensic contexts so that appropriate supports, which promote their 'access to justice', can be provided for men and women with intellectual disabilities.

References

American Law Institute (1962). *Model Penal Code*. Washington, DC: American Law Institute.

Balandin, S. (2000). Witnessing without words. In: T. Shaddock, M. Bond, I. Bowen and K. Hales (eds), *Intellectual Disability and the Law: Contemporary Australian Issues*. Callaghan, NSW: Australian Society for the Study of Intellectual Disability.

Bailey, A. and Barr, O. (2000). Police policies on the investigation of sexual crimes committed against adults who have a learning disability. *Journal of Learning Disabilities*, 4:129–139.

Baroff, G., Gunn, M., and Hayes, S. (2004). Legal issues. In: W. R. Lindsay, J. L. Taylor, and P. Sturmey (eds), *Offenders with Developmental Disabilities*, pp. 37–65. Chichester: John Wiley & Sons.

Beail, N. (2002). Interrogative suggestibility, memory and intellectual disability. *Journal of Applied Research in Intellectual Disabilities*, **15**:129–137.

Bonnie, R. J. (1992). The competence of criminal defendants: a theoretical reformulation. *Behavioral Sciences and the Law*, **10**:291–316.

Borum, R. (2003). Not guilty by reason of insanity. In: T. Grisso (ed.) *Evaluating Competencies: Forensic Assessments and Instruments*, 2nd edn, pp. 193–227. New York: Kluwer Academic/Plenum Publishers.

Borun, R. and Grisso, T. (1996). Establishing standards for criminal forensic reports: An empirical analysis. *Bulletin of the American Academy of Psychiatry and the Law*, **24**:297–317.

Cardone, D. and Dent, H. (1996). Memory and interrogative suggestibility: The effects of modality of information presentation and retrieval conditions upon the suggestibility scores of people with learning disabilities. *Legal and Criminological Psychology*, **1**:34–42.

Clare, I. C. H. (2003). Psychological vulnerabilities of adults with mild learning disabilities: Implications for suspects during police detention and interviewing. Unpublished PhD thesis, Institute of Psychiatry, King's College London, UK.

Clare, I. C. H. and Gudjonsson, G. H. (1993). Interrogative suggestibility, confabulation, and acquiescence in people with mild learning disabilities (mental handicap): Implications for reliability during police interview. *British Journal of Clinical Psychology*, **32**:295–301.

Clare, I. C. H. and Gudjonsson, G. H. (1995). The vulnerability of suspects with intellectual disabilities during police interviews: A review and experimental study of decision-making. *Mental Handicap Research*, **8**:110–128.

Clare, I. C. H., Gudjonsson, G. H., and Harari, P. M. (1998). Understanding of the current police caution (England and Wales). *Journal of Community and Applied Social Psychology*, **8**:323–329.

Cooke, D. J. and Philip, L. (1998). Comprehending the Scottish caution: Do offenders understand their right to remain silent? *Legal and Criminological Psychology*, **3**:13–27.

Cooke, P. and Davies, G. (2001). Achieving best evidence from witnesses with learning disabilities: new guidance. *British Journal of Learning Disabilities*, **29**:84–87.

Davis, C. (2000). Systemic abuse: Intellectual disability and the criminal justice system. In: T. Shaddock, M. Bond, I. Bowen, and K. Hales (eds), *Intellectual Disability and the Law: Contemporary Australian Issues*. Callaghan, NSW: Australian Society for the Study of Intellectual Disability.

Dinerstein, R. D. and Buescher, M. (1999). Capacity and the courts. In: R. D. Dinerstein, S. S. Herr, and, J. L. O'Sullivan (eds), *A Guide to Consent*. Washington, DC: American Association on Mental Retardation.

Dunn, L. M., Dunn, L. M., Whetton, C., and Burley, J. (1997). *The British Picture Vocabulary Scale*, 2nd edn. London: GL Assessment.

Ericson, K. I. and Isaacs, B. (2003). Eyewitness identification accuracy: A comparison of adults with and those without intellectual disabilities. *Mental Retardation*, **41**:161–173.

Ericson, K. I. and Perlman, N. B. (2001). Knowledge of legal terminology and court proceedings in adults with developmental disabilities. *Law and Human Behavior*, **25**:529–545.

Everington, C. T. and Fulero, S. M. (1999). Competence to confess: Measuring understanding and suggestibility of defendants with mental retardation. *Mental Retardation*, **37**:212–220.

Everington, C. and Luckasson, R. (1992). *Competence Assessment for Standing Trial for Defendants with Mental Retardation: CAST-MR*. Worthington, OH: IDS Publishing Corporation.

Fenner, S., Gudjonsson, G. H., and Clare, I. C. H (2002). Understanding of the current police caution (England and Wales) among suspects in police detention. *Journal of Community and Applied Social Psychology*, **12**:83–93.

Finlay, W. M. L. and Lyons, E. (2002). Acquiescence in interviews with people who have mental retardation. *Mental Retardation,* **40**:14–29.

Fulero, S. M. and Everington, C. T. (1995). Assessing competency to waive Miranda rights in defendants with mental retardation. *Law and Human Behavior*, **19**:533–543.

Fulero, S. M. and Everington, C. T. (2004). Mental retardation, competency to waive Miranda rights and false confessions. In: G. D. Lassiter (ed.), *Interrogations, Confessions and Entrapment*, pp. 163–179. New York: Kluwer Academic.

Grisso, T. (1981). *Juveniles' Waiver of Rights: Legal and Psychological Competence*. New York: Plenum Press.

Grisso, T. (1986). *Evaluating Competencies: Forensic Assessments and Instruments*, 1st edn. New York: Kluwer Academic/Plenum Publishers.

Grisso, T. (2003). *Evaluating Competencies: Forensic Assessments and Instruments*, 2nd edn. New York: Kluwer Academic/Plenum Publishers.

Grubin, D. H. (1991a). Unfit to plead in England and Wales 1976–1988: A survey. *British Journal of Psychiatry*, **158**:540–548

Grubin, D. H. (1991b). Unfit to plead, unfit for discharge: Patients found unfit to plead who are still in hospital. *Criminal Behaviour and Mental Health*, **1**:282–294.

Gudjonsson, G. H. (1991). The 'Notice to Detained Persons', PACE Codes and reading ease. *Applied Cognitive Psychology*, **5**:89–95.

Gudjonsson, G. H. (1992*). The Psychology of Interrogations, Confessions and Testimony*. Chichester: John Wiley & Sons.

Gudjonsson, G. H. (1995). 'Fitness for interview' during police detention: A conceptual framework for forensic assessment. *Journal of Forensic Psychiatry*, **6**:185–197.

Gudjonsson, G. H. (1997). *The Gudjonsson Suggestibility Scales*. Hove, UK: Psychology Press.

Gudjonsson, G. H. (2003). *The Psychology of Interrogations and Confessions: A Handbook*. Chichester: John Wiley & Sons.

Gudjonsson, G. H., Clare, I. C. H., Rutter, S., and Pearse, J. (1993). *Persons at Risk During Interviews in Police Custody: The Identification of Vulnerabilities*. The Royal Commission of Criminal Justice, Research Study No. 12. London: HMSO.

Gudjonsson, G. H. and Grisso, T. (2008). Legal competencies in relation to confession evidence. In: A. Felthous and H. Sass (eds), *The International Handbook of Psychopathic Disorders and the Law, Vol. II*, pp. 177–187. New York: John Wiley & Sons.

Gudjonsson, G. H. and Henry, L. (2003). Child and adult witnesses with intellectual disability: The importance of suggestibility. *Legal and Criminological Psychology*, **8**:241–252.

Gudjonsson, G. H., Murphy, G. H., and Clare, I. C. H (2000). Assessing the capacity of people with intellectual disabilities to be witnesses in court. *Psychological Medicine*, **30**:307–314.

Hamlyn, B., Phelps, A., Turtle, J., and Sattar, G. (2004). *Are Special Measures Working? Evidence from Surveys of Vulnerable and Intimated Witnesses* (Study 283). London: Home Office Research, Development and Statistics Directorate.

Hawker, D. S. J. and Boulton, M. J. (2000). Twenty years' research on peer victimization and psychosocial adjustment: A meta-analytic review of cross-sectional studies. *Journal of Child Psychology and Psychiatry*, **41**:441–445.

Henry, L. and Gudjonsson, G. H. (1999). Eyewitness memory and suggestibility in children with mental retardation. *American Journal on Mental* Retardation, **104**:491–508.

Henry, L. and Gudjonsson, G. H. (2003). Eyewitness memory, suggestibility and repeated recall sessions in children with mild and moderate intellectual disabilities. *Law and Human Behavior*, **27**:481–505.

Herr, S. S. (1999). Capacity for consent to legal representation. In: R. D. Dinerstein, S. S. Herr, and J. L. O'Sullivan (eds), *A Guide to Consent*, pp. 77–94. Washington, DC: American Association on Mental Retardation.

Hollins, S., Stone, K., Sinason, V., and Brighton, C. (2007). *Supporting Victims*. London: RCPsych Publications and St George's University of London.

Home Office (1990). *Provision for Mentally Disordered Offenders*. Home Office Circular 66/90. London: Home Office.

Home Office (2002). *Achieving Best Evidence in Criminal Proceedings: Guidance for Vulnerable or Intimidated Witnesses, including Children*. Report of the Memorandum Project Steering Group. London: Home Office Communication Directorate (see also http://www.homeoffice.gov.uk).

Home Office (2005). *Police and Criminal Evidence Act 1984. Codes of Practice A–G*. London: The Stationery Office.

Home Office (2007). *Modernising Police Powers. Review of the Police and Criminal Evidence Act (PACE) 1984*. Consultation Paper. London: Home Office (see also http://www.homeoffice.gov.uk).

James, A. (1996). *Life on the Edge: Diversion and the Mentally Disordered Offender*. London: Mental Health Foundation.

James, D. V., Duffield, G., Blizard, R., and Hamilton, L. W. (2001). Fitness to plead. A prospective study of the inter-relationships between expert opinion, legal criteria and specific symptomatology. *Psychological Medicine*, **31**:139–150.

Johnson, W. G., Nicholson, R. A., and Service, N. M. (1990). The relationship of competency to stand trial and criminal responsibility. *Criminal Justice and Behavior*, **17**:169–185.

Kassin, S. M. and Norwick, R. J. (2004). Why suspects waive their Miranda rights: The power of innocence. *Law and Human Behavior*, **28**:211–221.

Kebbell, M. R., Hatton, C., and Johnson, S. D. (2004). Witnesses with intellectual disabilities in court: What questions are asked and what influence do they have? *Legal and Criminological Psychology*, **9**:23–25.

Laski, F. J. (1992). Sentencing the offender with mental retardation: Honouring the imperative for intermediate punishments and probation. In: R. W. Conley, R. Luckasson, and G. N. Bouthilet (eds), *The Criminal Justice System and Mental Retardation*, pp. 137–152. Baltimore, MD: Paul H. Brookes.

Lawson, E., Johnson, M., Adams, L., Lamb, J., and Field, S. (2005). *Blackstone's Guide to The Domestic Violence, Crime and Victims Act 2004*. Oxford: Oxford University Press.

Luckasson, R. (1992). People with mental retardation as victims of crime. In: R. W. Conley, R. Luckasson, and G. N. Bouthilet (eds), *The Criminal Justice System and Mental Retardation*, pp. 209–220. Baltimore, MD: Paul H. Brookes.

Mackay, R. D. and Kearns, G. (2000). An upturn in unfitness to plead? Disability in relation to the trial under the 1991 Act. *Criminal Law Review*, 532–546.

Malpass, R. and Devine, P. (1984). Research on suggestion in lineups and photospreads. In: G. Wells and E. Loftus (eds), *Eyewitness Testimony*, pp. 64–91. Cambridge: Cambridge University Press.

McBrien, J., Hodgetts, A., and Gregory, J. (2003). Offending and risky behaviour in community services for people with intellectual disabilities in one Local Authority. *Journal of Forensic Psychiatry and Psychology*, **14**:280–297.

McCarthy, M. and Thompson, D. (2007). *Sex and the 3 Rs: Rights, Risks and Responsibilities*. 3rd edn. Brighton, UK: Pavilion Publishing.

McGarry, A., Curran, W., and Kenefick, D. (1968). Problems of public consultation in medico-legal matters: A symposium. *American Journal of Psychiatry*, **125**:42–45.

Medford, S., Gudjonsson, G., and Pearse, J. (2003). The efficacy of the appropriate adult safeguard during police interviewing. *Legal and Criminological Psychology*, **8**:253–266.

Mencap (1999). *Living in Fear*. London: Mencap.

'Michael' with the assistance of Pathak, M. (2007). My life. *Ann Craft Trust Bulletin*, **61**:3–8.

Milne, R., Clare, I. C. H., and Bull, R. (1999). Using the cognitive interview with adults with mild learning disabilities. *Psychology, Crime and Law*, **5**:81–101.

Milne, R., Clare, I. C. H., and Bull, R. (2002). Interrogative suggestibility among witnesses with mild intellectual disabilities: The use of an adaptation of the GSS. *Journal of Applied Research in Intellectual Disabilities*, **15**:8–17.

Monaghan, G. and Pathak, M. (2000). Silenced witnesses. *Community Care*, 27 April, 20–21.

Murphy, G. H. (2007). Intellectual disability, sexual abuse, and sexual offending. In: A. Carr, G. O'Reilly, P. Noonan Walsh, and J. McEvoy (eds), *The Handbook of Intellectual Disability and Clinical Psychology Practice*, pp. 831–866. Hove, UK: Routledge.

Murphy, G. H. and Clare, I. C. H. (1995). Adults' capacity to make legal decisions. In: R. Bull and D. Carson (eds), *Handbook of Psychology in Legal Contexts*, 1st edn, pp. 97–128. Chichester: John Wiley & Sons.

Murphy, G. H. and Clare, I. C. H. (2003). Adults' capacity to make legal decisions. In: D. Carson and R. Bull (eds), *Handbook of Psychology in Legal Contexts*, 2nd edn, pp. 31–66. Chichester: John Wiley & Sons.

Murphy, G. H. and Clare, I. C. H. (2006). The effect of learning disabilities on witness testimony. In: A. Heaton-Armstrong, E. Shepherd, G. H. Gudjonsson, and D. Wolchover (eds), *Witness Testimony: Psychological, Investigative and Evidential Processes*, pp. 43–60. Oxford: Oxford University Press.

Murphy, G.H. and Mason, J. (2007). People with intellectual disabilities who are at risk of offending. In: N. Bouras (ed.), *Psychiatric and Behavioural Disorders in Intellectual and Developmental Disabilities*, 2nd edn, pp. 173–201. Cambridge: Cambridge University Press.

Murphy, G. H. and O'Callaghan, A. C. (2004). Capacity of adults with learning disabilities to consent to sexual relationships, *Psychological Medicine*, **34**:1–11.

Nihira, K., Leland, H., and Lambert, N. (1993). *Adaptive Behavior Scale—Residential and Community Version*, 2nd edn. Austin, TX: Pro-ed.

O'Kelly, C. M. E., Kebbell, M. R., Hatton, C., and Johnson, S. D. (2003). Judicial intervention in court cases involving witnesses with and without learning disabilities. *Legal and Criminological Psychology*, **8**:229–240.

Olley, M. C. and Ogloff, J. R. P. (1993). *Competency to understand charter cautions: A preliminary investigation*. Paper presented at the Annual Meeting of the Canadian Psychological Association, Montreal, Quebec.

Ormerod, D. and Roberts, A. (2006). The admissibility of expert evidence. In: A. Heaton-Armstrong, E. Shepherd, G. H. Gudjonsson, and D. Wolchover (eds), *Witness Testimony: Psychological, Investigative and Evidential Processes*, pp. 401–423. Oxford: Oxford University Press.

Palmer, C. and Hart, M. (1996). *A PACE in the Right Direction?* Sheffield, UK: Institute for the Study of the Legal Profession, University of Sheffield.

Pattenden, R. (1990). *Judicial Discretion and Criminal Litigation*. Oxford: Clarendon Press.

Perlman, N. B., Ericson, K. I., Esses, V. M. and Isaacs, B. J. (1994). The developmentally handicapped witness. *Law and Human Behavior*, **18**:171–187.

Poythress, N., Nicholson, R., Otto R., et al. (1999). *The MacArthur Competence Assessment Tool—Criminal Adjudication: Professional Manual*. Odessa, FL: Psychological Assessment Resources.

Rasch, W. (1990). Criminal responsibility in Europe. In: R. Bluglass and P. Bowden (eds), *Principles and Practice in Forensic Psychiatry*, pp. 299–305. London: Churchill-Livingstone.

Richardson, P. J. (1993). *Archbold—Pleading, Evidence and Practice in Criminal Cases*, 43rd edn. London: Sweet & Maxwell.

Rock, F. (1999). *Caution? What does that mean?* Paper presented at the Conference of the International Association of Forensic Linguists, Birmingham, UK.

Roesch, R., Zapf, P., and Eaves, D. (2006). *Fitness Interview Test—Revised*. Sarasota, FL: Professional Resource Press.

Scottish Office (1998). *Interviewing People who are Mentally Disordered: 'Appropriate Adults' Schemes* (Circular No. SWSG 8/98). Edinburgh: Scottish Office.

Schonell, F. J. and Goodacre, E. J. (1974). *The Psychology and Teaching of Reading*, 5th edn. Harlow, UK: Oliver & Boyd/Longmans, Oliver & Boyd.

Smith, S. A. (1993). Confusing the terms "guilty" and "not guilty": Implications for alleged offenders with mental retardation. *Psychological Reports*, **73**:675–678.

Smith, S. A. and Hudson, R. L. (1995). A quick screening test of competency to stand trial for defendants with mental retardation. *Psychological Reports*, **76**:91–97.

Sparrow, S., Balla, D., and Cicchetti, D. (2005). *Vineland Adaptive Behavior Scales*, 2nd edn. Oxford: Pearson Assessment.

Steadman, H. J., Monahan, J., and Hartson, E. (1982). Mentally disordered offenders: A national survey of patients and facilities. *Law and Human Behaviour*, **6**:31–38.

VOICE UK (1998). *Competent to Tell the Truth. A report of a VOICE UK Working Party* (Chair: Professor Michael Gunn). Derby, UK: VOICE UK.

Wechsler, D. (1999). *Wechsler Adult Intelligence Scale*, 3rd edn. Oxford: Pearson Assessment.

Wilson, B. A., Greenfield, E., Clare L., *et al.* (2007). *The Rivermead Behavioural Memory Test*, 3rd edn. Oxford: Harcourt Assessment.

Winkler, J. D., Kanouse, D. E. and Ware, J. E. (1982). Controlling for acquiescence response set in score development. *Journal of Applied Psychology*, **67**:555–561.

Chapter 4

Attention-deficit hyperactivity disorder

Susan Young

In recent years, there has been growing concern about the association between attention deficit hyperactivity disorder (ADHD), antisocial behaviour, and crime (reviewed by Young, 2007). The reported high rates of recidivism may reflect the fact that people with ADHD have cognitive problems that cause them to be unsuccessful criminals, i.e. they commit poorly planned, opportunistic crimes. This chapter outlines the developmental course of ADHD and the vulnerabilities of youths and adults with ADHD in the criminal justice system. There follows detailed guidance on the assessment of ADHD for legal purposes, including important issues that need to be considered and how these relate to the legal instructions. The chapter will focus exclusively on the criminal justice system as this is the most common source of request for an expert opinion. Nevertheless, experts may also be requested to advise on civil matters, the assessment for which will be relatively similar to that presented here.

The developmental course of ADHD

It is estimated that around 5% of the childhood population has ADHD (Polanczyk *et al.*, 2007). Symptoms gradually remit with maturity, and a meta-analysis of 32 publications that followed ADHD children, as well as controls, into adulthood reported a rate of persistence of approximately 15% at the age of 25. However, the rate of individuals fulfilling the *Diagnostic and Statistical Manual of Mental Disorders—Fourth Edition* (DSM-IV) definition of ADHD in partial remission (i.e. persistence of some symptoms associated with significant clinical impairments) was substantially higher at around 50% (Faraone *et al.*, 2006). One London epidemiological longitudinal study that measured ADHD behaviours in boys at 7, 17 and 26 years found that the persistence of hyperactive behaviour was strongly associated with poor social adjustment at age 17 in terms of lack of friends, occupation, and constructive activity. By the age of 26, deficits associated with high levels of psychiatric morbidity were also found (Asherson *et al.*, 2007). Studies are yet to follow child cohorts into mid-adulthood, but my clinical experience is that some adults continue to be symptomatic into their 40s or even 50s.

The persistence of symptoms has been associated with general and specific learning problems, academic underachievement, employment, and relationship problems (Nutt *et al.*, 2007). Comorbid problems are the rule rather than the exception and include (childhood proportion in brackets) oppositional defiant disorder (40%), language disorders (30–35%), conduct disorder (20%), specific learning disability (15–25%), anxiety disorder (20–25%), mood disorder (15–20%), smoking (19%), substance use disorder (15%), autistic spectrum disorders (10%), and tics (15–20%). The most common comorbid conditions are the disruptive disorders of conduct disorder and oppositional defiant disorder, which together affect 40–60% of children and adolescents with ADHD (Wolraich *et al.*, 1996). Substance use and mood disorders predominate in adulthood (Nutt *et al.*, 2007).

A sizeable subgroup engage in criminal behaviour (reviewed by Young, 2007), and the link between ADHD and crime is likely to be associated with symptoms and/or personality factors that are associated with their symptoms. In particular, reckless/sensation-seeking behaviour, poor behavioural controls, inattention, compliant personality traits, labile temperament, and a confrontational interpersonal style are all important factors.

Sensation-seeking behaviour/recklessness

Feelings of restlessness will cause the individual to become quickly bored with monotonous routine tasks. The individual will find it difficult to settle down to such tasks and will have the urge to quit what they are doing and seek out a more 'interesting' occupation. Because people with ADHD have a low boredom threshold, they may be motivated to engage in high-stimulus and sensation-seeking behaviours. Dangerous or reckless acts may gratify a desire for a state of arousal and excitement. Furthermore, their aversion to delayed gratification will positively reinforce recklessness because thrilling or 'sensation-seeking' behaviour will satisfy a craving for excitement. This is also likely to accelerate reckless behaviour.

A lack of internal controls

An impulsive nature means that individuals will act without thinking and are unlikely to stop and think about the consequences of a course of action or behaviour. People with ADHD do not have the internal controls that may prevent them from engaging in dangerous acts, as they do not effectively engage in a process of problem-solving that causes them to consider multiple solutions to a problem and consideration of the most effective. Engaging in a rapid decision-making process will often result in the wrong decisions being made (if one can call it a 'decision' at all). An opportunity will present itself and the ADHD offender will simply act immediately on a whim, without thought; for example, theft, breaking and entering, and joyriding.

Inattention

The symptom of inattention will affect people with ADHD in many ways. One factor that commonly affects inattention is distraction, which can be caused by both internal and external factors. When an individual becomes distracted, they do not attend sufficiently to all of the information available to them. Distraction may occur 'internally' by thoughts, ruminations, and/or daydreams. The ADHD mind is never at rest and is constantly whirring in a sea of ceaseless mental activity, resulting in a loss of concentration, such as losing their train of thought mid-sentence, not recalling a question, or difficulty focusing on a lot of detailed documentation. It is not helped by the individual 'switching off' and daydreaming, or by feelings of anxiety, which will exacerbate the problem. Secondly, they are distracted by external factors; for example, they may be distracted in interviews (with police or legal representatives), by a noise coming from outside the room, by interruptions from others walking in/out of the room, or by a person fidgeting and shuffling papers.

Compliant personality

A recent study of Icelandic male prison inmates meeting screening criteria for ADHD has found an association between a compliant personality style and ADHD (Gudjonsson et al., 2008). This finding needs to be replicated. Nevertheless, it raises important questions regarding the potential for ADHD youths and adults being led, manipulated, or pressured into criminal activities by others.

Labile temperament and a confrontational interpersonal style

A difficulty with self-monitoring their internal state means that people with ADHD have difficulty with self-regulation and emotional control. Consequently, they experience rapid mood swings and are perceived by others as having a labile temperament. Because of their history of underperformance (compared with their own expectations and those of others), people with ADHD are often hypersensitive to criticism. This means they may respond to perceived slights or insults in a defensive and/or aggressive way. This hypersensitivity, together with an emotional lability, may escalate the problem, resulting in the person becoming confrontational, especially if they are unable to inhibit the urge to behave in a verbally and/or physically aggressive manner.

Vulnerabilities of individuals with ADHD and the legal system

Because of their symptoms, youths and adults with ADHD are psychologically vulnerable in the criminal justice system at various stages and in various roles, such as a suspect, witness, defendant, prison inmate, and/or under the supervision of probation services. There are two potential problems in relation to vulnerabilities. Firstly, vulnerabilities are often not recognized, which means that these individuals lack the protection they require. Secondly, going through the various stages of the criminal justice system is a demanding and stressful process; therefore, problems associated with their respective vulnerabilities are likely to be exacerbated, for example they may become more inattentive or impulsive. Experts are increasingly being asked to write reports to advise the court and/or to assist in their management. They may also be requested to conduct *de novo* assessments for individuals suspected of having symptoms (Collins & White, 2002).

The police interview

People with ADHD may be 'at risk' during a police interview, in that they may unwittingly provide the police with unreliable accounts of events including a false incriminating statement (Gudjonsson, 1993, 2003). This may be due to them not fully understanding the significance of the questions put to them, the implications of their answers, or because they are unduly influenced by short-term gains or interviewers' suggestions. In addition, if detainees are unable to listen to or understand the police caution and/or their legal rights, this has important practical and legal implications (Gudjonsson, 2003). One consequence of their vulnerabilities is that they may, in certain circumstances, make a false confession. Gudjonsson *et al.* (2008), in a study of 90 Icelandic male prison inmates, found that 24% of the 27 inmates meeting screening criteria for ADHD claimed they had made a false confession at some time in their lives, the most common reason being because they wanted to leave the police station. Their vulnerabilities mean that people with ADHD may make admissions or give factually incorrect information (which is perceived as being evasive or deliberately misleading) for several reasons, as described below.

Maladaptive coping strategies

When faced with stressful situations, people with ADHD apply maladaptive coping strategies comprised of confrontation, escape avoidance, and lack of planning in problem-solving (Young, 2005). This means that they are unlikely to cope or function well in stressful situations, and they may feel overwhelmed and respond with an overarching desire to avoid the source of stress by withdrawing and/or becoming confrontational.

Need for immediate gratification

People with ADHD think about short-term, immediate gain. They are unable to delay gratification or anticipate longer-term rewards. This means that ADHD detainees may be strongly motivated to escape the situation and get out of the confines of the police interview room or police cell by withholding important information or lying, and they may not realize or think about the longer-term consequences of their actions. They may not wait for a solicitor to arrive, which means that the police interview will proceed without the individual having legal advice.

Attentional problems

An important vulnerability for people with ADHD is that they may have difficulty sustaining attention during the police interview, or may become distracted and say the first thing that springs to mind. A person with ADHD may be further disadvantaged by their symptoms and may pay even less attention to the caution than their peers in the general population. Attentional deficits will be exacerbated by acute feelings of distress and anxiety. It is the middle sentence of the caution, warning of possible adverse inferences, that creates the greatest problem, and this is the most important part of the caution as it advises a person of the potential ramifications of withholding information or giving false information.

Interrogative suggestibility

Interestingly, ADHD adults seem to cope just as well with interrogative pressure as persons in the 'general population'. Nevertheless, they appear to do so by adopting a specific strategy of giving a disproportionate number of 'don't know' answers. This may be associated with poor behavioural inhibition, memory problems, or lack of confidence in their capacity to give correct answers (Gudjonsson *et al.*, 2007).

Memory problems

Working memory or short-term memory deficits have been reported in adults with ADHD (Hervey *et al.*, 2004; MacLean *et al.*, 2004; Young *et al.*, 2006). Gudjonsson *et al.* (2007) found that ADHD adults had significant verbal memory impairments on an experimental measure of interrogative suggestibility. They also had a significant tendency to respond to questioning by giving 'don't know' rather than 'yes/no' replies. There appeared to be at least two reasons for this 'don't know' response style: the first one relates to behavioural inhibition and the second to distrust of their memory, lack of confidence, and use of avoidance as a coping strategy when faced with demanding questioning. The findings suggest that behavioural inhibition and lack of confidence in memory ability may be more important than memory deficits per se in understanding how people with ADHD cope with questioning.

Presence of an appropriate adult

The police interviews of vulnerable suspects, including all juveniles, must be conducted in the presence of an appropriate adult, whose primary role is to give advice to all relevant parties, to further communication, and ensure that the interview is conducted in a fair way (Medford *et al.*, 2003). This person is likely to be a parent, and given the strong genetic link with ADHD (Levy & Hay, 2001), this will possibly be a parent with (undiagnosed) residual ADHD who will also struggle with the interview process and encourage the child to 'agree' or 'own up' so that they can get out of the police station and go home.

Fitness to plead and stand trial

Experts are often asked to consider whether a defendant is fit to plead and stand trial and, if so, to advise about modifications to the trial process in order to optimize participation. In England and Wales, fitness to plead and stand trial requires certain criteria to be met (*R v Pritchard* (1836) 7 C&P 303). Namely, the defendant must be able to comprehend the proceedings of the trial, be able to challenge a juror to whom he might wish to object, understand the details of evidence, instruct counsel, follow proceedings, and give evidence. For example, the individual has to be able to keep up with the pace of the trial, to sustain concentration, to listen to what is being said, and to understand and assimilate it. For a defendant with a severe attention deficit and who is easily distracted, this can be a challenging and difficult task. If a defendant is very impulsive, this may have implications for him or her giving evidence as they may 'blurt out' the first answer in their mind, irrespective of whether it is accurate and rational or not. They may be inconsistent and give conflicting evidence. Emotional lability may also be a problem when testifying as they may become distressed and/or angry in the witness box, especially under cross-examination. They may not be able to inhibit a verbally aggressive response. These vulnerabilities are likely to be misinterpreted by a jury unless these are carefully explained to them by a suitably qualified expert.

A landmark case heard in the Court of Appeal on 12 October 2004 opened the gates for ADHD defendants who come before the courts (*R v Billy Joe Friend* [2004] EWCA Crim 2661). The court determined that Billy Joe Friend had undiagnosed ADHD at the time of his trial and that his significant impairment in attention, impulsivity, and behavioural control meant that he was unlikely to have participated or to have given evidence effectively in the trial proceedings. This case set a legal precedent that has important implications for defendants with ADHD who come before the courts, as well as for suspects interviewed by the police, especially if individuals have significant deficits and are not receiving medication. This may be because young people are not taking their medication on a regular basis, as in the case of Blackender (see next section) or because they have discontinued medication prematurely and/or through choice.

However, many young people have grown up without recognition of a diagnosis of ADHD and have received treatments for alternative diagnoses with little effect (Asherson et al., 2007). In particular, screens have indicated an overrepresentation of individuals with symptoms consistent with ADHD in the criminal justice system (Young, 2007; Young et al., 2009a). Thus, the diagnosis may be identified for the first time in the course of a comprehensive psychiatric and/or psychological assessment for the courts that has involved a detailed clinical and developmental assessment, psychometric testing, and a review of historical records. This means that recommendations in the report may include suggested special considerations to be adopted by the courts in some cases, for example, for those who are unmedicated and/or have severe symptoms. By taking some simple precautions, a vulnerable defendant may be better supported and less disadvantaged; these might include the provision of brief regular breaks during the trial or asking one question at a time using simple language. This will help to ensure that the defendant has a fair trial and that he or she is fit to stand trial and give evidence.

Criminal responsibility

Court assessments may be commissioned to establish whether the diagnosis of ADHD has relevance to an offence, i.e. to negate criminal responsibility and/or to mitigate punishment. Psychological evidence often complements psychiatric evidence at trial (Leslie et al., 2007), which typically focuses on mental disorder in relation to the defence of insanity, infanticide, diminished responsibility (in cases where the charge is murder), and non-insane automatism. Gudjonsson & Haward (1998) considered this issue in detail and commented that psychologists are most likely to be instructed to evaluate a defendant concerning their *mens rea* with relation to: (i) duress and coercion; (ii) absentmindedness, and (iii) diminished responsibility. The term *mens rea* refers to the defendant's state of mind at the time of the alleged offence; the focus is on the question of guilty intent and knowledge of the wrongfulness of the act. It has to be proved that the offence was committed either recklessly or intentionally.

The defence of duress can only succeed if the defendant can show that he or she was placed in an unavoidable dilemma, for example, by presenting an immediate threat to which an individual is in some way psychologically vulnerable (e.g. abnormally compliant and fearful, very young or very old) and from which there was no opportunity of escaping from the threat. More often, psychological findings are used at the sentencing stage to mitigate the severity of the sentence.

Absentmindedness or forgetfulness is often raised as a defence in cases of shoplifting (Gudjonsson & Haward, 1998). Absentmindedness is a condition that is exacerbated during a period of stress as individuals become preoccupied and distracted. This has implications for defendants with deficits in attention and memory, and who are easily distracted.

Diminished responsibility involves 'malice aforethought' (i.e. an intention to kill another person or inflict grievous bodily harm), but there are mitigating circumstances that reduce the charge of murder to manslaughter. This reduced conviction provides the trial judge with a number of sentencing possibilities including probation orders. Importantly, one has to demonstrate 'substantial impairment' in perception, judgement, or willingness, and this has been argued successfully in cases of depression, psychosis, and personality disorder. Gudjonsson & Haward (1998) suggested that psychological evaluations may include, in addition to a mental state examination, testing of intellectual functions, neuropsychological assessment, and psychometric tests. Psychological assessments that provide information about an individual in a standardized and valid way are very helpful in the court's requirement to demonstrate 'substantial impairment'. For example, the standardized format of psychometric tests provides robust and objective data. They measure differences between individuals in relation to abilities, personality traits, and clinical problems. Psychometric tests can be used to generate, as well as test out, hypotheses. Individual test results are compared with a normative sample and this provides information about whether an individual deviates or not from 'normal' functioning. This will be discussed more fully with respect to ADHD in the section on Results from cognitive/neuropsychological assessment.

The leading case that argued that ADHD should be considered as a mental disorder that may impair criminal responsibility was heard at the 'Old Bailey' (Central Criminal Court) in June 2002. David Blackender pleaded guilty to manslaughter on the basis of diminished responsibility arising from his history of ADHD. Blackender, who was only 16 at the time of the offence, was of average intellectual ability and had ADHD/combined type at the time of the offence and at trial 1 year later. Although Blackender had been diagnosed with ADHD several years beforehand and prescribed medication, he had been taking it somewhat sporadically for several years and, crucially, was not taking his medication at the time of the offence.

> You pleaded guilty to manslaughter on the basis of diminished responsibility, primarily due to the condition from which all the doctors agree that you suffer, namely attention deficit hyperactivity disorder, which substantially, but of course not fully, impaired your responsibility for your actions ... The offence in itself is, in my judgment, sufficiently serious to justify a long sentence, even at your age.
>
> *R v David Blackender*, Central Criminal Court, 18 July 2001, p. 3.

The offence was that, one night when he was out with friends, Blackender became involved in an argument that resulted in him fatally stabbing the victim with a knife. Blackender claimed that someone handed him the knife, but witnesses claimed that he walked away from the victim to seek and obtain the knife and returned to assault the victim. Clearly, the second scenario implies an element of planning and, whilst both scenarios may have been spur-of-the-moment actions, the latter afforded more time to think about what he was proposing to do and consider the consequences.

Mitigation of sentence

Psychologists are commonly asked to provide reports about factors that are relevant to mitigation and sentencing. This involves consideration of treatment options and prognosis, and for people with ADHD, this will often include their treatment needs for core symptoms, comorbid problems (e.g. anxiety, anger, and antisocial personality characteristics) and criminogenic needs (e.g. understanding their offending, a lack of prosocial skills, and poor victim empathy). The sentence imposed depends primarily on the nature and seriousness of the case, as well as the aggravating features, surrounding circumstances, and mitigating factors. Financial penalties are generally imposed for less serious offences, whereas a probation order, a community service order, or a prison sentence is given for more serious offences.

In the case of Blackender, His Honour Judge Stokes requested that I write a supplementary psychological report to assist in his sentencing. In particular, he posed the following questions:

1. What is the severity of David Blackender's ADHD and the effect of Ritalin on his symptoms?
2. How long is he likely to suffer from ADHD?
3. What is the likelihood of him re-offending if he continues to suffer with ADHD?
4. What is the danger to the public that David Blackender poses if he continues to suffer with ADHD?

5. What other characteristics may make David Blackender a danger to the public?

These were difficult questions to answer, particularly because although Blackender reported a reduction in his ADHD symptoms when taking stimulant medication, the high frequency of aggressive and disruptive behavioural problems recorded in his inmate files while on remand suggested that the medication was not entirely successful in treating the core symptoms. This is not uncommon and most likely explained his history of poor compliance with taking his ADHD medication. Secondly, it is impossible to say for exactly how long a person will remain symptomatic. ADHD is a heterogeneous disorder and symptoms do not remit conveniently or uniformly, although one can of course provide the court data on the age-dependent decline in symptoms discussed earlier (Faraone et al., 2006). Similarly, it was not possible to predict whether Blackender would reoffend and/or be violent towards others in the future, although there was a greater likelihood that he would reoffend if he remained symptomatic and untreated. The 'other characteristics' that need to be considered with respect to the last question will include the presence of personality disorder (particularly antisocial personality disorder, which has been shown to be highly predictive of recidivism and impulsivity, particularly among males) (Gudjonsson et al., 2006).

In this case, the Judge accepted manslaughter on the basis of diminished responsibility. He gave a life sentence but recommended a minimum sentence provided Blackender took his medication and satisfied the parole board panel that he would not be a risk to the public in the community. He was, however, on license for life. Thus, the judgement was effective, because it minimized the risk to the public but allowed Blackender maximum advantages provided he cooperated with treatment.

> … the future is very much in your hands. It may be, and I very much hope, that you having pleaded guilty, and I give you every credit for that, now realise the very great danger that you pose if you do not take your medicine and pay very great attention to how you are going to spend the rest of your life. The sentence of the Court is detention for life under Section 91 of the Powers of Criminal Courts (Sentencing) Act. Had I been passing a determinate sentence, in view of your age if would have been one of 6 years. So for the purposes of Section 28 of the Crime Sentences Act of 1997 the Court specifies a period of 2 years and 4 months. This means that your case will not be considered by the Parole Board until you have served at least that period in custody. After that time the Parole Board will be entitled to consider your release. When, and only when, it is satisfied that you need no longer be confined in custody for the protection of the public it will be able to direct your release. Until it is so satisfied you will remain in custody. If you are released it will be on terms that you are subject to a licence for

the rest of your life and liable to be recalled to prison if at any time your licence is revoked, either on the recommendation of the Parole Board or if it is thought expedient in the public interest by the Secretary of State.

R v David Blackender, Central Criminal Court, 18 July 2001, p. 6.

This begs the question of what is appropriate 'treatment' for antisocial youths and adults with ADHD. Medication, particularly with stimulant drugs, is an effective means of reducing ADHD symptoms and behaviours in adulthood. Such treatment will help individuals to be more attentive, develop better listening skills, manage their time better, make plans, and settle down to a task. It will predispose individuals to positive change by helping them to engage better in prison programmes designed to provide basic education, further education, and occupational skills. There are various 'broad-brush' offender rehabilitation programmes, but current thinking emphasizes the need to provide treatments that map closely to individuals' needs, attributions, and motivations. Thus, specific treatment programmes for ADHD antisocial youths and adults should be provided as these may reduce risk and accelerate early release (Young & Ross, 2007).

Assessment of ADHD and legal considerations

ADHD is characterized by high levels of inattentiveness, restlessness, overactivity, impulsiveness, emotional lability, disorganization, and memory problems, and, as for many psychiatric disorders such as anxiety and depression, ADHD symptoms are continuously distributed throughout the population (Asherson, 2004). Clinical thresholds are therefore determined on the basis of usual clinical practice, which considers the impact of the symptoms on a person's functional ability and identifies 'disorder' when these symptoms are sufficiently frequent or severe to cause personal distress, distress to others, interference with psychosocial function, or health complications. Symptoms remit with age but not uniformly, and whilst some individuals will continue to experience 'impairment' in all symptoms, others will continue to experience marked problems related to some symptoms but not others. Thus, the aims of an ADHD assessment are to establish the presence of core symptoms and the level of associated functional impairment.

Classification of symptoms

Formal diagnostic classifications cite three core symptoms of ADHD—inattention, hyperactivity, and impulsivity. There are 18 items that are required to make a diagnosis of ADHD. These items are the same in International

Table 4.1 Classification of DSM-IV symptoms for ADHD diagnosis

Predominantly inattentive type	6 out of 9 inattentive symptoms rated as 'often'
Predominantly hyperactive–impulsive type	6 out of 9 hyperactive/impulsive symptoms rated as 'often'
Combined type	Both 6 out of 9 inattentive symptoms rated as 'often' AND 6 out of 9 hyperactive/impulsive symptoms rated as 'often'

Reprinted with permission from Young & Bramham (2007).

Classification of Diseases and Related Health Problems 10th revision (ICD-10) and DSM-IV. Both classification systems require that symptoms are maladaptive, inconsistent with developmental level, and present for the past 6 months. Overall, there must be clear evidence of clinically significant impairment in social, academic, or occupational functioning (i.e. pervasive across different environments).

ICD-10 adopts a more restricted definition of 'hyperkinetic syndrome' than DSM-IV and requires that all three symptoms are present independently. Thus, DSM-IV is more commonly applied to diagnose the three distinct typologies (see Table 4.1).

ADHD combined type represents the more severe 'hyperkinetic' form and predominantly inattentive type or predominantly hyperactive–impulsive type may account for heterogeneity or remitting symptoms. Also included is a category for disorders with prominent symptoms of inattention or hyperactivity–impulsivity that fall short of diagnostic criteria, known as 'ADHD not otherwise specified'.

It is useful to screen for current symptoms using a checklist of symptoms in a semi-structured interview format (see Table 4.2, which shows how this may be completed for a client with predominantly inattentive symptoms). It is recommended that each positive self-rating is endorsed by the assessor on the basis of supplementary questioning or other information (e.g. independent documentation or information from a different source). Item 'B' in Table 4.2 asks whether symptoms were present before the age of 7, and this needs to be ascertained either by retrospective report (by the defendant and/or by an informant) and/or by collateral documentation that contains contemporaneous records of childhood (see section on The assessment process).

Partial remission of symptoms

The heterogeneous nature and trajectory of the ADHD disorder means that for each individual the experience of the disorder and their response to treatment

Table 4.2 DSM-IV checklist of symptoms

	In the past 6 months, do you think you:	Never 0	Sometimes 1	Often 2
	Failed to give close attention to details or made careless mistakes in studying, work or other activities?			✓
	Had difficulty sustaining attention in tasks or leisure activities?			✓
	Have not seemed to listen when spoken to directly?		✓	
	Did not follow through on instructions and failed to finish studies, chores or duties in the workplace (not due to oppositional behaviour or failure to understand instructions)?			✓
	Had difficulty organizing tasks and activities?			✓
	Avoided, disliked or were reluctant to engage in tasks that require sustained mental effort (e.g. studying, homework, leisure activities)?		✓	
	Lost things necessary for tasks or activities (e.g. pens, books, tools, study papers)?		✓	
	Were easily distracted by outside events and stimuli?			✓
	Were forgetful in daily activities?			✓
1	**Inattention criteria met?** (i.e. 6 or more items rated 'often')			**(Yes)/No**
	Fidgeted with hands or feet or squirmed in seat?			✓
	Left seat in situations where remaining seated is expected (e.g. in classes, church, movies)?			✓
	Experienced feelings of restlessness, especially in situations where it is inappropriate?		✓	
	Had difficulty engaging in leisure tasks quietly?			✓
	Felt 'on the go' or as if driven by a motor?	✓		
	Talked excessively?			✓
	Blurted out answers before questions have been completed?	✓		
	Had difficulty waiting turn?		✓	
	Interrupted or intruded on others (e.g. butting into conversations)?		✓	

Table 4.2 (continued) DSM-IV checklist of symptoms

	In the past 6 months, do you think you:	Never 0	Sometimes 1	Often 2
2	**Hyperactivity/impulsivity criteria met?** (i.e. 6 or more items rated 'often')			Yes/**No**
A	Either 1 and 2 (or both rated yes)			✓
B	Were some hyperactive–impulsive or inattentive symptoms present before age 7?			✓
C	Some impairment from the symptoms is present in two or more settings (e.g. in educational setting, work setting, at home)?			✓
D	Is there clear evidence of clinically significant impairment in social, academic or occupational functioning?			✓
E	The symptoms do not occur exclusively during the course of a severe psychiatric illness (e.g. schizophrenia) and are not better accounted for by another mental disorder (e.g. mood disorder, anxiety disorder, dissociative disorder or a personality disorder).			✓
3	**Combined (A–E and items 1 and 2 rated yes)**			Yes/**No**
4	**Predominantly inattentive type** (A–E and item 1 rated yes)			**Yes**/No
5	**Predominantly hyperactive–impulsive type** (A–E and item 2 rated yes)			Yes/**No**
6	**Total score obtained for symptoms by applying ratings of 0 = never, 1 = sometimes, 2 = often**			26 N/A
7	**In partial remission of symptoms? If (3), (4) and (5) above are scored 'no' and if score obtained for (6) above is 17 or greater**			Yes/**No**

Reprinted with permission from Young & Bramham (2007).

is different. Symptoms do not conveniently and uniformly remit, and many individuals are 'in partial remission' of their symptoms (Young & Gudjonsson, 2008). However, DSM-IV does not provide clarification of how to ascertain this other than to say that *'if clinically significant symptoms remain but criteria are no longer met for any of the subtypes, the appropriate diagnosis is Attention-Deficit/Hyperactivity Disorder, In Partial Remission'*. One way of ascertaining partial remission is to score the DSM-IV checklist responses as '0 = never', '1 = sometimes', and '2 = often'. A score of 17 on the DSM-IV checklist of symptoms represents one standard deviation above the mean average score obtained in a normal control group (Young, 1999), i.e. falling at the 84th percentile. Thus, individuals who are below the threshold of the categorical diagnosis but who continue to experience the persistence of some symptoms associated with significant clinical impairments may be identified using this method.

The assessment process

Because ADHD symptoms may have been unrecognized and/or misdiagnosed, often in criminal cases the question relates firstly to determining whether the person has ADHD, before this can subsequently be related to the legal issue. Thus, sometimes an assessment of ADHD is being made for the first time in young adulthood, which may be hampered by a lack of contemporaneous records and a dependency on self-reported childhood symptoms. There are two fundamental questions to be answered when conducting an assessment of ADHD: did the defendant have ADHD as a child, and, if so, to what extent does the defendant remain symptomatic? As difficulties stemming from childhood are central to diagnosis, wherever possible it is essential to support self-reported childhood symptoms with those of other sources, the best being contemporaneous documentation recorded in childhood (e.g. school records, probation records, and professional assessments). In practice, it is not always possible to obtain these records, and there may be other time and/or financial constraints that will limit what the expert can achieve. However, the ideal 'best practice' assessment will include the following:

1. Review of childhood records.
2. Interview with the defendant (including a comprehensive developmental history, assessment of mental state, and differential diagnosis).
3. Interview with informant(s) (e.g. parent, teacher, partner, good friend, probation officer, or social worker) regarding the defendant's past and current functioning, with the aim of obtaining collaborative information from independent sources.
4. Observation of behaviour during the assessment and testing.
5. Completion of child and adult rating scales.
6. Neuropsychological assessment (including intellectual functioning, attention and vigilance, impulsiveness, and effort).
7. Assessment of the current mental state, including a psychometric assessment of anxiety and depression.

When conducting a *de novo* assessment of ADHD in adults, it will be helpful to have the following checklist in mind:

1. Obtain a comprehensive developmental history, particularly with respect to the presence and severity of ADHD core symptoms in childhood across settings.

2. Evaluate the presence of current ADHD symptoms across settings and determine their severity.
3. Assess the evidence that these symptoms are causing the defendant significant impairment in their everyday life (e.g. in educational or occupational achievement, and emotional and psychosocial adjustment).
4. Assess for differential diagnoses and determine whether these symptoms can be better explained by an alternative primary diagnosis.
5. Assess for the existence of comorbid conditions and problems.

Once the assessment has been completed, the expert then has to consider the severity of the ADHD symptoms and their relationship to the issue under instruction. This is not always straightforward and may involve the expert having to disentangle inconsistent information from different sources. This is especially the case when relying on the fallible memory of informants going back several years, and more weight should be put on contemporaneous records if these are available. When writing the court report, it is important that this begins with a statement about what you have been instructed to do and why, and, if this included an assessment of ADHD, the methodology used.

Table 4.3 summarizes a suggested format for presenting the findings of an assessment in a court report and provides guidance about important areas that should be considered. Each item of the report is discussed more fully below (for a more detailed discussion regarding specific assessment tools, see Chapter 2 on Assessment in Young & Bramham, 2007).

Table 4.3 The court report: what to report and what to consider

What to report:	Developmental history and interview with defendant
	Interviews with others
	Information from contemporaneous records
	Presentation and behaviour during testing
	Medication status
	Results from rating scales
	Results of cognitive/neuropsychological assessment
	Effort
	Mental state
What to consider:	Consistency of findings across tests
	Consistency of findings across different sources
	Consistency of findings across time
	Differential diagnosis versus comorbid issues
	Relating findings to instruction and making recommendations

Developmental history and interview with defendant

The assessment must include a comprehensive and thorough developmental history that is considerably more detailed than that usually taken by clinicians working in general adult psychiatric services. This should be generated drawing on documentation available and an interview with the defendant and/or informants, as follows:

1. Presentation to child and adolescent services, including the outcome of referrals to agencies, e.g. contacts with educational psychology services, child guidance clinics, social services, and child psychiatry or paediatric services.
2. Family: relationship with parents, siblings, and extended family; problems within the family (e.g. psychiatric, and substance misuse); stressful life events (e.g. bereavements, periods in care, financial problems and unemployment, neglect, and physical and emotional abuse).
3. School progress and educational achievement: type of school attended (mainstream or pupil referral units), information from Statements of Special Educational Need, additional support provided in school, academic achievement/qualifications, truancy/school refusal, attitude and motivation, behavioural problems in school, suspensions/expulsions, and relationships with peers and teachers.
4. Further education history and qualifications obtained: note drop outs.
5. Occupational history: number of jobs, types of job, reasons for leaving, periods of unemployment, and future intentions; occupation of family members.
6. Antisocial behaviour: verbal and physical aggression, history of conduct problems/oppositional behaviour, and police contact and offending.
7. Substance misuse: onset, frequency, and severity of use of drugs and alcohol misuse, drug of preference, level of dependency, and reason for misuse.
8. Social functioning: activities, friendships, and intimate relationship problems.

Interviews with others

Adults may be more accurate than children in describing their ADHD symptoms (Danckaerts *et al.*, 1999; Murphy & Schachar, 2000; Smith *et al.*, 2000; Young & Gudjonsson, 2005). Nevertheless, in order to make a diagnosis with confidence, especially one involving retrospective accounts, it is advisable to include an informant interview whenever possible. Parents may be a useful source of information for childhood functioning, but partners may be more helpful regarding current symptoms and psychosocial functioning. In some cases, it may be helpful to obtain the perspective of individuals who are not emotionally involved with the defendant in order to obtain an objective perspective (e.g. teachers, probation officers, or work colleagues).

Information from contemporaneous records (child and adult)

De novo adult assessments can be made with relative confidence when contemporaneous records are available from childhood. It is more tenuous in the absence of such records. The report should summarize the relevant information from these records, for example, school reports, Statements of Special Educational Need, educational psychology assessments, paediatric and/or child psychiatry reports, probation reports, and social services reports. If the records contain past psychology test results (e.g. intellectual test scores), then these should be reported and compared with current test results. Contemporaneous records are also important sources of information to corroborate self-reported information, in addition to that provided by others. For example, if a person is on remand, then perusal of the inmate prison report is very helpful as this will provide information about how cooperative he or she has been, and whether he or she has been restless, distractible, disruptive, labile, impulsive, argumentative, etc. In particular, the expert should look for consistent 'real life' expressions of core symptoms and mood instability, especially as symptoms may decrease in situations that are highly novel or salient to the individual, such as neuropsychological testing.

Presentation and behaviour during testing

Behavioural observation is an extremely important aspect of the assessment and should not be overlooked. This aspect of the report should include information about a person's demeanour (e.g. whether they presented as polite, friendly, circumspect, anxious, quiet, or evasive), attitude (e.g. cavalier, careful, or thoughtful) and behaviour during testing. It is important to state whether the individual cooperated with the assessment, how well he or she concentrated and over what period, and how many breaks were required. It should be stated whether questionnaires had to be read to the individual, if the defendant frequently requested clarification of the meaning of words or appeared to respond without fully understanding, and whether the defendant seemed able to understand and follow instructions. It is also important to comment on the defendant's response style when completing cognitive tests. A typical approach to tests is for the defendant to race through them rapidly but making lots of errors. Inattention will be evidenced by requests for instructions to be repeated, becoming distracted, and daydreaming; hyperactivity by fidgeting, foot tapping, leg shaking, standing up and walking about, and fiddling with items on the desk; and impulsivity by rapid shifts in conversation, turning the pages of tests prematurely, blurting out irrelevant answers or questions, and favouring speed over accuracy. Deterioration in performance may be evidenced from a difficulty sustaining concentration over a protracted period and expressed as a lack of motivation to perform tasks (they give up easily, stop trying, give lots of 'don't know' answers), refusal to complete tasks, somatic complaints (e.g. headache), complaints about the duration of the assessment, and requests for breaks (for cigarettes, coffee, or the toilet).

Medication status

It is essential to comment on the defendant's medication status as this will strongly influence the interpretation of test results. ADHD symptoms in adults show the same responsiveness to stimulant and non-stimulant medication as that seen in children (Faraone et al., 2004; Simpson & Plosker, 2004). Thus, deficits may not be found on neuropsychological testing of individuals tested while on medication, and ratings completed on scales that ask about functioning within a set period may bias towards the norm. This issue is especially important if an offence was committed while the defendant claimed not to be taking medication at the time. One way forward is to ask individuals taking medication to complete rating scales twice, once for 'on medication' and the second for 'off medication' (if they have had periods in the recent past off medication and so can comment on this). Similarly, cognitive assessments can be administered both on and off medication, and when this is possible, this provides helpful information regarding the potential for treatment response. I have, however, found that prison establishments are often reluctant to stop a defendant's medication for this purpose. On one occasion, staff reported that they were anxious about how they would cope with an increase in aggression and the potential disruption that this would cause on the wing. However, on some occasions it has been agreed that short-acting stimulant medications can be stopped 48 hours prior to the assessment (which means that there may remain some small effect).

Results from rating scales

Rating scales cannot be used as a sole basis for diagnosing ADHD. Nevertheless, they are useful for several reasons. Firstly, they can be used as screening measures because, if base rates (childhood and adulthood) are low, then it is unlikely that the person has ADHD. Secondly, these are usually standardized so the defendant's results can be compared with a normative sample to determine the extent to which they differ from 'normal' functioning. Thirdly, they can be used to monitor and quantify progression of the disorder and treatment response. In addition to the DSM-IV checklist of symptoms described above (which could also be used to obtain retrospective ratings of childhood behaviour), there are several scales in common practice including Conners' Child and Adult Rating Scales (Conners, 2000; Conners *et al.*, 1998), the Wender Utah Rating Scale (Ward *et al.*, 1993), the Brown Attention Deficit Disorder Scales (BADDS) (Brown, 1996), the DuPaul ADHD Rating Scale (DuPaul, 1990), and the Barkley Symptom Scales (Barkley & Murphy, 1998). The disadvantage of using rating scales is that the questions are answered subjectively and have 'face validity'. Thus, they are easy to fake if a person is motivated to present themselves as a person with ADHD. Therefore, it is important to seek corroborative ratings and/or objective support wherever possible (e.g. information in records and documentation).

Results from cognitive/neuropsychological assessment

A cognitive assessment is important for several reasons. Firstly, it may contribute to the assessment and diagnostic evaluation of ADHD and support the diagnosis. Secondly, it can be helpful in excluding other diagnoses such as learning disabilities or diffuse brain injury leading to a global impairment, rather than specific attentional and/or impulse control difficulties. Thirdly, it provides a benchmark from which an individual's psychosocial functional performance can be compared, such as academic and occupational attainment. Fourthly, and perhaps for court cases most importantly, it provides an evaluation of the defendant's relevant strengths and weaknesses, which will assist the judge and jury in their decision-making because findings can be compared with a normative frame of reference. Standardized scores indicate the number of standard deviations above or below the mean at which a score falls. Percentile ranks perform a similar function as these express the percentage of people in the standardization groups who fall above or below a given raw score. This provides information about the severity of functional deficits or symptoms. This is language that the courts understand, as a person's functioning can be measured and in turn can indicate a level of statistically significant impairment. For example, evidence can be framed in terms of performance falling in, say, the 5th percentile (i.e. the bottom 5% of the normative population); in other words, 95% of the 'normal' population would obtain a higher score. Furthermore, confidence intervals will estimate the certainty of a score falling within a given range.

As a minimum, the neuropsychological assessment should include an assessment of intelligence, attention, and response inhibition. Depending on the legal issues, it may also be helpful to include other executive functions such as planning ability.

However, there are two caveats: neuropsychological tests lack specificity, and the presence of cognitive deficits may be explained by different underlying problems or pathology, such as anxiety, ADHD, and learning disability. Secondly, people with ADHD may do well in neuropsychological tests as these are usually conducted in an optimal quiet environment, which helps them to concentrate better; they receive structure, encouragement, and feedback from the tester, which is a motivating factor; and they tend to do well on novel and interesting tasks. Thus, the absence of deficits will not reject the diagnosis, and the presence of the deficits needs to be considered in terms of differential diagnoses.

Effort

Effort is very important to assess, because if individuals lack effort during testing or deliberately underperform, then this is likely to render the forensic evaluation unreliable. Gudjonsson & Haward (1998, p. 96) state *'the incentive for clients to fake on psychological tests is often compelling and must be considered as a possibility in every civil and criminal case. There is no room for complacency with regard to the possibility of faking'*. Poor motivation to do the best one can is more difficult to identify objectively than deliberate faking, but it can sometimes be revealed by the client's demeanour during testing (e.g. giving up very easily on items or giving many 'don't know' answers). There are specific tests that can be applied to detect deliberate underperformance on cognitive tests, such as Raven's Standard Progressive Matrices and the Test of Memory Malingering; these are discussed in Chapter 11.

Mental state

An evaluation of the client's mental state normally forms a part of any psychological assessment conducted for civil or criminal proceedings. This includes an assessment of the individual's cooperation and motivation, mental alertness, orientation, attention and concentration, depression, anxiety, language problems, reading problems, response style and consideration of cultural factors (Gudjonsson and Haward, 1998). The tester should also include a psychometric assessment of anxiety and depression as this will help determine whether symptoms of inattention are associated with ADHD (i.e. the person would have a childhood history of ADHD, continuation of symptoms and/or possible comorbid anxiety/depression) or whether these are primary (e.g. the person has no childhood history of ADHD, but reports many attentional problems that seem to be more associated with anxiety or depression). In some adult cases it may be appropriate to administer an instrument that assesses a broader range of psychopathology such as the Symptom Checklist-90-R (Derogatis, 1994) or the Millon Clinical Multiaxial Inventory III measure of clinical syndromes and personality patterns and which also provides information about response styles (Millon, 1997).

Consistency of findings across tests

This involves a comparison of all of the test results, taking into account the source of reporting and their objectivity. This may also involve comparing results obtained from rating scales with neuropsychological test results, as in the following case study.

Case Study 1

Mr Smith self-rated himself to have some residual inattention and impulsive/hyperactive symptoms on the DSM-IV checklist of ADHD symptoms. The results were supported by the results of the cognitive assessment which indicated that he continues to have severe deficits of attention (95th percentile on the Letter Cancellation Test assessment of selective attention and 98th percentile on errors of omission on the Continuous Performance Test of sustained attention and vigilance) and impulse control (98th percentile on the Matching Familiar Figures Test and >99th percentile for errors of commission on the Continuous Performance Test). The scores suggest that Mr Smith generally adopted a strategy that favoured speed over accuracy resulting in numerous errors. The rating scale scores do not indicate the severity of symptoms found from the cognitive assessment and this may reflect that Mr Smith has generated functional strategies that help him cope with his symptoms on a daily basis.

Consistency of findings across different sources

This involves comparing self-reporting, informant reports, contemporaneous records, and psychometric/cognitive test scores, for example: comparing IQ scores with the defendant's educational and/or occupational achievement; comparing the defendant's educational/occupational achievement with that of siblings; comparing the findings of the assessment with his or her psychosocial progress.

Case Study 2

Mr Adams obtained a score of 64 on the Wender Utah Rating Scale which means he self-rated himself to have a childhood history consistent with ADHD. This finding is strongly supported by the contemporaneous childhood documentation completed by multi-disciplinary professionals between the age of 8–15 years. These documents consistently record Mr Adams had problems with attentional control and poor behavioural controls (impulsivity) from a very young age and these problems caused him to underachieve academically. Because of these problems, Mr Adams was referred to special schools but excluded from three units for aggressive behaviour towards staff and teachers. The cognitive and behavioural problems contained within this detailed documentation are consistent with a history of Attention Deficit Hyperactivity Disorder in childhood. Mr Adams appears to have responded very well to the structure provided by the Franklin Youth Treatment Service where his behaviour and learning ability considerably improved. The reports demonstrate that following a very unsettled period initially, Mr Adams' behaviour improved illustrating how he responded positively in a structured setting employing a token economy system (i.e. one with clear rules and expectations of behaviour and one that provides rewards to positively reinforce achievement). Mr Adams is reported to have engaged very well with education sessions and his Record of Incidents shows a gradual reduction in incidents over the period in terms of both frequency and severity. In order to achieve this standard, Mr Adams required bi-weekly monitoring as opposed to weekly meetings commonly provided to his peers as 'this enables him to achieve positive results over a shorter time period'. This is entirely consistent with what would be expected from an ADHD child learning in this type of environment, away from a large class where there is ample opportunity for distraction. Indeed, this is an optimum environment for achievement both academically and in terms of learning behavioural control as specific care plans can be structured, the child can receive more individual attention and immediate feedback. Nevertheless his symptoms remained evident (slow progress, constant individual feedback, poor concentration, poor behavioural controls) and, had he undergone an appropriate psychiatric assessment at the time, he may have been prescribed medication which in turn may have significantly helped him.

Consistency of findings across time

This comparison will indicate the developmental process of the disorder, for example, whether a person remains fully symptomatic and/or whether they are in partial remission of their symptoms. This will involve consideration of information from all of the available different sources and evaluation of whether the individual continues to experience a level of functional impairment in one or more symptoms in his or her personal, social, or occupational life.

Differential diagnosis versus comorbid issues

A difficulty with attentional control is common to many psychiatric disorders, and poor impulse control is commonly associated with conduct and antisocial behaviours. Early rearing in deprived conditions, and disrupted and disordered early attachments have been reported to predispose ADHD-like behaviour (Rutter, 2005), as these experiences leave children more vulnerable to problems of self-regulation, characterized by poor impulse control, impatience, and disinhibition, all of which are phenomena associated with ADHD (Cassidy, 1994; Young *et al.*, 2009). These experiences, however, should not automatically preclude the diagnosis. Nevertheless, when considering whether a diagnosis is differential or comorbid, it is helpful to bear in mind the age of onset. Comorbid problems such as anxiety, depression, emotional lability, and/or substance misuse are likely to have a later onset than childhood ADHD. The mental state assessment, supplemented by a psychometric assessment of anxiety and depression, will assist in this decision. Other problems may concurrently co-occur and/or be primary, such as oppositional defiant disorder, pervasive developmental disorder and Tourette syndrome. In adulthood, these problems include personality disorder (particularly antisocial), bipolar disorder, obsessive–compulsive disorder and, rarely, psychotic disorders.

Relating findings to instruction and making recommendations

The legal instruction will determine the issues that need to be considered and discussed. The manner in which functional impairments relate to legal issues will vary, and range from consideration of the reliability of statements given in police interviews, the ability to follow trial proceedings, and the ability to give evidence, to the question of abnormality of mind in cases of those charged with murder. For example, in a case of fitness to plead and stand trial, one must consider whether the defendant's cognitive impairments will prevent him or her from effectively participating in the trial proceedings and/or giving evidence. In the case of criminal responsibility, one may need to consider the extent to which they influence the ability to form intent. An important issue is the medication status of the individual at the relevant time (i.e. at the time of the offence, during police interviews, and/or at the time of court appearance). Two questions arise:

1. Has he or she taken medication in the past and, critically, was he or she taking medication at the time of the offence and/or during the police interviews? If so, was it taken on a regular or sporadic basis?
2. Is he or she currently taking medication, or does he or she need to be taking medication to help control symptoms during the court appearance?

Recommendations should be made to help support the ADHD defendant, especially for lengthy trials and/or in complex cases involving multiple defendants and their respective counsel. Individuals who are unmedicated and exhibiting active symptoms should be referred for a psychiatric assessment to determine whether medication would be helpful. During the trial, the expert may also recommend taking regular breaks during the trial, avoiding lengthy questions and complex language structure, and making sure that important information is put across directly and simply. These precautions may prevent unnecessary and costly interruptions to the court process and prevent the defendant from being unfairly disadvantaged.

Conclusions

Prison and correctional facilities are reporting rates of adults and youths with ADHD that far exceed those found in the 'normal' population. This recognition will be accompanied by scientific advances in the understanding and needs of this subgroup. These young people are vulnerable and often disadvantaged at several stages in their interface with the criminal justice system and many become 'revolving-door' offenders. Whilst the association between ADHD and offending is becoming increasingly recognized and acknowledged by the courts, the greatest challenge still lies ahead, as nothing will change in the long-term unless institutional settings accept that specific treatments (both pharmacological and psychological) are necessary to help individuals control their ADHD symptoms and improve pro-social competence.

References

Asherson, P. (2004). Attention-deficit hyperactivity disorder in the post-genomic era. *European Child and Adolescent Psychiatry*, **13**:150–170.

Asherson, P., Chen, W., Craddock, B., and Taylor, E. (2007). Adult attention-deficit hyperactivity disorder: Recognition and treatment in general adult psychiatry. *British Journal of Psychiatry*, **190**:4–5.

Barkley, R. A. and Murphy, K. R. (1998). *Attention-Deficit Hyperactivity Disorder: A Clinical Workbook*, 2nd edn. New York: The Guildford Press.

Brown, T. E. (1996). *Brown Attention-Deficit Disorder Scales*. San Antonio, TX: Harcourt Brace.

Cassidy, J. (1994). Emotional regulation: Influences of attachment relationships. In: N. Fox (ed.), *The Development of Emotional Regulation: Biological and Behavioural Considerations*. Monographs of the Society for Research in Child Development, **59**, (Serial no. 240:2–3), 228–249.

Collins, P. and White, T. (2002). Forensic applications of attention deficit hyperactivity disorder (ADHD) in adulthood. *Journal of Forensic Psychiatry*, **13**:263–284.

Conners, C. K. (2000). *Conners' Rating Scales—Revised: Technical Manual*. New York: MHS.

Conners, C., Erdhardt, D., and Sparrow, E. (1998). *The Conners Adult ADHD Rating Scale (CAARS)*. Toronto: Multi-Health Systems Inc.

Danckaerts, M., Heptinstall, E., Chadwick, O., and Taylor, E. (1999). Self-report of attention deficit and hyperactivity disorder in adolescents. *Psychopathology*, **32**:81–92.

Derogatis, L. R. (1994). *Symptom Checklist-90-R (SCL-90-R): Administration, Scoring and Procedures Manual*, 2nd edn. Minneapolis: National Computer Systems.

DuPaul, G. (1990). *The ADHD Rating Scale: Normative data, reliability, and validity*. Unpublished manuscript, University of Massachusetts Medical Centre, Worcester, MA.

Faraone, S. V., Spencer, T., and Aleardi, M. (2004). Meta-analysis of the efficacy of methylphenidate for treating adult attention-deficit/hyperactivity disorder. *Journal of Clinical Psychopharmacology*, **24**:24–29.

Faraone, S. V., Biederman, J., and Mick, E. (2006). The age-dependent decline of attention deficit hyperactivity disorder: A meta-analysis of follow-up studies. *Psychological Medicine*, **36**:159–165.

Gudjonsson, G. H. (1993). Confession evidence, psychological vulnerability and expert testimony. *Journal of Community and Applied Social Psychology*, **3**:117–129.

Gudjonsson, G. H. (2003). *The Psychology of Interrogations and Confessions. A Handbook.* Chichester: John Wiley & Sons.

Gudjonsson, G. and Haward, L. R. C (1998). *Forensic Psychology: Guide to Practice.* London: Routledge.

Gudjonsson, G. H., Einarsson, E., Bragason, O. O. and Sigurdsson, J. F. (2006). Personality predictors of self-reported offending in Icelandic students. *Psychology, Crime and Law,* **47**:361–368.

Gudjonsson, G. H., Young, S., and Bramham, J. (2007). Interrogative suggestibility in adults diagnosed with attention-deficit hyperactivity disorder (ADHD). A potential vulnerability during police questioning. *Personality and Individual Differences,* **43**:737–745.

Gudjonsson, G. H., Sigurdsson, J. F., Einarsson, E., Bragason, O. O., and Newton, A. K. (2008). Interrogative suggestibility, compliance and false confessions among prison inmates and their relationship with attention deficit hyperactivity disorder. *Psychological Medicine,* **38**:1037–1044.

Hervey, A. S., Epstein, J. N., and Curry, J. F. (2004). Neuropsychology of adults with attention-deficit/hyperactivity disorder: A meta-analytic review. *Neuropsychology,* **18**:485–503.

Leslie, O., Young, S., Valentine, T., and Gudjonsson, G. (2007). Criminal barristers' opinions and perceptions of mental health expert witnesses. *Journal of Forensic Psychiatry and Psychology,* **18**:74–89.

Levy, F. and Hay, D. (2001). Attention, genes and ADHD. Philadelphia, PA: Brunner-Routledge

MacLean, A., Dowson, J. H., Toone B., *et al.* (2004). Characteristic neurocognitive profile associated with adult attention-deficit/hyperactivity disorder. *Psychological Medicine,* **34**:681–692.

Medford, S., Gudjonsson, G. H., and Pearse, J. (2003). The efficacy of the appropriate adult safeguard during police interviewing. *Legal and Criminological Psychology,* **8**:253–266.

Millon, T. (1997). *Manual for the Millon Clinical Multiaxial Inventory-III (MCMI-III),* 2nd edn. Minneapolis: National Computer Systems.

Murphy, P. and Schachar, R. (2000). Use of self-ratings in the assessment of symptoms of attention deficit hyperactivity disorder in adults. *American Journal of Psychiatry,* **157**:1156–1159.

Nutt, D. J., Fone, K., Asherson, P., *et al.* (2007). Evidence-based guidelines for management of attention-deficit/hyperactivity disorder in adolescents in transition to adult services and in adults: Recommendations from the British Association for Psychopharmacology. *Journal of Psychopharmacology,* **21**:10–41.

Polanczyk, G., de Lima, M. S., Horta, B. L., Biederman, J., and Rohde, L. A. (2007). The worldwide prevalence of ADHD: A systematic review and metaregression analysis. *American Journal of Psychiatry,* **164**:942–948.

Rutter, M. (2005). Environmentally mediated risks for psychopathology: Research strategies and findings. *Journal of Child Psychology and Psychiatry,* **44**:3–18.

Simpson, D. and Plosker, G. L. (2004). Atomoxetine: A review of its use in adults with attention-deficit hyperactive disorder. *Drugs,* **64**:205–222.

Smith, B. H., Pelham, W. W. E, Gnagy, E., Molina, B., and Evans, S. (2000). The reliability, validity, and unique contributions of self-report by adolescents receiving treatment for attention-deficit/ hyperactive disorder. *Journal of Consulting and Clinical Psychology*, **68**:489–499.

Ward, M. F., Wender, P. H., and Reimherr, F. W. (1993). The Wender Utah Rating Scale: An aid in the retrospective diagnosis of childhood attention deficit hyperactivity disorder. *American Journal of Psychiatry*, **150**:885–890.

Wolraich, M. L., Hannah, J. N., Pinnock, T. Y., *et al.* (1996). Comparison of diagnostic criteria for attention-deficit hyperactivity disorder in a country-wide sample. *Journal of American Academy of Child and Adolescent Psychiatry*, **35**:319–324.

Young, S. (1999). Psychological therapy for adults with attention deficit hyperactivity disorder. *Counselling Psychology Quarterly*, **12**:183–190.

Young, S. (2005). Coping strategies used by adults with ADHD. *Personality and Individual Differences*, **38**:809–816.

Young, S. (2007). Forensic Aspects of ADHD. In: M. Fitzgerald, M. Bellgrove, and M. Gill (eds), *Handbook of Attention Deficit Hyperactive Disorder*, pp. 90–108. Chichester: Wiley, UK.

Young, S. and Bramham, J. (2007). *ADHD in Adults: A Psychological Guide to Practice*. Chichester: John Wiley & Sons.

Young, S. and Gudjonsson, G. (2005). Neuropsychological correlates of the YAQ-S self-reported ADHD symptomatology, emotional and social problems, and delinquent behaviour. *British Journal of Clinical Psychology*, **44**:47–57.

Young, S. and Gudjonsson, G. (2008). Growing out of attention-deficit/hyperactivity disorder: The relationship between functioning and symptoms. *Journal of Attention Disorders*, **12**:162–169.

Young, S.J. and Ross, R.R. (2007). R&R2 for ADHD Youths and Adults. A Handbook for Teaching Prosocial Competence.

Young, S., Morris, R. G., Toone, B. K., and Tyson, C. (2006). Spatial working memory and strategy formation in adults diagnosed with Attention Deficit Hyperactivity Disorder. *Personality and Individual Differences*. **41**:653–61.

Young, S., Gudjonsson, G., Wells J., *et al.* (2009a). Attention deficit hyperactivity disorder and critical incidents in a Scottish prison population. Personality and Individual Differences, **46**:265–269.

Young, S., Chesney, S., Sperlinger, D., Misch, P., and Collins, P. (2009b). A qualitative study exploring the life-course experiences of young offenders with symptoms and signs of ADHD who were detained in a residential care setting. *Criminal Behaviour and Mental Health*, **19**:54–63.

Chapter 5

Autism spectrum conditions

Isabel Clare and Marc Woodbury-Smith

Over the past two decades, there has been an enormous amount of interest in what are increasingly known as autism spectrum conditions (ASCs). However, with a few striking exceptions (for example, Powell, 2002; Howlin, 2004), much of this interest has focused on children rather than adults, and on nosological and aetiological, rather than practical, issues. It is not perhaps surprising, therefore, that very little guidance is available to clinicians about the ways in which men and women with suspected or diagnosed ASCs might best be understood and supported when they come into contact with the civil or criminal justice systems. The purpose of this chapter is to explore the contribution that a neuropsychological perspective might make.

The 'spectrum' of ASCs

ASCs comprise a group of biologically based behavioural syndromes (for more details, see Volkmar *et al.*, 2005; Bauman & Kemper, 2006) of childhood onset, characterized by a core clinical phenotype of qualitative impairments in (i) reciprocal social interaction, and (ii) verbal and non-verbal communication, together with (iii) a restricted and repetitive range of behaviours, interests and activities, the so-called 'triad of impairments' (Wing, 1976). It is now accepted that, because of the heterogeneity of the population, these syndromes are best thought of as a 'spectrum' (Wing, 1997) of conditions. At present, they are defined using the criteria in the DSM-IV (American Psychiatric Association, 1994) or ICD-10 (WHO, 1992).

Recent findings from children (Baird *et al.*, 2006) suggest that just over half of those with ASCs also have a significant intellectual impairment (a full-scale IQ score below 70). This means that, in adulthood, they would meet at least one of the usual eligibility criteria for specialist services for people with intellectual disabilities. Some may be able to participate meaningfully in the civil and/or criminal justice systems (see Chapter 3 of this volume); others may not. In this chapter, we focus on the significant minority of individuals whose intellectual ability is not significantly impaired, and who are sometimes referred to as 'high functioning'. These men and women, who have been (and sometimes still are) known as people with 'autism', 'Asperger's syndrome' or 'high-functioning autism', have often been regarded as 'mildly affected' by their ASC and consequently have traditionally received little understanding and support. Such a view is not only unhelpful but is also unwarranted (Howlin, 2004).

Despite attempts to challenge the view that, for 'high-functioning' individuals, ASCs are necessarily a disability (Happé, 1999; Baron-Cohen, 2000), the everyday lives of most of these men and women are bleak. They have limited opportunities for employment, independent accommodation, participation in social activities, and intimate relationships, and are at risk of social exclusion (Barnard et al., 2001; Powell, 2002; Howlin, 2004). The findings of a study by Mawhood et al. (2000) of 19 men aged 21–26 years, with non-verbal IQ scores ranging from 70 to 117 are, unfortunately, typical. Although five of the group had attended college or university, only three were living independently (one in sheltered accommodation), three were employed (two under special arrangements), and three were described as having friends. Fifteen had never had a close friendship or a sexual relationship, and 13 were described as having moderate to severe behavioural difficulties, associated with restricted interests and repetitive behaviours.

The self-reported experiences of these 'high-functioning' men and women are no less discouraging. Autobiographical accounts (Williams, 1992; Sainsbury, 2000) often include moving descriptions of a range of adverse experiences including bullying and other kinds of victimization, and painful and unwanted feelings of social isolation. The limited empirical literature based on self-reported personality measures paints a similar picture. Compared with 'general population' controls, this group of people with ASCs have higher levels of introversion, social discomfort, dysphoria, and unhappiness (Ozonoff et al., 2005).

Among a few individuals with an ASC, adverse experiences seem to provoke strong feelings of resentment or powerlessness that can lead to behaviour that is illegal (Wing, 1997; Woodbury-Smith et al., 2006) or intended to cause shock and disruption (Tantam, 1999). Despite receiving considerable attention, however (see review by Woodbury-Smith et al., 2006), such outcomes are rare. A small study of self-reported offending and 'official' statistics from the Home Office Offenders' Index in a community sample of men and women with ASCs ($n = 25$, mean full-scale IQ of 104.7, SD 17.7; 6:1 male:female ratio; Woodbury-Smith et al., 2006) suggested that the rate of law-breaking was very low. Indeed, overall, it was significantly lower than that of a stringent comparison group of people in full-time employment ($n = 20$, full-scale IQ 118.7, SD 10.0; 2:1 male:female ratio). Where extreme violence or other offending is carried out by a person with a diagnosed ASC, this may not be related to any aspect of the core phenotype, such as a particular circumscribed interest (Woodbury-Smith, 2005). Rather, it may reflect some comorbid developmental disorder such as psychopathy (as diagnosed with the PCL-R; Hare, 2003) or antisocial personality disorder (Woodbury-Smith et al., 2005a).

As Mawhood et al. (2000) suggested, the lives of men and women with ASCs are often affected very negatively by their restricted interests and range of behaviours. The way in which such problems are best understood continues to be debated. Less controversially, there is accumulating evidence that, compared with the general population, these individuals are at increased risk of mood disorders, particularly clinical depression (Ghaziuddin et al., 1992; Lainhart & Folstein, 1994) and anxiety disorders (Kim et al., 2000; Gillott et al., 2001). Nevertheless, some people with ASCs do seem to lead successful and happy adult lives. Both outcome studies and anecdotal self-reports suggest that the extent to which this is possible depends largely on the support available from their families and others.

The prevalence of men and women with ASCs whose intellectual ability is not significantly impaired remains uncertain. A meta-analysis (Williams et al., 2006) of 42 methodologically adequate studies in different countries has provided an estimated prevalence of all forms of ASC of 20.0 per 10,000 of the population, but the range of estimates is enormous (95% confidence interval: 4.9–82.1). Higher estimates reflect the use of the two main classification systems: ICD-10 (WHO, 1992) and DSM-IV (American Psychiatric Association, 1994) versus other diagnostic criteria, younger age at diagnosis, even during childhood years, and urban rather than rural locations. Apart from the association with intellectual disability, the only area in which there is broad agreement is that ASCs predominantly affect men rather than women (at a ratio of about 4:1) (Fombonne, 2005; Baird et al., 2006). This sex imbalance is particularly marked among those who are 'high functioning'. From a forensic perspective, the issues on which clinical advice is most likely to be sought involve men. This is reflected in two case studies of people we have worked with.

Case Study 1

Mr A, a university graduate, runs an IT consultancy business from home. He is married, with two very young children, and lives on a housing estate. He has no clinical diagnosis but describes himself as a 'bit of a loner' who 'likes to do his own thing'. He has a long history of interpersonal difficulties, and the relationship with his wife has not always been easy. He was arrested by the police because of his threatening behaviour towards neighbours who held a late night party. Mr A's wife, who cared for the children at home in the day, found herself very isolated and eventually left him, taking the children. She has now initiated divorce proceedings and will have custody. The couple have not been able to agree access arrangements.

Mr A has been described in reports as 'cold' and 'rigid', but he has always been clear that he wishes to continue seeing his children regularly. Since the start of the divorce proceedings, his concentration has been impaired, he has had problems sleeping, and he has lost weight. He is receiving treatment from his GP for depression. Mr A's solicitor has now asked for a psychological report to contribute to the court's decision-making.

Case Study 2

Mr B is a young man who lives with his parents. He has no clinical diagnosis but attended a residential boarding school because of his behavioural difficulties. He was excluded from a college course and work experience because of problems in participating. He has an estimated full-scale IQ score of 89 on an abbreviated form of the WAIS-III. Mr B often speaks of his wish for a girlfriend. He has no history of sexually inappropriate behaviour. Recently, he has been visiting a nightclub on the way home from a snooker hall. One night, he approached a woman who was dancing, reached under her skirt and tried to pull down her underwear, while kissing her rather forcefully. She attempted to push him away and started shouting and crying. The security staff arrived to eject Mr B, who became agitated. The police were called and arrested him. On the way to the police station, he gave a full account of what happened. Despite legal advice and the presence of an appropriate adult, he repeated the same account during his police interview. Mr A was charged with indecent assault and released on bail. He was referred by his solicitor for a psychological report to address issues relating to court proceedings and disposal.

Receiving a referral: what are the relevant questions?

Diagnosis is undeniably important because, as Grisso (1986) has pointed out, it provides '*data ... to assist ... in addressing causal, predictive, and remediation questions*'. However, a diagnosis, or even the difficulties it summarizes, does not, on its own, provide an adequate basis for a forensic assessment. One of the most salient criticisms (see Grisso, 2003) of a diagnostic approach is that it provides no direct information to address the kinds of legal decisions that the civil and criminal justice systems frequently have to make. Many such decisions relate to the person's capacity, or ability, to carry out a particular 'task' in a forensic context, such as that of a criminal suspect detained by the police for interviewing.

In recent years, the use of diagnosis on its own has given way to a functional approach, and this now has considerable empirical support (e.g. Wong *et al.*, 2000; Suto *et al.*, 2005) and legal support both in case law (e.g. Re C [1994] 1 All E R 819) and statute in the UK (e.g. the Sexual Offences Act 2003, the Adults with Incapacity (Scotland) Act 2000, the Mental Capacity Act (England and Wales) 2005) and elsewhere. This approach focuses on:

- the person's 'functional abilities, behaviours or capacities' (Grisso, 1986), i.e. what he or she understands, knows, believes, or can do that is directly relevant to the forensic context at issue (such as managing the role of a defendant in a criminal trial)

- the extent to which these functional abilities meet the demands of a particular situation within a given forensic context (for example, within the context of a criminal trial, a single appearance at a magistrates' court versus several days in a crown court).

Where there is a mismatch between the person's functional abilities and the particular situation, then consideration needs to be given as to whether it would be possible either to improve the person's relevant abilities (for example, by providing treatment or support) and/or to simplify or otherwise amend the situation (Murphy & Clare, 2003).

Unfortunately, clinical experience suggests that, perhaps reflecting uncertainty among criminal justice practitioners about how best to think about men and women with ASCs, many requests for assessments focus primarily, or even solely, on issues of diagnosis; such an approach is unhelpful and may, at times, be discriminatory. One of the first tasks is often to ensure that the 'referral' (in whatever form this is received) focuses on a set of questions that a neuropsychologist can appropriately address. Examples for the two illustrative case studies are given below:

Case study 1:

- What is the nature of Mr A's difficulties?
- What is the relevance of these difficulties to Mr A's expressed wish to have access to his children?
- Is there anything that might be done to minimize the effect of Mr A's difficulties?
- What recommendations might be submitted to inform the court's decision about Mr A's access to his children?

Case study 2:

- What is the nature of Mr B's difficulties?
- How can the alleged offence best be understood?
- Is Mr B fit to plead?
- If Mr B is found guilty, what recommendations might be made about sentencing?

Issues in diagnosis

Interacting with the person

The core phenotype of ASCs means that, even when individuals are verbally fluent, their understanding of non-verbal communication and complex language is likely to be limited. Questions that involve hypothetical situations

('Suppose you were in a situation where ....'; 'How do you think she felt when you did that ...') are particularly difficult. Based on the findings of experimental 'theory-of-mind' tests that are easily solved by adults who do not have significant intellectual impairments, it is sometimes asserted that people with an ASC 'tell it like it is'. This is not the case. Like others, they may make mistakes; they may also leave out or (less often) invent information deliberately.

Good practice in diagnosis

For children, 'good practice' in diagnosis involves a detailed interview with the child and with at least one informant, normally a parent, who can provide details of the developmental trajectory of that child's social interaction, communication, and behaviour. This material is usually supplemented by records of family, medical, social, and psychiatric history, and psychological assessments of intellectual and language functioning. A number of structured and semi-structured diagnostic interviews and checklists have been developed to aid this process. Increasingly, as parents have realized the importance of a diagnosis in terms of accessing appropriate support, children are diagnosed early in life.

Many people, however, remain undiagnosed until adulthood or their diagnosis is based on very superficial information. A request for the diagnosis of an adult often takes place in the context of major difficulties in the person's life, such as severe mental illness, loss of employment, or contact with the civil or criminal justice systems. Clinical diagnosis in such circumstances can be difficult, and often has to remain tentative unless the kinds of complementary materials required for 'good practice' in childhood diagnosis are available.

This does not mean, however, that it is not still useful to carry out screening to help distinguish men and women with ASCs from those with other conditions that may present as superficially similar (such as depression, personality disorder, and anxiety disorder) but that arise from different causes (Rutter *et al.*, 1999) and have different implications for treatment and support. For these purposes, a self-report measure, the Autism Quotient (Baron-Cohen *et al.*, 2001a; Woodbury-Smith *et al.*, 2005b), a 50-item questionnaire assessing five different areas (social skills, attention switching, attention to detail, communication, and imagination) or an informant completed measure, the Social Communication Questionnaire (SCQ), previously known as the Autism Screening Questionnaire (Berument *et al.*, 1999), are both useful.

Where diagnosis is possible, one of the 'gold standard' measures, such as the Autism Diagnostic Interview—Revised (ADI-R; Lord *et al.*, 1994), the Diagnostic Interview for Social and Communication Disorders (DISCO; Wing *et al.*, 2002) or preferably, as it is particularly helpful in identifying the subtle difficulties of 'high-functioning' people with ASCs, the Autism Diagnostic Observation Scale—Generic (ADOS-G; Lord et al., 2003) should be used. However, it is important to note that these are intended to approximate good clinical judgement and all of them require intensive formal training.

The ADOS-G comprises four modules to cover the range of children and adults of different chronological and developmental ages. Module 4 is the most advanced, and is used for adolescents and adults who can use language to provide information. The format is that of an interview, lasting approximately 30–45 minutes and comprising a series of questions probing the person's understanding of friendships, closer relationships, and a range of basic emotions. The person is encouraged to talk about his or her personal experiences, and cues are given for him or her to engage in reciprocal conversation and to ask the interviewer similar questions. In addition, there are a number of tasks (most of them optional) examining topics such as imagination, story telling, and the ability to explain an everyday procedure.

At the end, an overall rating is made that is used, through an algorithm, to produce a preliminary diagnosis, which can be confirmed when other material becomes available. However, even after training, it requires practise in administration, scoring, and note-taking during its presentation so that the clinician can focus fully on observing the person.

Confusing issues in diagnosis: autism, AS, or HFA?

It is not unusual to find clinical notes in which a person whose intellectual functioning is not significantly impaired has acquired a list of diagnoses containing the words 'autism' or 'high-functioning autism' (HFA) and 'Asperger's syndrome' (AS), and there remains considerable confusion around their use. The main reasons for this are as follows:

1. HFA is not included in DSM-IV and ICD-10. Whilst the two main diagnostic classification systems, the DSM-IV (American Psychiatric Association, 1994) and the ICD-10 (WHO, 1992), define the criteria for a range of conditions within the 'spectrum', neither includes HFA.

2. DSM-IV and ICD-10 definitions of AS do not match Asperger's original clinical descriptions of the condition (Miller & Ozonoff, 1997).

3. The distinction between autism and AS in DSM-IV and ICD-10 is unclear. As Baron-Cohen et al. (2005) have pointed out, according to DSM-IV (as for ICD-10), the two conditions seem essentially similar, differing only in that a diagnosis of autism, but not of AS, can be made regardless of intellectual functioning or language ability. In both of the established psychiatric classifications, autism and AS are also mutually exclusive. So a person

who has received a diagnosis of autism should not later receive a diagnosis of AS; the reverse is also true (see Howlin, 2000, for a very clear example of the confusion this can lead to). In an attempt to resolve the uncertainty about whether or not there is a fundamental difference between autism and AS, a number of research studies have been carried out (see the detailed review in Howlin, 2004). Many of these are methodologically flawed: the samples are small and/or poorly matched on variables such as intellectual functioning that have a major impact on clinical presentation and outcome, and there are inconsistencies in the use of diagnostic criteria. Where the methodology has been acceptable, however, no consistent empirical evidence has been found for a distinction (Howlin, 2004).

4. In recent years, HFA has often been used by clinicians as a synonym for AS. However, there is a good deal of variation. Other clinicians prefer 'autism' as a 'catch all' for people with AS and HFA (Howlin, 2004), whilst yet others use HFA to refer to people whose intellectual ability lies more than one standard deviation below the mean (i.e. <85) but who do not have significant intellectual impairments, and restrict AS for those whose intellectual ability lies within or above the average range. It should be emphasized that none of these approaches has a clinical or empirical basis.

How may these issues be resolved? Where justified, it is probably best simply to diagnose an ASC, rather than a particular condition within the 'spectrum'.

Case Study 1

Mr A was interviewed at home, where it was found that:

- he presented as awkward, with little idea of 'social niceties'
- he gave a history of failure in developing peer relationships compatible with his description of himself as a 'loner'. Prior to meeting his wife, he had had no intimate relationships
- he seemed unable to think of any reason why his wife left him
- he talked at length, and not in a way that was easily interrupted, about the supposed 'crimes' (such as leaving his car dirty and not keeping his drive well swept) of the neighbour he had threatened
- his interpersonal difficulties had led him to be dismissed from paid employment on a couple of occasions. His only social life seemed to involve monthly meetings with a former colleague to play chess.

Consistent with the interview data, Mr A scored 38 on the AQ (see Baron-Cohen et al., 2001b; Woodbury-Smith et al., 2005b). Since Mr A was depressed, an informant-based measure (the ADI-R) was used to assist in making a diagnosis. After some hesitation, Mr A agreed to his mother being interviewed; her report of his history supported the other findings. There seemed little doubt that it was appropriate to diagnose an ASC.

Case Study 2

Mr B was visited on bail at his home. He agreed to his parents being interviewed. They appeared to be good informants and consistently highlighted the differences between Mr B's development and that of his siblings. Mr B, whose reported estimated full-scale IQ score was 89, received a preliminary diagnosis of an ASC:

- he had a history of failure to form friendships with his peers (corroborated by his parents)
- he made no eye contact and muttered under his breath about what he was doing
- during his interview, he smiled constantly, even when the alleged incident was being discussed, and kept interrupting with irrelevant facts and questions (about snooker competitions, local history, etc.).

The findings of the algorithm, completed from the ADOS-G Module 4, on the basis of the interview, supported the diagnosis.

Beyond diagnosis: exploring the core clinical phenotype

In such a heterogeneous group as adults with ASCs, diagnosis is only a starting point, alerting to the presence of the triad of impairments. A huge experimental literature has developed that has attempted to explain this core clinical phenotype in terms of impairments in specific neuropsychological processes. Three such explanations have dominated: social cognition, executive function, and central coherence (for a recent overview, see Frith & Hill, 2004). Some of the measures that have been developed, or used, to test out hypotheses relating to each of these explanations have been rather removed from everyday life, but others are clinically relevant in a forensic context.

Social cognition

Social cognition includes any cognitive process involved in interpersonal behaviour (Hoffman, 2000; Baron-Cohen *et al.*, 2002), and it has been argued that the social difficulties of people with ASCs reflect impairments in the ability to understand others' minds and emotions (Baron-Cohen, 1995). 'Theory of mind' is generally used to describe the understanding of others' desires, beliefs, thoughts, and opinions that enables us to understand irony, sarcasm, deception, and the motivations underlying the behaviour of others. It has been established that although 'high-functioning' adults with ASCs pass simple, first-order theory-of-mind tests, designed for people at a younger developmental level, they fail in more advanced 'second-order' and 'faux pas' tests (Golan *et al.*, 2006).

Recently, there has been increasing interest in the affective aspects of social cognition, particularly empathy (Baron-Cohen et al., 2001b; Golan et al., 2006). Empathy is generally used to describe the process of emotional understanding, which includes discriminating and labelling affective states in others, sharing these states, and responding emotionally (Hoffman, 2000), enabling us to react to distress, anger, and other feelings in others. Emotion recognition is one of the basic building blocks of empathy. In contrast with performance on 'theory-of-mind' tasks, the experimental evidence for impaired emotion recognition in ASCs is mixed (Hobson, 1986a, b; Ozonoff et al., 1990; Adolphs et al., 2001).

From a clinical perspective, both advanced 'theory-of-mind' tests and emotion recognition tasks can be very useful in making sense of the difficulties of a person with ASC. The main tasks that are suitable for 'high-functioning' people with ASCs are summarized in Tables 5.1 and 5.2. In everyday practice, some of them are difficult to carry out (for example, assessments using electrodermal responses) or raise problems of ecological validity (for example, the 'ice cream van' test).

Executive functioning

The rigid and inflexible behaviours, difficulty adapting to new situations, and perseverative speech that are often seen, even in intellectually able men and women with ASCs, may all be explained by deficits in executive functioning (EF), the mental operations that enable a person to perform tasks requiring organization, decision-making, and inhibiting prepotent responses (Hughes et al., 1994; Russell, 1997). This suggests that, despite continuing controversy over the concept of EF (Burgess et al., 1998; Parkin, 1998), it is a useful area to explore. Whilst a wide variety of tests is available (for details, see Lezak et al., 2004), unfortunately there is no one test in which all participants with an ASC have demonstrated a weaker performance than neurotypical controls and different studies have demonstrated different patterns of EF strengths and vulnerabilities among people with ASCs (Woodbury-Smith, 2005).

Central coherence

The premise of central coherence is that people with ASCs have limited ability to process complex stimuli into coherent and meaningful wholes, instead perceiving them as a collection of parts (see Plaisted et al., 2004). It focuses on the restricted and repetitive behaviours that form part of the core phenotype: intense resistance to change in the environment, the preoccupation with parts of objects, and highly circumscribed interests. Evidence in support of this theory comes from the superior performance of people with ASCs on the Block Design Test and the Embedded Figures Test (Jolliffe & Baron-Cohen, 1997), and has been used to argue that this group of men and women have a

Table 5.1 Summary of tests of Theory of Mind (ToM)

Name of test	Type of test	Description of method	Examples of studies using test
Ice Cream Van Test (Baron-Cohen, 1989)	Second-order ToM	Two people are introduced (John and Mary) who are playing in a park. When an ice cream van arrives, John goes home to get some money. The ice cream van leaves the park to drive to the church. It passes John on the way and tells him it will be selling ice creams at the church. The critical belief question asked is, when Mary calls for John and is told that he has gone to buy an ice cream, where will she think he has gone?	(Baron-Cohen, 1989; Ozonoff et al., 1991)
Strange Stories (Happé, 1994)	Advanced ToM	A series of vignettes is presented involving situations where a person has deceived, lied, or bluffed, and questions requiring mental state attribution are asked.	(Blair et al., 1996)
Faux Pas Test (Stone et al., 1998; Baron-Cohen et al., 1999a)	Advanced ToM	A series of stories is presented describing different social situations. In some of the stories ($n=10$), a faux pas has occurred. A series of questions follows each story to determine whether the participant understands that the faux pas was the consequence of a false belief rather than an action with malicious intent.	(Stone et al., 1998; Baron-Cohen et al., 1999a)
Adult Eyes Test (Baron-Cohen et al., 2001b)	Advanced ToM	A series of 36 photographs of the eye region of different male and female actors/actresses is presented. Four complex mental state descriptions are presented for each image, with one (the target word) correctly identifying the mental state of the person in the photograph.	(Richell et al., 2003)

'different' cognitive style (Happé, 1999). Whilst such an argument has important implications for the support of people with the condition, at present, central coherence is not associated with any methodologies that are routinely helpful in addressing specific forensic issues.

Other aspects of ASCs—restrictive and repetitive patterns of behaviour, interests, and activities

Surprisingly, perhaps, given their impact on the lives of people with ASCs (Mawhood et al., 2000), relatively little attention has been paid by researchers to the restrictive and repetitive patterns of behaviour, interests, and activities

Table 5.2 Summary of tests of emotional understanding and empathy

Type of test	Description of method	Examples of studies using test
Emotion recognition (matching task)	Involves matching a facial expression with gestures, vocalizations, and contexts. The control task simply requires the participants to match objects without emotional salience.	(Hobson, 1986a, b; Ozonoff et al., 1990)
Emotion recognition (sorting task)	Involves sorting a pack of cards on which are photographs of faces displaying different basic facial expressions. The participants are asked to sort according to identity (control task) and then facial expression.	(Ozonoff et al., 1990)
Emotion recognition (labelling tasks)	Involves identifying the correct emotional label to describe the expression portrayed in a series of still images of faces. One such test is the Facial Expressions of Emotion Stimuli and Tests—Emotion Hexagon Test (FEEST; Young et al., 2001), comprising six facial expressions morphed to create a series of images that form a continuum along the axis of happiness–surprise–fear–sadness–disgust–anger. Happiness and anger are joined to create an 'emotional hexagon'. There are 30 morphed images, created from 90, 70, 50, 30 and 10% morphs between two emotions. The task is to identify the emotion that each image, shown randomly on a computer screen, most resembles.	(Macdonald et al., 1989; Woodbury-Smith et al., 2005a)
Moral/ conventional distinction	Comprises a series of vignettes, which require an understanding that, whilst under modified rule conditions conventional transgressions become permissive (e.g. if a rule allowing talking in the library was implemented), this is not so for moral transgressions (such as hitting another).	(Blair, 1995)
Electrodermal studies	Autonomic arousal to images that are unpleasant, threatening, or fearful is recorded using skin conductance responses.	(Blair, 1999; Blair et al., 1997)
Self-report	Involves describing the extent to which the respondent believes himself or herself to be someone with or without empathy (for example, 'I can tune into how someone feels rapidly and intuitively'; Baron-Cohen & Wheelwright, 2004).	(Baron-Cohen & Wheelwright, 2004; Baron-Cohen et al., 2005)

that form part of the core clinical phenotype (WHO, 1992; American Psychiatric Association, 1994). This domain manifests in different ways for different people, but some people have stereotyped patterns of interests, which are abnormal in either intensity or focus, and can be conceptualized as 'circumscribed interests'.

Since Tantam's (1988a, b) important set of case descriptions, forensic clinicians have investigated the possible link between the circumscribed interests of people with ASCs and their antisocial behaviour (see Woodbury-Smith, 2005), and exploration of this domain often appears important. Unfortunately, there is, as yet, no accepted method for documenting these interests. At present, there are three main approaches, described below.

The Autism Diagnostic Interview—Revised

The Autism Diagnostic Interview—Revised (ADI-R; Lord *et al.*, 1994) provides a detailed typology of interests. These fall into two categories: (i) circumscribed interests, which are described as pursuits that differ from ordinary hobbies in their intensity, their limited nature (their tendency not to develop into a broader context of knowledge), their non-social quality, and their tendency to persist but not progress (develop) over time, and (ii) unusual preoccupations (for example, pylons, insulators). Both categories are coded according to the degree of their intrusiveness into other activities. This approach provides clear criteria, but means that people who would otherwise be diagnosed with an ASC would be excluded if the interests/preoccupations were 'social' or showed 'progress' over time. However, there are examples of men and women with ASCs whose interests have led to improved socialization or employment opportunities (Baron-Cohen *et al.*, 1999b).

The Cambridge University Obsessions Questionnaire

The Cambridge University Obsessions Questionnaire (CUOQ; Baron-Cohen & Wheelwright, 1999) was originally developed for use in children and was designed to be rated by a parent or other primary carer to provide a taxonomy of interests. Nineteen categories of interest are included, with an extra 'other' category. For each category, the parent/carer is asked to indicate whether the child has ever had an 'obsession' (in the lay sense) of that kind and then to provide details. This is a useful measure that allows information to be collected about the different interests that someone may have had at different times. However, it has limitations:

- There are no data regarding its inter-rater and test–retest reliabilities.
- It focuses on the nature of the interest, not on other aspects, such as the extent of its sociability.
- It does not enable the intensity of the interest to be coded.
- It does not enable detailed information to be collected to ensure that the interest is consistent with DSM-IV and ICD-10 classifications.

Interview analysis

Mercier *et al.* (2000) adopted a different approach, based on qualitative analyses of interviews with six 'high-functioning' adults with an ASC. This focused on the content of the interests, their evolution over time, the time devoted to them, feedback from family members regarding them, perceived positive and negative aspects for the person, and adaptation to environmental demands. Whilst sophisticated and detailed, the main drawback of this approach is that it is very time-consuming, with each interview lasting between 25 and 90 minutes.

For practical purposes, a briefer semi-structured schedule was developed by Woodbury-Smith (2005). This includes questions about (i) the nature of current and past interests, (ii) the interests themselves, to obtain a detailed account, and (iii) the average time spent, the extent to which the interest is shared with others, and the perceived positive and negative aspects of the interest. While no test–retest or inter-rater agreement data are available, the measure has been used experimentally with people with ASCs (Woodbury-Smith, 2005), and an interview covering the same areas may be helpful in addressing a forensic referral.

Forensic assessments in practice

Mr A—main findings and recommendations

Mr A's score on the Hamilton Depression Scale (Table 5.3), which was carried out at the initial assessment, indicated that his depression was not being treated effectively. It was recommended to the court (and accepted by the court) that interim arrangements should be made for Mr A to have supervised access to his children while he received psychiatric support. After 4 months, Mr A had progressed well and the assessment was resumed:

- As Mr A's depression was resolved, he appeared less hostile and rigid, and became a little more tolerant of the perceived failings of others.
- Mr A's ability to recognize emotional facial expressions fell well within the range expected of the general population, although his empathy score on the EQ was unchanged.
- The observational and interview assessments of Mr A's parenting skills indicated that, while he remained rather rigid and 'rule-bound', he had an adequate understanding of his children's needs. There was no evidence that they would come to harm. The findings were consistent with his responses to the 'faux pas' and prosocial functioning tasks.
- Mr A's parents were able, and willing, to provide him with social support.
- Encouragingly, Mr A's response to the Significant Others Scale indicated that he felt that his social isolation was problematic and he was motivated to try to change.

Table 5.3 Summary of assessments for Mr A

Area of assessment	Test used	Rationale
Depression	Hamilton Depression Scale (Hamilton, 1960).	Impact of treatment of depression.
Further assessment of his ASC	ADOS-G Module 4 (Lord et al., 2003).	Information about his social interactions and emotional strengths and vulnerabilities.
Empathy	EQ (Baron-Cohen & Wheelwright, 2004; repeated following treatment).	Impact of treatment on his ability to empathize with others.
Recognition of emotional expressions in his children and others	FEEST (Young et al., 2001).	One of the basic skills in empathy. Whilst the stimuli are static, the morphing means that the expressions are more subtle than those of other measures.
Ability to avoid attributing unfortunate outcomes to malicious intent	Faux pas test (Stone et al., 1998; Baron-Cohen et al., 1999a)	To address concerns that he might present a risk to his children by misattributing their intentions.
Ability to put children's needs before his own	Vignettes showing situations in which a protagonist has to make a decision about whether to help another at his or her personal expense (Eisenberg et al., 1991), adapted to include Mr A's current situation.	To assess prosocial functioning.
Understanding of the physical and psychological needs of his children	Interview focusing on specific issues (such as Mr A's own history of being parented and understanding of safety; drawn from Tymchuk, 1992; Friedman & Chase-Lansdale, 2002).	Factors known to increase likelihood of adequate parenting.
	Observations of the quantity and quality of stimulation and support provided by Mr A during access visits to his children, using the Home Observation for Measurement of the Environment (HOME) (Caldwell & Bradley, 1984).	Addresses difficulty for people with ASCs of tasks involving imagination. The HOME is well-established and discriminates between families in which there are difficulties and those in which there are not (Bradley, 1985).
Extent of social support available during access periods	Simplified form of the Significant Others Scale (Power et al., 1988).	Information about Mr A's current and ideal relationships to establish his motivation for engaging in more interaction.
	Interview with Mr A's parents.	Information about support available from extended family.

Mr A found discussion of an ASC diagnosis and its implications very helpful in making sense of his past and current experiences of 'being different'. His parents attended one of these meetings and, importantly, his ex-wife agreed to meet with the treating clinician on her own on one occasion and with Mr A on another. She also read some relevant material (Slater-Walker & Slater-Walker, 2002), which she found helpful in understanding her marital life. The discussions about the children became much more constructive.

It was recommended to the court that Mr A was a 'good enough' parent and that he should be allowed regular access to his children. In part, this recommendation reflected Mr A's positive response to the suggestion that he continue taking antidepressant medication until it was judged clinically unnecessary and attended sessions of cognitive behavioral therapy at regular intervals to monitor his progress, solve difficulties, and maintain his mental well-being. The court accepted this recommendation. When access was resolved, Mr A decided to move to a neighbourhood closer to his parents, where he did not have a history of poor relationships. He offered his skills to a local community project so that he could develop his social network. Mr A and his ex-wife agreed that, as the children grew up, they should be informed about the nature of their father's difficulties.

Mr B—main findings and recommendations

It was not easy to engage Mr B in the tasks, and the assessment took a number of sessions to complete (Table 5.4):

- Mr B had some understanding of the objectives of court proceedings, but his appreciation of their personal relevance was very limited. Time constraints meant that it was not possible to carry out any work to improve his 'functional abilities' relating to a court appearance.

- Mr B responded well to information that was presented pictorially or in a way that made use of his visuospatial skills, but his ability to deal with verbal information was limited. There was a discrepancy between different areas of Mr B's language, so that, whilst he expressed himself competently, his comprehension was much weaker. He repeated statements, such as '*I must not do that sex dirty thing again*' that he did not seem to fully understand. Consistent with this finding, he was very suggestible (he obtained the maximum score of 20 on the shift subtest of the GSS2).

- Nevertheless, and consistent with his behaviour when he was arrested, Mr B did realize that what he did to the alleged victim was against the law.

- As expected from the ADOS-G interview, Mr B's understanding of complex social situations and his knowledge and understanding of personal

Table 5.4 Summary of assessments for Mr B

Area of assessment	Test used	Rationale
Intellectual functioning	WAIS-III (UK).	Reported FSIQ score on an abbreviated form of the WAIS-R concealed an 18-point discrepancy in favour of his performance IQ over his verbal IQ.
Further assessment of his ASC	ADOS-G Module 4 (Lord et al., 2003; already carried out).	Information about his social interactions and emotional strengths and vulnerabilities.
Ability to understand complex social situations	Faux pas test (Stone et al., 1998; Baron-Cohen et al., 1999a).	Understanding of social awareness.
Understanding of emotional expressions	FEEST (Young et al., 2001).	Information about one of the basic skills in empathy.
Emotion recognition matching and sorting tasks	Hobson (1986a, b); Ozonoff et al. (1990).	Information about very basic skills in recognizing emotions.
Sexual knowledge and understanding of relationships, and of his behaviour towards the alleged victim	Sex-Ken ID (McCabe, 1994; adapted by Murphy and O'Callaghan, 2004); Understanding of consent and abuse (Murphy & O'Callaghan, 2004).	Detailed information on understanding of sexual behaviour, including issues around consent.
	Interview.	Self-reported view of meaning of a 'girlfriend' and expectations of a relationship.
		Understanding of the alleged offence.
Social networks	Social Network Map (Forrester-Jones, 1998; see O'Callaghan & Murphy, 2002).	Scope of current relationships.
Executive functioning	Behavioural Assessment of the Dysexecutive Syndrome (BADS; Wilson et al., 1996).	Instructions are reasonably straightforward and provide information on a broad range of planning and problem-solving tests.
Language functioning	OWLS: Listening Comprehension (LC) and Oral Expression (OE) Scales (Carrow-Woolfolk, 1995).	Takes less than 15 minutes; has normative data for young adults around Mr B's age and provides information about whether he is likely to understand court proceedings.

Table 5.4 (continued) Summary of assessments for Mr B

Area of assessment	Test used	Rationale
Suggestibility	Gudjonsson Suggestibility Scale, Form 2 (GSS-2; Gudjonsson, 1997).	Information about the extent to which he is likely to be (mis)led by leading information.
Fitness to plead	Fitness Interview Test—Revised (FIT-R; Roesch et al., 2006).	Flexible structured interview that covers the main relevant areas in English law (Lawson et al., 2005).
Support available if found guilty and given community sentence	Interviews with family members, and letters and telephone calls to statutory and independent health and social care agencies.	Advice for the court about support and treatment for Mr B that would also meet the needs of public protection.

(including sexual) relationships and issues relating to consent and abuse were all limited. Consistent with his performance on the FEEST (in which his score of 52 was more than two standard deviations below the mean for offenders with ASCs; Woodbury-Smith et al., 2005a), he had great difficulty with identifying abuse and consent from the victim's facial expression and body language. His skills in matching and sorting 'fear' and 'anger' were particularly poor. Where appropriate normative data were available, it was found that Mr A's performance on tasks of social cognition, sexual knowledge, and relationships fell well within the range normally expected of people with a learning disability.

- Mr B performed well on experimental tasks such as the Block Design and Object Assembly of the WAIS-III, but his scores on the more ecologically valid tasks of the BADS were poor, even for a person with his limited verbal ability. This seemed surprising, given his particular interest in snooker. A visit with him to the snooker hall indicated that, despite his seemingly encyclopaedic knowledge of the game, he was unable to plan and problem-solve sufficiently well to allow him to play meaningfully.

- Despite all that was learned about Mr B, it remained difficult to understand the offence. There was no evidence that Mr B was upset in any way before he went to the nightclub or when he arrived. He had visited before without apparent difficulties. He was unable to explain what had attracted him to the victim.

- Mr B had a history of behavioural difficulties but no previous history of contact with the criminal justice system. His social network barely went beyond his immediate family, who cared for him without any additional formal or informal support. The clinician involved believed that, with an appropriate framework, he could be managed in the community. There was no reason to believe that treatment needed to be carried out in hospital. What was needed, however, was additional support. The local community-based forensic service only saw people with a mental illness, whilst initially the integrated health and social care learning disability service deemed him ineligible. Following negotiations between commissioners, it was agreed that, because of his difficulties in dealing with verbal information, Mr B's needs were best met within the service for people with learning disabilities.

The court accepted the argument made by Mr B's defence that he was not fit to plead. A 'trial of the facts' took place, at which the alleged victim and witnesses gave evidence. Mr B was found guilty of indecent assault. Based on the clinician's recommendations, he received a supervision order to be managed by the Probation Service with a condition of treatment. This meant that he received assistance that began to address his difficulties and included meaningful daytime activities, individual and group support to help him learn social and sexual rules, sex education, and social groups for people with ASCs. The supervision framework provided by the Probation Service included a contract to which Mr B had to agree. The recommendations included the suggestion that, as such contracts are often too complex for people with impaired verbal intellectual functioning (Mason & Morris, 2000), advice should be sought from a speech and language therapist on presenting the information in a format that was more accessible to him.

Conclusions

Forensic neuropsychology involving the heterogeneous group of 'high-functioning' people with ASCs is still at an early stage. This is likely to change, however, as both the condition and its relevance to a range of forensic issues becomes increasingly recognized. Undoubtedly, further developments are needed, for example, to address the confusion around issues of diagnosis and the lack of agreed ways of assessing aspects of the core clinical phenotype (such as circumscribed interests). Nevertheless, by carrying out detailed investigations and providing recommendations for further assessment, treatment, and support, a forensic neuropsychological perspective can make an important contribution to the lives of men and women with an ASC who come into contact with the civil and criminal justice systems.

Acknowledgements

We are grateful to Dr Susan Young, Professor Gisli Gudjonsson, and Professor Tony Holland for advice and support in writing this chapter.

References

Adolphs, R., Sears, L., and Piven, J. (2001). Abnormal processing of social information from faces in autism. *Journal of Cognitive Neuroscience*, **13**:232–240.

American Psychiatric Association (1994). *Diagnostic and Statistical Manual of Mental Disorders*, 4th edn. Washington, DC: American Psychiatric Association.

Baird, G., Simonoff, E., Pickles, A., et al. (2006). Prevalence of disorders of the autism spectrum in a population cohort of children in South Thames: The Special Needs and Autism Project (SNAP). *The Lancet*, **368**:210–215.

Barnard, J., Harvey, V., Prior, A., and Potter, D. (2001). *Ignored or Ineligible? The Reality for Adults with Autistic Spectrum Disorders*. London: National Autistic Society.

Baron-Cohen, S. (1989). The autistic child's theory of mind: A case of specific developmental delay. *Journal of Child Psychology and Psychiatry*, **30**:285–298.

Baron-Cohen, S. (1995). *Mindblindness: An Essay on Autism and Theory of Mind*. Boston: MIT Press, Bradford Books.

Baron-Cohen, S. (2000). Is Asperger syndrome/high functioning autism necessarily a disability? *Development and Psychopathology*, **12**:489–500.

Baron-Cohen, S. and Wheelwright, S. (1999). Obsessions in children with autism or Asperger syndrome: A content analysis in terms of core domains of cognition. *British Journal of Psychiatry*, **175**:484–490.

Baron-Cohen, S. and Wheelwright, S. (2004). The empathy quotient (EQ). An investigation of adults with Asperger syndrome or high functioning autism, and normal sex differences. *Journal of Autism and Developmental Disorders*, **34**:163–175.

Baron-Cohen, S., O'Riordan, M., Jones, R., Stone, V., and Plaisted, K. (1999a). Recognition of faux pas by normally developing children and children with Asperger syndrome or high- functioning autism. *Journal of Autism and Developmental Disorders*, **29**:407–418.

Baron-Cohen, S., Wheelwright, S., Stone, V., and Rutherford, M. (1999b). A mathematician, a physicist and a computer scientist with Asperger syndrome: performance on folk psychology and folk physics tests. *Neurocase*, **5**:475–483.

Baron-Cohen, S., Wheelwright, S., and Hill, J. (2001a). The 'Reading the Mind in the Eyes' test revised version: A study with normal adults, and adults with Asperger syndrome or high-functioning autism. *Journal of Child Psychiatry and Psychiatry*, **42**:241–252.

Baron-Cohen, S., Wheelwright, S., Skinner, R., Martin, J., and Clubley, E. (2001b). The autism spectrum quotient (AQ): Evidence from Asperger syndrome/high-functioning autism, males and females, scientists and mathematicians. *Journal of Autism and Developmental Disorders*, **31**:5–17.

Baron-Cohen, S., Wheelwright, S., Griffin, R., Lawson, J., and Hill, J. (2002). The exact mind: Empathising and systemising in autism spectrum conditions. In: U. Goswami (ed.), *Handbook of Cognitive Development*, pp. 491–508. London: Blackwell.

Baron-Cohen, S., Wheelwright, S., Robinson, J., and Woodbury-Smith, M. R. (2005). The Adult Asperger Assessment (AAA): A diagnostic method. *Journal of Autism and Developmental Disorders*, **35**:807–819.

Bauman, M. and Kemper, T. (2006). *The Neurobiology of Autism*, 2nd ed. Baltimore, MD: Johns Hopkins University Press.

Berument, S. K., Rutter, M., Lord, C., Pickles, A., and Bailey, A. (1999). Autism Screening Questionnaire: diagnostic validity. *British Journal of Psychiatry*, **175**:444–451.

Blair, R. J. R. (1995). A cognitive developmental approach to morality: Investigating the psychopath. *Cognition*, **57**:1–29.

Blair, R. J. R. (1999). Psychophysiological responsiveness to the distress of others in children with autism. *Personality and Individual Differences*, **26**:477–485.

Blair, R. J. R., Sellars, C., and Strickland I., *et al.* (1996). Theory of mind in the psychopath. *Journal of Forensic Psychiatry*, **7**:15–25.

Blair, R. J. R., Jones, L., Clark, F., and Smith, M. (1997). The psychopathic individual: A lack of responsiveness to distress cues? *Psychophysiology*, **34**:192–198.

Bradley, R. H. (1985). The HOME inventory: Rationale and research. In: J. E. Stevenson (ed), *Recent Research in Developmental Psychopathology*, pp. 191–202. Oxford: Pergamon Press.

Burgess, P. W., Alderman, N., Evans, J., Emslie, H., and Wilson, B. A. (1998). The ecological validity of tests of executive function. *Journal of the International Neuropsychological Society*, **4**:547–558.

Caldwell, B. and Bradley, R. H. (1984). *Home Observation for Measurement of the Environment.* Little Rock, AR: University of Arkansas at Little Rock.

Carrow-Woolfolk, E. (1995). OWLS: Listening Comprehension (LC) Scale and Oral Expression (OE) Scale. London: NFER Nelson.

Eisenberg, N., Miller, P. A., Shell, R., McNalley, S., and Shea, C. (1991). Prosocial development in adolescence: A longitudinal study. *Developmental Psychology*, **27**:849–857.

Fombonne, E. (2005). Epidemiological studies of pervasive developmental disorders. In: F. R. Volkmar, A. Klin, R. Paul, and D. J. Cohen (eds), *Handbook of Autism and Pervasive Developmental Disorders*, pp.42–69. New Jersey: John Wiley & Sons.

Forrester-Jones, R. (1998). *Social Networks and Social Support Development and Proposal.* Departmental Working Paper, Tizard Centre, University of Kent (used by O'Callaghan, A. C. and Murphy, G. H. (2002)).

Friedman, R. J. and Chase-Lansdale, P. L. (2002). Chronic adversities. In: M. Rutter and E. Taylor (eds), *Child and Adolescent Psychiatry*, pp.261–276. Oxford: Blackwell.

Frith, U. and Hill, E. (2004). *Autism: Mind and Brain.* Oxford: Oxford University Press.

Ghaziuddin, M., Tsai, L., and Ghaziuddin, N. (1992). Co-morbidity of autistic disorder in children and adolescents. *European Child and Adolescent Psychiatry*, **1**:209–213.

Gillott, A., Furniss, F., and Walter, A. (2001). Anxiety in high-functioning children with autism. *Autism*, **5**:277–286.

Golan, O., Baron-Cohen, S., and Hill, J. (2006). The Cambridge Mindreading (CAM) Face-Voice Battery: Testing complex emotion recognition in adults with and without Asperger syndrome. *Journal of Autism and Developmental Disorders*, **36**:169–183.

Grisso, T. (1986). *Evaluating Competencies: Forensic Assessments and Instruments*, 2nd edn. New York: Kluwer Academic/Plenum.

Grisso, T. (2003). *Evaluating Competencies: Forensic Assessments and instruments,* 2nd edn. New York: Kluwer Academic/Plenum.

Gudjonsson, G. H. (1997). *The Gudjonsson Suggestibility Scales Manual.* Hove: Psychology Press.

Hamilton, M. (1960). A rating scale for depression. *Journal of Neurology and Psychiatry*, **23**:56–62.

Happé, F. (1994). An advanced test of theory of mind: Understanding of story characters' thoughts and feelings by able autistic, mentally handicapped, and normal children and adults. *Journal of Autism and Developmental Disorders*, **24**:129–154.

Happé, F. (1999). Autism: Cognitive deficit or cognitive style? *Trends in Cognitive Sciences*, **3**:216–222.

Hare, R. D. (2003). *The Hare Psychopathy Checklist—Revised*, 2nd edn. Toronto: Multi-Health Systems.

Hobson, R. P. (1986a). The autistic child's appraisal of expressions of emotion. *Journal of Child Psychology and Psychiatry*, **27**:321–342.

Hobson, R. P. (1986b). The autistic child's appraisal of expressions of emotion: A further study. *Journal of Child Psychology and Psychiatry*, **27**:671–680.

Hoffman, M. L. (2000). *Empathy and Moral Development: Implications for Caring and Justice*. Cambridge: Cambridge University Press.

Howlin, P. (2000). Assessment instruments for Asperger syndrome. *Child Psychology and Psychiatry Review*, **5**:121–129.

Howlin, P. (2004). *Autism: Preparing for Adulthood*, 2nd edn. London: Routledge.

Hughes, C., Russell, J., and Robbins, T. (1994). Specific planning in autism: Evidence of a central executive dysfunction. *Neuropsychologia*, **32**:477–492.

Jolliffe, T. and Baron-Cohen, S. (1997). Are people with autism or Asperger syndrome faster than normal on the Embedded Figures Task? *Journal of Child Psychology and Psychiatry*, **38**:527–534.

Kim, J. A., Szatmari, P., Bryson, S. E., Streiner, D. L., and Wilson, F. J. (2000). The prevalence of anxiety and mood problems among children with autism and Asperger syndrome. *Autism*, **4**:117–132.

Lainhart, J. E. and Folstein, S. E. (1994). Affective disorders in people with autism: A review of published cases. *Journal of Autism and Developmental Disorders*, **24**:587–601.

Lawson, E., Johnson, M., Adams, L., Lamb, J. and Field, S. (2005). *Blackstone's Guide to The Domestic Violence, Crime and Victims Act 2004*. Oxford: Oxford University Press.

Lezak, M. D., Howieson, D. B., and Loring, D. W. (2004). *Neuropsychological Assessment*, 4th edn. Oxford: Oxford University Press.

Lord, C., Rutter, M., and Le Couteur, A. (1994). Autism Diagnostic Interview—Revised. *Journal of Autism and Developmental Disorders*, **24**:659–686.

Lord, C., Rutter, M., DiLavore, P., and Risi, S. (2003). *Autism Diagnostic Observation Schedule*. Los Angeles, CA: Western Psychological Services.

Macdonald, H., Rutter, M., Howlin, P., et al. (1989). Recognition and expression of emotional cues by autistic and normal adults. *Journal of Child Psychology and Psychiatry*, **30**:865–877.

Mason, J. and Morris, L. (2000). Improving recall and understanding of the probation service contract. *Journal of Community and Applied Social Psychology*, **10**:199–210.

Mawhood, L., Howlin, P., and Rutter, M. (2000). Autism and developmental receptive language disorder—a follow-up comparison in early adult life, I. Cognitive and language outcomes. *Journal of Child Psychology and Psychiatry*, **41**:547–559.

McCabe, M. P. (1994). *Sexuality Knowledge, Experience and Needs Scale for People with Intellectual Disability*, 4th edn. Burwood, VA: Australia: School of Psychology, Deakin University.

Mercier, C., Mottron, L., and Belleville, S. (2000). A psychosocial study of restricted interests in high-functioning persons with pervasive developmental disorders. *Autism*, **4**:406–425.

Miller, J. N. and Ozonoff, S. (1997). Did Asperger's cases have Asperger disorder? A research note. *Journal of Child Psychology and Psychiatry*, **38**:247–251.

Murphy, G. H. and Clare, I. C. H. (2003). Adults' capacity to make legal decisions. In: D. Carson and R. H. C. Bull (eds), *Handbook of Psychology in Legal Contexts*, 2nd edn, pp. 32–66. Chichester: John Wiley & Sons.

Murphy, G. and O'Callaghan, A. (2004). Capacity of adults with intellectual disabilities to consent to sexual relationships. *Psychological Medicine*, **34**:1–11.

O'Callaghan, A. C. and Murphy, G. H. (2002). *Capacity to Consent to Sexual Relationships in Adults with Learning Disabilities*. Final Report to the Nuffield Foundation.

Ozonoff, S., Pennington, B., and Rogers, S. (1990). Are there emotion perception deficits in young autistic children? *Journal of Child Psychology and Psychiatry*, **31**:343–363.

Ozonoff, S., Pennington, B., and Rogers, S. (1991). Executive function deficits in high-functioning autistic children: Relationships to theory of mind. *Journal of Child Psychology and Psychiatry*, **32**:1081–1106.

Ozonoff, S., Nicanor, G., Clark, E., and Lainhart, J. E. (2005). MMPI-2 personality profiles of high-functioning adults with autism spectrum disorders. *Assessment*, **12**:86–95.

Parkin, A. J. (1998). The central executive does not exist. *Journal of the International Neuropsychological Society*, **4**:518–522.

Plaisted, K., Saksida, L., Alcantara, J., and Weisblatt, E. (2004). Towards an understanding of the mechanisms of weak central coherence effects: Experiments in visual configural learning and auditory perception. In: U. Frith and E. Hill. *Autism: Mind and Brain*, pp.187–210. Oxford: Oxford University Press.

Powell, A. (2002). *Taking responsibility. Good Practice Guidelines for Services: Adults with Asperger Syndrome*. London: The National Autistic Society.

Power, M. J., Champion, L. A., and Aris, S. J. (1988). The development of a measure of social support: The Significant Others Scale (SOS). *British Journal of Clinical Psychology*, **27**:349–358.

Richell, R. A., Mitchell, D. G. V., Newman, C., Leonard, A., Baron-Cohen, S., and Blair, R. J. R. (2003). Theory of mind and psychopathy: Can psychopathic individuals read the 'language of the eyes'? *Neuropsychologia*, **41**:523–526

Roesch, R., Zapf, P., and Eaves, D. (2006). *FIT-R: Fitness Interview Test—Revised*. Sarasota, FL: Professional Resource Press.

Russell, J. (1997). *Autism as an Executive Disorder*. Oxford: Oxford University Press.

Rutter, M., Anderson-Wood, L., Beckett C., et al. (1999). Quasi-autistic patterns following severe early global privation. *Journal of Child Psychology and Psychiatry*, **40**:537–549.

Sainsbury, C. (2000). *Martian in the Playground: Understanding the School Child with Asperger's Syndrome*. Bristol: Lucky Duck Publishing.

Slater-Walker, G. and Slater-Walker, C. (2002). *An Asperger Marriage*. London: Jessica Kingsley Publishers.

Stone, V., Baron-Cohen, S., and Knight, K. (1998). Frontal lobe contributions to theory of mind. *Journal of Cognitive Neuroscience*, **10**:640–656.

Suto, W. M. I., Clare, I. C. H., Holland, A. J., and Watson, P. C. (2005). Capacity to make financial decisions among people with mild intellectual disabilities. *Journal of Intellectual Disability Research*, **49**:199–209.

Tantam, D. (1988a). Lifelong eccentricity and social isolation, I. Psychiatric, social, and forensic aspects. *British Journal of Psychiatry*, **153**:777–782.

Tantam, D. (1988b). Lifelong eccentricity and social isolation, II. Asperger's syndrome or schizoid personality disorder? *British Journal of Psychiatry*, **153**:783–791.

Tantam, D. (1999). Malice and Asperger syndrome. Paper presented at Autism99 International Online Conference (organized by the National Autistic Society, The Shirley Foundation, and RMR plc). Available at: http://www.autismconnect.org/autism99

Tymchuk, A. (1992). Predicting adequacy of parenting by persons with mental retardation. *Child Abuse and Neglect*, **16**:165–178.

Volkmar, F. R., Kiln, A., Paul, R., and Cohen, D. J. (2005). *Handbook of Autism and Pervasive Developmental Disorders*, 3rd edn. New Jersey: John Wiley & Sons.

WHO (1992). *ICD-10: International Statistical Classification of Diseases and Related Health Problems*, 10th edn. Geneva: World Health Organization.

Williams, D. (1992). *Nobody Nowhere*. London: Corgi Books.

Williams, J. G., Brayne, C. E. G., and Higgins, J. P. T. (2006). Systematic review of prevalence studies of autism spectrum disorders. *Archives of Disease in Childhood*, **91**:8–15.

Wilson, B. A., Alderman, N., Burgess, P. W., Emslie, H., and Evans, J. J. (1996). *Behavioural Assessment of the Dysexecutive Syndrome*. San Antonio, TX: Harcourt Assessment.

Wing, L. (1976). Diagnosis, clinical description and prognosis. In: L. Wing (ed.), *Early Childhood Autism*, 2nd edn, pp. 15–64. Oxford: Pergamon.

Wing, L. (1997). Asperger's syndrome: Management requires diagnosis. *Journal of Forensic Psychiatry*, **8**:253–257.

Wing, L., Leekham, S. R., Libby, S. J., Gould, J., and Larcombe, M. (2002). The Diagnostic Interview for Social and Communication Disorders: Background, inter-rater reliability and clinical use. *Journal of Child Psychology and Psychiatry*, 43:307–325.

Wong, J. G., Clare, I. C. H., Holland, A. J., Watson, P. C., and Gunn, M. (2000). The capacity of people with a 'mental disability' to make a health care decision. *Psychological Medicine*, **30**:295–306.

Woodbury-Smith, M. R. (2005). *An investigation of offending among adults with high functioning autism or Asperger syndrome*. PhD thesis, University of Cambridge, Cambridge, UK.

Woodbury-Smith, M. R., Clare, I. C. H., Holland, A. J., Kearns, A., Staufenberg, E., and Watson, P. (2005a). A case–control study of offenders with high functioning autistic spectrum disorders. *Journal of Forensic Psychiatry and Psychology*, **16**:747–763.

Woodbury-Smith, M. R., Robinson, J., Wheelwright, S., and Baron-Cohen, S. (2005b). Screening adults for Asperger syndrome using the AQ: A preliminary study of its diagnostic validity in clinical practice. *Journal of Autism and Developmental Disorders*, **35**:331–335.

Woodbury-Smith, M. R., Clare, I. C. H., Holland, A. J., and Kearns, A. (2006). High-functioning autistic spectrum disorders, offending and other law-breaking: Findings from a community sample. *Journal of Forensic Psychiatry and Psychology*, **17**:108–120.

Young, A., Perrett, D., Calder, A., Sprengelmeyer, R., and Ekman, P. (2001). *Facial Expressions of Emotion: Stimuli and Tests (FEEST)*. San Antonio, TX: Harcourt Assessment.

Chapter 6

Amnesia

Natalie Pyszora, Eli Jaldow, and
Michael Kopelman

Amnesia (i.e. pathological memory loss) is commonly encountered when assessing and treating offenders, especially perpetrators of violent crimes, and memory complaints commonly arise in those being assessed for civil purposes. Despite this, the exact aetiology of such memory disorders is often poorly understood. This chapter provides a guide for forensic practitioners assessing those presenting with memory problems in criminal and civil settings by summarizing key aspects of the literature and examining the legal implications for those before the criminal courts who claim some degree of amnesia for their offence.

Amnesia in criminal cases

Assumptions are often made regarding the validity of claims of amnesia in criminal cases, based on little or no empirical evidence, and this can have important implications at trial for criminal offenders. There is very little understanding of whether amnesic offenders can be expected to have some return of memory over time, which in turn presents problems in terms of risk assessment and management, including offence-related treatment interventions. Unresolved amnesia may therefore impede offence-related work and delay discharge or release. The inability to fully understand an offence because of amnesia may perplex the forensic practitioner, cause distress to the offender, and impede the ability to understand and come to terms with the offence.

Associations

Amnesia is more commonly associated with violent crimes and is relatively rare in non-violent crimes (Taylor & Kopelman, 1984). Studies describe rates of amnesia for homicide or serious violence varying from 23 to 70% (Leitch, 1948; Guttmacher, 1955; O'Connell, 1960; Tanay, 1969; Bradford & Smith,

1979; Parwatiker *et al.*, 1985; Gudjonsson *et al.*, 1989; Gudjonsson *et al.*, 1999; Cima *et al.*, 2003; Pyszora *et al.*, 2003).

Memories must be encoded for them to be retrieved later, and therefore any factors that impair registration and encoding will in turn affect recall. Examples include factors that impair or narrow attention, such as intoxication or high emotional states (Bradford & Smith, 1979), florid psychosis (Taylor & Kopelman, 1984), and other mental illnesses (Power, 1977). Thus, a failure of encoding in these circumstances can result in amnesia.

It is widely acknowledged that 'crimes of passion', associated with emotionally aroused states, are associated with amnesia and this has been described consistently in the literature (Hopwood & Snell, 1933; Tanay, 1969; Taylor & Kopelman, 1984; Pyszora *et al.*, 2003). Amnesia in this context typically has its onset at the height of the emotional arousal, for example during an argument, and may include the beginning of the attack, and there is then typically a continuous amnesic period for several seconds or minutes until the offender 'comes round' and usually realizes what he has done. Such states have also been described as 'red-outs' (Swihart *et al.*, 1999).

Amnesia has been found to be more common in those with a history of psychiatric disorder (Taylor & Kopelman, 1984; Pyszora *et al.*, 2003), and there is some evidence that personality factors may also be important, specifically hysterical personality (O'Connell, 1960; Parwatiker *et al.*, 1985). Any other association with personality disorders has not been widely explored, although there may be a link with antisocial personality; Cima *et al.* (2003) found that their amnesic subjects had significantly higher rates of antisocial personality disorder than non-amnesic subjects, although there was no difference in scores between the two groups on the screening version of the Psychopathy Check List (Hart *et al.*, 1995).

Offenders claiming amnesia are also more likely to have a previous history of alcohol abuse or dependence (Hopwood & Snell, 1933; Taylor & Kopelman, 1984; Pyszora *et al.*, 2003), and previous 'blackouts', i.e. transient amnesic episodes (Pyszora *et al.*, 2003). Amnesic offenders have been found to be older than non-amnesic offenders by between 3 (Pyszora *et al.*, 2003) and 8 years (Taylor & Kopelman, 1984), but no differences have been found in terms of sex, ethinicity, or IQ.

Mechanisms underlying amnesia

It is important to have some understanding of the mechanisms underlying amnesia for several reasons. Firstly, during assessment, the forensic practitioner needs to look for evidence of an underlying cause of the amnesia, for example, mental illness, alcohol dependence, or previous dissociative experiences. One also needs to be able to provide evidence to the court as to why the offender has experienced amnesia for the offence, based on robust empirical evidence where this exists. Lastly, understanding the underlying mechanisms should aid risk assessment and management of the offender, and may give some indication as to whether memory is likely to recover.

The distinction between medical or 'organic' and psychogenic or 'functional' amnesia can be difficult (Kopelman, 1987b, 2002a), especially as both may be present in offenders, although for the purpose of this chapter they will be examined separately.

Medical causes

The main body of literature in this area has been reviewed previously by Kopelman (1987b, 2002a, b) who divided organic memory impairment into discrete and persistent loss. Medical disorders that produce a discrete episode of memory loss include toxic confusional states (including alcohol intoxication), head injury, epileptic seizures, alcoholic blackouts, hypoglycaemic attacks, post-electroconvulsive therapy confusional states, and the transient global amnesia syndrome. Persistent memory impairment occurs within the amnesic syndrome, which can result from a number of possible pathologies or as part of a dementing illness. Fenwick (1990) outlined some medical factors that may very occasionally be associated with amnesia for a criminal offence and result in impaired consciousness or 'automatisms'. Examples include internal factors such as epilepsy, sleepwalking, cerebral tumour, and transient global amnesia, and external factors such as a blow to the head or administration of insulin resulting in hypoglycaemia (see Chapter 7 of this volume).

However, medical pathology accounts for only a very small minority of cases of amnesia in the context of offending, and in general no association has been found between amnesia and organic pathology (Taylor & Kopelman, 1984; Pyszora *et al.*, 2003). However, Cima *et al.* (2003) found that their amnesic group had poorer executive function than non-amnesic controls, perhaps indicating some neurological impairment. Cases of automatism are very rare, despite their importance medico-legally (Fenwick, 1990). Moreover, there is little convincing evidence of an association between adult learning disability and amnesia for offences (Hopwood & Snell, 1933; O'Connell, 1960), although Cima *et al.* (2003) found amnesic patients to have significantly lower performance IQ on the WAIS. The only study to assess visual and verbal memory function formally in a cohort of amnesic violent offenders did not find any association with neuropsychological impairment (Pyszora, 2006).

Of all the possible neuropsychiatric disorders underlying amnesia for violent offences, alcohol and drug intoxication at the time of the offence are the most common (see Chapter 8 of this volume). Over half of all offenders who commit a violent crime are intoxicated with alcohol at the time of the offence (Petursson & Gudjonsson, 1981; Hamilton et al., 1993; Leong & Silva, 1995), and it is commonly assumed that acute alcohol intoxication can cause genuine memory loss. Some previous studies have suggested that amnesic offenders are more likely to be intoxicated with drugs and/or alcohol at the time of the offence than non-amnesic offenders (O'Connell, 1960; Bradford & Smith, 1979; Parwatiker et al., 1985; Gudjonsson et al., 1989). It is also possible that alcohol and high emotional arousal can interact to cause the memory loss (Kopelman, 1987b), and a recent study suggested that acute intoxication in those who are alcohol dependent (but not those who are non-dependent) potentiates the amnesic effects of a dissociative state (Pyszora, 2006).

Memory loss in the context of alcohol may occur either through state-dependent effects or so-called alcoholic blackouts. The state-dependent hypothesis suggests that information is mainly accessible in the same physiological state in which it was learned, and is not available in another state. In the context of alcohol use, alcohol intoxication determines the physiological state, and suggests that memories would be available if the intoxicated state was repeated, but would not be available in the sober state. Although an attractive hypothesis, which has been supported by some evidence in the non-offender population (Goodwin, 1971), it has not been extensively investigated in the offender population. The one small study carried out failed to provide empirical support for this mechanism (Wolf, 1980). Alcoholic blackouts have been defined as 'amnesia for events occurring during a drinking episode, where events are ordinarily memorable in a sober state' (Goodwin, 1971). These have been categorized into two types: 'fragmentary' blackouts, with islets of preserved memory and shrinkage of the amnesic gap over time, and 'en bloc' blackouts, where islets of memory are rare and the amnesia rarely recovers (Goodwin et al., 1969). Some authors (for example, Taylor & Kopelman, 1984; Kopelman, 1987b) have argued that, in alcohol abusers, amnesia is accounted for by alcoholic blackouts or alcohol-induced state-dependent memory, although other authors remain less convinced. Cima et al. (2002) suggested that offenders use the fact of alcohol intoxication as a 'partial excuse for the essentially inexcusable'.

Fenwick (1990) suggested that acts carried out during a period of alcoholic blackout can be automatisms, with sleep deprivation and physical exhaustion tending to precipitate the automatic state. He cited Redeski's (1975) account of some defendants who had been acquitted because of alcoholic automatism, recorded as total intoxication, as distinct from partial intoxication. It is known that at 200 mg/100 ml blood (approximately 12 units of alcohol) there is marked clouding of consciousness (Fenwick, 1990). Cima *et al.* (2002) cited the case of an intoxicated rapist judged to have suffered an alcoholic automatism. The suggestion that those who become so intoxicated that they cannot remember their crimes may actually be acting in a state of automatism is controversial and the issue is generally dealt with in a more pragmatic way by the courts for policy reasons. The legal implications of intoxication are more thoroughly reviewed later in this chapter.

The problem of drug intoxication in association with amnesia has received relatively little attention in the offender literature, and accounts have generally been anecdotal. The empirical evidence for drug intoxication in the context of offending is equivocal (Bradford & Smith, 1979; Taylor & Kopelman, 1984; Parwatiker *et al.*, 1985), and no robust studies have been done to examine the issue, although amnesia in the context of drug intoxication is quite common in clinical practice. Fenwick (1990) highlighted the fact that any drug that depresses the central nervous system can lead to confusion and amnesia. Fauman & Fauman (1982) noted that defendants charged with crimes of violence in which phencyclidine (PCP) has been implicated often claim to have no memory of the crime. Generally, the PCP was taken 2 or 3 days before the crime, and the violence was characterized by severe disorganized behaviour, usually uncoordinated and chaotic, with characteristics of an acute toxic brain disorder. It is an uncommon dose-related effect and there is usually either no memory for the event or a very distorted recollection with a bizarre quality, distorted body image, and a delusional idea about the victim. The amnesic effects of various drugs on victims in the context of drug-assisted sexual assault have been reviewed by Pope & Shouldice (2001) and Curran (2006). All of the drugs have a similar profile in that they have a rapid onset of action, and they induce sedation and anterograde amnesia (inability to remember events following ingestion). Flunitrazepam (Rohypnol) is a potent, fast-acting benzodiazepine. Amnesia can last up to 12 hours. It can only be detected within 72 hours of ingestion. GHB (gamma-hydroxybutyrate) acts on $GABA_B$ receptors and causes direct central nervous system depression. Amnesia is common, although large doses may cause coma and respiratory depression. Ketamine is a widely used general anaesthetic that causes amnesia and there is no detection test. MDMA (ecstasy) is also reported to cause memory impairment and has been used in the context of sexual assault. It would not be unexpected for these drugs to have similar effects in perpetrators of offences, and amnesia for offences has been described in the context of benzodiazepine use (Medawar & Rassaby, 1991), and such cases are indeed encountered clinically.

In summary, amnesia for criminal offences (especially violent offences) is rarely caused solely by medical or 'organic' factors, other than drug and alcohol use or dependence. However, where medical factors are involved, they can have significant medico-legal implications, which are explained later in this chapter.

Psychological factors

Most of the literature to date suggests that psychogenic factors are more common than organic factors in the context of amnesia for offending (Kopelman, 1987b), although neuropsychiatric disorders, especially intoxication, and psychogenic factors commonly co-exist and may interact (Pyszora, 2006).

Past theories regarding the underlying mechanisms in psychogenic amnesia for offending have largely reflected those fashionable at the time, with a dominance of repression theories until the 1970s. More recently, dissociation has been more commonly proposed as a possible mechanism, perhaps because of the renewed interest occurring in research on traumatic memories (Putnam, 1989; Van der Hart & Horst, 1989; Van der Kolk & Fisler, 1995). However, until recently, there has been little empirical evidence to support these mechanisms in offenders.

Studies in the earlier part of the twentieth century generally argued in favour of repression. It was thought that, in order to cope with the internal conflict caused by an act alien to the superego and resulting depression, individuals repressed from consciousness the memory of their violent actions. Hopwood & Snell (1933) argued that both dissociation and repression may be important in amnesia, but that repression was more common, accounting for some of the cases where memory for the crime was initially present but subsequently lost, or where memory was more hazy. They also argued that repression would account for cases where total amnesia was temporary and memory later recovered as the conflict became less acute with time. Leitch (1948) argued that repression was the primary mechanism underlying amnesia and that this was more common in (although not exclusive to) those with 'hysterical tendencies'. Leitch recognized the protective element of amnesia against possible suicide. He divided psychogenic amnesia into hysterical (akin to malingering and evasion of responsibility in his view) and affective (involving repression of the painful and usually highly emotional memories). Likewise, O'Connell (1960) felt that amnesia was secondary to repression, being more easily achieved in those with hysterical personalities, although he believed it could be exhibited in others given sufficient stress. Bradford & Smith (1979) also argued that repression was the mechanism in operation for highly emotionally charged events. Some authors have used measures related to the idea of repression, such as over-control, to explain amnesia. For example, Tanay (1969) reported that the homicide offenders he had seen displayed dissociative phenomena at the time of the offence in association with 'severe or overdeveloped superegos'. Most of these individuals experienced anger in the form of sudden explosions. They displayed an overall rigidity and 'personality impoverishment', and they were said to exhibit primary defence mechanisms of denial, repression and reaction formation. However, there has been little in the way of empirical evidence to support this. Gudjonsson *et al.* (1999) found that high scores on measures of over-controlled hostility and over-control (measured by the superego score on the Arrow-Dot Test) were not associated with amnesia. Pyszora (2006) found that there was no direct correlation between amnesia and a repressive coping style (as defined by Weinberger *et al.*, 1979).

By the end of the twentieth century, several studies had examined the phenomenon of dissociation in the context of violent offences, although few specifically examined the phenomenon of amnesia for the offence. Smith (1965) described three cases of adolescent murderers who clearly displayed dissociative amnesia for the actual attacks, following provocation from the victim, and he believed that the amnesia may have protected against suicide. Meyerson (1966) described two cases of women who killed their children and experienced dissociative amnesia, stating that dissociation was a diagnosis that was generally not considered by others at the time. Tanay (1969) found that 70% of the 53 homicide offenders he assessed pretrial in his American sample had evidence of dissociative reactions, with faulty recollection ranging from complete amnesia to 'spotty' memory. He found that an altered state of consciousness occurred in the perpetrator *before* the act at a time when a weapon (usually a gun) was available. Tanay (1969) believed that dissociative reactions occurred in response to an 'aggressive flooding of the ego'. Most of the homicides involved killing someone who was emotionally close, following a quarrel. Carlisle (1991) gave qualitative accounts of 20 men convicted of violent offences, who reported dissociative symptoms at the time of the offence. These symptoms included inner voices, depersonalization, 'deaffectualization' (the process of dissociating emotions), and trance states, as well as amnesia ranging from minutes to hours in three of the offenders.

A more systematic study of severe dissociation in offenders was provided by Lewis *et al.* (1997) of New York University. They evaluated 'approximately 150' murderers for legal purposes over a 13-year period, including 29 on death row. Fourteen (9%) met DSM-IV criteria (American Psychiatric Association, 1994) for dissociative identity disorder. The study focused on the 12 subjects in whom objective evidence was available for long-standing dissociative symptoms and signs (all 12) and child abuse (11 cases out of 12). All of these subjects had impaired memory for both violent and non-violent behaviour, although unfortunately no comment was made on the rates of amnesia for the killings themselves.

A study of life-sentence prisoners who had committed a range of violent crimes (Pyszora, 2006) has provided the first empirical evidence of an association between dissociation at the time of the offence and amnesia for it. Previous research had shown dissociation in the victims of violent crime (Mechanic et al., 1998) and in those experiencing other traumatic events (Spiegal & Cardena, 1991). Other factors may help to explain why some offenders experience dissociation during a particular type of offence and others do not; for example, concurrent or pre-existing psychopathology is often found in dissociative amnesia (Cercy et al., 1997), some people have an innate capacity to dissociate (Porter et al., 2001), and unpremeditated crimes may be particularly associated with amnesia (Porter et al., 2001). Despite the growing evidence, some are sceptical about the notion of dissociative amnesia in offenders (e.g. Cima et al., 2002). The process of dissociation has some similarities to the theory of emotional state-dependent memory. Both processes involve intense emotional arousal and subsequent unavailability of memory. However, in emotional state dependency, the theory suggests that the affective state becomes so intense that the person may not be able to integrate these feelings within their usual repertoire of emotions, but that the memories can be retrieved at a later time if the original emotional state is restored.

There are obvious problems involved in examining the state-dependent memory of violent offenders: it would be unethical, and probably impossible, to induce such a negative affective state in the laboratory. Therefore, research has had to rely on less robust, more naturalistic studies of the phenomenon in offenders, which are, by definition, retrospective in nature. Swihart et al. (1999) explored several explanations for the phenomenon of circumscribed amnesia (or what they called 'red-outs') for assaults on partners or 'crimes of passion'. They suggested that one possible explanation is that a person who severely abuses or kills his or her partner may be in such a uniquely negative affective state, with such high intensity (rage), that it is not possible to retrieve the memory of the abuse when no longer in the rage state, i.e. mood/state-dependent memory may be an underlying factor. This model is consistent with the claims of some amnesic individuals that they remember events leading up to the crime and events after the crime, when the intensity of their emotions was somewhat lower, as these states of arousal are not as drastically different from normal angry or upset states. Occasionally offenders will give an account of the offence immediately afterwards, but subsequently develop amnesia for it, and Swihart et al. (1999) saw this as consistent with the state-dependent proposal. However, it is possible to explain this pattern of memory loss as a result of failure of encoding, secondary to intense emotional arousal, in which case recall would be impossible whatever the mood state at retrieval.

In summary, there is some knowledge about the mechanisms that may underlie amnesia for an offence, with empirical evidence to support them in some cases. It is likely that, at least in violent offenders, amnesia can be induced by three main mechanisms, which are not mutually exclusive:

1. Intense emotional arousal leading to impaired encoding and/or state-dependent effects.
2. As part of a dissociative state.
3. As part of an alcoholic blackout.

There is a reasonable understanding of typical patterns of memory loss associated with each mechanism, and 'typical' case examples for each are given below.

Case Study 1

Mr B was 23 at the time of his offence. He had a stormy relationship with his girlfriend and had been violent to her prior to the index offence. He was jealous and possessive. He had abused alcohol for the past 14 months to cope with stress over his career and financial problems and suffered from occasional impotence. On the morning of the offence, he had not been drinking. They argued about his accusations of infidelity and his financial problems. They made up and started to have sexual intercourse, but he then lost his erection. He said she then manually stimulated him but she 'looked repulsed' and he 'lost his head and went for her'. He struggled with her and strangled her and when he 'came round' his foot was on her throat. He had strangled her and then stood on her neck, killing her. Afterwards he thought of killing himself but was persuaded not to by his brother. He handed himself in to the police.

At trial, he was convicted of murder, being unsuccessful in his defence of provocation, and sentenced to life with a tariff of 10 years. He had no change in memory over the following 7 years.

Mr B—interpretation of amnesia

Mr B's brief amnesic gap is a classical 'red-out' in the context of extreme emotional arousal.

Case Study 2

Mr V was 44 years old at the time of his offence. He had suffered an anxiety state 13 years previously and received treatment from the GP. Two years before the offence, he became depressed as a result of the breakdown of his marriage and he received antidepressants for 6 months and saw a consultant psychiatrist. The following year, he was noted to be low secondary to relationship difficulties, and this was exacerbated when he was sacked from work some weeks prior to the offence, as well as experiencing ongoing financial pressures and difficulties gaining access to his son. There was no history of alcohol or drug abuse.

He met the victim 5 months prior to the offence when she advertized in a lonely hearts column. Two days prior to the offence, he found out that she was having an affair but felt unable to confront her. He brooded over this and became angry. They agreed to meet at her flat on the evening of the offence. He arrived early and spent an hour pacing the pavement, brooding over her infidelity and becoming more angry. The victim arrived late, and he shouted at her as she got out of her car. She then told him that the relationship was over. He grabbed her and repeatedly smashed her head against the pavement and a wall. He described clear memories for events preceding the attack and for the beginning of the assault. His next memory was walking somewhere in the rain to the bus station, although this was patchy. Back in his flat, he stated that the 'shock of seeing blood brought me round' and he knew that something had happened, although he was unsure what. The following day, he sat with the dog all day and then walked him. He stated that he was focusing on the dog instead of what had happened and was 'cutting off'. When the police attended in the evening, he described relief that it was 'all out of his hands'.

Mr V successfully pleaded guilty to manslaughter on the basis of diminished responsibility. In all, seven psychiatrists and psychologists provided evidence that he suffered with a personality disorder and depression. He was sentenced to life imprisonment with a tariff of eight years. He had no change in his memory over the next seven years, despite stating that he wanted to remember the attack so that he could accept what he had done.

Mr V—interpretation of amnesia

Significant findings 7 years after the offence were that he scored highly on a measure of post-traumatic symptomatology related to the offence. He also scored highly on a measure of dissociation at the time of the offence, which was consistent with his description of his mental state during and following the offence. It is likely that dissociation was the most significant factor underlying his amnesia because of the very high peritraumatic dissociation score, absence of organic factors (including drugs or alcohol), and a classical description of a dissociative state during and following the offence. It is notable that even 7 years after the event he had no return of memory, but still had significant post-traumatic symptoms, particularly those of an intrusive nature.

Case Study 3

Mr D was 36 and living on the streets at the time of the offence. He had nine previous convictions, including one for actual bodily harm when he assaulted a stranger who refused to give him money. He had a 6-year history of alcohol dependence and a 4-year history of alcohol-related blackouts, with associated episodes of (unprosecuted) violence. He had no psychiatric history or history of head injury.

Mr D was convicted of the murder of a 46-year-old female stranger, although they had drunk together on the day of the offence. She had been beaten, resulting in a broken jaw, and strangled, and was found floating in the canal. Mr D was seen by witnesses acting aggressively towards the victim during the evening. He had amnesia for the events of the whole day. At trial, he pleaded not guilty as he believed he had not committed the offence, but also put forward a defence of Majewski lack of intent. No psychiatric reports were conducted. Mr D was given a 12-year tariff and appealed post-conviction as he believed he could not have committed the offence 'not having it in him to hurt a woman'. His appeal was unsuccessful.

At first, Mr D had no memory at all for the day and believed he had been 'stitched up' by the police. His last memory was getting off the bus in the morning and starting to drink with his friends. His next memory was talking with his friends the next morning, with an amnesic gap of approximately 24 hours. He had no idea of what had happened and was arrested at lunchtime. About a year after the offence, he started having flashes consisting of islets of memory, and 7 years later his last memory was of a fight with his friend, and his next memory was looking at the sky and then the victim's face. He also had flashes of memory of seeing people in the subway.

Mr D—interpretation of amnesia

It is likely that the main factor causing the amnesia was an alcoholic blackout. However, psychometric measures classified him as a repressor, which raised the possibility of motivated forgetting. The negative affect, which for him may have been associated with having been violent to a woman, may have been repressed, together with memory of the crime itself.

Length and nature of the amnesia gap

Descriptions of the length of the amnesic gap in criminal offenders have varied in the literature (Kopelman, 1987a) and are generally unhelpful, being described as 'a few seconds to the offender's whole life' (Leitch, 1948), 'hours to days' (Hopwood & Snell, 1933) to 'less than 24 hours with the majority less than 30 minutes' (Bradford & Smith, 1979). However, in a more systematic assessment of 31 amnesic life-sentence prisoners, Pyszora (2006) found that amnesic offenders generally fell into one of two groups: those with long amnesic gaps, averaging 2 hours and apparently mediated by alcoholic blackouts and/or dissociation, and those with short amnesic gaps of approximately 1 minute, which appeared to be mediated by intense emotional arousal in the context of crimes of passion. It is important to remember that, in clinical practice, there is rarely one factor working alone and thus the picture of the amnesia and the aetiology of an amnesia is often more complicated.

Recovery of memory

Unfortunately, little is known about the recovery of memory in those offenders who claim amnesia for their offence. Hopwood & Snell (1933) attempted to follow up 100 amnesic cases in Broadmoor Hospital. Thirty of the 78 cases they judged to have 'genuine' amnesia recovered their memory, usually within 6 months of the crime. This process was gradual and was not due to any conscious attempt to recollect the crime. They argued that some patients may assert that they remember their previously forgotten crimes in order to help obtain their discharge from a secure psychiatric hospital, and that other patients may hear the story of their crime so often that they eventually come to believe that they remember it. If either of these factors were true (and many clinicians continue to worry about these possibilities), it would lead to an overestimation of the rate of recovery of memory. In their study of life-sentence prisoners, Pyszora et al. (2003) found that 59% of amnesic offenders reported at least some recovery of memory at 3 years post-conviction. Pyszora (2006) found that those with long amnesic gaps in the context of an alcoholic blackout and/or dissociation seemed to have at least some recovery of memory 7 years later, although the central amnesic gap of a few seconds or minutes was generally permanent. This permanent memory gap appeared to reflect a common underlying mechanism related to intense emotional arousal. Recovered memories of the offence were not generally different from memories of the offence in the non-amnesic offenders, except that amnesic offenders recalled less perceptual information, possibly because of attentional narrowing in the context of extreme emotional arousal (Pyszora, 2006). It is clear that more research needs to be done on this topic, as recovery of memory has important implications for risk assessment and offence-related work.

Legal aspects of amnesia for criminal offences

It is a general principle of criminal law that a person may not be convicted of a crime unless the prosecution has proved beyond reasonable doubt both (i) that he has caused a certain event, and that responsibility is to be attributed to him for the existence of a certain state of affairs, which is forbidden by criminal law (the *actus reus*), and (ii) that he had a defined state of mind in relation to the causing of the event or the existence of the state of affairs (the *mens rea*) (Smith & Hogan, 1996). Furthermore, the *actus reus* must be willed, i.e. the act must be voluntary.

Amnesia for the offence is potentially relevant in relation to both fitness to plead and criminal responsibility and courts will almost inevitably raise the issue of possible malingering.

Fitness to plead

The concept of fitness to plead, or competency to stand trial, is confined to countries relying on an adversarial system of justice such as England, Australia, Canada and the USA, but not in countries with an inquisitorial approach such as Denmark, Switzerland and Austria. In the UK, the legal position has been that amnesia does not affect fitness to plead. In his study of all those found unfit to plead in England and Wales between 1976 and 1988, Grubin (1996) found that, although amnesia for an offence was mentioned in 14 (5%) of cases, it appeared to be the prime reason underlying the psychiatric recommendation in two cases. Taylor & Kopelman (1984) found that all of the amnesic men on remand in their study were regarded as fit to plead.

In the UK, the most commonly cited case of amnesia is that of Podola, which was reviewed by Bradford & Smith (1979). On 13 July 1959, Podola shot and killed a policeman. He was arrested 3 days later as the prime suspect. The door to his flat was rammed just as he was opening it, and it hit him in the face, after which the police landed on top of him. He was admitted to hospital the next day for 3 days, where he was monosyllabic but found to be engaging in a difficult jigsaw puzzle and playing chess. He was amnesic for all events prior to his arrest. He was diagnosed with severe retrograde amnesia, post-concussional syndrome, and cerebral contusion. The defence attempted to establish that he was unfit to plead on the grounds that he was unable to instruct counsel due to amnesia for the whole of his past life. The case came to trial in September. Medical evidence concluded that an organic basis for his amnesia was unlikely. The issue then revolved around whether his amnesia was hysterical or malingered. The Crown highlighted that he had no other hysterical features and that he retained various (procedural) skills, therefore implying that his amnesia was malingered. Of course, this assumption is now known to be neuropsychologically unsound. The jury found his amnesia to be not genuine and therefore found him fit to plead. Thus, the issue of whether he would have been competent, had his amnesia been genuine, was never examined, but the case is still quoted in relation to amnesia and fitness to plead. Podola was convicted of murder and sentenced to death.

The slightly different approach adopted in the USA is worthy of mention. Here, the equivalent guidance on fitness to plead was outlined in *Dusky v United States* 362 US 402 (1960) and has been summarized by Rubinsky & Brandt (1986). Competency is judged on the basis of whether the defendant 'has sufficient present ability to consult with his lawyer with a reasonable degree of rational understanding and whether he has a rational as well as a factual understanding of the proceedings against him' (Rubinsky & Brandt, 1986, p. 402). Given this standard, courts have held that amnesia is a factor that should be considered when determining a defendant's competence. An accused who cannot recall the crime may be unable to meaningfully assist in the defence and therefore should not be considered competent. However, it is not a sufficient factor alone to negate competency, and Rubinsky & Brandt

(1986) could find no cases where amnesia was judged to be a bar to competency, the rationale being identical to that in the UK, i.e. that the defendant may be feigning amnesia.

Roesch & Golding (1986) highlighted the fact that amnesia has posed a special problem in relation to competency assessments and that approaches to the evaluation of competency are inconsistent and that some decisions are invalid. These concerns reflect those of Grubin (1996) in his study of fitness to plead in the UK. An important case addressing the issue of amnesia in the USA was *Wilson v United States*, 391 F.2d 460 (DC Cir. 1968). The defendant had permanent retrograde amnesia and appealed against his conviction on the grounds that his amnesia deprived him of his right to a fair trial. The court suggested six criteria by which to determine whether the defendant had received a fair trial, which included whether the amnesia inhibited the defendant's ability to assist his lawyer and testify on his own behalf, and also included the strength of the prosecution's case. Thus, according to these criteria, if the prosecution evidence is weak, amnesia becomes more relevant in determining the fairness of the trial. These criteria promote a functional case-by-case approach, and are more stringent than the Duskey criteria. Many courts in the USA have not adopted the Wilson criteria, although R. Roesch and S. Golding, Professors of Psychology in Canada and the USA, respectively, support the idea of their adoption. Under most US state laws, a finding of incompetency leads to dismissal of charges if the defendant is unlikely to regain his competency in the foreseeable future, whereas in the UK, being found unfit to plead will lead to a trial of the facts.

Criminal responsibility

It has been established that amnesia for the offence per se does not stop offenders assuming responsibility for their actions (Kopelman, 1987a; Stein, 2001). Contrary to common assumptions, a recent study has shown that amnesic offenders are actually less likely to deny their offence, i.e. to say they did not do it, than non-amnesic offenders (Pyszora *et al.*, 2003). Although the presence of amnesia for a criminal offence does not provide a defence in itself, it may indicate the presence of an underlying or associated disorder that may give rise to a medical or legal defence, either reducing or negating criminal responsibility. However, the presence of amnesia in itself does not imply that, at the time of the offence, the defendant did not know right from wrong (Goodwin, 1995; Swihart *et al.*, 1999), and it does not have any implications with respect to the defendant's motives or conduct at the time of the crime (Rubinsky & Brandt, 1986). There has only been one study to date that has examined issues at trial for those who claim amnesia for their offence, finding that amnesic offenders were more likely to use defences of diminished responsibility, provocation, and Majewski lack of intent, even if these were unsuccessful (Pyszora et al., 2003).

In assessing amnesic offenders, it is important to look for an underlying disorder in cases of amnesia that may provide a defence of Diminished Responsibility under s.2 of the Homicide Act 1957, or may be indicative of another disorder that would provide a defence under the McNaughton Rules for insanity. Amnesia may be associated with an underlying mental disorder, most commonly depression and psychosis (Taylor & Kopelman, 1984), which can provide a defence of diminished responsibility. Alcohol intoxication in the context of dependence may also provide a defence of diminished responsibility if the defendant is suffering with alcoholism that renders the taking of the 'first drink' of the day involuntary (*R v Tandy* [1989] 1 All ER 267).

As highlighted earlier in the chapter, amnesia commonly occurs in the context of a 'crime of passion', and provocation (as defined in s.3 of the Homicide Act 1957) may be relevant in these circumstances. The defendant must be provoked to lose his self-control (the subjective condition), and, if so, provocation must be enough to make a reasonable man or woman do as he or she did (the objective condition). It had been established that special characteristics of the defendant, such as depression, could be considered (*R v Smith* (Morgan) [2001] 1 AC 146, 168) in determining the 'objective condition', i.e. the degree of self-control that could be expected from a defendant with those special characteristics. However, a recent judgement by the Court of Appeal (*R v James* and *R v Karimi* [2006] EWCA Crim 14) chose to follow the precedent of a Privy Council decision, which ruled that the only characteristics that could be taken into account (in considering the objective condition) were those directly relevant to the provocation itself, and not general characteristics that simply affected a person's ability to control himself or herself. This suggests that special characteristics can no longer be considered by the English courts in relation to the 'objective' test.

Generally, voluntary intoxication with alcohol or drugs, which may be associated with amnesia, will not provide a defence. However, voluntary intoxication may negate specific intent (*DPP v Majewski* [1976] 2 All ER 142). In the Majewski case, the defendant was charged with three counts of actual bodily harm and three counts of assault on police at a public house in Basildon. He had consumed large quantities of drugs and alcohol prior to the offence and claimed to have 'blanked out' and not to have known what he was doing when he threatened to kill the police officers. The trial judge directed the jury to ignore the subject of drink and drugs as being in any way a defence. His appeal to the House of Lords was dismissed. The 'Majewski approach' established that, where the defendant is charged with a crime of specific intent, he will be convicted of the offence of 'basic' intent. For example, where the charge is one of s.18 Offences Against the Person Act 1861, he or she may be convicted of an offence under s.20 of the 1861 Act, which only requires proof that the defendant was aware that his act might cause physical harm to a person, but that requirement is not a specific intent.

The issue of involuntary intoxication was examined in the case of *R v Kingston* [1994] 3 All ER 353. In this case, the defendant had paedophiliac homosexual inclinations. An attempted blackmail was set up, whereby it was arranged for the defendant to come to a flat, where a 15-year-old boy had been lured and drugged. The defendant abused him sexually and was photographed and audiotaped. He claimed that his drink had been laced with drugs and that he could not remember anything after seeing the boy lying on the bed. He was convicted and on appeal the conviction was upheld. The House of Lords ruled that involuntary intoxication was only a defence if the defendant was so intoxicated that he could not form intent.

Involuntariness for an offence may arise from automatism. Automatism has been defined as 'an involuntary piece of behaviour over which an individual has no control' (Fenwick, 1990, p. 4) and its presence negates criminal responsibility altogether. Automatism, by definition, occurs when there is a significant disturbance of consciousness. Afterwards, the individual may have no recollection, or only partial or confused memory, for his actions (Fenwick, 1990). Thus, the presence of amnesia for a criminal offence may, albeit rarely, indicate the presence of an underlying disorder that would provide a defence of automatism (Schacter, 1986; Fenwick, 1986; Fenwick, 1987; Hindler, 1989; Kopelman, 2002a, b). The law on automatism is complex and remains unsatisfactory in its division between sane and insane automatism (Fenwick, 1990; Mackay, 1995). It states that, if the automatism results from an external factor (for example an injection of insulin or anaesthetic, or blow to the head), this is a 'sane' automatism, whereas, if it arises from an internal factor, i.e. a 'disease of the mind' (for example dementia, epilepsy, or a brain tumour), it is 'insane' (*R v Quick* [1973] 3 All ER 347). This distinction is of fundamental importance for the defendant, as those found 'sane' will be acquitted at trial, whereas those found 'insane' will receive a disposal under the Criminal Procedure (Insanity and Unfitness to Plead) Act 1991. Although the 1991 Act provides a greater range of disposals than the old 1964 Act, including an absolute discharge, the defendant still carries the stigma of having been found insane (Fenwick, 1984; Fenwick, 1999). In addition, until March 2005, those found guilty of the act of murder still had to be committed to hospital, however inappropriate this was clinically. Murder now has the same range of disposals as other crimes under the provisions of the Domestic Violence, Crime and Victims Act 2004.

Psychogenic automatism has not been extensively accepted in the courts in the UK, although it has in other countries. It has been defined by Fenwick (1990, p. 22) as 'a complex sequence of behaviour which appears to be well motivated and directed, with no evidence of organic confusion'. In the case of *R v Issitt* [1978] RTR 211 in the UK, the clear principle was established that, if it could be shown that there was a clear set of purposeful acts with the mind apparently functioning in the presence of a hysterical amnesia for the events, then automatism could not be used as a defence, although the medical evidence could be used in mitigation. Other countries have also examined this issue in court, e.g. Febbo *et al.* (1993–1994). The fundamental issue is that, during a dissociative state, control over one's actions may be diminished, making it relevant in establishing criminal responsibility (Porter *et al.*, 2001). The Canadian and Australian courts have taken contrasting approaches to crimes committed by individuals while in a state of dissociation (McSherry, 1998). In Canada, dissociative states are seen as falling within the defence of mental disorder (insane automatism), whilst in Australia evidence of dissociation generally leads to a complete acquittal (sane automatism). These contrasting approaches hinge on the respective laws of 'automatism', and arbitrary distinctions between sane and insane have been made in cases where the defendant is in a state of dissociation at the time of the offence. Whether a mental condition is deemed to give rise to sane or insane automatism will depend on whether it is classified as a 'disease of the mind'. The argument for accepting the defence of psychogenic automatism remains unconvincing, if only for policy reasons, when one considers that a large number of homicide offenders will experience a dissociative state at the time of the offence (Tanay, 1969; Pyszora, 2006). It is likely that this will remain the strongest argument against adopting such a defence, and it is likely that other causes of automatism, such as concussion or hypoglycaemia, are accepted because of the relative rarity of such cases being associated with violent crime. The pivotal issue remains: During a dissociative state, what control does the defendant have over his actions and therefore how criminally responsible should he or she be judged to be? (Porter *et al.*, 2001).

Malingering

The assessment of malingering in those claiming amnesia is examined in more detail in Chapter 11 of this volume, but some general points are worthy of mention here. The major research over the past 30 years aimed at developing methods to detect malingered amnesia has become increasingly sophisticated with time. Wiggins & Brandt (1988) recognized the incentives to feign or exaggerate memory impairments, both in criminal and civil litigation, for secondary gain. In the USA, significant amnesia may still render a defendant either temporarily or permanently incompetent to stand trial, or make an adjournment for recovery of memory advisable (Schacter, 1986). Frederick (2000) highlighted the advantages to the defendant of a finding of incompetency, including postponement of trial (with lower likelihood of successful prosecution), the introduction of tenable mental state defence evidence, and, in some cases, a decision not to prosecute.

Many people, especially within the legal profession, believe that amnesia is easily faked, and practically impossible to disprove, and that many criminal defendants may submit claims of amnesia simply to avoid punishment (Wiggins & Brandt, 1988). There may be several motivations for falsifying amnesia (Porter *et al.*, 2001). Feigned amnesia may serve to support a legal defence, to elicit sympathy from jurors or family members, to raise doubt about involvement in a crime, or to avoid using the much more risky and more cognitively taxing approach of explicit deception (e.g. concocting an alibi). In psychopathic offenders, it may simply reflect pathological lying or 'duping delight'. Cercy *et al.* (1997) argued that most who present with isolated amnesia for the past are either feigning or have dissociative amnesia (defined in part by the absence of an observed neurological abnormality).

However, it is important to recognize that some offenders have little to benefit from malingering amnesia, such as those who admit their guilt (Stein, 2001), and many claims of amnesia are likely to be genuine (Porter *et al.*, 2001). Some evidence for this is provided by the fact that amnesia also occurs in sanctioned homicides; for example during combat killings (Van der Hart *et al.*, 1999), and a knowledge of common patterns of amnesia and associated factors should aid the forensic practitioner in assessing defendants claiming amnesia for their offence.

Assessment of the amnesic defendant

In many respects, this follows the guidelines for any thorough forensic assessment.

1. A full history needs to be obtained including:
    + Organic/medical history (head injury, epilepsy, diabetes, sleepwalking, current medication)
    + Past psychiatric history and personality assessment
    + Past history of childhood sexual and physical abuse, or other trauma, and previous dissociative symptoms
    + Alcohol and drug history
    + Evidence of psychiatric disorder at the time of the offence
    + Alcohol and drug intoxication at the time of the offence

- Exact pattern of the amnesia (last thing remembered, next continuous memory, and any islets of memory, as well as length of amnesic gap). It is vital that the defendant gives an account of what he or she actually remembers, not what he or she has been told has happened.
2. Depositions must be read and any inconsistencies in the account of the amnesia noted. Witness accounts of behaviour during the amnesic gap provide valuable information. The amnesia may improve with time but accounts should be consistent.
3. Neuropsychological and psychometric testing may be of value where neuropsychiatric and psychological factors appear significant. An EEG and MRI should be completed where appropriate, i.e. when there is evidence of neuropsychological impairment.
4. Malingering instruments are increasingly used in criminal cases in the UK but may be of limited value where there is a discrete episode of memory loss.

Neuropsychological assessment

In both civil and criminal cases, solicitors will usually request a neuropsychological assessment when either the plaintiff claims compensation for cognitive impairment following a trauma or the defendant claims amnesia for the alleged offence. Head injuries (e.g. after a road traffic accident or a criminal assault) and medical negligence cases (e.g. hypoxic brain damage following anaesthesia) are two areas where a request for a comprehensive neuropsychological assessment is often made.

In the UK, the neuropsychological assessment of both civil and criminal cases should ideally always be carried out by a Practitioner Full Member of the Division of Neuropsychology of the British Psychological Society. It is also helpful and advisable to have a neuropsychiatric evaluation to ascertain medical and mental health issues that might be contributing to cognitive dysfunction. The neuropsychologist will want to establish from the medical records such factors as: the duration of retrograde and post-traumatic amnesia, the Glasgow Coma score and neurological signs at admission, and the presence or history of skull fractures, haematomas, neurosurgical interventions, etc.

There are essentially two general aims when neuropsychologically assessing clients, either for criminal or civil purposes: firstly, to establish whether cognitive difficulties are present, and secondly, to establish the extent, pattern, and severity of difficulties so identified.

The areas of cognitive function that would normally be assessed in most cases are: general intellectual function, memory (particularly relevant when assessing an amnesic plaintiff or defendant), planning and organization (so-called executive function), naming, and perceptual abilities. Equally, it is important to be flexible in the administration of tests so that they address the particular questions asked by the commissioning solicitors. It is important in any neuropsychological assessment to be cognizant of emotional factors (e.g. depression and anxiety) as well as motivational factors (e.g. exaggeration of or even fabrication of impairment) as they will, of course, influence test scores. Assessment of motivational factors can be of extreme importance in both civil and criminal cases where compensation is at stake or a plea of diminished responsibility is entered. The examples of particular tests below are not meant to be exhaustive; neuropsychologists will often have their own preferred battery to assess particular areas of cognitive function.

Assessment of general intellectual function

It is normally helpful to have some idea of the expected level of an individual's intellectual function. This is particularly relevant after a sustained head injury, when there may well have been a deterioration from premorbid levels. One simple way of establishing premorbid levels is by considering demographic variables, in particular education and occupation. A more validated approach, however, is to administer a reading test, from which a more precise measure of premorbid intellectual function can be derived. Both the National Adult Reading Test—Second Edition (Nelson & Willison, 1994) and the Wechsler Test of Adult Reading (WTAR; Wechsler, 2001) are widely used in clinical neuropsychological practice (Bright et al., 2002).

There are a number of tests available that assess general intellectual function, although the most widely used is the Wechsler Adult Intelligence Scale—Third Edition (WAIS-III; Wechsler, 1999a). It comprises subtests that assess language function, i.e. the ability to comprehend, reason, and express oneself in the English language (other language versions also exist), as well as non-language based tests (so-called performance tests), that assess a person's ability to reason, plan, and organize material, primarily using visual stimuli. The WAIS-III allows the calibration of an overall full-scale IQ, a verbal IQ, and a performance IQ. In addition, more detailed indexes can be calculated, giving information on an individual's information processing speed as well as working memory, i.e. the ability to retain information in one's mind briefly and process it.

Memory

When assessing an amnesic plaintiff or defendant, it is important to assess memory for the learning of new material (anterograde memory) and to have some idea of both visual and verbal memory. It is also important to test both recall (the ability to retrieve information without the help of any prompts) and recognition (the ability to identify previously seen items). Memory is normally assessed immediately after items are presented and again after a short delay. In criminal cases, particularly where loss of past memories is a key point of contention, it can be helpful to assess stored memories (remote memory), focusing on autobiographical memories as well as past news events.

A number of tests are currently on the market, with the Wechsler Memory Scale—Third Edition (WMS-III; Wechsler, 1999b), Warrington's Recognition Memory Test (Warrington, 1984) and the Doors and People Memory Test (Baddeley *et al.*, 1994) in wide use. The WMS-III is a particularly useful test to administer as it is normed against both the WTAR and the WAIS-III, allowing for calculation of expected scores based on predicted and obtained IQ. If time is of prime concern, then the Doors and People Memory Test, which can be administered in about 40 minutes, offers an elegant and compact alternative. Warrington's Recognition Memory Test, apart from assessing recognition memory for words and faces, can also serve as a useful measure of motivation (see below). The most widely employed test for the assessment of autobiographical memories is the Autobiographical Memory Interview (Kopelman *et al.*, 1990). It is of particular use in the assessment of psychogenic amnesia (Kopelman, 2002b).

Planning and organization

These abilities are normally referred to as 'executive function', as they implicate the overall cognitive processes that enable one to attend to the task in hand, free from extraneous distractions, as well as allocating mental resources appropriately. Executive function also includes the ability to inhibit inappropriate social responses, and thus has a significant bearing on social adjustment and criminal behaviour.

The most widely used test to assess executive function is the Wisconsin Card Sorting Test (Berg, 1948), although often modified shorter versions are used (e.g. Nelson, 1976; Kongs *et al.* 2000), which enable reasonably quick administration. The Hayling Sentence Completion Test (Burgess & Shallice, 1997) and the Brixton Spatial Anticipation Test (Burgess & Shallice, 1997) are also widely used tests assessing executive function, although the authors caution its use in people with a low IQ (<85). The Behavioural Assessment of the Dysexecutive Syndrome (Wilson *et al.*, 1996) uses a more ecologically valid range of executive tests, and appropriate subtests can be selected. Fluency tests that require the generation of words beginning with specific letters or examples of particular categories (e.g. animals, or items in a supermarket) under a time constraint are also sensitive to executive function (see Spreen & Strauss, 1998).

The Delis Kaplan Executive Function System (DKEFS; Delis *et al.*, 2001) has a wide selection, and elaboration of, classic executive tests including tests of fluency and trail-making.

Naming

These tests reflect semantic memory and are related to an individual's verbal intelligence. The two most widely used tests are the Graded Naming test (McKenna & Warrington, 1983) and the Boston Naming Test (Goodglass & Kaplan, 2001). They can reflect relative early progressive cognitive change, and should be used if there is a suspicion of cognitive decline.

Perception

A widely used test to assess perceptual abilities, in the presence of normal visual acuity, is the Visual Object and Space Perception Battery (Warrington & James, 1991). The tests in this battery are sensitive to brain damage in areas that subserve perceptual abilities.

Anxiety and depression

The assessment of depression and anxiety is normally carried out as part of the clinical interview, supplemented by the use of self-administered questionnaires, for example the Beck Depression Inventory—Second Edition (Beck *et al.*, 1996) and the Beck Anxiety Inventory (Beck & Steer, 1990).

Motivation

The assessment of motivational factors, in particular possible exaggeration or even fabrication of symptoms, often crucial in both civil and criminal cases, is not an easy matter (see Chapter 11 of this volume). There are tests available that appear to the uninitiated as complex, but in reality can easily be passed by people with even fairly significant brain injury, such as the Test of Memory Malingering (Tombaugh, 1996) and the Pictorial Recognition Memory Test (Warrington, 1996). Poor performance on these tests, in the absence of clearly established severe amnesia or dementia, should raise suspicion of motivational factors.

In a recent study (Kelly *et al.*, 2005), healthy participants were asked to imagine that they had been involved in a road traffic accident and were claiming compensation. They were also told that that the more affected they appeared, the more financial compensation they were likely to receive. A number of neuropsychological tests were administered to this group and their results compared with a group of patients with an acquired brain injury. Two tests, the Coin-in -Hand Test (Kapur, 1994) and the Mental Control Test from the

WMS-III (Wechsler, 1999b), provided high sensitivity and specificity in separating simulators from patients.

It is also possible to analyse test scores, especially from forced-choice recognition tasks, to see if any scores fall below chance levels, implying possible motivation to perform especially poorly. Warrington's Recognition Memory Tests (Warrington, 1984) are useful to administer in this respect.

All of these tests and analyses are important in a comprehensive neuropsychological assessment. However, in the final analysis, it is only the pooling of all the relevant data from the incident, medical, and psychiatric histories and investigations, information from informants, clinical interview, and neuropsychological testing that can give a sense as to whether the data 'fit'.

Case studies

The cases described below are typical examples of the kind of issues for which a neuropsychological assessment is often sought.

Case Study 4

Mr J aged 20 was involved in a road traffic accident aged 18 whilst a back-seat passenger in a car driven by an acquaintance. He sustained a severe head injury, with a post-traumatic amnesia of about 8 days and retrograde amnesia of several hours. His Glasgow Coma Scale ranged between 9 and 12, indicating a moderately severe head injury. However, a CT scan was reported as showing no neurological injury or skull fracture. His parents described him as having been a happy child and popular in school. After the road traffic accident, his personality had changed and he had become depressed, with some persistent symptoms of post-traumatic stress disorder, and memory and concentration difficulties, as well as disinhibited behaviour. He now found it difficult both making and keeping friends. The substance of the instructions from the solicitors was to document the severity of Mr J's current cognitive impairments, possible treatment, and prognosis.

The Beck Depression Inventory indicated a current mild level of depression. A brief test sensitive to motivational factors, the Pictorial Recognition Memory Test, (Warrington, 1996), showed that Mr J was motivated to perform well obtaining a perfect score. The National Adult Reading Test—Second Edition (Nelson & Willison, 1994) predicted Mr J's IQ to fall in the average range. IQ testing on the WAIS-III (Wechsler, 1999a), however, revealed a young man now with a low average IQ. On the Doors and People Memory Test (Baddeley *et al.*, 1994) and one visual recall test from the WMS-III (Wechsler, 1999b), scores showed good verbal but poor visual memory. On executive tests, the Hayling Sentence Completion Test (Burgess & Shallice, 1997), the Brixton Spatial Anticipation Test (Burgess & Shallice, 1997), the Wisconsin Card Sorting Test (Berg, 1948) and verbal fluency (Spreen & Strauss, 1998), there was evidence of suboptimal performance across tests, with specific difficulties on response inhibition and verbal fluency.

The conclusion reached was that Mr J did indeed have cognitive difficulties in a number of domains, particularly marked on executive tests. It was suggested that Mr J receive cognitive rehabilitation to address these difficulties and that in light of his residual depression and post-traumatic stress symptoms, he also be assessed by a neuropsychiatrist. It was hoped that Mr J would continue to improve but that, in light of his executive difficulties and personality changes, he might indeed find it difficult both to obtain and to remain in full-time employment.

Cases are not always as relatively straightforward as the case described above, and there are situations when testing has to be repeated before a meaningful conclusion can be reached. The next case describes such a situation.

Case Study 5

Mr P was a 25-year-old man who was involved in an road traffic accident sustaining a fractured jaw and mild head injuries. Approximately 2 years prior to the accident, Mr P had been assaulted and knocked unconscious, remaining in a coma for 2 weeks. He had made a good recovery from that assault. The request for a neuropsychological assessment was to clarify whether there had been any further cognitive changes beyond those sustained in the assault, attributable to the subsequent road traffic accident.

IQ testing revealed a young man of borderline to low average intelligence, consistent with premorbid estimates of IQ. Memory testing, however, was poor across all tests, with chance performance on some tests. Executive test scores were also at impaired levels. In summary, although general IQ was at premorbid levels, there was impaired performance across both memory and executive tests. The impression from testing appeared to confirm current significant cognitive difficulties. However, as noted, there was chance performance on some memory tests. The Test of Memory Malingering (Tombaugh, 1996) was administered, where Mr P performed worse than people with a known dementia. It therefore raised the possibility of motivational factors influencing test scores. There was also evidence of significant depression. The conclusion reached was that, given the possibility of motivational factors, a reliable evaluation of Mr P's cognitive functioning could not be given at this point in time. It was recommended that he be reassessed once his depression had lifted and he was genuinely motivated to perform well.

Mr P's depression improved with treatment and, on subsequent testing where Mr P was encouraged to try his best, his memory and executive scores were much more in line with his IQ. It was concluded that there was unlikely to have been any new or additional cognitive impairment due to the road traffic accident.

Conclusions

In summary, amnesia or pathalogical memory loss can be issues in both the criminal and civil courts. In both, the need to detect or identify faking or exaggeration of memory impairment is an important one, but this is certainly not the only topic where a neuropsychologist can provide important information. In this chapter, we have summarized what is known about the circumstances giving rise to amnesia for an offence and to its maintenance or recovery through time, and we have outlined the basic principles of memory and neuropsychological assessment in civil and criminal cases. Many issues remain unresolved, and further research into both of these topics, amnesia for an offence and sophisticated neuropsychological testing, is desirable, involving psychologists with forensic and/or neuropsychological expertise.

References

American Psychiatric Association (1994). *Diagnostic and Statistical Manual of Mental Disorders*, 4th edn. Washington, DC: American Psychiatric Association.

Baddeley, A., Emslie, H., and Nimmo Smith, I. (1994). *Doors and People*. Bury St Edmunds, UK: Thames Valley Test Company.

Beck, A. T. and Steer, R. A. (1990). *Beck Anxiety Inventory*. Oxford, UK: Harcourt Assessment.

Beck, A. T., Steer, R. A., and Brown, G. K. (1996). *Beck Depression Inventory-II*. Oxford: Harcourt Assessment.

Berg, E. A. (1948). A simple objective treatment for measuring flexibility in thinking. *Journal of General Psychology*, **39**:15–22.

Bradford, J. and Smith, S. M. (1979). Amnesia and homicide: The Padola case and a study of thirty cases. *Bulletin of the American Academy of Psychiatry and the Law*, **7**:219–231.

Bright, P., Jaldow, E., and Kopelman, M. D. (2002). The National Adult Reading Test as a measure of premorbid intelligence: A comparison with estimates derived from demographic variables. *Journal of the International Neuropsychological Society*, **8**:847–854.

Burgess, P. W. and Shallice, T. (1997). *The Hayling and Brixton Tests*. Bury St Edmunds, UK: Thames Valley Test Company.

Carlisle, A. L. (1991). Dissociation and Violent Criminal Behaviour. *Journal of Contemporary Criminal Justice*, **7**:273–285.

Cercy, S. P., Schretlen, D. J., and Brandt, J. (1997). Simulated amnesia and the pseudo-memory phenomena. In: R. Rogers (ed.), *Clinical Assessment of Malingering and Deception*, 2nd edn, pp. 85–107. New York: Guilford Press.

Cima, M., Merckelbach, H., Nijman, H., Knauer, E., and Hollnack, S. (2002). I can't remember Your Honor: Offenders who claim amnesia. *German Journal of Psychiatry*, **5**:24–34.

Cima, M., Merckelbach, H., Hollnack, S., and Knauer, E. (2003). Characteristics of psychiatric prison inmates who claim amnesia. *Personality and Individual Differences*, **35**:373–380.

Curran, H. V. (2006). Effects of drugs on witness memory. In: A. Heaton-Armstrong, E. Shepherd, G. Gudjonsson, and D. Wolchover (eds), *Witness Testimony*, pp. 77–89. Oxford: Oxford University Press.

Delis, D. C., Kaplan, E., and Kramer, J. H. (2001). *Delis–Kaplan Executive Function System*. San Antonio, TX: The Psychological Corporation.

Fauman, B. J. and Fauman, M. A. (1982). Phencyclidine abuse and crime: A psychiatric perspective. *Bulletin of the American Academy of Psychiatry and the Law*, **10**:171–176.

Febbo, S., Hardy, F., and Finlay-Jones, R. (1993–1994). Dissociation and psychological blow automatism in Australia. *International Journal of Mental Health*, **22**:39–59.

Fenwick, P. (1984). Epilepsy and the Law. *British Medical Journal*, **299**:1938–1939.

Fenwick, P. (1986). Murdering whilst asleep. *British Medical Journal*, **293**:574–575.

Fenwick, P. (1987). Somnambulism and the law: A review. *Behavioural Sciences and the Law*, **5**:343–357.

Fenwick, P. (1990). Automatism, medicine and the law. *Psychological Medicine*, Monograph Supplement 17.

Fenwick, P. (1999). Witness testimony in sleep and dream related contexts. In: A. Heaton-Armstrong, E. Shepherd, and D. Wolchover (eds), *Analysing Witness Testimony*, pp. 76–93. London: Blackstone Press.

Frederick, R. I. (2000). A personal floor effect strategy to evaluate the validity of performance on memory tests. *Journal of Clinical and Experimental Neuropsychology*, **22**:720–730.

Goodglass, H. and Kaplan, E. (2001). *The Assessment of Aphasia and Related Disorders*, 3rd edn. Philadelphia: Lippincot Williams & Williams.

Goodwin, D. W. (1971). Two species of alcoholic 'blackout'. *American Journal of Psychiatry*, **127**:1665–1670.

Goodwin, D. W. (1995). Alcohol amnesia. *Addiction*, **90**:315–317.

Goodwin, D. W., Crane, J. B., and Guze, S. B. (1969). Phenomenological aspects of the alcoholic 'blackout'. *British Journal of Psychiatry*, **115**:1033–1038.

Grubin, D. (1996). *Fitness to Plead in England and Wales*. Maudsley Monograph 38. London: Psychology Press.

Gudjonsson, G. H., Petursson, H., Skulason, S., and Sigurdardottir, S. (1989). Psychiatric evidence: A study of psychological issues. *Acta Psychiatrica Scandinavica*, **80**:165–169.

Gudjonsson, G. H., Hannesdottir, K., and Petursson, H. (1999). The relationship between amnesia and crime: The role of personality. *Personality and Individual Differences*, **26**:505–510.

Guttmacher, M. S. (1955). *Psychiatry and the Law*. New York: Grune & Stratton.

Hamilton, J., Kopelman, M. D., Maden A., *et al.* (1993). Addictions and dependencies: their associations with offending. In: J. Gunn & P. J. Taylor (eds), *Forensic Psychiatry: Clinical, Legal and Ethical Issues*, pp. 435–489. Oxford: Butterworth-Heinemann.

Hart, S. D., Cox, D. N., and Hare, R. D. (1995). *The Hare PCL:SV Psychopathy Checklist: Screening Version*. Toronto: Multi-Health Systems.

Hindler, C. G. (1989). Epilepsy and violence. *British Journal of Psychiatry*, **155**:246–249.

Hopwood, J. S. and Snell, H. K. (1933). Amnesia in relation to crime. *Journal of Mental Science*, **79**:27–41.

Kapur, N. (1994). The coin-in-hand test: A new 'bedside' test for the detection of malingering in patients with suspected memory disorder. *Journal of Neurology, Neurosurgery and Psychiatry*, **57**:385–386.

Kelly, P. J., Baker, G. A., Van den Broek, M. D., Jackson, H., and Humphries, G. (2005). The detection of malingering in memory performance: The sensitivity and specificity of four measures in a UK population. *British Journal of Clinical Psychology*, **44**:333–341.

Kongs, S. K., Thompson, L. L., Iverson, G. L., and Heaton, R. K. (2000). *Wisconsin Card Sorting Test-64 Card Version*. Oxford: Harcourt Assessment.

Kopelman, M. D. (1987a). Amnesia: Organic and psychogenic. *British Journal of Psychiatry*, **150**:428–442.

Kopelman, M. D. (1987b). Crime and amnesia: A review. *Behavioural Sciences and the Law*, **5**:323–342.

Kopelman, M. D. (2002a). Disorders of memory. *Brain*, **125**:2152–2190.

Kopelman, M. D. (2002b). Psychogenic amnesia. In: A. D. Baddeley, M. D. Kopelman, and B. A. Wilson (eds), *Handbook of Memory Disorders*, 2nd edition, pp.451–473. Chichester: John Wiley & Sons.

Kopelman, M. D., Wilson, B. A., and Baddeley, A. D. (1990). *The Autobiographical Memory Interview*. Bury St Edmunds, UK: Thames Valley Test Company.

Leitch, A. (1948). Notes on amnesia in crime for the general practitioner. *Medical Press*, **219**:459–463.

Leong, G. B. and Silva, J. A. (1995). Psychiatric-Legal analysis of criminal defendants charged with murder: A sample without major mental disorder. *Journal of Forensic Sciences*, **40**:858–861.

Lewis, D. O., Yeager, C. A., Swica, Y., Pincus, J., and Lewis, M. (1997). Objective documentation of child abuse and dissociation in 12 murderers with dissociative identity disorder. *American Journal of Psychiatry*, **154**:1703–1710.

Mackay, R. D. (1995). *Mental Condition Defences in the Criminal Law*. Oxford: Clarendon Press.

McKenna, P. and Warrington, E. K. (1983). *Graded Naming Test*. Windsor, UK: NFER Nelson.

McSherry, B. (1998). Getting away with murder? Dissociative states and criminal responsibility. *International Journal of Law and Psychiatry*, **21**:163–176.

Mechanic, M. D., Resick, P. A., and Griffin, M. G. (1998). A comparison of normal forgetting, psychopathology, and information-processing models of reported amnesia for recent sexual trauma. *Journal of Consulting and Clinical Psychology*, **66**:948–957.

Medawar, C. and Rassaby, E. (1991). Triazolam overdose, alcohol, and manslaughter. *The Lancet*, **338**:1515–1516.

Meyerson, A. T. (1966). Amnesia for homicide ("pedicide"). Its treatment with hypnosis. *Archives of General Psychiatry*, **14**:509–515.

Nelson, H. (1976). A modified card sorting test sensitive to frontal lobe defects. *Cortex*, **12**:313–324.

Nelson, H. E. and Willison, J. R. (1994). *Restandardisation of the NART against the WAIS-R*. Windsor, UK: NFER Nelson.

O'Connell, B. A. (1960). Amnesia and homicide: A study of 50 murderers. *British Journal of Delinquency*, **10**:262–276.

Parwatiker, S. D., Holcomb, W. R., and Menninger, K. A. (1985). The detection of malingered amnesia in accused murderers. *Bulletin American Academy of Psychiatry and Law*, **13**:97–103.

Petursson, H. and Gudjonsson, G. H. (1981). Psychiatric aspects of homicide. *Acta Psychiatrica Scandinavica*, **64**:363–372.

Pope, E. and Shouldice, M. (2001). Drugs and sexual assault: A review. *Trauma, Violence, and Abuse*, **2**:51–55.

Porter, S., Birt, A. R., Yuille, J. C., and Herve, H. F. (2001). Memory for murder: A psychological perspective on dissociative amnesia in legal contexts. *International Journal of Law and Psychiatry*, **24**:23–42.

Power, D. J. (1977). Memory, identification and crime. *Medicine, Science and Law*, **17**:132–139.

Putnam, F. (1989). Pierre Janet and modern views of dissociation. *Journal of Traumatic Stress*, **2**:413–429.

Pyszora, N. (2006). *Amnesia for Criminal Offences in a Cohort of Life Sentence Prisoners.* Unpublished PhD thesis, University of London, UK.

Pyszora, N. M., Barker, A. F., and Kopelman, M. D. (2003). Amnesia for criminal offences: A study of life sentence prisoners. *Journal of Forensic Psychiatry and Psychology*, **14**:475–490.

Redeski, C. (1975). Medico-legal aspects of automatism. *Australian and New Zealand Journal of Psychiatry*, **9**:187–191.

Roesch, R. and Golding, S. (1986). Amnesia and competency to stand trial: A review of legal and clinical issues. *Behavioural Sciences and the Law*, **4**:87–97.

Rubinsky, E. and Brandt, J. (1986). Amnesia and criminal law: A clinical overview. *Behavioural Sciences and the Law*, **4**:27–46.

Schacter, D. L. (1986). Amnesia and crime: How much do we really know? *American Psychologist*, **41**:286–295.

Smith, J. and Hogan, B. (1996). *Criminal Law*, 8th Edition, pp. 38–40. Oxford: Oxford University Press.

Smith, S. (1965). The adolescent murderer: A psychodynamic interpretation. *Archives of General Psychiatry*, **13**:310–319.

Spiegal, D. and Cardena, E. (1991). Disintegrated experience: The dissociative disorders revisited. *Journal of Abnormal Psychology*, **100**:366–378.

Spreen, O. and Strauss, E. (1998). *A Compendium of Neuropsychological Tests.* Oxford: Oxford University Press.

Stein, A. (2001). Murder and memory. *Contemporary Psychoanalysis*, **37**:443–451

Swihart, G., Yuille, J., and Porter, S. (1999). The role of state-dependent memory in 'red-outs'. *International Journal of Law and Psychiatry*, **22**:199–212.

Tanay, E. (1969). Psychiatric Study of Homicide. *American Journal of Psychiatry*, **125**:1252–1258.

Taylor, P. J. and Kopelman, M. D. (1984). Amnesia for criminal offences. *Psychological Medicine*, **14**:581–588.

Tombaugh, T. N. (1996). *Test of Memory Malingering (TOMM).* Florida: Psychological Assessment Resources.

Van der Hart, O. and Horst, R. (1989). The dissociation theory of Pierre Janet. *Journal of Traumatic Stress*, **2**:397–413.

Van der Hart, O., Brown, P., and Graafland, M. (1999). Trauma-induced dissociative amnesia in World War I combat soldiers. *Australian and New Zealand Journal of Psychiatry*, **33**:37–46.

Van der Kolk, B. A. and Fisler, R. (1995). Dissociation and the fragmentary nature of traumatic memories: Overview and exploratory study. *Journal of Traumatic Stress*, **8**:505–525.

Warrington, E. K. (1984). *Recognition Memory Test.* Windsor, UK: NFER Nelson.

Warrington, E. K. (1996). *The Camden Memory Tests.* Hove, UK: Psychology Press.

Warrington, E. K. and James, M. (1991). *Visual Object and Space Perception Battery.* Bury St Edmunds, UK: Thames Valley Test Company.

Wechsler, D. (1999a). *Wechsler Adult Intelligence Scale—3rd UK Edition.* Oxford: Harcourt Assessment.

Wechsler, D. (1999b). *Wechsler Memory Scale—3rd UK Edition*. Oxford: Harcourt Assessment.

Wechsler, D. (2001). *Wechsler Test of Adult Reading*. Oxford: Harcourt Assessment.

Weinberger, D. A., Schwartz, G. E., and Davidson, R. J. (1979). Low-anxious, high-anxious, and repressive coping styles: Psychometric patterns and behavioural and physiological responses to stress. *Journal of Abnormal Psychology*, **88**:369–381.

Wiggins, E. C. and Brandt, J. (1988). The detection of simulated amnesia. *Law and Human Behaviour*, **12**:57–78.

Wilson, B. A., Alderman, N., Burgess, P. W., Emslie, H., and Evans, J. J. (1996). *Behavioural Assessment of the Dysexecutive Syndrome*. Bury St Edmunds, UK: Thames Valley Test Company.

Wolf, A. S. (1980). Homicide and blackout in Alaskan Natives: A report and reproduction of five cases. *Journal of Studies on Alcohol*, **41**:456–462.

Chapter 7

Epilepsy and automatism

Jonathan Bird, Margaret Newson, and Krystyna Dembny

This chapter will review clinical and forensic aspects of automatism from neuroscientific and legal perspectives. The clinical aspects will focus on epilepsy and sleepwalking, with some mention of dissociative states, after which a legal perspective referring to statute and key case law decisions will be taken. It will be seen that the clinical and legal attitudes to the often complex and vexatious issues of automatic behaviours and responsibility for actions can frequently prove difficult to reconcile.

Automatism is not an issue that arises in the civil courts and therefore this chapter will deal solely with criminal matters. Automatism is behaviour that lacks voluntariness. This statement embodies the fundamental differences between the medical and the legal approaches to human behaviour. The law requires certainty and dichotomy (guilty or innocent, voluntary or involuntary), whilst medicine generally recognizes the essential dimensionality and diversity of behaviour, personality, and biology. The concept of automatism raises profound questions of moral and legal responsibility, and challenges the ability of the neurosciences to provide worthwhile 'real life' answers to these problems.

A moral philosophy view is that guilty actions must be 'willed actions', actions that the actor takes himself to be doing. Automatism removes the individual's opportunity for choice, and therefore punishment should be preserved for those who make unlawful choices. Problems, however, arise in the presence of culpable internal motives if there is some evidence of awareness of surroundings, as is often the case, for instance, in somnambulistic automatism. Complete lack of consciousness and control rarely accompanies a potentially criminal act; hence, difficult judgements need to be made about the degree of loss of awareness and attention at the specific time.

Automatism is a complete defence to any criminal charge if it goes to the *actus reus* (guilty act), as well as to nearly all crimes (other than strict liability crimes) if it goes to the *mens rea* (guilty mind). In order to prove guilt, the prosecution must prove beyond reasonable doubt that both the *actus reus* and the *mens rea* were present at the material time. Automatism is of two types, insane and non-insane. Both types will be explored in this chapter. The different but related defence (in the UK) to a charge of murder, diminished responsibility (the 'special verdict') will also be discussed.

It is hoped that this chapter will provide an overview of the current state of the law (largely Anglo-American law) and of neuroscience in this area. It will also draw attention to the conflicts in approach that can result in confusion and frustration, and arrive at some helpful pointers for those attempting to operate across the borderlands to which a survey of automatism inevitably brings us.

In medical/psychological terms, automatism can arise as a result of the following underlying causes:

- epileptic seizures and their sequelae
- sleepwalking (somnambulism)
- psychological dissociation
- intoxication (alcohol, drugs)
- metabolic causes (e.g. low blood sugar)
- concussion and head injury
- psychoses.

The three main neuropsychiatric conditions that might allow of a defence of automatism are epilepsy, sleepwalking, and dissociative states. An outline of these conditions will be given before proceeding to the legal perspective.

The idea of an insane, or endogenous, automatism versus a non-insane, or exogenous, automatism illustrates how medical and legal notions of automatism differ. From a medical point of view, differentiating between an internal and external cause often makes little sense. For example, hypoglycaemia may occur due to a so-called internal event (e.g. due to a pancreatic tumour) or an external event (e.g. due to excess insulin via injection), and in both cases the clinical presentation is the same. However, in legal terms, the cause of hypoglycaemia has significant repercussions with regard to the defence that can be used in court. In the former case, the defence of insane automatism would be used, but in the latter case, the defence of sane automatism would be used (Fenwick, 1997).

If an offence is related to epileptic activity, the person's mental state is more akin to unconsciousness than insanity, and using the insanity plea in the case of epilepsy is, in medical terms, nonsensical (Fenwick, 1997).

There are a number of examples illustrating the controversy over the differentiation between sane and insane automatism. For example, if a person is sleepwalking, the sane automatism defence has been used in Canada, but the insane automatism defence was used in England (Beran, 2002; McSherry, 2002; Lowenstein, 2004). In the former case, the behaviour was considered to be secondary to external factors, but not in the latter cases. The debate with regard to sleepwalking has to do with medical opinion about whether sleepwalking has an internal or external cause. This discrepancy illustrates the potential difficulty in determining what are endogenous or exogenous factors affecting a person's behaviour (Beran, 2002). Stress can be considered endogenous or exogenous, depending on the circumstances (Beran, 2002). A sane automatism defence could be used in cases of extreme stress in a person with no previous mental illness (Beran, 1997), but in other cases, stress could be considered a state of mind and therefore an insane automatism defence should be used.

There may be cases in which the risk of an offending automatism can be foreseen, i.e. even though an offender was not in control of his or her behaviour, steps could perhaps have been taken to prevent the offence from occurring. For example, if someone has previously driven a car during an automatism, then car keys should be kept in a secure location. It is possible that the person could be found negligent if the automatism and offending behaviour could have been foreseen and prevented (van Rensburg *et al.*, 1994; Beran, 1997; Heinz-Dietrich, 1997). If, however, a person is fully aware that there is a risk of an automatism that is dangerous or could result in criminal behaviour, and does nothing to minimize that risk, the person could be held negligent if offending behaviour occurs. For example, if a person chooses to drive despite having epilepsy, then they are responsible for any criminal act (e.g. vehicular manslaughter) that might occur as a result of driving (Treiman, 1986).

The neuroscience perspective

Epilepsy, complex partial seizures, and automatisms

The term epilepsy refers to a heterogeneous group of neurological disorders in which seizures occur repeatedly. The term seizure (also called ictus) refers to an '*altered state of brain function*' (DeLorenzo & Towne, 1989) resulting from the abnormal synchronized discharges of group of neurons. The manifestation of a seizure involves sensory, experiential, or motor phenomena, either in isolation or in combination. The particular clinical manifestation of the seizure depends on the site of the focus in the cortex of the brain and on the location and extent of connected sites (Adams & Victor, 1993). A seizure is a symptom or sign of dysfunction in the grey matter of the brain rather than a disease in itself.

In medical terms, an 'epileptic automatism' is a state of clouding of consciousness, which occurs during or immediately after a seizure, during which the individual retains control of posture and muscle tone, but performs simple or complex movements without being aware of what is happening. The impairment of awareness varies. The behaviour itself is usually inappropriate to the circumstances and may be out of character for the individual. It can be complex, coordinated, and apparently purposeful and directed, although lacking in judgement. Afterwards, the individual may have no recollection, or only partial and confused memory, of his actions.

Determining whether a behaviour is truly an automatism is subject to interpretation. For example, how does one determine that a behaviour is involuntary, particularly if the behaviour in question can be carried out voluntarily? In addition, at what point does one differentiate between awareness and lack of awareness, or among consciousness, altered consciousness, and unconsciousness?

Classification and description of epileptic automatisms

Coining the term 'automatism' has been attributed to the nineteenth-century neurologist Hughlings-Jackson, as a way to ease communication about the range of automatic behaviours observed during complex partial seizures (Quesney, 1986). A typical epileptic automatism occurring during a complex partial seizure is usually simple, stereotyped, and repetitive (Bacon & Benedek, 1982). Complex, goal-directed activities are not typical, but can occur. The areas of brain most likely to give rise to epileptic automatisms are the temporal and frontal lobes. Automatisms can also occur during complex absence seizures (Beran, 2002), such as the ictal or interictal phases of petit mal status epilepticus (Bacon & Benedek, 1982). They are also thought to occur during the postictal 'twilight' phase of a complex partial or generalized tonic clonic seizure (Bacon & Benedek, 1982).

In a study by Knox (1968), reports of seizure semiology in 43 cases suggested that most automatisms (82%) last less than 5 minutes, with some (12%) lasting up to 15 minutes.

Aggression and violence during or following epileptic automatisms

Fenwick (1986, 1997) reviewed 'aggression and epilepsy' and cited a number of other studies in his review. When aggressive or violent behaviour arises during an epileptic automatism, it is typically disordered, uncoordinated, and non-directed, with altered or absent consciousness (Fenwick, 1997). There is evidence that seizures involving temporal lobe structures, including the hippocampus, amygdala, and hypothalamus, may be implicated in aggressive automatisms (Fenwick, 1990, 1997). Postictal aggression can occur, particularly if the person is confused and feels threatened by others trying to help or restrain him or her.

There are few published cases in which the relationship between aggressive behaviour and an ictal event has been clearly established (Treiman, 1991). After reviewing the evidence from 38 case studies, Treiman (1991, p. 354) concluded that *'there are no documented cases of ictal aggression in which an organized or directed attack toward another individual or object occurred as the initial or sole manifestation of an epileptic seizure and which could not otherwise be diagnosed on the basis of at least some concomitant typical features of complex partial or generalized tonic clonic seizures'*. Therefore, ictal automatisms are likely to be non-aggressive even if violent (i.e. non-directed). Given these observations, *'it is unlikely that organized and directed aggression, especially aggression involving complex acts, can truly be part of a complex partial seizure'* (Treiman, 1986, p. 599).

Directed aggression is more likely to occur as a reactive automatism with onset after a complex partial seizure or as resistive violence during a postictal confused state. Treiman (1986) suggested that 'resistive' aggression or violence might occur because some areas of the brain recover faster than others following a seizure. This notion leads to the conjecture that the prefrontal cortex may recover more slowly than the motor areas and limbic system, such that the patient is capable of producing a physical and emotional response to external stimuli, with a delay in the ability to moderate such responses. Treiman & Delgado-Escueta (1983) reviewed 29 cases, reported over 109 years, in which violence was alleged to have occurred as a result of epileptic activity. They concluded that there was strong evidence of a relationship between a seizure and a violent automatism in only three of these cases, each being in the context of postictal automatism.

Factors that can influence the manifestation of epileptic automatism

There are interictal, preictal, ictal, and postictal factors that can affect the particular manifestation of an automatism (van Rensburg et al., 1994). The interictal factors include personality characteristics. In theory, an individual's personality may predispose to certain behaviours during an epileptic automatism, and unconscious desires may come to the fore in the absence of conscious control of behaviour (reviewed by van Rensburg et al., 1994). Whilst there are individual cases that suggest this notion, there is little scientific evidence to support it.

There are also a number of cases in which the person's behaviour immediately preceding the onset of a seizure influenced the manifestation of an automatism (van Rensburg, *et al.*, 1994). Thus, some aspect of the preictal behaviour continued during the automatism, which resulted in a criminal act (e.g. holding a knife and slicing bread before the seizure, and then slicing a child's arm during an automatism). The ictal factors include seizure type and location of seizure focus. In particular, temporal lobe epilepsy is more commonly associated with ictal automatisms that include aggression, rage, paranoia, and fear (van Rensburg *et al.*, 1994). If control of higher cortical functions is lost, the resultant loss of control of emotions could lead to aggression and violence (Joubert *et al.*, 1997).

Postictal factors include confusion and misinterpreting the behaviour of others. Well-meaning attempts to assist a person following a seizure could be misinterpreted as threatening if the person is in a confused state (van Rensburg *et al.*, 1994). In the postictal state, there may be less control over emotions (Joubert *et al.*, 1997). On the other hand, in some cases postictal psychosis may underlie change in behaviour rather than a postictal automatism occurring in a confused state. The presence of hallucinations and/or delusions during the behaviour may help to differentiate between postictal psychosis and automatism (van Rensburg *et al.*, 1994).

Epileptic automatisms and criminal behaviour

At the end of the nineteenth century and beginning of the twentieth century, the view that epilepsy was correlated with violent behaviour was frequently promoted. This opinion was held into the second half of the twentieth century, as documented in textbooks of neurology and psychiatry (Rodin, 1973; Treiman, 1999). It appears that this view was based on clinical lore rather than scientific proof (Treiman, 1986) and it has been discredited in a number of studies from the late 1960s onwards.

Rodin (1982) reviewed early attitudes toward the relationship between epilepsy and aggression, and described a split between views from neurologists and psychiatrists. Historically, neurologists such as Hughlings-Jackson, Turner, and Gowers experienced very little evidence of a direct link between epilepsy and aggressive behaviour. In contrast, psychiatrists, such as Maudsley and Lombroso, often noted the relationship between mental disorder and epilepsy, particularly among the criminally insane (for a review of these historical matters, see Finger, 1994).

After reviewing the evidence of a link between epilepsy and criminal behaviour among inmates in prisons and mental hospitals, Rodin (1982, p. 195) concluded that *'while epileptic patients may intermittently show violent behaviour, a direct link between a murderous act and an epileptic attack is extremely uncommon, especially if accidental killing is expected*'. However, as Fenwick (1990) noted, the relative paucity of published cases of ictal aggression could reflect the difficulty in ascertaining whether an aggressive behaviour is truly ictal in origin, when the behaviour in question does not coincide with video-EEG monitoring.

Serious crime during the interictal, ictal, and postictal phases of an epileptic seizure is rare (Hindler, 1989; Hughes & Devinsky, 1994; Beran, 1997; Fenwick, 1997). For example, as of 1997, no cases of crime committed during a seizure have been reported in Germany (Heinz-Dietrich, 1997). Even so, such cases exist. Examples of automatisms that have been associated with criminal offending behaviour are driving offences, assault, theft, murder, and arson, but not rape (Joubert *et al.*, 1997). When a crime is committed during an epileptic automatism, it is more often committed by a man. Often minor offences (shoplifting) may be overlooked, so frequency may be underestimated (Fenwick, 1990).

Prevalence of aggression, violence, and criminal behaviour associated with epilepsy

The evidence does not support a direct relationship between epilepsy and violent crime (Gunn, 1977). Stated another way, epilepsy does not predispose one towards violent crime. In a review of the evidence of the prevalence of epilepsy among prisoners, Treiman (1986) concluded that, whilst there is a slightly increased prevalence of epilepsy among those who have been convicted of crime when compared with the general population, the prevalence rate of epilepsy is in keeping with expectations when compared with a sample with a socio-economic status typical of prisoners. Thus, there is no clear evidence to indicate that epilepsy is related to violence or criminal behaviour. Treiman concluded that there is evidence for increased violence among young men with low intelligence, other neurological deficits, and early onset or severe epilepsy. However, among samples in which individuals with these traits or with psychiatric disturbance were excluded, there was no increased prevalence of violent behaviour. Treiman also found no differences in violent behaviour or aggressive personality traits when comparing individuals with temporal lobe or generalized epilepsy. People with temporal lobe epilepsy were no more likely to commit violent crime than people with other types of epilepsy or people without epilepsy.

Studies investigating base rates of aggressive or violent behaviour—observation of patients (not convicts)

Knox (1968) examined the association between automatism and violence in a series of 434 patients with epilepsy: 43% had a history of automatism during their seizures and 49% were diagnosed with 'psychomotor' epilepsy. Six cases (1.4%) resisted restraint during an automatism, but none had exhibited violent behaviour. Only one case (0.2%) had a clear history of violent behaviour during automatism. Based on this study, Knox (1968, p.104) made the following conclusions:

1. Acts of violence are very unusual in epileptic automatism.
2. The abnormal activity tends to appear suddenly; there will be no evidence of planning or premeditation.
3. Automatic behaviour usually lasts for only a few minutes.
4. There will probably be no attempt to conceal the acts.
5. There will be no amnesia for events prior to loss of consciousness.
6. There does not need to be a history of automatism with previous epileptic fits.
7. Whilst an abnormal EEG may support a diagnosis of automatism due to epilepsy, a normal EEG does not exclude this.

Delgado-Escueta et al. (1982) documented the manifestations of complex partial seizures in 79 patients to examine the relationship between location of seizure focus and ictal behaviour. Seven patients (8.8%) fought restraint during automatism, three (3.7%) showed thrashing or flailing of arms, and three showed kicking or rolling movements.

Other research investigating the semiology of patients with temporal lobe epilepsy undergoing video-EEG monitoring suggests that aggressive or violent automatisms are quite rare in a controlled observation setting. Most studies do not report such automatisms (e.g. Maldonado et al., 1988; Gil-Nagel & Risinger, 1997; Williamson et al., 1998; Maillard et al., 2004; Carreno et al., 2005). Indeed, the lack of recent studies reporting data on violent or aggressive automatisms suggests a decline in interest in this area, perhaps due to the rarity of potential data.

In some studies, postictal confusion was observed (e.g. 25% of cases in Maillard et al., 2004), but again violence or aggression was not reported. However, some behaviour such as flailing or thrashing movements, karate postures, facial grimace, screaming, or even staring could be interpreted as aggressive in some circumstances, particularly by some individuals who are unfamiliar with the signs of a complex partial seizure. Thus, outside of the controlled hospital setting, environmental influences such as the reactions of other individuals could theoretically trigger behaviour that is interpreted as aggressive or violent.

Studies investigating base rates of aggressive or violent behaviour in people with epilepsy and a history of aggression

Ramani & Gumnit (1981) monitored the behaviour of 19 patients with refractory epilepsy and histories of aggressive behaviour over an average period of 6 weeks. None demonstrated ictal violence or aggression. Their observations indicated that interictal aggression is multifactorial in origin, not necessarily related to seizure activity.

In 1981 (Delgado-Escueta, 1981), 18 epileptologists reviewed the video telemetry of patients chosen from among approximately 5400 potential participants because they had been suspected of aggressive behaviour during seizures. Aggressive behaviour was documented in seven patients. Of these, six were mentally retarded and five had a history of mental disorder. The aggressive behaviour was spontaneous and non-directed; in four it occurred during a seizure, but in three it occurred at the end of a seizure, apparently in response to being restrained.

Studies investigating base rates of aggressive, violent, or criminal behaviour in convicted offenders with epilepsy

Gunn & Fenton (1971) surveyed all convicted offenders with epilepsy in England and Wales in 1967. They evaluated 158 prisoners with unequivocal epilepsy and considered 14 cases in which their offences could possibly be related to seizure activity. In one case, the offence appeared to be related to postictal confusion. There was no clear association between ictal automatic behaviour and offending behaviour. The authors also evaluated all 46 persons with epilepsy at Broadmoor Secure Hospital in 1966; of the 29 cases with adult epilepsy who had committed offences, three had a definite seizure within 12 hours of their criminal act. The surveys of Gunn & Fenton (1971) suggested that seizure activity is a rare explanation for offending behaviour and, if violence does occur, it is more likely to occur during a period of postictal confusion rather than during an ictal automatism.

A defence of epileptic automatism—practical advice

An expert clinician may be asked to form an opinion about whether an offence was committed during an epileptic automatism. There are a number of criteria sets for determining this. Fenwick (1990) has set out six points to assist in a decision as to whether a defence of epileptic automatism is a possibility:

1. The person should be known to have epilepsy. It is clearly unlikely that a crime will be committed during a first seizure.
2. The act should be out of character for the individual and inappropriate to the circumstances. Clearly, if the defendant is habitually aggressive and

commits a violent and aggressive crime, it is much more difficult to substantiate the diagnosis of epileptic automatism than if the act was committed by a normally mild mannered and tolerant person.

3. There must be no evidence of premeditation or concealment. An epileptic automatism must arise *de novo* from ongoing behaviour. If there is any suggestion that there was preplanning before the act, then it is not possible to substantiate a diagnosis of automatism. Concealment after an automatism is also unlikely.
4. If a witness is available, he or she should report a disorder of consciousness at the time of the act.
5. When an act occurs during an automatism or a postictal confusional state, a disorder of memory is the rule. It is unlikely that an epileptic automatism can occur in the setting of clear consciousness. Thus, memory for the act should be impaired. It is essential that there is no loss of memory antedating the event. During a seizure, loss of memory starts with the onset of the seizure and not before it. Thus, any loss of memory that antedates the episode suggests that it may not be an epileptic automatism.
6. The diagnosis of automatism is a clinical diagnosis. Although weight will clearly be given to abnormal investigations, such as a focal lesion on a CT scan, evidence of focal neuropsychological deficit, or of generalized or focal EEG epileptiform discharges, none of these make the diagnosis of epilepsy.

Treiman (1986, p. S102) concluded that *'even well documented epilepsy should not be considered in the defence of criminal aggression unless the aggressive episode indeed occurred during an unequivocal epileptic seizure'*. He did say that most cases of aggression *'have shown resistive violence while being restrained at the end of a seizure rather than directed aggression'*.

Sleepwalking (somnambulism) and automatism

Violent behaviours arising during sleep appear to occur in about 2% of the adult population (Hublin *et al.*, 1997). A predisposition to sleepwalking is based on genetic susceptibility, but priming factors, including conditions and substances that increase slow-wave sleep or that make arousal from sleep more difficult, may precipitate an episode of sleepwalking and, potentially, violence. Such conditions may include alcohol, certain medications, stress, and sleep deprivation (including that associated with shift working). Complex interactions between these various factors and the circumstances in which an individual behaves in a violent fashion ensure that cases of alleged automatism whilst sleepwalking will require careful assessment. Associated sleep disorders, such as sleep-disordered breathing and periodic leg movements, along with sudden noise or touch in an individual with a predisposition to partial arousals from slow-wave sleep may act as immediate triggers to an episode. Confusional arousals, usually resulting from forced awakening from slow-wave sleep, may be associated with significantly disturbed behaviour such that it may be referred to as 'sleep drunkenness'.

A diagnosis of sleepwalking and related disorders remains largely based on a clinical history along with witness accounts. Sleep laboratory studies, particularly polysomnography, tend to lack both sensitivity and specificity. They have a rather limited medico-legal role and form only part of the clinical assessment of an individual. Over-reliance on sleep laboratory findings should be avoided. Unless a sleepwalking episode is observed rising out of or as part of slow-wave sleep in the laboratory, sleep studies may be unhelpful, although some indicators of sleepwalking tendencies will include evident arousals from slow-wave sleep, hypersynchronous slow-wave activity and, possibly, an increase in the cyclical alternating pattern during sleep. If anything, these only indicate a possibly increased likelihood of sleepwalking in an individual; they cannot confirm or refute the contention that sleepwalking has resulted in some violent act (Pressman, 2007).

Whilst a family history of sleepwalking in a first-degree relative increases the chances of developing this disorder significantly, genetic testing lacks sensitivity and specificity and is unhelpful in the legal setting. Similarly, an increase in the quantity of slow-wave sleep during a recording, whilst associated with sleepwalking, again lacks specificity and sensitivity such that an individual with a normal percentage of slow-wave sleep may still sleepwalk. Frequent arousals during slow-wave sleep may be more of a diagnostic marker, but, again, there is significant variation in an individual, and frequent arousals may be associated with other sleep disorders including sleep apnoea and periodic leg movements. Sleep deprivation is often seen as a possible priming factor in sleepwalking; however, this does not seem to be particularly associated with frequent arousals from slow-wave sleep on polysomnographic recording.

Sleepwalking has often been believed to be associated with a wide variety of medications, according to a long tradition of single case histories. Almost all types of psychotropic medication and many other forms of medication are said to have been associated with sleepwalking. However, most of these case histories are unreliable, idiosyncratic, and complex. Many of the cases described do not give real evidence of definite sleepwalking in any event. Most occur in individuals with psychiatric disorder and under considerable personal stress. They often consist merely of nocturnal wandering rather than clear sleepwalking.

The use of alcohol prior to sleep has frequently been reported as being associated with sleepwalking; on the other hand, alcohol may actually reduce a tendency to sleepwalk in clinical situations rather than forensic situations. There is no scientific data as to how alcohol affects the sleep of known sleepwalkers or the frequency of sleepwalking. Intake of alcohol is often combined with multiple other factors, including medication, personality difficulties, stress, and psychiatric disorder. Whilst 'alcohol-induced sleepwalking' has been used as an automatism defence in many criminal cases, criminal behaviour associated merely with alcohol ingestion is obviously very much more common and is usually a much more likely explanation. So-called 'alcohol provocation studies' to induce sleepwalking lack any basis in accepted practice or science. They result in a drunken individual who may behave in a disturbed fashion, but this is not proof that an individual has a tendency to sleepwalk.

Specific cases in which sleepwalking has been used to support an automatism defence will be discussed later, in particular the landmark Canadian case, *R v Parks* [1992] 2 SCCR 871; 95 DLR (4th) 27, in which the defendant drove his car some 23 km along a busy road, negotiating six turns and eight sets of traffic lights prior to attempting to strangle his father-in-law before knifing both his father-in-law and mother-in-law. In this case, Parks claimed that the attacks took place whilst he was asleep and were therefore somnambulistic acts for which he was not responsible. The court accepted that this was a case of somnambulism, which was found not to be categorized as a mental illness or disease of the mind, even though he experienced a disorder of sleep, but that it was not this that caused the impairment of his relevant faculties. There was, therefore, it was judged, no question of insanity. Of importance, there was no evidence of a regular previous pattern of violence during sleep, in which case it would have been possible to label the condition as a mental disorder and resort to insane automatism as a defence.

A very different view was taken in the English Court of Appeal in the case of *R v Burgess* [1991] 2 WLR 1206, again discussed later. In this case, the condition was regarded as having internal status, it manifested in violence, and it was felt likely to recur. It was, therefore, believed to result from a disease of the mind and it was believed that sleep was a normal condition but that sleepwalking, particularly with violence, was abnormal. In the case of Parks, sleepwalking was regarded as a normal function, whereas in Burgess it was regarded as an abnormality of brain functioning. Much depended upon the nature of the medical evidence in court.

These two cases point to the complexities seen in many sleepwalking cases. However, the first and most important factor must be to decide whether sleepwalking was, in fact, the cause for some criminal act. Good evidence for this is often lacking. Guidelines have been proposed in order to determine the possible role of a sleep disorder in a specific violent act. However, there is little scientific validity for a number of these items. Nevertheless, the general guidelines are as follows:

1. There should be good reason to suspect a sleep disorder (on the basis of personal history, family history, and investigations).
2. The violent action is typically brief, lasting perhaps just seconds or minutes.
3. The violent behaviour may seem senseless and lacking in motivation.
4. The victim of the violent behaviour is usually somebody who merely happens to be present, although recognizing that this may often be a family member.
5. After the violent act, the individual should appear perplexed and horrified and should not attempt to cover up the act.
6. There should be partial or complete amnesia of the events.
7. In the case of sleepwalking and confusional arousals, these should occur in the first third of the night, typically 1 or 2 hours after sleep onset.
8. In the case of sleepwalking, they may be precipitated by attempts to awaken the subject.
9. Typically, they may be associated with alcohol, sedatives, or sleep deprivation.

For a challenging review of these factors, see Pressman (2007).

The relatively recently recognized disorder of 'REM sleep behaviour disorder' or RBD (Schenck *et al.*, 1986; Schenck & Mahowald, 2002) is a different sleep disorder, tending to occur in older individuals, usually male. It may be associated with the development of Parkinson's disease or other brain disorders. Typically, the individual shows disturbed behaviour, often hitting out and shouting as if acting on dreams. The individual usually remains in bed and therefore violence may be directed towards a bed partner but very rarely towards anybody else. Violence under these circumstances is usually obviously due to what is readily accepted as a medical condition and it very rarely results in severe wounding so that criminal cases associated with this condition are rare.

Dissociative states

The term 'dissociative disorders' may be one of the least satisfactory of the diagnoses that result in a possible defence of automatism. The essential feature of dissociative disorders is said to be '*a disruption in the usually integrated functions of consciousness, memory, identity or perception*' (DSM-IV; American

Psychiatric Association, 1994). Thus, there may be dissociative amnesia, characterized by the inability to recall important personal information, dissociative fugue characterized by sudden unexpected travel away from one's customary place, dissociative identity disorder (multiple personality disorder), and other feelings of dissociation or depersonalization. There is significant overlap with somatoform disorders and conversion disorder. The experience of dissociation may, indeed, not be abnormal at all and may well be an accepted expression of religious experience or a normal defence mechanism in response to stress. An individual in a state of dissociation is not regarded as unconscious as they are aware of and responsive to their surroundings. Dissociative fugue states and sleepwalking contain significant overlaps and, indeed, in the case of Burgess above it was proposed by one of the medical experts (Fenwick in *R v Burgess* [1991]) that this was actually a dissociative state rather than sleepwalking. Dissociative disorders, however, are more commonly associated with personality disorders and psychiatric illness. Dissociative disorders of this kind can occur under any circumstances and not particularly in sleep. In general, the courts have not been willing to accept dissociative conditions as a defence, especially for non-insane automatism. However, the Australian case of *R v Falconer* (1990) 65 Aus LJR 20 held that there was a dissociative state as a result of severe psychological trauma, which would have caused a 'sound mind' to malfunction transiently. This did produce the effect required for a defence of insanity, but as this could happen to an ordinary human individual and was external, a defence of sane automatism could be allowed. However, a proviso here was that the condition was one that should not be likely to recur. This is an example of the pragmatism of the law, which may decide things on principal but only to a certain extent.

The legal perspective

Lawton LJ in *R v Quick* [1973] QB 910 referring to the 'defence' of automatism said it is a *'quagmire of law seldom entered nowadays save by those in desperate need of some kind of defence'*.

The defence comes in two guises; non-insane and insane automatism. The latter is best referred to as a 'defence of insanity'. Both rely on the premise that liability pertains to prohibited conduct where that conduct is carried out 'voluntarily'. Conduct may not be 'voluntary' if carried out under duress or in self-defence. These defences are 'mitigatory' in that the essential elements of the criminal act are admitted to but that there is an 'excuse' for these actions.

In the cases of automatism and insanity 'defences', the issue goes to one of the core elements that makes up the crime. The result is that, if successfully pleaded, the verdict is that there is no criminal act although the act may have caused a prohibited result such as 'the death of another'. These defences come under the group called 'exemptions', which have been extracted from the group of defences termed 'excuses'.

Both automatism and insanity attract a great deal of academic commentary, yet in practical terms they engage little of the courts' time. Statistical evidence from 1991 shows that there were 60 findings of diminished responsibility and only two of insanity.

The Fitness to Plead and Insanity Act 1991

The Fitness to Plead and Insanity Act 1991 changed the law so that a person convicted of insane automatism could be sentenced to a range of disposals, from freedom to indefinite detention. The sentence could be determined to fit the nature of the crime and the condition of the person (Fenwick, 1997; Beran, 2002). Therefore, in current practice, it is at the sentencing phase of a trial that medical evidence may be most useful in influencing the outcome.

Research comparing the 5 years prior to the Act and 5 years after it revealed a doubling of successful insanity pleas from 20 to 44, mostly involving offences of serious but non-fatal violence.

Use of the automatism defence over the past 50 years

Fenwick (1988, 1990) has provided a review of case law as it pertains to the use of automatism as a defence. A brief review of these cases illustrates changes in interpretation of the law over time, and contradictions that result when applying the non-sane dichotomy (see also Wasik, 1990).

Case Study

In the case of *R v Charlson* in 1955, the defence used was sane automatism. Mr Charlson, who had a cerebral tumour, hit his son on the head with a hammer and threw him out of a window into a river. The judge found that he was not in control of his actions and *'in the same position as a person in an epileptic fit'* (*R v Charlson* [1955] WLR 317, cited in Fenwick, 1990, p. 6). As a result, Mr Charlson was not responsible for his crime and he was acquitted (see also McSherry, 2002).

However, in 1957 this conclusion was contradicted in the case of *R v Kemp* [1957] 1 QB 399 (Hindler, 1989; Fenwick, 1997). Mr Kemp suffered from arteriosclerosis, which was believed to have caused a lapse in consciousness during which he assaulted his wife. Since his mind was affected by his medical condition, he was judged to be suffering from a disease of the mind when he committed the crime. Therefore, the McNaughton rules were applied. As a result, only the defence of insane automatism was allowed.

The interpretation that only an insane automatism defence could be used in the case of a disease of the mind was upheld in the subsequent murder case of *Bratty v Attorney General for Northern Ireland* [1963] AC 411. There was evidence that he may have had epilepsy and committed the murder during an automatism. Initially, a plea of automatism was not allowed, due to lack of evidence, and Bratty was convicted of murder. The appeal was heard in the House of Lords, and in his response Lord Denning stated the following (cited in Wasik, 1990, p. 257): '*It seems to me that any mental disorder which has manifested itself in violence and is prone to recur is a disease of the mind. At any rate it is the sort of disease for which a person should be detained in hospital rather than be given an unqualified acquittal.*'

The *Bratty v AG* [1963] ruling cemented the notion that an epileptic seizure should be considered a disease of the mind and, therefore, only insane automatism could be used as a defence for a crime that was committed during an epileptic automatism (Fenwick, 1997). This conclusion was further tested in the case of *R v Sullivan* [1983] 3 WLR 123.

Sullivan was known to have epilepsy and during a complex partial seizure he assaulted his neighbour (Fenwick, 1985, 1990, 1997). He was not able to use the defence of sane automatism, due to the precedent set in *Bratty v AG* [1963]. At that time, if Sullivan had used the plea of 'insane automatism' successfully, he would have seen sent to a special hospital for an unknown period. Therefore, his lawyers persuaded him to plead guilty, even though he did not remember the offence and he had no control over it (Fenwick, 1997). The verdict was later appealed and it was rejected. This confirmed the notion that epilepsy is considered to be a disease of the mind for the purposes of the legal system and, therefore, only the defence of insane automatism can be used.

The law

Liability for offending conduct depends on the forbidden act being carried out with the requisite blameworthy mind in circumstances where there is no defence. This statement has three basic elements:

1. The *actus reus*, literally meaning the 'guilty act', which the law prohibits; murder, rape, burglary, fraud, etc.
2. The *mens rea*, the 'guilty mind', which encompasses specific and basic intention, recklessness, and, in some circumscribed instances, gross negligence. The *mens rea* accords with the definition of a specific crime. For murder, this is the intention to kill or an intention to cause grievous bodily harm, the latter going beyond the outcome itself. The *mens rea* for theft is twofold: dishonesty and intention to permanently deprive (see s.1(1) of the Theft Act 1968). In the case of wounding and causing grievous bodily harm with intent, the offence must be committed 'maliciously' and with 'intent' (s.18 of the Offences against the Person Act 1861).
3. Defences come under two headings, 'general' and 'specific'. 'General' implies that the defence is available to all crimes, an example being self-defence.

However, there are exceptions. Duress is not available for murder, and intoxication only applies to crimes of 'specific intent', which include murder, s.18 of the Offences Against the Persons Act 1861, theft, and 'attempts' (for example, attempted burglary, attempted fraud). General defences have been classified into (i) justifications, (ii) excuses, and (iii) exemptions. Specific defences apply to a particular crime. For murder, there are specific partial defences of provocation or diminished responsibility, which, if successfully pleaded, reduce the charge to manslaughter.

Actus reus

The *actus reus* of most crimes is composed of two or more of the following components: an act or omission to act, occurring in defined surrounding circumstances, and causing a requisite prohibited consequence. One of the fundamental requirements for liability to arise is that the *actus reus*, or the act, must be performed voluntarily. It is, therefore, an implicit requirement that a defendant's muscular movements, which constitute the 'conduct', are under the control of the defendant's conscious mind. If they are not, then the defendant is taken not to have performed the act and hence there is no *actus reus*. The expression that is used to denote involuntary conduct is 'automatism'. The courts have given examples of what constitute actions that have not been willed, e.g. a driver attacked by a swarm of bees or a reflex action or convulsion. Automatism in this sense has been kept very narrow, as it is difficult to substantiate. Furthermore, if the defendant is at fault for getting himself or herself into the situation, he or she will probably not escape liability.

Mens rea

The link between responsibility and criminal liability is the hallmark of a free society (Clarkson & Keating, 2003). Therefore, blame and censure is only appropriate if the offender was morally responsible for his or her behaviour. If the offender is a child, or is insane, they lack the capacity to appreciate some aspect of 'wrongness' in their actions. Hence, a mentally disordered individual who does harm is exonerated from blame and therefore punishment (although that individual may be restrained in order to protect society from recurrence).

Mens rea is not a 'single' state of mind. It is related solely to the particular harmful act. Liability for a particular prohibited act may require specific intent, or basic intent or recklessness. There are two levels of culpability: that of recklessness or negligence and that of intention. Thus, the charge of manslaughter generally carries a lesser sentence than that for murder.

General defences

The rationale for these defences is that they absolve the actor of the prohibited harm of 'blameworthiness'. Initially, defences were broadly classified into those that justified the defendant's conduct and those that excused it. Paul Robinson (1982, p. 213) wrote:

> Conduct is correct behaviour, which is encouraged or at least tolerated. An excuse represents a legal conclusion that the conduct is wrong, undesirable, but that the criminal liability is appropriate because some characteristic of the actor vitiates society's desire to punish him. Justification is seen in such defences as: self defence, public authority, discipline and consent. Excuses encompass: mistake, provocation, intoxication and duress. Exemptions emerged out of excuses. Defences operating in this field include: insanity, diminished responsibility, automatism and lack of age.

Specific defences

Diminished responsibility

Automatism and insanity defences will be examined in detail; however, any discussion of the insanity defence cannot be isolated from the defence of diminished responsibility. It is useful to juxtapose these two defences.

The defence of diminished responsibility was introduced by the Homicide Act 1957, at a time when the death penalty existed for murder. The intention behind the Act was to provide a 'partial defence' for those mentally disordered offenders who fell outside the narrow legal definition of insanity. The defence is restricted to reducing murder to manslaughter, but the prosecution must still establish the *mens rea* for murder; therefore, the defence acts only as a mitigating factor. Section 2 of the Homicide Act 1957 reads:

> Where a person kills or is party to a killing of another he shall not be convicted of murder if he was suffering from such an abnormality of mind (whether arising from a condition of arrested development of mind or any inherent causes or induced by disease or injury) as substantially impaired his mental responsibility for his acts and omissions in doing or being party to the killing.

It is worth examining at this point the wording of this section, particularly the judicial interpretation of the phrase 'abnormality of mind'. It forms a useful contrast with the judicial approach in respect of the term 'disease of mind', which forms part of the McNaughton definition of legal insanity (McNaughton (1843)10 Cl and F200 HL*Eng. Rep. 718).

Lord Parker in *Byrne* [1960] 2 QB 396 defined 'abnormality of mind' as '*a state of mind so different from that of ordinary human beings that the reasonable man would term it abnormal*'.

The burden of proof is on the accused to establish the defence on the balance of probability (see s.2(2) of the Homicide Act 1957). Exceptionally, the judge may raise the issue, but never the prosecution. This contrasts with insanity, where the prosecution may prove insanity (on the balance of probability) provided that the defendant has adduced some evidence with respect to his or her mental state by, for example, pleading non-insane automatism or diminished responsibility.

Insanity (insane automatism)

Clarkson & Keating (2003) wrote, *'The defence of insanity ... has been the source of more debate and heart searching than almost any other area of criminal law'*, even though there are only about nine finds of insanity per year in England and Wales.

There are moral considerations regarding the punishment of individuals who at the time of committing a wrongdoing are not responsible for their actions because of some illness that affects their ability to reason or control their movements. *'The criminal law exists to punish those who would choose to do wrong. If they cannot exercise choice, they cannot be deterred and it is a moral outrage to punish them'* (Morris, 1982, pp. 31–32).

The common law proceeds on the assumption that individuals are rational and autonomous human beings who are responsible for their actions. If they step outside the limits of legal action, they are justifiably blamed and punished. If, on the other hand, they are suffering from a serious mental disorder that removes their rationality and autonomy, they cannot be held responsible for the wrongful acts they perform and punitive sanctions are inappropriate.

The defence of insanity has a long history and has been available since the 1800s. It is a defence open to all crimes but it was rarely used as the only available response to a successful plea was for the judge to order the defendant to be detained in a mental institute until such time as the medical establishment considered the individual to be no longer a danger to the public. This detention could be indefinite and long. It was therefore rarely pleaded unless the crime was murder, where, before the abolition of capital punishment, the sanction was death by hanging.

If a defendant raises the defence of automatism (non-insane), it is open to the prosecution to contend that it was a 'disease of the mind' that prevented the defendant's conscious mind from being in control of his muscular movements and therefore the defendant was legally insane at the 'relevant time'. This also applies to diminished responsibility. If the defendant raises this defence, the prosecution can contend that the defendant was in fact insane.

The definition of legal insanity was set out by Lord Tindal CJ in McNaughton's (1843) case:

> To establish a defence on the grounds of insanity, it must be clearly proved that, at the time of the committing of the act, the party accused was labouring under such a defect

of reason, from a disease of the mind, as not to know the nature and quality of the act he was doing; or, if he did know it, that he did not know he was doing what was wrong.

There are two parts to this definition:

1. The defendant must know '*the nature and quality of the act*'. An example given is that by Kenny (2003, p. 76): '*The madman who cuts a woman's throat under the idea that he is cutting a piece of bread*' does not know the nature and quality of his acts. This has been extended to include states of 'unconsciousness' or 'unawareness' as may exist in cases of sleepwalking, epilepsy, hyperglycaemia, arteriosclerosis, etc. In this case, there is no *mens rea* (*R v Antoine* [2000] 2 All ER 208).

2. Alternatively it must be shown that, although the defendant knew what he was doing and therefore had the *mens rea* for the *actus reus*, he did not know that his acts were wrong. This aspect of McNaughton's insanity definition excludes from its ambit many of those individuals who would qualify for sectioning under the Mental Health Acts, such as people with severe and untreated schizophrenia and other psychoses, as well as psychopaths.

In contrast, the other component of the McNaughton definition, namely '*defect of reason, from a disease of the mind*' appears to 'broaden' the scope of 'insanity' to include those who, by medical definition, are clearly not mad. It is not enough that the defendant should not know the nature and quality of his or her acts or that they are wrong. This has to be due to a 'disease of the mind'. '*Mind*', said Devlin, '*is used in the ordinary sense of the mental faculties of reason, memory and understanding*' (*R v Kemp* [1957]).

This 'suspension' of reason, memory, and understanding is common to both insane and non-insane automatism and has been recognized in *R v Kemp* [1957] and in *R v Sullivan* [1983]. In the latter case, Lord Diplock, agreeing with Devlin (in *R v Kemp* [1957]), stated:

> I do not regard that learned judge as excluding the possibility of non-insane automatism (for which the proper verdict would be a verdict of 'not guilty') in cases where temporary impairment (not being self induced by consuming drink or drugs) results from some external factor such as a blow to the head causing concussion or the administration of an anaesthetic, for therapeutic purposes.

It is clear from this statement that, for a non-insane automatism defence to succeed, it must be shown that:

- the impairment or suspension of 'reason, memory and understanding' is temporary
- it is due to external factors, not an inherent defect within the brain or body

- it is not self-induced as in the case of failing to eat after taking insulin and exacerbating the situation by the consumption of alcohol, knowing it may bring on a hypoglycaemic event
- it is something 'out of the ordinary' and 'unpredictable'.

When a 'disease', i.e. something internal to the body, impairs the functioning of the 'mind', *'it matters not whether the aetiology of the impairment is organic, as in epilepsy, or functional, or whether the impairment itself is permanent or is transient and intermittent provided that it subsisted at the time of commissioning of the act'* (Lord Diplock writing in *R v Sullivan* [1983]).

In *Bratty v AG* [1963], Lord Denning defined 'disease of the mind' as *'any mental disorder, which has manifest itself in violence and is likely to recur'*. In *R v Sullivan* [1984] AC 156, the requirement of 'recurrence' was abandoned from the definition. Instead, Lord Diplock was of the opinion that it should only be relevant at the point of deciding how best to deal with the defendant once the 'special verdict' was in.

This would accord with the 1991 Act, which now places discretion on the judge as to how the defendant is to be 'managed'. In exercising this discretion, the judge would look at applicable factors such as the danger to the public with respect to the level of violence, the potential for recurrence, the ability to treat the condition, and so forth.

In this case, Mr Sullivan was charged with inflicting grievous bodily harm, contrary to s.20 of the Offences Against the Person Act 1861, after he attacked a friend during the postictal stage of an epileptic seizure. When the trial judge ruled that the defendant's actions during the postictal phase amounted to insanity, the defendant pleaded guilty to the lesser offence of assault occasioning actual bodily harm. He then appealed; the appeal was dismissed.

This case, as well as that of *R v Burgess* [1991] and the earlier case of *R v Quick* [1973] has added to the narrowing of the 'non-insane automatism' defence and the increase in the ambit of the 'insanity' plea. The cases have all stressed the requirement that some 'external factor' operates in automatism. The various examples include a swarm of bees, a malevolent passenger, and prescribed drugs correctly taken (*R v Hardie* [1984] 3 All ER 848, CA).

In *R v Burgess* [1991], D attacked his girlfriend with a bottle and then a tape recorder, finally putting his hand round her throat. He claimed that he was sleepwalking at the time and was therefore unconscious. Sleepwalking was taken to be an internal disorder and therefore a 'disease of the mind'. The fact that violent recurrence was very unlikely and that it was 'transient' did not exclude it from the ambit of legal insanity.

The internal/external distinction is problematic as can be demonstrated by two cases, those of *R v Quick* [1973] and *R v Hennessy* [1989] 1 WLR 287, CA.

In the former, the defendant, having taken insulin, failed to have anything to eat and he drank alcohol. He then became violent with a patient under his care, occasioning grievous bodily harm. The defendant, supported by medical evidence, contended that he was in a hypoglycaemic state. The trial judge ruled that the evidence could only support a defence of insanity. The defendant appealed but lost.

In *R v Hennessy* [1989], the police found a car that had been stolen. They kept it under watch and saw the defendant get into the car, but before he could drive off the police arrested him. The defendant was taken to hospital where he appeared confused. He had failed to take his insulin with the result that he had became hypoglycaemic. In evidence, the defendant stated that he was suffering from stress, anxiety, and depression at the time, which the medical evidence suggested could increase blood sugar levels. Paraphrasing Lawton in *R v Quick* [1973], Lord Lane said, '*Hyperglycaemia, high blood sugar, caused by an inherent defect and not corrected by insulin is a disease and if, as the defendant was asserting here, it does cause a malfunction of the mind, the case may fall within the McNaughton rules.*'

Two points need to be made about these cases:

1. The external cause must be external. In *R v Hennessy* [1989], Lane said '*In our judgment, stress, anxiety and depression can no doubt be the result of the operation of external factors, but they are not it seems, in themselves separately or together external factors of the kind capable in law of causing or contributing to a state of automatism.*'

2. The automatism must not be self-induced. Therefore, if the defendant takes a drug, other than prescribed (*R v Lippman* [1970] 1 QB 152, CA), fails to eat food after taking insulin for his diabetes, or takes alcohol against advice whilst on medication (*R v Ante and Bailey* [1983] 1 WLR 760), his automatism is self-induced. In the case of crimes of specific intent such as murder or s.18 assault, there is a partial defence reducing the offence to a lesser crime, i.e. manslaughter and s.20 assault. However, the defendant is guilty of basic intent crimes despite the fact that he did not have the requisite *mens rea* if the automatism is brought about by alcohol or non-prescribed drugs. The theory behind this is that it is general knowledge that such substances can give rise to automatic states, resulting in unpredictable and aggressive behaviour. By taking these substances, the defendant is acting recklessly, which is sufficient *mens rea* for crimes of basic intent.

   If the automatism is due to the taking of a non-dangerous drug or to some other cause such as a diabetic's failure to eat after taking insulin, the defendant will not be convicted of a basic intent crime unless the prosecution can prove the necessary element of subjective recklessness occurred before the onset of the automatism. The defendant's knowledge and hence risk-taking will have to be shown.

The other subcategory, which is a contentious one, is where the defendant claims unconsciousness or partial consciousness during the performance of the wrongful act. How does one prove that the defendant was in fact sleepwalking, or having a fit, or in a hypoglycaemic state? It is only the defendant's word. In *Bratty v AG* [1963], there was tenuous evidence of psychomotor epilepsy; therefore, the defendant's contention that he was in this state could be rejected. Other cases are not so clear, especially where there is a known medical history of, for example, diabetes or epilepsy.

Thus, the 'automatism/insanity' dichotomy is based on pragmatism. How best to do justice to the actor, the victim, and the public? The 'rules' established through legislation and case law attempt to meet the evidential challenge.

World-wide recent and possible legal reforms

There is much made of the label pertaining to the verdict 'not guilty by reason of insanity'. It may be that by changing the label much of the controversy will be removed. In 1975, the Butler Report gave a number of recommendations to change the law in order to update the insanity defence (Mawson, 1990). One of these recommendations was to rename the defence '*not guilty on evidence of mental illness*', and another was '*to give the judge discretion as to disposal*' (Mawson, 1990). Prior to 1991, a successful insane automatism defence always led to a sentence such as indefinite detention in a special hospital.

The reforms set out in the Draft Criminal Code Bill provide for a defence of automatism, which would apply to all offences, including strict liability offences (Law Com. No. 177, clause 33). It would apply where:

- the defendant is conscious but his act is a 'reflex, spasm or convulsion' *and*
- the defendant is '*in a condition (whether of sleep, unconsciousness, impaired consciousness or otherwise) depriving him of effective control of the act*'.

However, clause 33(1)(b) removes this defence where:

- the act or condition is due to voluntary intoxification *or*
- something is 'done or omitted with the fault required for the offence'.

Therefore, if, in a crime of recklessness or negligence, the defendant exhibits recklessness or negligence in getting himself into the automatous state, he will be guilty. This is an exception to the rule that the *mens rea* must be linked to the *actus reus*. Clause 36 provides that if the automatism is attributable to a 'mental disorder', the verdict must be '*not guilty on evidence of mental disorder*' (Keating, 2003, p. 163). It would appear that little would change for the epileptic or hypoglycaemic defendant, although the sleepwalker would be protected if the sleepwalking was not due to an underlying condition and would be unlikely to recur.

In the USA, the concept of an 'unconsciousness defence' has gained credence in some jurisdictions (Treiman, 1986). This is similar to the doctrine of *mens rea*, as the defence is based on the fact that the alleged offender was unaware of the act, and unable to control it, at the time it was committed.

In Canada, it has been proposed to use the defence 'not criminally responsible on account of mental disorder' instead of the defence of insane automatism (Joubert *et al.*, 1997; McSherry, 2002). The benefits of this approach include removing the dubious distinction between an external and an internal cause of the automatism (McSherry, 2002).

In Australia, McSherry (2002, p. 1) suggested a specific new defence to cover automatism: '*A person is not criminally responsible for an offence if he or she was suffering from cognitive dysfunction at the time of the commission of the offence such that his or her ability to reason was substantially impaired.*'

In non-common-law countries, other pleas are available to persons who commit crimes during an automatism. There is no concept of sane versus insane automatism as the McNaughton rules do not apply. For example, in Norway the plea 'not guilty by virtue of automatism' exists (Falk-Pedersen 1997). Also, an act cannot be punished if the person is unconscious when it is carried out, and automatisms are considered to be due to 'relative unconsciousness' (Falk-Pedersen, 1997).

Using an automatism defence to gain an acquittal could deny people access to treatment that they would otherwise get if they were found guilty. It could also place members of the public in danger if the criminal behaviour might occur again. This should be taken into consideration when considering changes to current law.

A 'last' word from Cross (1962):

> Although they are still comparatively rare, pleas of non insane automatism are becoming increasingly frequent and questions may be legitimately raised concerning the sufficiency of the courts' powers. Is it right that someone who has been acquitted on the grounds of non insane automatism should inevitably go free?

Forty-five years later and the 'problems' remain unresolved.

Conclusions

Clinicians and lawyers think differently. It is to be hoped that this chapter, with perspectives taken from both angles, may inform both professions in their understanding of automatisms. However, whilst the clinician will have views based on neuroscience and experience, he or she must remember that in court, the law is in charge. It behoves any clinician venturing into the courtroom to remember that and to be informed of the legal methods of analysis, always entirely logical and well argued, but sometimes requiring a degree of shoe-horning and selective vision that is unfamiliar and sometimes unwelcome to a scientist or physician. The law must make a decision; clinicians can often leave questions unanswered. However, the law is decided upon and imposed by mankind and can be changed, whereas the underpinnings of science and illness are part of a natural order and cannot.

References

Adams, R. D. and Victor, M. (1993). *Principles of neurology*, 5th edn. New York: McGraw Hill.

American Psychiatric Association (1994). *Diagnostic and Statistical Manual of Mental Disorders*, 4th edn. Washington, DC: American Psychiatric Association.

Bacon, P. D. and Benedek, E. P. (1982) Epileptic psychosis and insanity: Case study and review. *Bulletin of the American Academy of Psychiatry and the Law*, **10**:203–210

Beran, R. G. (1997). Epilepsy should not be an accepted defense in criminal proceedings. *Medicine and Law*, **405**:1–6

Beran, R. G. (2002). Automatism: Comparison of common law and civil law approaches—a search for the optimal. *Journal of Law and Medicine*, **10**:61–68

Carreno, M., Donaire, A., Perez Jimenez, M. A., et al. (2005). Complex motor behaviors in temporal lobe epilepsy. *Neurology*, **65**:1805–1807.

Clarkson, C. M.V. and Keating, H. M. (2003) *Criminal Law*, 5th edn. London: Sweet & Maxwell.

Cross, R. (1962). Reflections on the Bratty Case. 78 LQR 236, 238–239.

Delgado-Escueta, A. V. (1981). The nature of aggression during epileptic seizures. *New England Journal of Medicine*, **305**:711–716

Delgado-Escueta, A. V., Bacsal, F. E., and Treiman, D. M. (1982). Complex partial seizures on closed-circuit television and EEG: A study of 691 attacks in 79 patients. *Annals of Neurology*, **11**:292–300.

DeLorenzo, R. J. and Towne, A. R. (1989). Epilepsy. In: S. H. Appel (ed.), *Current Neurology*, pp. 27–76. Chicago: Mosby Year Book.

Falk-Pedersen, J. K. (1997). Automatisms in non common law countries. *Medicine and Law*, **16**:359–365.

Fenwick, P. (1985). Introduction—Regina v Sullivan: The trial and the judgment. In: P. Fenwick and E. Fenwick (eds), *Epilepsy and the Law—A Medical Symposium on the Current Law*. Royal Society of Medicine International Congress & Symposium Series No. 81, pp. 3–8. London: Royal Society of Medicine.

Fenwick, P. (1986). Aggression and epilepsy. In: M. R. Trimble and T. G. Bolwig (eds), *Aspects of Epilepsy and Psychiatry*, pp. 31–60. Chichester: John Wiley & Sons.

Fenwick, P. (1988). Epilepsy and the law. In: T. A. Pedley and B. S. Meldrum (eds), *Recent Advances in Epilepsy*, No. 4, pp. 241–51. Edinburgh: Churchill Livingstone.

Fenwick, P. B. (1990). Automatism, medicine and the law. *Psychological Medicine. Monograph Supplement*, **14**:1–27.

Fenwick, P. B. (1997). Epilepsy, automatism and English law. *Medicine and Law*, **349**:1–6.

Finger, S. (1994). *Origins of Neuroscience*. Oxford: Oxford University Press.

Gil-Nagel, R. and Risinger, M. W. (1997). Ictal semiology in hippocampal versus extra-hippocampal temporal lobe epilepsy. *Brain*, **120**:183–192.

Gunn, J. (1977). *Epileptics in Prison*. London: Academic Press.

Gunn, J. and Fenton, G. (1971). Epilepsy, automatism and crime. *Lancet*, **7710**:1173–1176.

Heinz-Dietrich, B. (1997). Epilepsy, its place as a legal defence. *Medicine and Law*, **413**:1–4.

Hindler, C. G. (1989). Epilepsy and violence. *British Journal of Psychiatry*, **155**:246–249.

Hublin, C., Kaprio, J., and Partinen, M. (1997). Prevalence and genetics of sleepwalking. *Neurology*, **48**:177–181.

Hughes, J. T. and Devinsky, O. (1994). Legal aspects of epilepsy. *Neurologic Clinics*, **12**:203–223.

Joubert, A. F., Verschoor, T., Rensburg, P. (1997). Epilepsy and the law. *Medicine and Law*, **769**:1–4.

Keating, R. (2003). *Criminal Law*, 3rd edn. London: Sweet & Maxwell.

Kenny (2003). *Outlines of Criminal Law*, 17th edn. Cambridge: Cambridge University Press.

Knox, S. J. (1968). Epileptic automatism and violence. *Medicine Science and the Law*, **8**:96–104.

Lowenstein, L. F. (2004). Automatism: Psychological and legal aspects. *Justice and Peace*, **165**:284–288.

Maillard, L., Vignal, J. P. and Gavaret, M., et al. (2004). Semiologic and electrophysiologic correlations in temporal lobe seizure subtypes. *Epilepsia*, **45**, 1590–1599.

Maldonado, H. M., Delgado-Escueta, A. V., Walsh, G. O., Swartz, B. E., and Rand, R. W. (1988). Complex partial seizures of hippocampal and amygdalar origin. *Epilepsia*, **29**, 420–433.

Mawson, D. (1990). Specific defences to a criminal charge: Assessment for court. In: R. Bluglass and P. Bowden (eds), *Principles and Practice of Forensic Psychiatry*, pp. 215–222. London: Churchill Livingstone.

McSherry, B. (2002). Epilepsy and law. *Medicine and Law*, **133**:1–12.

Morris, N. (1982). *Madness and Criminal Law*. Chicago: University of Chicago Press.

Pressman, M. (2007). Factors that predispose, prime and precipitate NREM parasomnias in adults: Clinical and forensic implications. *Sleep Medical Review*, **11**:5–30.

Quesney, L. F. (1986). Clinical and EEG features of complex partial seizures of temporal lobe origin. *Epilepsia*, **27** (Suppl. 2): S27–S45.

Ramani, V. and Gumnit, R. J. (1981). Intensive monitoring of epileptic patients with a history of episodic aggression. *Archives of Neurology*, **38**:570–571.

Robinson, P. (1982). *Criminal Law Defences: A Systematic Analysis*. 82 Col L R, 213:221:229.

Rodin, E. A. (1973). Psychomotor epilepsy and aggressive behaviour. *Archives of General Psychiatry*, **28**:210–213.

Rodin, E. A. (1982). Aggression and epilepsy. In: T. L. Riley and A. Roy (eds), *Pseudoseizures*, pp. 185–212. Baltimore: Williams & Wilkins.

Schenck, C. H. and Mahowald, M. W. (2002). REM sleep behaviour disorder: Clinical, developmental and neuroscience perspectives 16 years after its formal identification in SLEEP. *Sleep*, **25**:120–138.

Schenck, C. H., Bundles, R., Ettinger, M. G., and Mahowald, M. W. (1986). Chronic behavioural disorders of human REM sleep: A new category of parasomnia. *Sleep*, **9**:93–306.

Treiman, D. M. (1986). Epilepsy and violence. Medical and legal issues. *Epilepsia*, **27** (Suppl. 2): S7–S104.

Treiman, D. M. (1991). Psychobiology of ictal aggression. *Advances in Neurology*, **55**:341–356.

Treiman, D. M. (1999). Violence and the epilepsy defense. *Neurologic Clinics*, **17**:245–255.

Treiman, D. M. and Delgado-Escueta, A. V. (1983). Violence and epilepsy: A critical review. In: T. A. Pedley and B. Meldrum (eds), *Recent Advances in Epilepsy*, pp. 179–209. Edinburgh: Churchill Livingstone.

van Rensburg, P., Gagino, C. A., and Verschoor, T. (1994). Possible reasons why certain epileptics commit unlawful acts during or directly after seizures. *Medicine and Law*, **13**:373–379.

Wasik, M. (1990). Insanity, diminished responsibility and infanticide: Legal aspects. In: R. Bluglass and P. Bowden (eds), *Principles and Practice of Forensic Psychiatry*, pp. 255–263. London: Churchill Livingstone.

Williamson, P. D., Thadani, V. M., French, J. A., *et al.* (1998). Medial temporal lobe epilepsy: Videotape analysis of objective clinical seizure characteristics. *Epilepsia*, **39**, 1182–1188.

Chapter 8

Alcohol and drug misuse

Helen Miles and Andrew Johns

Substance use is increasing in our society, and excessive use of alcohol and drugs is associated with significant physical, psychological, and social consequences to individuals, families, and communities. These are both acute problems, requiring short-term health or forensic interventions (e.g. intoxication, overdose, accidents, or criminal behaviours such as violence or acquisitive offending), as well as more chronic problems of dependency, which require specific longer-term treatment interventions (Marshall & Farrell, 2003).

Regarding prevalence rates for substance use, a UK national survey of psychiatric comorbidity in 2000, which also assessed substance use in the general population (Coulthard et al., 2002), found that almost half of the UK population (48%) drank alcohol more than twice a week, whilst a quarter (26%, although more men than women) scored in the hazardous drinking range on the Alcohol Use Disorders Identification Test (AUDIT; Piccinelli et al., 1997). Rates of illegal substance use were also noted to have increased from previous years (Coulthard et al., 2002), with 12% of the general population reporting having used an illegal drug in the past year, males more than females. Moreover, whilst cannabis was the most commonly used drug (25% of the population having ever used, compared with 7% reporting use of amphetamines, 4% reporting use of ecstasy, cocaine, or LSD, and less than 1% reporting use of 'hard' drugs such as crack cocaine, heroin and non-prescribed methadone), most substance users abused more than one substance. From the same survey, Coid et al. (2006) found that people with antisocial personality disorder and substance misuse are more likely to report involvement in violent incidents—hazardous drinking was by far the largest risk factor for serious and repetitive violence.

It follows that a neuropsychological assessment in a forensic setting will need to be informed by a detailed understanding of substance use. This chapter will briefly examine the relationship between use of alcohol and drugs and offending, followed by an overview of medico-legal issues, especially that of criminal responsibility. This is followed by a review of the neuropsychological impact of substance use, before considering practical issues in undertaking the neuropsychological assessment of substance users in criminal and civil cases, and in forensic clinical settings.

Relationship between offending and substance use

Those who misuse drugs or alcohol may also commit crimes due to a number of reasons that have to be understood in order to manage the health and risk of offending of individual patients. Such offences can be classed as (i) violent offences, often involving an altered mental state, (ii) acquisitive offences, and (iii) miscellaneous offences, such as breaking laws to control the misuse of drugs, driving under the influence of alcohol, and the impact of substance misuse on parenting (Johns, 2000).

Violent offences

Aggression is not an inevitable consequence of misusing alcohol or any particular drug, but may arise from many factors, including expectancy effects, pattern of consumption, individual responses to intoxication or withdrawal, peer influences, and interpersonal issues.

Alcohol consumption is the single factor most associated with violence. It is a repeated finding from the British Crime Surveys that alcohol is a key factor in at least half of interpersonal assaults, with a greater contribution to assaults on strangers and domestic violence. By comparison and as a group, drug misusers are overwhelmingly more likely to commit acquisitive offences.

The risk of violence is further increased by the comorbidity of major mental illness and substance misuse. From the USA, the Epidemiological Catchment Area survey of 10 000 individuals (Swanson, 1994) found that the prevalence of violent behaviour in the previous year was 2% for those with no mental disorder, 7% in 'major mental illness', 20% for 'substance misuse disorder', and 22% for comorbid respondents.

Among English patients with first-episode psychoses (Milton et al., 2001), just under 10% demonstrated serious aggression when psychotic, and 23% showed lesser degrees of aggression. Those comorbid for drug misuse were nine times more likely to show aggression after service contact—primary drug-related psychoses or alcohol misuse was not associated in this way. However, again in the UK (Shaw et al., 2006), alcohol or drug misuse contributed to two-fifths of homicides, and 17% were committed by patients with severe mental illness and substance misuse. Alcohol- and drug-related homicides were generally associated with male perpetrators who had a history of violence, personality disorders, mental health service contact, and 'stranger' victims.

Individuals with serious mental disorders who misuse drugs or alcohol may become violent for a host of reasons. Even low levels of consumption can lead to disinhibition and autonomic arousal, which lower the threshold for aggression. Intoxication on alcohol or other central nervous system depressants such as benzodiazepines or barbiturates may lead initially to apparently excited behaviour. Irritability and arousal may be produced by stimulants such as cocaine or amphetamines. Intoxication generally leads to impaired perception, impulse control, and judgement, whereas severe intoxication on alcohol or many drugs can lead to a toxic psychosis and the risk of highly disturbed behaviour. 'Pathological' intoxication, in which the consumption of moderate amounts of alcohol is followed by rapid onset of aggression, is of uncertain validity. In most cases, such aggression is better explained by alcohol-induced hypoglycaemia, head injury, or another organic disorder. Withdrawal effects can also increase the risk of violence. The withdrawal syndrome from alcohol and most drugs of dependence is a highly aversive state in which irritability and aggression may occur.

Acquisitive offending

The relationship between acquisitive crime and drug misuse problems is complex. From a large survey of British youth (Pudney, 2002), the average age of onset for truancy and crime are 13.8 and 14.5 years, respectively, compared with 16.2 years for drugs generally and 19.9 years for 'hard' drugs. Thus, crime tends to precede drug use rather than vice versa.

Of the 753 clients recruited to the National Treatment Outcome Research Study, Gossop *et al.* (2005) reported that, during the 90-day period prior to treatment, they carried out 17 000 offences. Yet half of the clients committed no acquisitive crimes during this period, whereas 10% committed 76% of the crimes. Statistically significant reductions in the mean number of convicted offences were found between treatment intake and 5-year follow-up. Reductions in convictions were found for acquisitive, drug-selling, and violent crimes.

It is clear that, whilst the majority of drug users have a history of acquisitive crime, those with a heavy drug use are at particular risk of impulsive acquisitive offending, including street robbery and burglary that involve violence (Macdonald *et al.*, 2008).

Miscellaneous offences

Drug offences In Britain, the non-medical use of drugs is subject to the Misuse of Drugs Act 1971, as subsequently amended, which contains a classification based on perceived harm. Class A drugs include ecstasy, LSD, heroin, cocaine, crack, magic mushrooms (if prepared for use), and amphetamines (if prepared for injection). Class B drugs include amphetamines, cannabis, and methylphenidate (Ritalin). Class C drugs include cannabis, tranquilizers, some painkillers, gamma-hydroxybutyrate (GHB) and ketamine. Cannabis was reclassified from a Class B to a Class C drug between January 2004 and January 2009. This legislation defines the penalties for supply, dealing, production, trafficking, and possession.

Drug use and parenting Substance misuse problems can have a considerable impact on parenting skills. Prenatal heroin and cocaine misuse can lead to developmental difficulties. Substance misuse can have a deleterious effect on children through psychological, environmental, and social factors (Barnes & Stein 2000). All of these issues are likely to be aggravated by comorbidity for mental illness or personality disorder. For these reasons, the family courts may request evaluation of the substance-misusing parent.

Other offences Other offences include driving cars, or public conveyances (such as trains) whilst under the influence of alcohol or other drugs.

Impact of substance use on criminal responsibility

With few exceptions, the voluntary use of drugs or alcohol is not a mitigating factor for an offence and it is argued that a drunken intent is still an intent. Under some narrowly defined circumstances, an altered mental state due to substance misuse can raise the question of a possible defence (Haque & Cumming, 2003). These include the following.

Voluntary intoxication and intent

In England and Wales, it has been determined by case law that offences such as murder, wounding with intent, theft, and burglary require a specific intent for which self-induced intoxication on alcohol or drugs may be a defence, but only if it can be shown that the accused was so intoxicated as to be unable to form the necessary intent. The assessor can only comment as to whether the accused had the capacity to form the specific intent, and it is a matter for the jury to determine whether the specific intent was present or not. It is suggested that the extent of purposive action before, during, and after the offence may be a clinical indication of the extent to which an individual was so intoxicated as to be unable to form a specific intent (Johns, 2000).

In the absence of such specific intent, the accused may still be convicted of a lesser offence. Other offences such as rape, manslaughter, and unlawful wounding require only a basic intent, which cannot be negated by intoxication.

Taking drugs or alcohol to make it easier to offend is commonly called 'Dutch courage' and does not reduce culpability.

Insanity

The McNaughton rules require that, at the time of the offence, the accused *'laboured under a defect of reason, from a disease of mind, as not to know the nature and quality of what he was doing, or not to know that what he was doing was wrong'*. Substance misuse may lead to a psychotic state that could meet the McNaughton requirements, but even if substance misuse leads to an insane automatism, the defence is not available if the consumption has been voluntary.

Diminished responsibility

Section 2 of the Homicide Act 1957 allows for the partial defence of diminished responsibility to a charge of murder. The accused has to suffer from an 'abnormality of mind' arising from one of the specified categories, such as to substantially impair mental responsibility. Alcoholism or drug misuse may lead to organic brain damage or to an inability to resist the impulse to drink—in either case the defence may apply. However, the sequelae of voluntary consumption of drink or alcohol are excluded as case law has held that the transient effects of alcohol do not arise from a category specified by the Act (Haque & Cumming, 2003). When substance misuse interacts with other factors such as depression, organic brain damage, or personality disorder, the effect of intoxication has to be set aside and it must be shown that the associated condition in itself was severe enough to lead to an abnormality of mind.

Amnesia This is claimed by about 30% of serious violent offenders and is associated particularly with a history of alcohol misuse, previous blackouts, psychiatric disorders, and crimes of passion (Pyszora *et al.*, 2003). It does not of itself affect fitness to plead, although it clearly complicates assessment (see Chapter 6 of this volume).

Impact of alcohol and drugs on neuropsychological functioning

Any psychoactive substance will have an impact on neuropsychological or cognitive functioning (Powell, 2004), through acute effects and/or long-term effects on performance, which may or may not be reversible. Moreover, as well as predictable and wanted effects from substances, possible side effects and withdrawal symptoms cannot be overlooked in assessment. Many substances produce homeostatic changes in brain functioning after long-term use, and abstinence may result in mood changes and effects on motivation, concentration, and attention, especially in the early stages.

The extent and duration of any effects of a psychoactive substance will depend upon a variety of factors, which must be considered as part of any neuropsychological assessment (Powell, 2004). These include the pharmacological characteristics of the substance (e.g. neurochemical actions, half-life, dose/amount used) and the mode of administration (e.g. smoked, injected). They also include the characteristics of the individual user (e.g. weight, age, gender, level of premorbid functioning, other medical health factors such as poor health, epilepsy, or vitamin deficiency, and psychological disturbance such as depression, stress, or agitation), as well as their previous experience with the substance (i.e. tolerance to the substance will affect the amount of performance deficit). Any other substance use, either that used concurrently or in the past as part of a substance-using career, must also be considered, as it is relatively rare in practice to find an individual only ever using one substance of abuse. Finally, the 'set and setting' of use may also have an impact on cognitive functioning, such as the user's expectations, attitudes towards the substance's effects, mood state, and social environment (O'Brien, 1996).

Consequently, it is often difficult in practice to evaluate precisely the effects of substance use on an individual's cognitive functioning. This difficulty is often compounded by the observation that many substance users are inaccurate in their own estimations of their use (i.e. denying or minimizing use) and there are obvious practical difficulties in objectively verifying the individual's pattern of use and purity or quantity of substances used. However, a basic awareness of the impact of the most common substances of abuse (both legal and 'illegal') on cognitive functioning and behaviour, and the factors affecting these, is essential for the neuropsychologist, whether in a forensic and/or a clinical setting. The reason is twofold: firstly, alcohol and drugs are commonly implicated in criminal behaviours; and secondly, such understanding aids the interpretation of neuropsychological test results.

Legal psychoactive substances

Alcohol

Alcohol primarily affects the $GABA_A$ receptors, inhibits glutamate receptors, and interacts directly or indirectly with opioid receptors. Alcohol intoxication results in euphoria, increased sociability, and disinhibition, although irritability and depression can occur and higher doses cause drowsiness, stupor, ataxia, blurred vision, slurred speech, and slowed reaction times, finally leading to respiratory depression or death. As alcohol is a central nervous system depressant, it is likely to affect cognitive functioning in a broad and non-specific manner (Powell, 2004) and can cause detectable impairments in cognitive functioning after only a few drinks (e.g. reaction times compromising driving skills). If an individual is intoxicated, they are likely to underperform on tests that require an individual to be alert and thus amplify any deficits. In addition, most other psychoactive substances interact with alcohol (Kerr & Hindmarch, 1998), some increasing any effect (e.g. benzodiazepines) and others reducing them (e.g. nicotine and caffeine). Therefore, neuropsychological testing should always be avoided within a couple of hours of a single drink and within 24 hours of a heavy drinking session (Powell, 2004).

Nevertheless, moderate social drinking appears to only have very subtle long-term cognitive effects. A review of 19 studies since 1986 by Parsons & Nixon (1998) found that cognitive deficits were unlikely in individuals drinking up to four standard drinks per day, mild cognitive deficits were likely at seven to nine drinks per day, and moderate cognitive deficits equivalent to those found in diagnosed alcoholics occurred at ten or more drinks per day. Some studies of social drinkers have shown a relationship between the amount and frequency of consumption and mild cognitive impairments, such as reduced short-term verbal recall, subtle deficits in concept formation and mental flexibility, and a mild perseverative tendency, although performance on most neuropsychological tests is unimpaired (Grant, 1987; Rourke & Løberg, 1996). Therefore, current evidence is inconclusive and inconsistent (Knight & Longmore, 1994).

However, large quantities of alcohol (i.e. 'binge drinking'; defined as consuming five or more drinks in about 2 hours for males, or four or more for women), especially if consumed quickly and without food, can lead to 'blackouts', even in non-dependent drinkers (White et al., 2002). Blackouts consist of transient episodes of anterograde amnesia, lasting anywhere from minutes to days, depending on how long the individual's blood alcohol level remains high. However, whilst any alcohol-induced amnesia may be an issue in forensic work, it is often difficult to evaluate without reliable blood alcohol levels.

Individuals who engage in heavy and prolonged alcohol abuse are likely to experience withdrawal symptoms, which include tremulousness, anxiety, poor memory and concentration, fleeting and poorly formed visual or auditory hallucinations, insomnia, increased temperature, elevated pulse and blood pressure, and possibly seizures. In severe cases, individuals may experience the 'delirium tremens', consisting of confusion, disorientation, vivid hallucinations, and possible death and/or 'alcohol hallucinosis', which, although it improves with abstinence, consists of auditory hallucinations, delusions of persecution or reference, fear, and irritability (Soyka, 1990). Generally, alcohol withdrawal peaks in 2–3 days, reducing in severity over the next 2–3 days, and generally resolves after approximately a week, although some residual symptoms may last longer. It is therefore important to determine the duration of abstinence in such individuals and to avoid neuropsychological assessments during any acute withdrawal phase (Powell, 2004).

Chronic alcohol use can damage nerve cells, particularly in the frontal cortex, hypothalamus, and cerebellum, and possibly the amygdala, hippocampus, and locus coeruleus (Harper, 1998). Some effects on cognitive functioning reverse over increasing periods of abstinence (e.g. Horner et al., 1999), although the greatest amount occurs in the first week (Ryan & Butters, 1986), slowing down rapidly thereafter, depending upon the individual's age (Munro et al., 2000). An early review by Kleinknecht & Goldstein (1972) noted that alcoholics performed worse than non-alcoholics on a variety of neuropsychological tests, including manifesting deficits in visual abstraction and visuospatial abilities, problem-solving, and tasks that involved speed of processing and complex perceptual spatial motor performance. Overall, intellectual functioning (IQ), attention, and language were not generally impaired, although verbal linguistic skills of a more demanding nature can be (Ryan & Butters, 1986). Similar results were also found by other reviewers and have cross-cultural stability (e.g. Løberg & Miller, 1986; Parsons et al., 1987; Rourke & Løberg, 1996).

Specifically, whilst visuospatial functions were essentially intact, chronic alcohol users performed poorly on tests requiring visuospatial organization such as the WAIS-III Block Design subtest or Part B of the Trail Making Test, visual and spatial searching, scanning, or learning such as the WAIS-III Digit Symbol Substitution subtest (De Renzi et al., 1984). In addition, deficits in executive functioning tasks are often observed (Grant, 1987), impairments that may have the most obvious implications for lessened effective functioning in everyday life. These include decreased cognitive flexibility, defective searching behaviour, simplistic problem-solving strategies, perseveration, and impaired organization and synthesis of elements, although the basic ability to make abstractions and generalize may be intact (Rourke & Løberg, 1996).

Memory impairments in chronic alcohol users are not usually serious or universal, are commonly in short-term learning and memory, and typically manifest as subtle, only becoming more evident as task difficulty increases (Ryan & Butters, 1986). Butters & Granholm (1987) have suggested that there are continuities in memory impairment between social drinkers and heavier drinkers, involving a gradual erosion of ability rather than a 'distinct' jump to amnesia. Chronic alcohol users have also been found to manifest more intrusions and recall errors, although they tend to have normal rates of forgetting, suggesting that the deficits are a result of encoding than retrieval problems (Ryan & Butters, 1986).

The underlying causes of any deficits in cognitive functioning remain unclear. Some studies have found that it is the toxic effect of high levels of alcohol consumption (De Renzi *et al.*, 1984), whilst duration of use is implicated in some studies (Ryan & Butters, 1986) but not others (Grant, 1987). Overall, whilst 'binge' drinkers are less prone to alcohol-related cognitive deficits than individuals with heavy daily consumption, consumption alone explains relatively little of neuropsychological test scores (Rourke & Løberg, 1996). Other factors such as diet (e.g. a thiamine deficiency in Korsakoff's syndrome; see below) may be implicated over and above the direct toxic effects of alcohol.

Moreover, chronic alcohol users are not a homogenous population. Whilst some researchers have found that deficits hold for both male and female alcoholics, the effect of alcohol use is greater in older than younger drinkers and other variables such as socio-economic level, race, and culture related to drinking practices have not been investigated with regard to neuropsychological differences (Vaillant, 1983). In addition, the presence of other psychological disorders (e.g. depression and anxiety), which may affect the onset, course, and outcome of treatment, have not been investigated with respect to their impact on neuropsychological impairments in this population, although they have been found to play a significant role in subjective complaints about cognitive deficits (Shelton & Parsons, 1987) and should be considered before making clinical inferences based on individuals' self-reported difficulties. Finally, any results obtained may also vary by neuropsychological assessment instruments used in comparisons.

Wernicke–Korsakoff syndrome (WKS) One of the most researched consequences of chronic long-term alcohol use is WKS. This is the development of amnesia (a dense and circumscribed deficit in memory in the context of otherwise preserved memory) as a consequence of chronic alcohol abuse and malnutrition, usually thiamine or vitamin B_{12} deficiency. The onset of the disorder is usually marked by an acute phase, known as Wernicke's encephalopathy, in which the individual is disorientated, confused, apathetic, and unable to maintain a coherent conversation, and may also have occulomotor problems and ataxia. Diagnosis is by at least two of the following: dietary deficiencies, occulomotor abnormalities, cerebellar dysfunction, and altered mental status (Caine *et al.*, 1997). Once the acute confusion clears, the individual may be left with an enduring dense amnesia—Korsakoff's syndrome (Korsakoff, 1889). However, Cutting (1978) noted that not all individuals have the initial

Wernicke's encephalopathy; it is more common in clinical practice for the onset to be more insidious or to have only transient periods of the acute state, especially in women. WKS has a poor prognosis, as the condition is long-lasting, requiring life-long care.

Regarding performance on neuropsychological assessments, Ryan & Butters (1986) noted that WKS individuals perform essentially normally on tests of general intellectual ability that are structured and untimed, for example, on tests of well-structured overlearned material such as the Vocabulary and Arithmetic subtests of the WAIS-III (Wechsler, 1999). Scores on other subtests decline only to the extent that speed and visuoperceptual and spatial organization are involved, as WKS individuals are thought to take longer to identify visually presented material due to slowed visual processing capacity. For example, WKS patients show deficits on tasks requiring visuospatial and visuoperceptive capacities, such as the Digit-symbol Substitution subtest of the WAIS-III, the Hidden or Embedded Figures Tests and Concept Formation tests, if they require sorting and discrimination of complex visual stimuli (Butters & Cermak, 1980; Brandt & Butters, 1986). WKS individuals also perform normally on tests of focused attention, although they are likely to show deficits on tests where they are required to divide or shift attention (Lezak, 2004). Moreover, whilst the rate of 'long-term' forgetting is normal (Kopelman, 1985), WKS individuals have variable performance on short-term forgetting tasks and manifest false recognition over repeated memory trials (Butters & Cermak, 1980).

The most marked deficits in WKS individuals are in the learning of new material and memory. There are many studies of the pattern of impaired and persevered memory in WKS (for more detailed reviews, see Baddeley, 1990; Squire & Butters, 1992; Kopelman, 1995) and there is general agreement about the pattern of deficits in WKS (Kopelman, 1995). WKS individuals commonly have a well-preserved working memory. However, although WKS individuals can repeat information in the absence of any delay (e.g. performing normally on tests of working memory that require information only to be retained for a short time, such as the Digit Span or Subtracting Serial Sevens), distraction for longer than about 10 seconds means that subsequence performance is markedly impaired and WKS individuals are unlikely to resume interrupted activities. Procedural learning (e.g. skills) and procedural memory are relatively unimpaired (Kopelman, 1995).

WKS individuals generally have profound and global memory and learning difficulties, the result of an increased sensitivity to interference (O'Connor & Verfaellie, 2002). This includes both anterograde amnesia (the loss of memory for items presented after WKS onset) and retrograde amnesia (the loss of memory for items presented before WKS onset) (Rourke & Løberg, 1996). One of the most striking features of WKS memory disorder is anterograde amnesia, with WKS individuals living in a 'time zone' of about 3–5 minutes. WKS individuals show major impairments on both verbal and non-verbal tests, regardless of modality of presentation (i.e. visual, auditory, or tactile) and type of material, and irrespective of whether retention is tested by free recall or recognition (O'Connor & Verfaellie, 2002). They also show little, if any, learning on repeated recall trials, have a tendency to perseverate errors or responses from one set of stimuli to next, and make intrusion errors in both verbal and visual modalities.

In addition, WKS individuals have profound retrograde amnesia. This is 'temporally graded', with poorest recall of the most recent events, improving as the time of original memory acquisition is more removed from the date of onset of WKS (Kopelman, 1995).

Another problem commonly displayed in (although not exclusive to) WKS individuals, is confabulation (e.g. Kopelman *et al.*, 1997). Confabulation is defined as 'honest lying'; therefore, the individual provides information that is patently false and sometimes self-contradictory without intention or awareness of lying. Confabulation occurs not just in verbal statements but also in actions and generally on occasions when individuals think they should know the answer. It is also most apparent when autobiographical recollection is required (Gilboa & Moscovitch, 2002) or in semantic memory (Kopelman *et al.*, 1997), although it should be distinguished from delusions and false recall/recognition (for a discussion of the differences, see DeLuca, 2000).

WKS individuals also show considerable evidence of frontal lobe or 'executive dysfunction' (e.g. Joyce & Robbins, 1991). For example, they show impairments in the Wisconsin Card Sorting Test, the verbal fluency task, and the cognitive estimates test (Kopelman, 1991).

Finally, WKS individuals also manifest problems in emotional and psychosocial behaviour (Lezak, 2004). They may be 'emotionally bland', albeit with a capacity for quick irritability, anger, or pleasure that disappears when the stimulus causing it is removed. They may also be apathetic (characterized by a total loss of initiative, insight, and interest, and a striking lack of curiosity about the past, present, or future), have low motivation, and be at the mercy of whatever is in their immediate environment.

Alcoholic dementia This is distinguished from WKS by the presence of widespread cognitive deterioration (i.e. loss of intellectual functioning), rather than just profound amnesia (Ryan & Butters, 1986; Rourke & Løberg, 1996). Alcoholic dementia also appears insidiously after many years of chronic and severe drinking, and is characterized by apathy, coarsening of personality, poor judgement, concreteness, poor memory, and minor signs of cortical atrophy, such as aphasia, apraxia, and agnosia.

Nicotine

Nicotine is the critical ingredient of cigarettes and is a cholinergic agonist acting on endogenous nicotinic receptors. An individual's blood nicotine concentration reaches its peak after 15 minutes, returning to baseline after about 2 hours. Nicotine enhances sustained, divided, and focused attention (Foulds et al., 1992; Kassel, 1997) and improves memory and performance upon complex tasks (Peeke & Peeke, 1984), as well as reaction time (Foulds et al., 1992) and information-processing speed, although it has also been shown to decrease response speed and some other aspects of cognitive performance including some adverse effects on spatial working memory (Park et al., 1999). However, a recent study found no substantial cognitive effects from long-term smoking (Schinka et al., 2002).

Nicotine is highly addictive, and withdrawal symptoms include dysphoria, craving, irritability, restlessness, increased appetite, insomnia, poor concentration, and low frustration tolerance, all of which may affect an individual's performance on a neuropsychological assessment. Therefore, regular smokers are likely to show disturbances associated with nicotine abstinence if tested more than 2 hours after smoking, such as impaired working memory (Blake & Smith, 1997) and reductions in motivation, verbal fluency, and digit span (Al-Adawi & Powell, 1997). Consequently, practitioners should allow an individual a cigarette break or provide nicotine replacement therapy (e.g. patches or gum), especially when undertaking prolonged neuropsychological assessments.

Anxiolytics

Whilst anxiolytics or benzodiazepines such as diazepam and lorazepam are usually prescribed, they can also be misused, often with alcohol or opiates. All benzodiazepines have anticholinergic neurochemical actions, acting on GABA (gamma-aminobutyric acid) receptors in brain regions such as the amygdala and hippocampus, although they vary in terms of their half-life, so it is important to know which type of benzodiazepines was taken, how long ago, and in what dose in order to consider properly any possible effects on cognitive functioning (Powell, 2004). Tolerance and addiction to benzodiazepines also occurs relatively quickly, and benzodiazepines have a withdrawal syndrome similar to alcohol, including seizures if rapidly discontinued, the time course of withdrawal depending upon the half-life of the benzodiazepine.

Therefore, as with alcohol, neuropsychological assessment during withdrawal is not recommended.

The effects of benzodiazepines on memory, whilst related to dose and half-life, are direct rather than secondary to the generalized sedation (Powell, 2004). Single doses in healthy adults do not affect attention span, executive function, retrograde memory, semantic memory, or procedural learning, although they do slow information processing and can produce temporary anterograde amnesia, forgetting information presented after drug administration, particularly in episodic memory. (Curran, 1991, 2000; Curran et al., 1994). Benzodiazepines affect the encoding and consolidation processes of memory, rather than retrieval, as once information is learnt, the rate of forgetting is normal (Curran & Weingartner, 2002).

'Illegal' psychoactive substances

It is extremely difficult to investigate the effects of many illegal drugs on cognitive functioning as it rare that they are used in isolation and experimental studies have obvious ethical and legal issues (Powell, 2004). In addition, whilst individuals are more likely to have clear effects while acutely intoxicated, the longer-term effects are less apparent.

Cannabis

The active part of the cannabis plant (tetrahydrocannabinol) has a half-life of 60 hours (for discussion of the biological properties of cannabis, see Ameri, 1999) and varies in form and strength, the dried-out leaves, buds, or resin of the plant being smoked with tobacco. Therefore, the acute effects of the drug are long lasting (up to 24 hours) and chronic users may have traces in their central nervous system for several weeks. Cannabis can produce a mild withdrawal state of restlessness, dysphoria, and insomnia (Duffy & Millin, 1996), and may trigger or exacerbate psychotic illness in vulnerable individuals at low doses as well as anxiety/panic and psychotic states in non-vulnerable individuals at higher doses (Arendt et al., 2005).

The effects of cannabis on cognitive functioning are most marked after acute intoxication, and consequently the neuropsychologist should avoid assessment if it is likely that the individual has smoked within the last 48 hours. The most consistently reported effect from numerous studies is alterations in memory functioning (Miller, 1984), suggested to be the consequence of dysfunctions in focusing attention and maintaining concentration, the failure to exclude irrelevant associations or extraneous stimuli from attention, and possible interference in the transfer of information from short-term to long-term memory (see reviews by Miller & Branconnier, 1983; Solowij, 1998).

For example, short-term memory is impaired although the extent is dose-dependent, free recall (although not always recognition) is impaired, and the frequency of intrusion errors increases. However, remote memory of previously learned information is not affected. Attention, concentration, and task accuracy are also affected, although again this is dose- and task-dependent, the greatest deficits being shown at higher doses and for more complex and demanding tasks, especially divided attention. However, sustained attention on simple visual and auditory tasks can also be impaired, although tasks generally need to be of a long duration (over 50 minutes).

Cannabis can also adversely affect motor skills, fine motor control, manual dexterity, and motor coordination, especially on skilled tasks (see reviews by Chait & Pierri, 1992; O'Brien, 1996). Simple reaction times are less likely to be affected, although impairments increase as task difficulty increases. In a review of cannabis effects on driving, Smiley (1986) found impairments in lane control but reductions in risk-taking, manifested by slower speeds and maintenance of a greater distance from the vehicle in front. However, again there were greater impairments in more complicated tasks. Acute intoxication with cannabis has also been found to cause loosening of associations so that the individual may be lost in fantasy and find it difficult to sustain goal-directed mental activity (Solowij, 1998), as well as having the experience of time passing more quickly relative to real time.

The chronic effects of cannabis use are more difficult to determine due to less research, methodological problems, and conflicting and equivocal evidence (see reviews by Pope *et al.*, 1995; Carlin & O'Malley, 1996; Solowij, 1998), as well as a lack of specificity and sensitivity. Clinical anecdotal evidence suggests that long-term use (i.e. more often than every 6 weeks for approximately 2 years) produces a 'dulling' of cognitive abilities, particularly difficulties in concentration and memory, although clinical improvement can be seen within 14 days of abstinence, returning to normal functioning after about 6 weeks (Lundquist, 1995). Pope & Yurgelun-Todd (1996) found that after 19 hours of supervised abstinence, almost daily cannabis users performed slightly more poorly on some neuropsychological tests (e.g. verbal fluency, although only for those with a pre-existing low verbal IQ) and had decreased mental flexibility and increased perseveration on the Wisconsin Card Sorting Test (Heaton *et al.*, 1993) although there was no association between test scores and lifetime consumption, suggesting no underlying structural damage.

MDMA (ecstasy)

MDMA (3,4-methylenedioxymethamphetamine) or ecstasy is increasingly being used as a recreational substance by young people, particularly within the 'dance' and 'clubbing' scenes. It is commonly taken in a pill form, producing effects of subjective well-being, feelings of being 'loved up' or 'rushes of euphoria', increased energy, and more intensely experienced sounds and colours, effects lasting 4–6 hours. MDMA is also associated with disturbances of mood; there is a 'come down' period rather than a specific withdrawal syndrome, which persists for several days after use (Curran & Travill, 1997). The effects tend to be transient and pass within a week (Parrott & Lasky, 1998). Therefore it is important to know the time since last use and to avoid neuropsychological assessment while the examinee is still likely to be adversely affected.

There is growing evidence of MDMA neurotoxicity in humans with regard to long-term depletion of serotonin levels and degenerative changes to serotonergic structures (e.g. McCann *et al.*, 2000), and small but significant impairments of immediate and delayed verbal and visual memory have been found in both light (only a few occasions) and heavy regular users (Parrott *et al.*, 1998). Bhattachary & Powell (2001), taking into account concurrent cannabis use, also demonstrated impairments of prose recall and verbal fluency, with immediate and delayed recall highly correlated with estimated lifetime consumption, although they did not find impairments on the Rey–Osterreith Test of visuospatial memory.

Cocaine

Cocaine primarily blocks the reuptake and facilitates the release of dopamine as well as norepinephrine (noradrenaline) and serotonin. It can either be combined with other chemicals and smoked (known as crack), with effects lasting for about 15 minutes, or inhaled nasally in powder form, with effects lasting for about 30–40 minutes. Cocaine causes increased alertness, arousal, libido, confidence, and motor activation, whilst withdrawal symptoms include dysphoria, irritability, restlessness, insomnia or hypersomina, and drug cravings, which generally resolve after a few days, occasionally lingering for up to a few weeks. Cocaine can also cause hypertension, other central nervous system overstimulation symptoms, agitation, paranoia, delusions and hallucinations, panic attacks, and self- or other directed violence (Taylor, 1999).

Regarding the effect of cocaine on cognition, impairments in verbal learning, attention and concentration, non-verbal problem-solving, visuospatial abilities, and memory are the most commonly reported deficits, although again the evidence is far from conclusive and appears to be dose-dependent (Ardila *et al.*, 1991). For example Berry *et al.* (1993), in a small sample of 16 cocaine users, found deficits in memory, visuospatial abilities, and concentration during the acute phase of withdrawal, with effects continuing for at least 2 weeks. O'Malley & Gawin (1990) found a normal performance on verbal subtests of the WAIS-III, but deficits on the arithmetic subtest, and Holman et al. (1991) found deficits in spatial learning and organization in some but not all users.

O'Malley & Gawin (1990) found that chronic cocaine-dependent patients who had been abstinent for up to 18 months could show persistent difficulty in tasks requiring concentration and recent memory. Beatty et al. (1995), controlling for concurrent cannabis use, found that deficits on a wide range of neuropsychological tests of intellectual ability, problem-solving/abstraction, perceptual motor speed/attention/visuospatial abilities, learning/memory and face naming persisted for at least 3–5 weeks after abstinence, closely resembling deficits of abstinent alcoholics (over the same period of abstinence). However, Azrin et al. (1992) suggested that some recovery of functioning may occur after more prolonged periods of abstinence.

Therefore, it is perhaps best for the neuropsychologist to avoid assessment if the examinee is likely to have used cocaine recently and to give due consideration to possible impairments in long-term cocaine-dependent individuals.

Opiates

Commonly abused opiates include heroin and methadone, as well as, less commonly, codeine and morphine. The effects of opiates occur through endogenous opiate receptors, involve an 'intense high' followed by a period of drowsy and a less intense euphoria, and can result in respiratory depression or death if overdosed. The opiate withdrawal syndrome includes dysphoria, yawning, intense bone and muscle pain, nausea, vomiting, abdominal cramping, diarrhoea, elevated temperature, and increased pulse and blood pressure, and usually begins about 6–12 hours after use, peaking after 2–3 days and lasting for about a week, although this depends on the half-life of the drug, and some residual symptoms may last longer. It is therefore important to determine the time since last use and the duration of abstinence to avoid neuropsychological assessments during any acute intoxication or withdrawal phase (Powell, 2004).

As with cocaine, there are few studies of the acute effects on cognitive functioning of opiates. Some studies have shown that long-term opiate users sustain permanent impairments on tests involving visuospatial and visuomotor activities (e.g. Grant et al., 1978; Carlin & O'Malley, 1996), although the former sample were also alcohol users. Other studies have reported a pattern of performance slowing and impaired verbal and visual memory, although verbal concept formation was intact (Sweeny et al., 1989). Curran et al. (2001) found significant impairments in delayed prose recall after administration of a full daily dose of methadone to opiate-dependent subjects currently in detoxification, although there was no effect when the dose was split. However, overall the prolonged use of opiates alone does not appear to significantly affect cognitive functioning. Most opiate users are polysubstance users, commonly also using cocaine and alcohol, so it is difficult to draw firm conclusions regarding the effects of opiates on cognitive functioning.

Methods and problems of neuropsychological assessment

Neuropsychological assessment is open to broad interpretation when the individual has a history of psychoactive drug use and/or polydrug use. Powell (2004) suggests that the ideal approach would be to ascertain the type and degree of cognitive impairment expected by the individual's substance use history and determine the extent to which the observed pattern of performance corresponds to that expected, with significantly different impairments from those expected being attributable to other factors. However, whilst the practitioner therefore needs a basic knowledge of the impact of different substances upon cognitive functioning, as reviewed above, in reality it is often difficult in individual cases to actually ascertain the form or severity of any substance effects due to the sheer range and combinations of prescribed, social, and/or illegal substance use. This is further complicated by inconsistencies in the research literature, much of which uses experimental measures rather than standard clinical assessments, although this can still provide guidance to the practitioner.

Therefore, whilst it is good practice to acknowledge that substance use may have had an effect on cognitive functioning in clinical or forensic reports, in order to strengthen any such conclusions, the neuropsychologist is advised not to rely solely on the profile of impairments obtained during neuropsychological assessment as a basis of any conclusions. This is particularly important in forensic work, where there are obvious and serious implications in over- or underestimating the extent to which substance use is responsible for an individual's presentation, either during the current neuropsychological assessment or on previous occasions that one may be asked to comment on (e.g. during the index offence or police interviews). It is good practice for any neuropsychological assessment to be carried out in conjunction with any forensic psychiatric assessment and to refer to this in any final report—for medico-legal purposes, it is necessary to obtain prior permission for this from the instructing solicitor.

The following (based on Johnson, 2003) are suggestions of areas to consider that may or may not be indicative of substance-use problems:

- Biological factors
  - Family history of substance use
  - Medical health problems (e.g. liver damage, diabetes, hypertension, ulcers, abscesses, scaring, weight fluctuations, rhinorrhea, lip/finger burns, overly dilated or constricted pupils (the former common in stimulant users, the latter in opiate users), excess perspiration, tremors, tachycardia, unexplained bruises, chronic pain, and track injection marks)
  - Other signs of intoxication/withdrawal outlined above
- Psychological factors
  - Depression, anxiety, or excessive mood swings
  - Loss of interest in friends, family, or leisure activities
  - Attention and concentration difficulties
  - Personality disorder
  - Suicidal ideation, talk, or gestures
- Behavioural factors
  - Legal problems
  - Poor employment history
  - Financial problems
  - Extreme talkativeness, poor judgement, or erratic behaviour
  - Frequent falls and frequent hospitalizations
  - Drug-seeking behaviours.

It is important to consider that the individual may not experience or perceive their substance use to be a problem and may not make the link with other problems (Johnson, 2003). Nevertheless, if substance use is suspected, it is important to undertake a substance use assessment, assertively enquiring about all aspects of the individual's substance use history. In all assessments, it is necessary to introduce screening questions early in the interview about possible misuse of drugs or alcohol. For medico-legal assessments relating to an index offence or event, it will be necessary to ask about this in detail, as outlined below. This should involve a clinical interview covering the following areas:

- Substance use history (of every substance, including alcohol)
  - age of first use
  - onset of regular use

- duration of use
- amount used on a typical day
- number of days typically used each week
- time since last used (i.e. is either acute intoxication or withdrawal likely to compromise performance?)
- any periods of abstinence (i.e. are any abstinence-related effects likely to have abated or are any enduring deficits likely?)
- route of administration (i.e. oral, smoked, or injected)
- duration of prescribed drug use (i.e. have they started to exert therapeutic effects or are still symptoms still present? Are there any side effects of mediation, such as sedation or tremors?)

- Any effects of substance use on functioning (i.e. consider biological, psychological, and social aspects in the short and long term)
- Any individual vulnerability factors that may make the individual abnormally sensitive to cognitive deficits (i.e. age, gender, family history of substance use, prior psychiatric or neurological conditions)
- Prior treatment history (if any), including when, where, what type, whether treatment completed or not, whether helpful or not, abstinent for how long, and what factors contributed to relapse
- Meaning, attitudes, beliefs, and motivations surrounding the individual's substance use, which could include a functional analysis to examine the reasons for use and reinforcing/maintaining factors
- Other compulsions/dependencies (e.g. food, shopping, gambling, and self-destructive behaviours).

For medico-legal purposes, the clinical interview should cover the effects of substance use on the individual's offending either immediately prior to or during the index offence. For example, the individual may have committed an offence to fund their substance use, or substance use may be a potentially mitigating factor in the severity of the offence (e.g. alcohol-fuelled aggression). It is also worth ensuring that a detailed history of previous offending is sought, and if possible this should be corroborated from independent sources, such as a police record. Moreover, the clinical interview should also examine the individual's degree of insight into their offending behaviour and substance use (i.e. do they believe there is a relationship between the two?). This may be important if the assessor is asked to comment on the individual's future likely willingness to address their substance use in treatment.

A variety of substance use screening instruments is available, including the Alcohol Use Disorders Identification Test (AUDIT; Piccinelli *et al.*, 1997), the

Severity of Dependence Scale (SDS; Gossop *et al.*, 1995), the Maudsley Addiction Profile (MAP; Marsden *et al.*, 1998), CAGE (Ewing, 1984), the Addiction Severity Index (ASI; McClellan *et al.*, 1980), and the Change Readiness & Treatment Eagerness Scale (SOCRATES; Miller & Tonigan, 1996). For others, see Johnson (2003).

Whenever possible, corroborating evidence should also be gathered (e.g. from family, friends, and work colleagues, and from objective measures such as urine drug screens), as self-reports of substance use are often unreliable.

There are many different neuropsychological assessments (see Lezak, 2004, for a comprehensive compendium) that can describe and quantify specific cognitive, perceptual, and emotional skills or behavioural controls that may (or may not) have been adversely affected by the individual's use of substances. Whilst neuropsychological assessment is essential for individuals with a long history of substance use, the specific tests to be administered will depend on those deemed appropriate following the questions posed by the instructing solicitor, and a thorough review of the case and the salient issues. For example, the neuropsychologist may want to consider any one or more of the following:

- Intellectual abilities (both current and premorbid functioning)
- Frontal lobe or executive functioning deficits
- Memory abilities
- Attention/concentration
- Visuoperceptual functioning
- Language.

In addition, the neuropsychologist may also consider the addition of other psychological assessments that are commonly used when assessing this population. For example:

- Sensation seeking
  - Sensation Seeking Scale, assessing exciting, interesting, stimulating, and risk-taking activities (SSS; Zuckerman, 1979)
- Personality
  - Millon Clinical Multiaxial Inventory—Third Edition (MCMI-III; Millon *et al.*, 1997)
  - Minnesota Multiphasic Personality Inventory—Second Edition (MMPI-II; Hathaway & McKinley, 1991)
  - Eysenck Personality Questionnaire—Revised (including the Addiction, Criminality and Impulsivity/Venturesomeness Scales) (EPQ-R; Eysenck & Eysenck, 1996)

- Mood and anxiety
  - Beck Depression Inventory (BDI; Beck, 1988)
  - Beck Anxiety Inventory (BAI; Beck, 1990)
- Suggestibility and compliance
  - Gudjonsson Suggestibility Scales: (GSS; Gudjonsson, 1997)
  - Gudjonsson Compliance Scale: (GCS; Gudjonsson, 1989).

An important general rule is that, if the individual is known to be a regular user of substances, the neuropsychologist should find out the length of time since last use. Assessment should be deferred by at least 24 and preferably 48 hours after last use, and test results will be most reliable for individuals who do not have dependency (Powell, 2004). In substance-dependent individuals (commonly alcohol and/or opiates), it is a matter of judgement as to the most appropriate time for neuropsychological assessment as there will be no time when the test results will be uncontaminated by the effects of acute intoxication or acute abstinence (Powell, 2004).

For the same reasons, a suspect may be unfit for police interview, rendering their answers to questions unsafe. The reliability of confessions obtained while suspects are intoxicated or withdrawing from substances has been challenged (e.g. Clark, 1991; Davison & Forshaw, 1993; Davison & Gossop, 1996, 1999), and forensic practitioners may be called on to comment on the reliability of such a testimony. For example, opiate withdrawal limits the ability for rational thinking, autonomy, and the ability to cope with interrogative pressure (Davison & Forshaw, 1993) as well as affecting the user's ability to formulate and prioritize goals (i.e. the suspect may focus on short-term need to obtain drugs over the long-term consequences of making a confession). In addition, the suspect may be vulnerable to making a false confession as they fear further detention and wish to avoid withdrawal symptoms; they may believe that, if they confess, they are more likely to receive treatment to relieve symptoms (Pearson *et al.*, 2000). Moreover, whilst different substances may have differing effects on suggestibility and compliance, there is some evidence that alcohol intoxication may decrease suggestibility and that alcohol withdrawal may increase suggestibility as the individual has less ability to cope with interrogative pressure (Gudjonsson *et al.*, 2002). Lader (1999) states that important drug-induced states that are relevant to the reliability of testimony are sedation, disinhibition, and paradoxical reactions (e.g. anxiety, anger, and violence), as well as alterations in concentration, memory, and learning. For further details on the effects of alcohol and drugs on the reliability of testimony and confessions, and related issues, see reviews by Davison & Forshaw (1993), Davison & Gossop (1999), Lader (1999), Gossop &Davison

(2000), and Gudjonsson (2003). Examples of specific cases can also be found in Gudjonsson (2003).

Substance misuse and risk assessment

Substance misuse is a highly relevant factor to consider when assessing risk of further violence or offending. Such a risk assessment starts with a clinical consideration of the impact of drugs or alcohol misuse on the offence or behaviour of concern, and should include reference to the effect of substance misuse on underlying mental disorder, insight, and plans for the future, especially the extent to which the subject will cooperate with treatment.

Structured Professional Judgement (SPS) approaches to risk assessment (e.g. HCR-20, RSVP) include specific consideration of substance misuse as a risk factor, and should be incorporated into any clinical assessment if possible.

Conclusions

Any neuropsychological assessment should include screening questions for substance misuse—a history of relevant misuse of drugs or alcohol should be followed by further detailed clinical investigation, if appropriate, involving standardized instruments and questionnaires, including reference to the results of biochemical tests, as described. Bear in mind that such a thorough assessment may not be feasible during a single interview, and, where possible and especially for medico-legal purposes, corroboration should be obtained from other sources, such as significant others, contemporaneous witness accounts, and police records.

References

Al-Adawi, S. and Powell, J. (1997). The influence of smoking on reward responsiveness and cognitive functions: A natural experiment. *Addiction*, **92**:1773–1782.

Ameri, A. (1999). The effects of cannabinoids on the brain. *Progress in Neurobiology*, **58**:315–348.

Ardila, A., Rosselli, M., and Strumwasser, S. (1991). Neuropsychological deficits in chronic cocaine abusers. *International Journal of Neuroscience*, **57**:73–79.

Arendt M., Rosenburg, R., and Foldager, L. (2005). Cannabis-induced psychosis and subsequent schizophrenia-spectrum disorders: a follow-up study of 535 incident cases. *British Journal of Psychiatry*, **187**:510–515.

Azrin, R. L., Millsaps, C. L., Burton, D. B., and Mittenberg, W. (1992). Recovery of memory and intelligence following chronic cocaine abuse. *Clinical Neuropsychologist*, **6**:344–345.

Baddeley, A. D. (1990). *Human Memory: Theory and Practice*. London: Lawrence Erlbaum.

Barnes, J. and Stein, A. (2000). Effects of parental psychiatric and physical illness on child development. In: M Gelder, J. Lopez-Ibor, and N. Andreasson (eds), *New Oxford Textbook of Psychiatry*, pp. 1848–1855. Oxford: Oxford University Press.

Beatty, W. W., Katzung, V. M., Moreland, V. J., and Nixon, S. J. (1995). Neuropsychological performance of recently abstinent alcoholics and cocaine abusers. *Drug and Alcohol Dependence*, **37**:247–253.

Beck, A. T. (1988). *Beck Depression Inventory (BDI)*. Sidcup: The Psychological Corporation.

Beck, A. T. (1990). *Beck Anxiety Inventory (BAI)*. New York: The Psychological Corporation.

Berry, J., Van Gorp, W. G., Herzberg, D. S., *et al*. (1993). Neuropsychological deficits in abstinent cocaine abusers: Preliminary findings after two weeks of abstinence. *Drug and Alcohol Dependence*, **32**:231–237.

Bhattachary, S. and Powell, J. H. (2001). Recreational use of 3,4-methylenedioxymethamphetamine (MDMA) or 'ecstasy': Evidence for cognitive impairment. *Psychological Medicine*, **31**:647–658.

Blake, J. and Smith, A. (1997). Effects of smoking and smoking deprivation on the articulatory loop of human memory. *Human Psychopharmacology—Clinical and Experimental*, **12**:259–264.

Brandt, J. and Butters, N. (1986). The alcoholic Wernicke–Korsakoff syndrome and its relationship to long-term alcohol abuse. In: I. Grant and K. M. Adams (eds), *Neuropsychological Assessment of Neuropsychiatric Disorders*, pp. 441–447. Oxford: Oxford University Press.

Butters, N. and Cermak, L. S. (1980). *Alcoholic Korsakoff's Syndrome: An Information Processing Approach to Amnesia*. New York: Academic Press.

Butters, N. and Granholm, E. (1987). The continuity hypothesis: Some conclusions and their implications for the etiology and neuropathology of alcoholic Korsakoff's syndrome. In: O. A. Parsons, N. Butters, and P. E. Nathan (eds), *Neuropsychology of Alcoholism: Implications for Diagnosis and Treatment*, pp. 176–206. New York: Guildford Press.

Carlin, A. S. and O'Malley, S. S. (1996). Neuropsychological consequences of drug abuse. In: I. Grant and K. M. Adams (eds), *Neuropsychological Assessment of Neuropsychiatric Disorders*, pp. 486–503. New York: Oxford University Press.

Caine, D., Halliday, G., Kril, J., and Harper, C. (1997). Operational criteria for the classification of chronic alcoholics: Identification of Wernicke's encephalopathy. *Journal of Neurology, Neurosurgery and Psychiatry*, **62**:51–60.

Chait, L. D. and Pierri, J. (1992). Effects of smoked marijuana on human performance: A critical review. In: L. Murphy and A. Bartke (eds), *Marijuana/Cannabinoids: Neurobiology and Neurophysiology*, pp. 387–423. Boca Raton: CRC Press.

Clark, M. D. B. (1991). Fit for interview? *The Police Surgeon*, **40**:15–18.

Coid, J., Yang, M., and Roberts, A. (2006). Violence and psychiatric morbidity in the national household population of Britain: Public health implications. *British Journal of Psychiatry*, **189**:12–19.

Coulthard, M., Farrell, M., Singleton, N., and Meltzer, H. (2002). *Alcohol and Drug Use and Mental Health: National Statistics*. London: Stationary Office.

Curran, H. V. (1991). Benzodiazepines, memory and mood: A review. *Psychopharmacology*, **105**:1–8.

Curran, H. V. (2000). Psychopharmacological perspectives on memory. In: E. Tulving and F. I. M Craik (eds), *The Oxford Handbook of Memory*, pp. 539–554. Oxford: Oxford University Press.

Curran, H. V. and Travill, R. A. (1997). Mood and cognitive effects of 3,4-methylenedioxymethamphetamine (MDMA: 'ecstasy'): Weekend 'high' followed by mid-week low. *Addiction*, **92**:821–831.

Curran, H. V. and Weingartner, H. (2002). Psychopharmacology of human memory. In: A. D. Baddeley, M. D. Kopelman, and B. A. Wilson (eds), *The Handbook of Memory Disorders*, pp. 123–141. Chichester, UK: John Wiley & Sons.

Curran, H. V., Bond, A., O'Sullivan, G., *et al.* (1994). Memory functions, alprazolam and exposure therapy: A controlled longitudinal study of patients with agoraphobia and panic disorder. *Psychological Medicine*, **24**:969–976.

Curran, H. V., Kleckham, J., Bearn, J., Strang, J., and Wanigaratne, S. (2001). Effects of methadone on cognition, mood and craving in detoxifying opiate addicts: A dose–response study. *Psychopharmacology*, **154**:153–160.

Cutting, J. (1978). The relationship between Korsakoff's syndrome and 'alcoholic dementia'. *British Journal of Psychiatry*, **132**:240–251.

Davison, S. E. and Forshaw, D. M. (1993). Retracted confessions: Through opiate withdrawal to a new conceptual framework. *Medicine, Science and the Law*, **33**:285–290.

Davison, S. E. and Gossop, M. (1996). The problem of interviewing drug addicts in custody: A study of interrogative suggestibility and compliance. *Psychology, Crime and Law*, **2**:185–195.

Davison, S. E. and Gossop, M. (1999). The management of opiate addicts in police custody. *Medicine, Science and the Law*, **39**:153–160.

DeLuca, J. (2000). A cognitive neuroscience perspective on confabulation. *Neuropsychoanalysis*, **2**:119–132.

De Renzi, E., Faglioni, P., Nichelli, P., and Pignattari, L. (1984). Intellectual and memory impairment in moderate and heavy drinkers. *Cortex*, **20**:525–533.

Duffy, A. and Millin, R. (1996). Case study: Withdrawal syndrome in adolescent chronic cannabis users. *Journal of American Academy of Child and Adolescent Psychiatry*, **35**:1618–1621.

Ewing, J. A. (1984). Detecting alcoholism: The CAGE questionnaire. *Journal of the American Medical Association*, **252**:1905–1907.

Eysenck, H. J. and Eysenck, B. G. (1996). *Manual of the Eysenck Personality Scales*. London: Hodder & Stoughton.

Foulds, J., Stapleton, J., Feyerabend, C., Vesey, C., Jarvis, M., and Russell, M. A. H. (1992). Effect of transdermal nicotine patches on cigarette smoking: A double blind crossover study. *Psychopharmacology*, **106**:421–427.

Gilboa, A. and Moscovitch, M. (2002). The cognitive neuroscience of confabulation: A review and a model. In: A. D. Baddeley, M. D. Kopelman, and B. A. Wilson (eds), *The Handbook of Memory Disorders*, pp. 315–342. Chichester, UK: John Wiley & Sons.

Gossop, M. and Davison, S. E. (2000). Arrest, interrogation, statements and confessions: The complications of drug dependence. *American Journal of Forensic Psychiatry*, **21**:49–68.

Gossop, M., Darke, S., and Griffiths, P. (1995). Psychometric properties of the SDS in English and Australian samples of heroin, cocaine and amphetamine users. *Addiction*, **90**:607–614.

Gossop, M., Trakada, K., Stewart, D., and Witton, J. (2005). Reductions in criminal convictions after addiction treatment: 5-year follow-up. *Drug and Alcohol Dependence*, **79**:295–302.

Grant, I. (1987). Alcohol and the brain: Neuropsychological correlates. *Journal of Consulting and Clinical Psychology*, **55**:310–324.

Grant, I., Adams, K. M., and Carlin, A. S. (1978). The collaborative neuropsychological study of polydrug users. *Archives of General Psychiatry*, **35**:1063–1064.

Gudjonsson, G. H. (1989). Compliance in an interrogation situation: A new scale. *Personality and Individual Differences*, **10**:535–540.

Gudjonsson, G. H. (1997). *The Gudjonsson Suggestibility Scales Manual*. Hove, UK: Psychology Press.

Gudjonsson, G. H. (2003). *The Psychology of Interrogations and Confessions: A Handbook*. Chichester, UK: John Wiley & Sons.

Gudjonsson, G. H., Hannesdottir, K., Petursson, H., and Bjornsson, G. (2002). The effects of alcohol withdrawal on mental state, interrogative suggestibility, and compliance: An experimental study. *Journal of Forensic Psychiatry*, **13**:53–67.

Haque, Q. and Cumming, I. (2003). Intoxication and legal defences. *Advances in Psychiatric Treatment*, **9**: 144–151.

Harper, C. (1998). The neuropathology of alcohol-specific brain damage, or does alcohol damage the brain? *Journal of Neuropathology and Experimental Neurology*, **57**:101–110.

Hathaway, S. R. and McKinley, J. C. (1991). *The Minnesota Multiphasic Personality Inventory Manual*. Minneapolis, MN: University of Minnesota Press.

Heaton, R. K., Chelune, G. J., and Talley, J. L. (1993). *Wisconsin Card Sorting Test Manual*. Odessa, FL: Psychological Assessment Resources.

Holman, B. L., Carvalho, P. A., and Mendelson, J. (1991). Brain perfusion is abnormal in cocaine-dependent polydrug users: A study using technetium-99m-HMPAO and ASPECT. *Journal of Nuclear Medicine*, **32**:1206–1210.

Horner, M. D., Waid, L. R., Johnson, D. E., Latham, P. K., and Anton, R. F. (1999). The relationship of cognitive functioning to amount of recent and lifetime alcohol consumption in outpatient alcoholics. *Addictive Behaviours*, **24**:449–453.

Johns, A. (2000) Forensic aspects of alcohol and drug disorders. In: M. Gelder, J. Lopez-Ibor, and N. Andreasson (eds), *New Oxford Textbook of Psychiatry*. Oxford: Oxford University Press.

Johnson, S. L. (2003). *Therapist's Guide to Substance Abuse Intervention*. San Diego, USA: Academic Press.

Joyce, E. M. and Robbins, T. W. (1991). Frontal lobe function in Korsakoff and non-Korsakoff alcoholics: Planning and spatial working memory. *Neuropsychologia*, **29**:709–723.

Kassel, J. D. (1997). Smoking and attention: A review and reformulation of the stimulus-filter hypothesis. *Clinical Psychology Review*, **17**:451–478.

Kerr, J. S. and Hindmarch, I. (1998). The effects of alcohol alone or in combination with other drugs on information-processing, task performance and subjective responses. *Human Psychopharmacology—Clinical and Experimental*, **13**:1–9.

Kleinknecht, R. A. and Goldstein, S. G. (1972). Neuropsychological deficits associated with alcoholism: A review and discussion. *Quarterly Journal of Studies on Alcohol*, **33**:999–1019.

Knight, R. G. and Longmore, B. E. (1994). *Clinical Neuropsychology of Alcoholism* Hillsdale, NJ: Erlbaum.

Kopelman, M. D. (1985). Rates of forgetting in Alzheimer-type dementia and Korsakoff's syndrome. *Neuropsychologia*, **23**:623–638.

Kopelman, M. D. (1991). Frontal dysfunction and memory deficits in the alcoholic Korsakoff's syndrome and the Alzheimer-type dementia. *Brain*, **114**:117–137.

Kopelman, M. D. (1995). The Korsakoff Syndrome. *British Journal of Psychiatry*, **166**:154–173.

Kopelman, M. D., Ng, N., and Van den Brouke, O. (1997). Confabulation extending across episodic memory, personal and general semantic memory. *Cognitive Neuropsychology*, **14**:683–712.

Korsakoff, S. S. (1889). Psychic disorder in conjunction with peripheral neuritis. Translated and republished by M. Victor and P. I. Yakovlev (1955). *Neurology*, 5:394–406.

Lader, M. (1999). The influence of drugs on testimony. *Medicine, Science and the Law*, **39**:99–105.

Lezak, M. D. (2004). *Neuropsychological Assessment*, 4th edn. New York: Oxford University Press.

Løberg, T. and Miller, W. R. (1986). Personality, cognitive, and neuropsychological correlates of harmful alcohol consumptions: A cross-cultural comparison of clinical samples. *Annals of the New York Academy of Sciences*, **472**:75–97.

Lundquist, T. (1995). *Cognitive Dysfunctions in Chronic Cannabis Users Observed During Treatment: An Integrative Approach*. Stockholm: Almqvist & Wiksell International.

Macdonald, S., Erickson, P., and Wells, S. (2008). Predicting violence among cocaine, cannabis, and alcohol treatment clients. *Addictive Behaviors*, **33**:201–205.

Marsden, J., Gossop, M., Stewart. D., et al. (1998). The Maudsley Addiction Profile (MAP): A brief instrument for assessing treatment outcome. *Addiction*, **93**:1857–1867.

Marshall, E. J. and Farrell, M. (2003). Introduction to Special Issue on Addiction Psychiatry—Part 1. *Psychiatry*, 2:1.

McCann, U. D., Eligulashvili, V., and Ricaurte, G. A. (2000). 3,4-Methylenedioxymethamphetamine ('ecstasy') induced serotonin neurotoxicity: Clinical studies. *Neuropsychobiology*, **42**:11–16.

McClellan, A. T., Luborsky, L., Woody, G. E., and O'Brien, C. P. (1980). An improved diagnostic evaluation instrument for substance abuse patients: The Addiction Severity Index. *Journal of Nervous and Mental Diseases*, **168**:26–33.

Miller, L. L. (1984). Marijuana: Acute effects on human memory. In: S. Agurell, W. L. Dewey, and R. E. Willette (eds), *The Cannabinoids: Chemical, Pharmacologic and Therapeutic Aspects*, pp. 21–46. Orlando, FL: Academic Press.

Miller, L. L. and Branconnier, R. J. (1983). Cannabis: Effects on memory and the cholinergic limbic system. *Psychological Bulletin*, **93**:441–456.

Miller, W. R. and Tonigan, J. S. (1996). Assessing drinkers' motivation for change: The Stages of Change Readiness and Treatment Eagerness Scale (SOCRATES). *Psychology of Addictive Behaviours*, **10**:81–89.

Millon, T., Davis, R., and Millon, C. (1997). *Manual for the Millon Clinical Multiaxial Inventory—III (MCMI-III*, 2nd edn. Minneapolis: National Computer Systems.

Milton, J., Amin, S., Singh, S. P., *et al.* (2001). Aggressive incidents in first-episode psychosis. *British Journal of Psychiatry*, **178**:433–440.

Munro, C. A., Saxton, J., and Butters, M. A. (2000). The neuropsychological consequences of abstinence among older alcoholics: A cross-sectional study. *Alcoholism, Clinical and Experimental Research*, **24**:1510–1516.

O'Brien, C. P. (1996). Drug addiction and drug abuse. In: J. G. Hardman, L. E. Limbird, P. B. Molinoff, R. W. Ruddon, and A. G. Gilman (eds), *Goodman and Gilman's The Pharmacological Basis of Therapeutics*, 9th edn, pp. 557–577. New York: McGraw-Hill.

O'Connor, M. and Verfaellie, M. (2002). The amnesic syndrome: Overview and subtypes. In: A. D. Baddeley, M. D. Kopelman, and B. A. Wilson (eds), *The Handbook of Memory Disorders*. Chichester, UK: Wiley.

O'Malley, S. S. and Gawin, F. H. (1990). Abstinence symptomatology and neuropsychological impairment in chronic cocaine abusers. In: J. W. Spencer and J. J. Boren (eds), *Residual Effects of Abused Drugs on Behaviour*. National Institute on Drug Abuse Research Monograph 101. US Department of Health & Human Sciences Pub. No. (ADM) 90-1719. Washington, DC: Supt. of Docs, US Government Printing Office.

Park, S., Knopick, C., McGurk, S., and Meltzer, H. (1999). Nicotine impairs spatial working memory while leaving spatial attention intact. *Neuropsychopharmacology*, **22**:200–209.

Parrott, A. C. and Lasky, J. (1998). Ecstasy (MDMA) effects upon mood and cognition: Before, during and after a Saturday night dance. *Psychopharmacology*, **139**:261–268.

Parrott, A. C., Lees, A., Garnham, N. J., Jones, M., and Wesnes, K. (1998). Cognitive performance in recreational users of MDMA or 'ecstasy': Evidence for memory deficits. *Journal of Psychopharmacology*, **12**:79–83.

Parsons, O. A. and Nixon, S. J. (1998). Cognitive functioning in sober social drinkers: A review of the research since 1986. *Journal of Studies on Alcohol*, **59**:180–190.

Parsons, O. A., Butters, N., and Nathan, P. E. (1987). Neuropsychology of alcoholism: Implications for diagnosis and treatment. New York: Guildford Press.

Pearson, R., Robertson, G., and Gibb, R. (2000). The identification and treatment of opiate users in police custody. *Medicine, Science and the Law*, **40**:305–312.

Peeke, S. C. and Peeke, H. V. S. (1984). Attention, memory, and cigarette smoking. *Psychopharmacology*, **84**:205–216.

Piccinelli, M., Tessari, E., Bortolomasi M., *et al.* (1997). Efficacy of the alcohol use disorders identification test as a screening tool for hazardous alcohol intake and related disorders in primary care: A validity study. *British Medical Journal*, **314**:420–424.

Pope, H. G., Jr and Yurgelun-Todd, D. (1996). The residual cognitive effects of heavy marijuana use in college students. *Journal of the American Medical Association*, **275**:521–527.

Pope, H. G., Gruber, A. J., and Yurgelun-Todd, D. (1995). The residual neuropsychological effects of cannabis: The current status of research. *Drug and Alcohol Dependence*, **38**:25–34.

Powell, J. (2004). The effects of medication and other substances on cognitive functioning. In: L. H. Goldstein and J. E. McNeil (eds), *Clinical Neuropsychology: A Practical Guide to Assessment and Management for Clinicians*. Chichester/New York: John Wiley & Sons.

Pudney, S. (2002). Home Office Research Study 253. The road to ruin? Sequences of initiation into drug use and offending by young people in Britain. Home Office Research, Development and Statistics Directorate.

Pyszora, N., Barker, A., and Kopelman, M. (2003). Amnesia for criminal offences: A study of life sentence prisoners. *Journal of Forensic Psychiatry and Psychology*, **14**:475–490.

Rourke, S. B. and Løberg, T. (1996). Neurobehavioural correlates of alcoholism. In:. I. Grant and K. M. Adams (eds), *Neuropsychological Assessment of Neuropsychiatric Disorders*. Oxford: Oxford University Press.

Ryan, C. and Butters, N. (1986). Neuropsychology of alcoholism. In: D. Wedding, A. M. Horton, Jr and J. S. Webster (eds), *The Neuropsychology Handbook*. New York: Springer Verlag.

Schinka, J. A., Vanderploeg, R. D., Rogish, M., and Ordorica, P. J. (2002). Effects of alcohol and cigarette use on cognition in middle-aged adults. *Journal of the International Neuropsychological Society*, **8**:683–690.

Shaw, K., Hunt, I. M., Flynn S., et al. (2006). The role of alcohol and drugs in homicides in England and Wales. *Addiction*, **101**:1117–1124.

Shelton, M. D. and Parsons, O. A. (1987) Neuropsychological performance in alcoholics: I. Self-assessment of everyday functioning. *Journal of Clinical Psychology*, **43**:395–403.

Smiley, A. (1986). Marijuana: On-road and driving simulator studies. *Alcohol, Drugs and Driving*, **2**:121–134.

Soyka, M. (1990). Psychopathological characteristics in alcohol hallucinosis and paranoid schizophrenia. *Acta Psychiatrica Scandinavica*, **81**:255–259.

Solowij, N. (1998). *Cannabis and cognitive functioning*. International Research Monographs in the Addictions (IRMA). Cambridge: Cambridge University Press.

Swanson, J. W. (1994) Mental disorder, substance abuse, and community violence: An epidemiological approach. In: J. Monahan J and H. J. Steadman (eds), *Violence and Mental Disorder—Developments in Risk Assessment*, pp. 101–136. London: University of Chicago Press.

Squire, L. R. and Butters, N. (1992). *Neuropsychology of Memory*, 2nd edn. New York: Guildford Press.

Sweeny, J. A., Meisel, L., Walsh, V. L., and Castrovinci, D. (1989). Assessment of cognitive functioning in poly-substance abusers. *Journal of Clinical Psychology*, **45**:346–351.

Taylor, M. A. (1999). *The Fundamentals of Clinical Neuropsychiatry*. New York: Oxford University Press.

Vaillant, G. R. (1983). *The Natural History of Alcoholism*. Cambridge, MA: Harvard University Press.

Wechsler, D. (1999). *Wechsler Adult Intelligence Scale—3rd UK Edition*. Oxford: Harcourt Assessment.

White, A. M., Jamieson-Drake, D. W., and Swartzwelder, H. S. (2002). Prevalence and correlates of alcohol-induced blackouts among college students: Results of an e-mail survey. *Journal of American College Health*, **51**:117–131.

Zuckerman, M. (1979). Development of a situation-specific trait-state test for the prediction and measurement of affective responses. *Journal of Consulting and Clinical Psychology*, **45**:513–523.

Chapter 9

Traumatic brain injury

Rodger Wood

The introduction of new Civil Procedure Rules in England and Wales in 1998 (Department for Constitutional Affairs, 1998a, b) promoted the role of clinical neuropsychologists as expert witnesses in personal injury litigation. Lawyers frequently ask for an assessment of cognitive and neurobehavioural deficits following traumatic brain injury to help the court understand the impact of head trauma on emotional adjustment, employability, mental capacity, and potential for community living (with or without support). In less serious cases, an opinion might be sought on the need for psychological therapy, in order to promote psychological adjustment and coping strategies. In cases of more serious injury, neuropsychologists may be asked to advise on a claimant's need for specialist post-acute brain injury rehabilitation (which is usually funded privately, through special damages) and whether such rehabilitation will improve psychosocial outcome. If poor psychosocial outcome is predicted, post-acute neurobehavioural rehabilitation may still be necessary to make the claimant easier to manage in a community setting. It may then be necessary for the neuropsychologist to give advice on alternative arrangements for long-term care, taking into consideration not only the claimant's cognitive difficulties but also any behaviour or personality problems that may influence the day-to-day management of the claimant.

The instructing solicitor may ask for neuropsychological advice on the type or level of case management and support worker involvement, giving reasons why particular support packages are necessary, and how long certain levels of care are required. In elderly claimants, the impact of brain injury on the ageing process will need to be considered. However, the impact of serious brain damage on the ageing process is also an important factor when claimants are young people and very long-term care arrangements are being considered. In this respect, recent research into the very long-term psychosocial outcome of serious head trauma suggests that prospects for very late 'recovery' may not be as bleak as was initially thought (Wood & Rutterford, 2006a).

Another important role of the neuropsychologist is to distinguish between problems of cognition, personality, and behaviour that are organically mediated from those that are psychogenic, reflecting emotional adjustment problems, or even deliberate embellishment for the purpose of financial gain (see Chapter 11 of this volume). It is therefore clear that, in order to address the complex cognitive and psychosocial issues arising from head trauma, clinical neuropsychologists engaging in medico-legal work need to have considerable experience, specifically with regard to acute and post-acute stages of recovery, head-injury rehabilitation (especially at a post-acute stage), and how well people function at later stages of recovery when they return to the community.

This chapter will try to elucidate how knowledge of the mechanical forces involved in head trauma can influence neuropsychological abilities generally (and test performance in particular) and how observations of behaviour made during neuropsychological examination can reveal aspects of brain dysfunction that supplement (or sometimes supersede) quantitative information obtained from formal tests. The chapter will not focus on specific neuropsychological approaches to assessment or on procedural issues surrounding forensic neuropsychology. These have already been addressed by Powell & Wood (2001), McKinlay & McGowan (2003), and Powell (2004), and are further addressed by in Chapter 10 of this volume.

Understanding the role of mechanical forces in head trauma

A relationship exists between mechanical forces at the time of injury and the consequent neuropathology, symptom pattern, and course of recovery. Understanding this relationship can improve the neuropsychologist's ability to interpret test results and predict psychosocial outcome.

Road traffic accidents and falls constitute the most frequent form of head trauma seen in a medico-legal context (Thurman *et al.*, 2007). Both types of injury involve sudden changes of velocity (with or without direct injury to the head), involving acceleration–deceleration forces that cause the brain to oscillate and rotate within the cranial vault, distorting a number of cerebral systems and structures. Impact is maximum at the frontal and temporal poles and the medial convexity of the temporal lobes (Shaw, 2002). Bigler (2001) reported that accidents involving acceleration–deceleration injury are far more likely to generate diffuse axonal injury (even in the absence of a direct blow to the head—as in whiplash injury) than the mechanical forces involved when head trauma is the result of a static concussion, such as in an assault or being struck by a falling object.

Frontotemporal neuropsychological systems mediate cognitive abilities and emotions important to social behaviour (Eslinger, 1999). The term 'neurobehavioural disability' has been coined to describe the combination of cognitive, emotional, behavioural, and personality changes resulting from injuries to these structures and systems (Levin *et al.*, 1982; Wood, 1987). Wood (2001) described five categories of neurobehavioural disability: (i) loss of cognitive control; (ii) executive dysfunction; (iii) disorders of drive and motivation; (iv) disorders of inhibitory control; and (v) altered personality (which would now be described as an emotional deficit disorder, reflecting alexithymia and loss of empathy; see Wood & Williams 2007, 2008). These categories are not mutually exclusive and usually interact to prevent or weaken a person's capacity to undertake social roles that define independent social behaviour. They all have neuropsychological relevance in the context of a medico-legal examination because, individually or collectively, they can influence a range of outcome characteristics relevant to judging quantum or deciding on interim awards for special damages to cover specialist rehabilitation, case management, or similar support services (for a detailed description of neurobehavioural disorders, see Wood, 2001, and Worthington & Wood, 2008). However, whilst many neurobehavioural problems have a major impact on psychosocial functioning, they are not easily identified using traditional neuropsychological tests, nor from the nomenclature of classification systems used in psychiatry (DSM-IV and ICD-10).

Measuring the severity of head trauma

An important starting point in any neuropsychological examination is to determine the severity of injury, which is then used as a framework for interpreting test results. Inexperienced clinicians sometimes use the test results as an index of injury severity; however, this reflects the logical fallacy—*post hoc ergo propter hoc* (arguing from correlations to causes). Test results can be influenced by a number of factors and it can be embarrassing to learn that someone designated as having suffered 'severe brain damage' on the basis of their poor test performance is later shown never to have been unconscious or have any other index of severe injury to support the test results (which may have to be explained on the basis of psychological factors or even deliberate embellishment). Two indices are regularly used to determine severity in medico-legal reports—the Glasgow Coma Score and post-traumatic amnesia. Neuroimaging procedures are also used to determine the presence of contusions or structural damage, reflecting 'objective' evidence of brain damage. These three methods are described below.

Glasgow Coma Score

The Glasgow Coma Score (GCS; Teasdale & Jennett, 1974) is the internationally accepted method of evaluating levels of consciousness in acute neurological disorders. The score comprises three response categories (eye opening, motor response, and verbal response). A GCS of 3–8 is regarded as a severe or very severe injury involving coma; 8–13 is a moderately severe injury, and 13–15 is mild concussion. Those who have a Glasgow Coma Score of 3–8 at the scene of the accident, or on admission to hospital, almost inevitably exhibit a number of neuropsychological deficits and long-term alterations to behaviour and personality that may have lifetime implications for relationships, employment, and independent living (Jennett, 1976).

The first point of reference for GCS should be the ambulance records as these report on the patient's level of awareness at the scene of the accident. The next point of reference will be at the time of admission to hospital. In many cases, an improvement in GCS score will be evident between the time of injury and admission to hospital, but some patients will show deterioration, due to brain swelling or subdural haemorrhage. In such cases, neurosurgical intervention may follow. Length of coma is an important indicator of early brain dysfunction and has prognostic significance for psychosocial outcome (Bishara et al., 1992). However, care needs to be taken in using length of coma as an estimate of severity as many patients who arrive at hospital in an unconscious or neurologically unstable condition are sedated and intubated, and then placed on a ventilator for a period of time until medically stable and capable of maintaining their own airway. This process will artificially extend the duration of coma after injury and cause it to be an unreliable indicator of severity. Therefore, it is important to study the hospital records carefully to determine what medical interventions have taken place that may influence the time taken to recover consciousness fully (GCS 15).

Post-traumatic amnesia (PTA)

PTA is usually obtained retrospectively by asking the patient open questions about what they remember of the scene of the accident, then subsequent events (with particular reference to the arrival of an ambulance, the journey to hospital, arrival at A&E, transfer to the ward, or, if not detained in hospital, conveyance home) (see McMillan et al., 1996). A period of amnesia lasting less than 1 hour indicates mild concussion; 1–24 hours indicates moderate concussion, and 24 hours to 7 days points to severe concussion, whilst PTA in excess of 7 days reflects very severe concussion (Russell, 1974). Many patients display islands of memory whilst still in PTA, but the point at which the amnesic interval ends is indicated by the patient's ability to recall general activities from one day to the next. Therefore, fragmented memories for events at the scene of the accident or shortly afterwards, or a description of events that lacks a clear timeframe (remembered incidents that seem to immediately follow each other when, logically, there are periods of time separating them) reflect discontinuity of information processing that contributes to an estimate of post-traumatic amnesia. In this respect, it is important to note that entries in the hospital records that signal recovery of consciousness often include the phrase 'orientated for time and place'. However, this observation should not be used as an indicator of the time when the patient recovered clear and continuous memory. Patients are capable of giving names, addresses, and dates of birth (overlearned information), yet have no memory of doing so at a later point in time.

Although believed by many to be a crude measure of injury severity, PTA is probably a more reliable indicator of long-term outcome from head trauma than Glasgow Coma Scores (Bishara et al., 1992). Clinicians must take care not to lead the patient about what they recall after the injury and to check the hospital records to see whether sedation, in the form of general anaesthetic or morphine-based analgesia, was administered because this will reduce the patient's ability to process information and will artificially extend the duration of PTA. It is also important to distinguish organically induced PTA from loss of memory that accompanies emotional trauma or extreme pain. In the case of severe emotional trauma, events associated with the scene of the accident can be blocked from conscious awareness. This is one of the criteria in DSM-IV for classifying post-traumatic stress disorder. Extreme pain can also interfere with information processing and give a misleading impression of PTA duration. The injured person may be so preoccupied or distressed by pain that they lack awareness of surrounding events and even lose track of time. Therefore, when asked about events following the accident, they can appear vague, even amnesic, but for reasons that are emotional and pain-related, not organic. Therefore, in cases where patients report long periods of amnesia, perhaps for several weeks, when there is no history of loss of consciousness or early neurological deficit, and no neuroimaging abnormality, neuropsychologists should be alert to the possibility that the amnesic interval (whilst genuinely reported) reflects emotional blocking of memories, not true PTA, placing the injury in the mild–moderate rather than the severe category.

Retrograde amnesia is sometimes used as an index of injury severity, but it does not have the same value as PTA because retrograde amnesia tends to 'shrink' with the passage of time (Russell & Nathan, 1946; Benson & Geschwind, 1967). In the weeks after injury, a patient may report a loss of memory for several days or weeks prior to the injury; however, with the passage of time, memories of this interval are recovered, to the point that the amnesic interval can shrink to a few minutes. Long periods of retrograde amnesia are rare after head trauma, unless there has been injury to hippocampal structures (Kopelman, 2002). These topics are discussed in more detail in Chapter 6 of this volume. In cases where there is no evidence of subcortical damage, yet the patient still describes loss of biographical memory for many years before the accident, it is probable that recall is blocked because of an extreme psychological reaction (dissociation). Long retrograde amnesia may also be reported in a forensic context, such as when a person, accused of a crime, claims to have no memory of the incident for which they are accused, especially if they have sustained a head injury after the alleged crime. Excessive alcohol and/or drug use, as well as extreme emotions, may also cause crime-related amnesia (Kopelman, 2002). Defendants in criminal cases may also simulate amnesia for the offence (Porter *et al.*, 2001; Cima *et al.*, 2002).

Symptom validity testing has been used to assess the veracity of memory loss in individuals who claim to have no recollections of a crime. Symptom validity testing is a forced choice procedure in which defendants are asked questions about a crime, each question having two equally plausible answers, one of which is correct. Genuine amnesia for a crime should result in random performance. Significantly below chance performance is an indication of malingering in the context of crime-related amnesia (e.g. Frederick *et al.*, 1995; Denney, 1996). It has been argued that this procedure has limited value because intelligent malingerers would easily understand its rationale (Rogers *et al.*, 1993). However, Merckelbach *et al.* (2002) found that nearly 60% of undergraduate psychology students performed significantly below chance on a symptom validity test designed to detect feigned amnesia for a mock crime. They argue that even intelligent people can have incorrect statistical notions, giving support to symptom validity testing as a method to use in such cases. The topics of suboptimal effort and malingering are discussed fully in Chapter 11 of this volume.

Neuroimaging

Neuroimaging scans provide the most obvious indication of brain damage per se, but a normal brain scan does not necessarily mean a normal brain, especially in a neuropsychological sense. Computerized tomography (CT) scans, for example, lack the resolution needed to identify punctuate haemorrhages associated with diffuse axonal injury (Bigler, 2001). Bigler also points out that it may be weeks or months before stable degenerative patterns can be established by neuroimaging techniques. CT scans obtained at the time of admission to hospital may therefore fail to reveal contusional injuries that later become evident on magnetic resonance imaging (MRI) scans (Groswasser et al., 1987; Wilson et al., 1998). However, contemporary imaging methods used in routine clinical examination only provide gross inspection of the macroscopic brain, whereas neuropsychological dysfunction often reflects microscopic damage—'even our best contemporary functional neuroimaging tools ... are limited in their ability to assess neurobehavioural correlates' (Bigler, 2001, p. 123).

In cases where there is clear evidence of neuropsychological dysfunction but a normal brain scan, the neuropsychologist may request a functional imaging scan, such as a PET (positron emission tomography) or SPECT (single positive emission tomography) scan. Only the latter is in regular clinical use. SPECT is a functional neuroimaging procedure that uses measures of cerebral blood flow to provide a 'picture' of the brain at work. Newton et al. (1992) reported that SPECT scans obtained between 3 and 36 months after injury found more lesions than CT or MRI scans, and a correlation between the number of cerebral blood flow defects and the functional status of the patient (measured by the Glasgow Outcome Score). However, SPECT remains a fairly crude form of functional neuroimaging as scans are open to various forms of interpretation. One reason for this is that abnormal cerebral blood flow can reflect alterations in levels of cortical arousal (in the context of mood or stress-related disorders), rather than brain damage per se (Gur et al., 1987).

The neuropsychological examination

The clinical interview

Most clinical interviews are semi-structured, with the aim of gaining details of the patient's personal history, accident details (and memories), and reported post-accident problems. However, the process of obtaining such details offers an opportunity to observe behaviour that may be neuropsychologically relevant, such as: impulsive or careless answers, social disinhibition, poor concentration, fatigue, difficulty with descriptive language, indifference to circumstances (possible euphoria), expressions of anger and resentment, an overinvestment in symptoms, a concrete style of thinking, denial of problems (or lack of awareness), and inappropriate affect. The manner in which questions are answered can also offer significant neuropsychological insights; for example, are the patient's comments direct and to the point, or are they given in a vague, rambling, circumstantial, and tangential manner. The examiner also needs to contrast a patient's ability to recall and describe recent events associated with reported neuropsychological problems and with their performance on standardized tests of memory, administered as part of the formal neuropsychological examination.

When describing the circumstances of the accident, or its impact on day-to-day functioning, it is important to note the reaction of patients; for example, do they reveal emotions and cry (reflecting some form of persisting emotional entanglement with the accident experience) or are they so objective in their account that they appear dispassionate, detached, or indifferent to circumstances, such as the death of another person involved in the accident. Some patients may exhibit over-inclusive thinking and provide too many details of the injury and its surrounding circumstances, often using dramatic language and gestures that appear to exaggerate the impact of the injury. The broad range of descriptions, expressions, and response styles to questions during interview should alert the clinician to the neuropsychological and emotional impact of injury and how this may affect performance on neuropsychological tests. For example, Rapoport et al. (2005) found that head-trauma patients who were depressed had significantly lower scores on measures of working memory, processing speed, verbal memory, and executive dysfunction.

It is not always easy to detect signs of neurobehavioural disability in a semi-structured consulting room interview because the structure implicit to formal clinical interviews can mask many subtle yet pervasive neurobehavioural weaknesses (e.g. Wood & Rutterford, 2004). It is therefore important to interview a close relative or friend who knew the patient prior to injury and is capable of commenting on changes in their ability, behaviour, or personality. Some clinicians prefer to interview relatives separately, in case they feel inhibited about making negative comments in front of the patient. Other clinicians prefer to interview relatives with the patient present, in order to see how the patient reacts to negative comments. Do they show surprise—indicating diminished awareness; anger or denial—implying problems of judgement (social interpretation); or indifference (in some cases the patient will laugh or make a joke about negative changes reported by relatives)? Such observations offer a rich source of information about neurobehavioural legacies of head trauma. However, judgement must be used when deciding how to structure the interview. Negative comments made by relatives when the patient is present may generate an antagonistic response that will have recriminations when the assessment has ended and could further compromise already fragile family relationships. It may be wise to elicit the bare bones of information from a relative whilst the patient is present but obtain a more detailed description at the end of the assessment process by interviewing relatives separately.

Information provided by patients and relatives during interview should be considered in the context of our knowledge about the sequelae associated with different degrees of injury severity. For example, if the injury was mild or moderate, the examiner needs to judge whether the reported symptoms appear consistent with those normally seen following such injuries. Secondly, understanding the nature of the injury (and the mechanical forces involved) gives an indication as to which functions of the brain are most likely to be affected, allowing the neuropsychologist to distinguish which behaviour problems reported by relatives (or the patient) are likely to be a direct consequence of the injury (such as mood swings reflecting loss of inhibitory control following damage to orbitofrontal mechanisms) and which are likely to be a consequence of psychological (adjustment) problems. These different aetiologies have different prognostic value and usually indicate different treatment approaches.

Observations obtained during interview should be compared with the content of self-report inventories used to explore personality or emotional adjustment. Some patients do not spontaneously express symptoms of post-traumatic anxiety during interview and may not appear anxious or depressed, yet they respond to self-report inventories in a way that suggests significant affective morbidity. Differences between the patient's appearance and comments during interview and their subsequent response to inventories needs to be reconciled by the neuropsychologist because they could have an impact on test performance or how performance is interpreted with respect to psychosocial functioning.

Examination of cognitive abilities

Most neuropsychological reports use standardized tests organized into sections that measure intelligence, attention, memory, mental speed, and executive function (however, see Wood, 2009, regarding the limitations of this approach). In addition, observations are usually made about language function, praxis, coordination, and perception, although after head trauma, these functions are not always formally tested, as they might be after stroke injuries. There is no prescription for using particular tests in a neuropsychological examination (see Powell & Wood, 2001; McKinlay & McGowan, 2003; Powell, 2004) and clinicians are free to select from a large range of tests, on the assumption that they are properly standardized for use on a particular category of brain injury (see Lezak *et al.*, 2004).

Intelligence

The majority of practitioners rely on the Wechsler Adult Intelligence Scale—Third Edition (WAIS-III; Wechsler, 1997a) to measure intelligence, a time-consuming process that may have only limited value as measures of intelligence cannot be relied on as an index of impairment or recovery after head trauma (Walsh, 1985), nor can they predict the psychosocial impact of brain injury (see Wood & Rutterford, 2004). It is therefore important that neuropsychologists distinguish intelligence, as a psychological construct measured by tests, from applied intelligence, as a form of socially adaptive executive behaviour, because there is often little relationship between them. Walsh (1985) noted that persons with seemingly preserved intelligence failed to cope with the demands of their occupation or profession and referred to this as the 'frontal lobe paradox'. Therefore, in a medico-legal context, neuropsychologists should be cautious about using measures of intelligence as an index of recovery from which one can predict return to employment and other forms of social functioning.

There is no particular relationship between severity of brain injury and type or degree of intellectual impairment (Shallice & Burgess, 1991). Many cases of severe brain injury show no reduction in measured levels of intellectual ability compared wih estimates of premorbid ability obtained from the National Adult Reading Test—Restandardised (NART-R; Nelson & Willison 1991), the Wechsler Test of Adult Reading (WTAR; Wechsler, 2001) or via a demographic index of ability (Crawford & Allan, 1997). It is therefore difficult to understand why some cases of relatively minor injury display blunted intelligence or a profile that suggests patchy impairment of ability. In the latter case, it is always important to obtain information about developmental abilities and school performance. Some people who exhibit an uneven scatter of subtest scores may have a history of mild developmental learning difficulty that would explain variations in intellectual performance unrelated to head trauma. A recent study has indicated that such cases are overrepresented in a head-trauma population (Wood & Rutterford, 2006b).

In the context of a medico-legal examination, it is important to distinguish between a person's ability to express knowledge about something (the idea of how a task is performed) from the actual ability itself (successfully implementing the task), what Teuber (1964) referred to as '*the curious dissociation between knowing and doing*'. This legacy of frontal injury is easily overlooked if one restricts oneself to testing a person's verbal knowledge (IQ) without establishing from relatives information regarding cognitive performance in real-life activities. This was illustrated by Wood & Rutterford (2004) in the case of MN, monitored for 18 years after a very serious head injury. From the earliest stages of recovery, he appeared bright and articulate, with a WAIS-R IQ in the superior range and few signs of attention, memory, or executive deficits on standardized tests. However, it soon became evident that he was not able to apply this intelligence to everyday life in the community. He stumbled from one low-paid job to another for a number of years, relying heavily on his parents for support and failing to function at a level commensurate with his measured cognitive abilities.

Attention and information processing

The amount of information we can process at any time depends largely on our attentional capacity, which itself relies on the ability to focus, sustain, divide, and switch attention, processes that are largely controlled by conscious effort (vigilance). Injury to the brain can disrupt these attention control mechanisms and increase distractibility, making it difficult to switch fluently between different attentional sets. This can influence what information is processed and how social situations are evaluated. Kreutzer (1993) argued that many social problems experienced by brain-damaged people occur because they do not perceive relevant social cues, what Van Zomeren & Brouwer (1994) described as social inattentiveness. Ironically, patients may be unable to evaluate their own social performance, even though they can recognize errors in other people's performance. Speed and efficiency of information processing is one of the more sensitive measures of cerebral dysfunction. However, performance on tests of mental speed can reflect the influence of anxiety, fatigue, and medication, making it necessary to exclude these as possible contributors to poor test performance.

Impairment of attention is an important factor contributing to diminished insight (Wood, 2001). Insight has been implicated as a factor predicting the quality of long-term psychosocial recovery (Brooks & McKinlay, 1983). Stuss & Benson (1986) described insight as the highest attribute of frontal function. It is an important factor in maturational development and thus one reason why adolescents who suffer brain injury are at risk of displaying late behavioural and social sequelae (Thomsen, 1989). Thomsen proposed that young people with head injuries lacked insight and a realistic attitude, arguing that this was responsible for delayed and incomplete maturational development. Insight is an important factor underpinning social judgement, which, in turn, depends on the capacity for both self-awareness and awareness of the needs of others. We may only become aware of deficits in self-awareness and social judgement from information provided by relatives, although Burgess et al. (1998) suggested that differences between the DEX-S (self-report) and the DEX-I scores (informant report) from the BADS may form an index of 'insight'.

Memory

Disorders of memory are one of the most frequent and socially intrusive legacies of head trauma. The Wechsler Memory Scale—Third Edition (WMS-III; Wechsler, 1997b) is the assessment tool used by the majority of clinicians, but an assortment of memory tests is available to examine specific aspects of memory in different modalities. However, some patients who complain of memory impairment in everyday life often manage to perform normally on clinical tests. This was originally noticed by Sunderland *et al.* (1983) and represents one of many dislocations between performance on clinical tests and performance in real-life settings. In the case of memory test performance, the dislocation may be explained by the particular kind of memory impairment associated with head trauma. Unlike cases of stroke or encephalitis, memory impairment after head trauma rarely presents as amnesia. The most frequent complaints of head-trauma patients relate to forgetfulness (a failure to recall at an appropriate time what is spontaneously recalled, or prompted into recall, at a later time)—a disorder of prospective memory. More often than not, such memory complaints reflect weaknesses of attention, involving depth of processing, described by patients as difficulty absorbing information during conversation, resulting in forgetfulness.

Discrepancies between (good) performance on clinical tests of memory in the consulting room, and problems reported by the patient (and relatives) encountered in everyday life can be explained by the cognitively advantageous nature of the test-taking situation. The assessment usually takes place in a quiet room. Efforts are made to relax the patient and administer tests in a way that does not exacerbate levels of fatigue. In such circumstances, patients are able to focus all their attention on a single task, whereas in real life, attention has to be divided simultaneously over a range of tasks and changing situations that have different attentional requirements, overwhelming the injured brain and resulting in 'forgetfulness'. Clinicians should therefore seek to balance test results with information from relatives about everyday memory performance.

Reason (1984) described everyday attentional lapses that underpin the type of forgetfulness seen after head trauma as 'actions not as planned'. Examples are: putting food in the oven instead of the freezer; putting things down and losing them within minutes; and going into a room to get something, then 'forgetting' what one is looking for. Such incidents are part of normal everyday experience; however, they are much more frequent and intrusive after head trauma and can disrupt a person's lifestyle, leading to anxiety and loss of confidence. Attentional lapses of memory reflect problems of working memory that can be explained on the basis of a faulty supervisory attentional system (Shallice, 1982), which may form part of an executive disorder.

Executive ability

The ability to organize and plan actions, structure and sequence activities, employ reasoning and judgement, and use initiative to decide when an action should be implemented are not directly related to intelligence but are central to the notion of 'executive behaviour'. Executive dysfunction is probably the most pervasive of all neurobehavioural legacies following serious head trauma. However, in mild or moderate forms, the disability can be quite subtle and may escape recognition in the context of a structured interview and assessment. People with executive deficits often give a plausible account of themselves and perform well on tests of intelligence and memory, yet their relatives describe a general loss of efficiency in daily life (one of a number of interesting dislocations between ability and performance in cognitive functions after head trauma).

A major challenge for neuropsychologists working in a medico-legal framework is to translate performance on office-based tests into cognitive interpretations of neurobehavioural problems in the course of everyday life, as reported by claimants or relatives. To address this problem, neuropsychological assessment is moving away from tests that have discriminative validity for diagnostic purposes to tests that have ecological validity. Chayton & Schmitter-Edgecombe (2003) describe two principles upon which neuropsychological tests are based: the principle of verisimilitude—the degree to which a test resembles the cognitive demands of real-life tasks, and the principle of veridicality—the degree to which performance on a neuropsychological test is empirically related to measures of everyday functioning.

The Multiple Errands Test (MET; Shallice & Burgess, 1991) and Behavioural Assessment of Dysexecutive Syndrome (BADS; Wilson et al., 1996) are founded on the principle of verisimilitude. The MET is described by Burgess (2003, pp. 315–316) as a test with *'the most obvious ecological validity in current use'*, one that is *'highly sensitive both to brain damage in general and to specific executive problems'*. However, the test is also time-consuming and is not conducive to most clinicians' idea of a routine clinical examination, principally because it is not an office-based test and has to be conducted in a community setting, subject to the vagaries of weather, public reaction, and occasional professional embarrassment. Recent refinements are attempting to address these limitations (Knight et al., 2002), but the procedure does not yet lend itself to medico-legal assessment.

BADS is composed of six tests administered conventionally in an office setting. The tests were evaluated on 78 brain-injured patients by Wilson et al. (1998). However, only 59% of the cohort had suffered a closed head injury, the remainder comprising patients who had suffered encephalitis, dementia, or stroke. In the initial validation studies, the ecological validity of BADS was measured using the Dysexecutive Questionnaire (DEX). DEX is a supplementary measure to BADS and is considered to be a sensitive and ecologically valid measure of dysexecutive symptoms among patients with different types of neurological disorders (Wilson *et al.*, 1998). Moderate, negative correlations (ranging from −0.31 for Key Search to −0.46 for Zoo Map) were established between DEX-I (informant report) and each of the six individual BADS tests. Therefore, the BADS subtests have different ecological validity and different relationships to informant ratings of real-life executive behaviours, as measured by DEX. However, Norris & Tate (2000) found that, in a head-trauma sample, only one of the BADS subtests (Zoo Map) correlated with independent ratings on DEX, but this was not in the expected direction. They found that the combined scores of three BADS subtests discriminated between a brain-injured and a control group, but this accounted for only 16.2% of the variance in general cognitive functioning across different domains. The generally poor relationships between BADS subtests and everyday performance may reflect the influence of general intelligence on executive test performance. Duncan *et al.* (1995) noted that many tests of executive function measure primarily a non-specific intellectual function, reminiscent of g (the general intelligence factor), a theoretical proposition that has received empirical support from studies on head-injured patients (Duncan *et al.*, 1997). Stokes & Bajo (2003) found that IQ should be taken into account when deciding whether a particular level of performance should be considered 'dysexecutive'. Using BADS, they found that only the Zoo Map and Key Search tests correlated with any factors on DEX before IQ was partialled out. Other new executive tests, such as the Hayling and Brixton tests also failed to show any correlations.

The Hayling and Brixton tests (Burgess & Shallice, 1997) seem to adhere to the principle of veridicality. Hayling and Brixton procedures are sensitive to executive functions assumed to be frequently impaired after frontal injury. The Hayling test measures initiation speed and response suppression, whilst the Brixton test measures rule detection. These cognitive functions are important in a range of social and functional activities. However, it is not clear whether the tests will be useful in an assessment of head trauma because they were standardized on 91 patients with circumscribed neoplastic and haemorrhagic lesions but not head injury. Several recent studies that used these measures with head-trauma patients failed to find correlations, or reported only weak correlations, between Hayling and Brixton tests and independent DEX ratings (Bajo & Nathaniel-James, 2001; Odhuba *et al.*, 2005; Wood & Liossi, 2006), implying that caution should be used when employing such tests for medico-legal purposes, especially when assessing claimants who have low premorbid estimates of intelligence, as this may influence relationships between test scores and everyday cognitive skills (Chayton & Schmitter-Edgecombe, 2003). Burgess & Alderman (2004) acknowledged that many executive tests in current use have yet to establish their clinical utility because performance on such tests does not always correlate with performance in real life.

The problem of 'capacity'

The England and Wales Mental Capacity Act (2005) has given neuropsychologists a central role in the assessment of capacity. Prior to the Act, neuropsychologists were asked to advise on a patient's mental capacity, but ultimately had to defer to the opinion of a medical doctor, such as a GP or psychiatrist, who may make a decision on far less 'evidence' than is available to a neuropsychologist. However, neuropsychologists are now able both to assess the patient and to sign the Court of Protection form. This form of empowerment does not come without far greater responsibility for making such an important decision. Therefore, clinical neuropsychologists are advised to read the Mental Capacity Act 2005, plus the Code of Practice 2007, as well as the BPS advisory document *Assessment of Capacity in Adults: Interim Guidance for Psychologists* (British Psychological Society, 2006) before taking on this responsibility.

The three components of this act (see also Chapter 10 of this volume) ask: (i) Does the person have a disability of mind? (ii) Is there evidence that the person is incapable of managing and administering their own affairs? and (iii) Does this incapacity result from the disability of mind? Lush (2001), as Master of The Court of Protection, provided a definition of 'capacity' as the ability to make a decision, enter into a transaction, engage in an activity, or exercise rights, which may have legal implications for the head-injured person, and others. A patient is not considered to have capacity if there is an impairment of, or disturbance in, the functioning of brain or mind that causes difficulty in decision-making because the individual: (i) is unable to understand information relevant to the decision; (ii) cannot retain the relevant information; (iii) is unable to use this information as part of the decision-making process; or (iv) cannot communicate the decision. Decisions on capacity in head-injury litigation usually relate either to a person's ability to conduct their own litigation (i.e. to give an informed opinion or take advice from a lawyer—and to evaluate legal advice), or to a person's capacity to manage their financial affairs, in particular any money that will be received as part of a litigation settlement.

Such decisions may appear to be a relatively straightforward for a clinical neuropsychologist because many patients who have suffered severe head injury have problems with memory and lack reasoning skills, self-awareness and/or social judgement. They are vulnerable to exploitation because they may forget the lessons of experience; they appear impulsive and spend money frivolously; they act to gain immediate reward without thought of the future or the needs of dependent others. However, it is not always easy, simply by relying on results of neuropsychological tests, to distinguish ability from disability in respect of mental capacity. Intellectual level is not a good measure of capacity, neither is any other neuropsychological measure used in isolation. Therefore, it is necessary for neuropsychologists to exercise judgement, based on results from a range of tests, combined with information from relatives and observations made during clinical interview, to estimate a claimant's ability for prospective memory, insight, social judgement, and self-regulation.

Many decisions relating to capacity are extremely complex and require a great deal of clinical judgement, using the Code of Practice as a frame of reference, because decisions on capacity still remain a legal, not a clinical decision. Capacity is context-specific. It depends on an individual's ability to understand information and reach a decision, not whether it is a good or bad decision, or how the decision was reached, or how vulnerable the patient may be to influence when making the decision, or the risks involved regarding the consequences of the decision. These criteria may be at odds with clinical judgement of neuropsychological disability. Many people who suffer serious brain injury have quite subtle deficits, which can still have serious implications for decision-making, or acting on decisions made. Simply basing a judgement on whether a person can understand a question or piece of advice in order to make a decision is inadequate because many patients understand information given in one situation, yet fail to apply that information in another setting, at a future time. Mental capacity is therefore situation-specific—individuals who have the capacity to make a decision in one context may not have capacity to make a similar decision in another, depending on the circumstances. The processes that contribute to decision-making are therefore dimensional and include the ability to understand, appreciate, reason, and express a choice about something.

Post-concussional syndrome

Between 6000 and 12 000 people per million of the population attend A&E departments and GP surgeries each year with symptoms that result from minor head injury (e.g. headache, tiredness, sleep-onset insomnia, irritability, difficulty concentrating, and forgetfulness) (Miller, 1993). Most recover quickly, usually by 3 months post-injury (Rutherford *et al.*, 1977; Levin *et al.*, 1982); however, a relatively small but clinically significant number of patients continue to report a persisting and intrusive pattern of cognitive and affective symptoms that represents the post-concussional syndrome, a condition that is often unresponsive to treatment and has the potential of imposing a lifetime of disability and handicap. Ruff *et al.* (1996) labelled this group the 'miserable minority', variously estimated to be around 15% of those who suffer minor head injury (Ponsford *et al.*, 2002).

There has been much debate about the aetiology of symptoms reported by patients after minor head injury (see Wood, 2004). Lishman (1998) proposed that organic factors are responsible only for the origin of post-concussional symptoms, arguing that psychological factors are responsible for the persistence of symptom clusters that evolve into a post-concussional syndrome. Kay (1992) introduced the concept of 'individual vulnerability' to explain the range of factors that contribute to this syndrome, i.e. the injury itself, the person's emotional reaction to the injury, the pre-accident circumstances of the individual, and the post-accident pressures or personal coping styles of the individual. Jacobson (1995) proposed a multi-factorial perspective, integrating biological, social, cognitive, affective, and behavioural factors to explain persisting post-concussional symptoms. In my experience, premorbid personality is an important factor contributing to coping style and emotional reaction to symptoms that (although transient) may persist for several weeks and force individuals to (temporarily) adjust their lifestyle. Those with a driving, achievement-orientated style of behaviour, or those who have a slightly obsessional approach to life, have great difficulty making life adjustments to accommodate the early symptoms of mild concussion or whiplash injury. Anxiety sensitivity is another personality factor that influences reactions to concussional symptoms. Tiredness experienced in the days following injury, contrasted with an inability to enjoy a good night's sleep, plus the inability to concentrate in order to read or converse sensibly, combined with persistent headaches and dizziness, can be interpreted catastrophically by someone with an anxious predisposition. This leads to an increase in arousal, which itself can be sufficient to replicate many of the symptoms originally caused by the concussion, meaning that the original symptoms are maintained beyond the point when they would normally resolve.

An important role of the neuropsychologist, therefore, is to determine whether persisting symptoms are organically based or a secondary psychological reaction to the injury experience. This often involves an assessment of effort and motivation (see Chapter 11 of this volume) as a means of establishing whether symptoms are likely to have an organic basis or to reflect psychological factors secondary to injury, which may imply a desire to deliberately underachieve. Lishman (1998) comments that the generality of embellishment in head-injured patients seeking compensation is hard to establish as few studies have compared litigant and non-litigant groups who have suffered comparable injury. Only two controlled studies have been conducted to examine the influence of litigation on neuropsychological performance after severe head trauma, and neither found any evidence of underachievement (McKinlay et al., 1983; Wood & Rutterford, 2006b). However, problems of effort and motivation are most often associated with litigation following minor injury. The vast majority of studies conclude that: (i) more post-concussional symptoms are reported by litigants than non-litigants; (ii) the symptoms last longer; (iii) they are more debilitating, in the sense that litigants take longer to return to work; and (iv) they generate higher levels of psychological distress (Miller & Donders, 2001; Paniak et al., 2002). A meta-analytical review by Binder & Rohling (1996), based on 18 study groups and 2353 cases, found a moderate overall effect size of 0.47, pointing to greater abnormality and disability in less severely injured patients when financial incentives were involved. If financial compensation was removed as a factor, the authors calculated that symptoms attributed to head injury would reduce by 23%.

Some neuropsychologists employ the revised version of the Minnesota Multiphasic Personality Inventory (MMPI-2; Butcher et al., 1989) to distinguish genuine from embellished symptoms. Heaton et al. (1978) suggested that the MMPI F scale was one of the best indicators of simulated malingering during forensic neuropsychological examinations. Berry et al. (1995) reported that several MMPI-2 validity scales (F, Fb, F(p), and Ds2) are sensitive to fabrication and exaggeration of head-injury symptoms by litigating head-injury patients. However, Greiffenstein et al. (1995) noted that the MMPI-2 F and F-K scales did not differ significantly between compensation-seeking (probable) malingerers and genuine head-injury patients. Factor analysis of MMPI-2 validity scales and motivational indices from these samples identified two distinct dimensions characterized as feigned emotional problems and feigned neurobehavioral deficits. MMPI-2 validity indices loaded on the emotional feigning but not neurobehavioral feigning factor. Greiffenstein et al. (1995) concluded that real-world traumatic-brain-injury (TBI) malingerers feigned neurobehavioral deficits such as amnesia rather than emotional problems, and that the MMPI-2F scale '*is not helpful in real world clinical-forensic settings*' (p. 238).

Miller & Donders (2001) compared MMPI-2 results from litigating and non-litigating mild TBI claimants with more severely injured non-compensation-seeking TBI patients. They found that 50% of the compensation-seeking mild TBI patients exceed the Fake Bad Scale (FBS) cut-off score, compared with only 4% of the severe TBI patients. However, 30% of the non-compensation-seeking mild TBI patients also exceeded this score, suggesting that the psychological impact of minor head injury on some patients can elicit a reaction that, whilst genuine, overlaps many of the characteristics displayed by those who deliberately embellish their difficulties. Therefore, the effectiveness of the MMPI-2 F family of scales for detection of feigned symptoms during neuropsychological assessment remains unclear. Larrabee (1998) argued that one reason for this relates to the structure of MMPI scales. Somatic complaints commonly seen after head trauma are represented on the MMPI-2 clinical scales Hs and Hy and therefore may inflate scores in a way that raises them above a threshold of reliability for the cohort used in the validation of MMPI scales. Larrabee (1998) recommends the Lees-Haley FBS (Lees-Haley et al., 1991) as a more sensitive indicator of feigned physical problems than traditional MMPI-2 indicators.

Conclusions

This chapter has attempted to outline some issues linking the legacies of head trauma with aspects of a neuropsychological examination, in order to elucidate the quality of neurobehavioural recovery. It is clear that clinicians need a broad spectrum of experience to understand some of the complex (even contradictory) features that emerge from the medico-legal examination of head-trauma patients, who suffer injuries that have different degrees of severity and include a combination of organically mediated and psychogenic problems. A narrow psychometric approach to assessment often fails to identify subtle but important features of executive dysfunction or to distinguish between poor performance that results from brain injury and cerebral dysfunction secondary to emotional factors, or even poor performance that is a result of deliberate underachievement. It should be clear that, without sufficient clinical experience, the neuropsychologist will not be able to provide expert advice to the court on the range of issues relating to the litigation process, particularly issues involving mental capacity. It is therefore important that neuropsychologists only accept instructions from solicitors at a stage in their career when their clinical skills have matured, based on a range of cases, giving them the experience necessary to enter medico-legal work as an 'expert' witness.

References

Bajo, A. and Nathaniel-James, D. (2001). The Hayling and Brixton Tests of Dysexecutive Syndrome. What do they measure in everyday life? Poster presentation at the 4th World Congress on Brain Injury, Turin, Italy.

Benson, D. F. and Geschwind, N. (1967). Shrinking retrograde amnesia. *Journal of Neurology, Neurosurgery and Psychiatry*, **30**:539–544.

Berry, D. T. R., Wetter, M. W., and Baer, R. A. (1995). Overreporting of closed-head injury symptoms on the MMPI-2. *Psychological Assessment*, **7**:515–523.

Bigler, E. D. (2001). The lesion(s) in traumatic brain injury: Implications for clinical neuropsychology. *Archives of Clinical Neuropsychology*, **16**:95–131.

Binder, R. L. and Rohling, M. L. (1996). Money matters: A meta-analytic review of the effects of financial incentives on recovery after closed head injury. *American Journal of Psychiatry*, **153**:7–10.

Bishara, S. N., Partridge, F. M., Godfrey, H. P.D., and Knight, R. G. (1992). Post-traumatic amnesia and Glasgow Coma Scale related to outcome in survivors in a consecutive series of patients with severe closed-head injury. *Brain Injury*, **6**:373–380.

British Psychological Society (2006). *Assessment of Capacity in Adults: Interim Guidance for Psychologists*. Leicester: British Psychological Society.

Brooks, D. N. and McKinlay, W. (1983). Personality and behavioral changes after severe blunt head injury: A relative's view. *Journal of Neurology, Neurosurgery and Psychiatry*, **46**:336–344.

Burgess, P. W. (2003). Assessment of executive function. In: P. W. Halligan, U. Kischka, and J. C. Marshall (eds), *Handbook of Clinical Neuropsychology*, pp. 322–340. Oxford: Oxford University Press.

Burgess, P. W. and Alderman, N. (2004). Executive dysfunction. In: L. H. Goldstein and J. E. McNeil (eds), *Clinical Neuropsychology: A Practical Guide to Assessment and Management for Clinicians*, pp. 185–209. Chichester, UK: John Wiley & Sons.

Burgess, P. W. and Shallice, T. (1997). *The Hayling and Brixton Tests*. Bury St. Edmunds, UK: Thames Valley Test Company.

Burgess, P. W., Alderman, N., Evans, J., Emslie, H., and Wilson, B. A. (1998). The ecological validity of tests of executive function. *Journal of the International Neuropsychological Society*, **4**:547–558.

Butcher, J. N., Dahlstrom, W. J., and Graham, W. G. (1989). Manual for the restandardized Minnesota Multiphasic personality Inventory: MMPI-2. Minneapolis: University of Minnesota Press.

Chayton, N. and Schmitter-Edgecombe, M. (2003). The ecological validity of neuropsychological tests: A review of the literature on everyday cognitive skills. *Neuropsychology Review*, **13**:181–197.

Cima, M., Merckelbach, H., Nijman, H., Knauer, E., and Hollnack, S. (2002). I can't remember your honor: Offenders who claim amnesia. *German Journal of Psychiatry*, **5**:24–34.

Crawford, J. R. and Allan, K. M. (1997). Estimating premorbid WAIS-R IQ with demographic variables: Regression equations derived from a UK sample. *Clinical Neuropsychologist*, **11**:192–197.

Denney, R. L. (1996). Symptom validity testing of remote memory in a criminal forensic setting. *Archives of Clinical Neuropsychology*, **11**:589–603.

Department for Constitutional Affairs (1998a). *Civil Procedure Rules Part 35: Experts and Assessors*. Department for Constitutional Affairs. Available at: http://www.dca.gov.uk/civil/procrules_fin/index.htm [accessed 18th May 2007].

Department for Constitutional Affairs (1998b). *Civil Procedure Rules Part 35 Practice Direction: Experts and Assessors* [online]. Department for Constitutional Affairs. Available at: http://www.dca.gov.uk/civil/procrules_fin/contents/practice_directions/pd_part35.htm [accessed 18th May 2007].

Duncan, J., Burgess, P., and Emslie, H. (1995). Fluid intelligence after frontal lobe lesions. *Neuropsychologia*, **33**:261–268.

Duncan, J., Johnson, R., Swales, M., and Freer, C. (1997). Frontal lobe deficits after head injury: Unity and diversity of function. *Cognitive Neuropsychology*, **14**:713–741.

Eslinger, P. J. (1999). Orbitofrontal cortex: Historical and contemporary views about its behaviour and physiological significance. *Neurocase*, **5**:225–229.

Frederick, R. I., Carter, M., and Powel, R. (1995). Adapting symptom validity testing to evaluate suspicious complaints of amnesia in medico-legal evaluations. *Bulletin of the American Academy of Psychiatry and the Law*, **23**:227–233.

Greiffenstein, M. F., Gola, T., and Baker, W. J. (1995). MMPI-2 validity scales versus domain specific measures in the detection of factitious traumatic brain injury. *Clinical Neuropsychologist*, **9**:230–240.

Groswasser, Z., Reider-Groswasser, I., Soroker, N., and Machtey, Y. (1987). Magnetic resonance imaging in head injured patients with normal late computed tomography scans. *Surgical Neurology*, **27**:331–337.

Gur, R. C., Gur, R. E., Resnick, S. M., Skolnick, B. E., Alavi, A., and Reivich, M. (1987). The effect of anxiety on cortical cerebral blood flow and metabolism. *Journal of Cerebral Blood Flow and Metabolism*, **7**:173–177.

Heaton, R. K., Smith, H. H., Lehman, R. A., and Vogt, A. J. (1978). Prospects for feigning believable deficits on neuropsychological testing. *Journal of Consulting and Clinical Psychology*, **46**:892–900.

Jacobson, R. (1995). The post concussional syndrome: Physiogenesis, psychogenesis and malingering. An integrated model. *Journal of Psychosomatic Research*, **39**:675–693.

Jennett, B. (1976). Prognosis after head injury. In: P. J. Vinken and G. W. Bruyn (eds), *Handbook of Clinical Neurology*, vol. 24, pp. 669–681. Amsterdam: North Holland Publishing Company.

Kay, T. (1992). Neuropsychological diagnosis: Disentangling the multiple determinants of functional disability after mild traumatic brain injury. *Physical Medicine and Rehabilitation*, **6**:109–127.

Knight, R. T., Alderman, N., and Burgess, P. W. (2002). Development of a simplified version of the Multiple Errands Test for use in hospital settings. *Neuropsychological Rehabilitation*, **12**:231–255.

Kopelman, M. D. (2002). Psychogenic amnesia. In: A. D. Baddeley, M. D. Kopelman, and B. A. Wilson (eds), *Handbook of Memory Disorders*, 2nd edn, pp. 451–471. Chichester, UK: John Wiley & Sons.

Kreutzer, J. S. (1993). Improving the prognosis of returning to work after brain injury. In: P. Frommelt and K. D. Wiedman (eds), *Neurorehabilitation: a Perspective for the Future*, pp. 26–29. Deggendorf Conference (reported in Van Zomeren, A. H. and Brouwer, W. H. (1994).) *Clinical Neuropsychology of Attention*. New York: Oxford University Press).

Larrabee, G. J. (1998). Somatic malingering on the MMPI and MMPI-2 in personal injury litigants. *Clinical Neuropsychologist*, **12**:179–188.

Lees-Haley, P. R., English, L. T., and Glenn, W. J. (1991). A Fake Bad Scale on the MMPI-2 for personal injury claimants. *Psychological Reports*, **68**:203–210.

Levin, H. S., Mattis, S., and Ruff, R. M. (1982). Neurobehavioural outcome following minor head injury: A three-centre study. *Journal of Neurosurgery*, **66**:234–243.

Lezak, M. D., Howieson, D. B., and Loring, D. W. (2004). *Neuropsychological Assessment*, 4th edn. New York: Oxford University Press.

Lishman, W. A. (1998). Physiogenesis and psychogenesis in the post-concussional syndrome. *British Journal of Psychiatry*, **153**:460–459.

Lush, D. (2001). Understanding and assessing capacity. In: R. Ll. Wood and T. M. McMillan (eds), *Neurobehavioural Disability and Social Handicap following Traumatic Brain Injury*, pp. 1–28. Hove, UK: Psychology Press.

McKinlay, W. M. and McGowan, M. (2003). Forensic issues in neuropsychology. In: P. W. Halligan, U. Kischka, and J. C. Marshall (eds), *Handbook of Clinical Neuropsychology*, pp. 677–697. New York: Oxford University Press.

McKinlay, W. M., Brooks, D. N., and Bond, M. R. (1983). Post-concussional symptoms, financial compensation and outcome of severe blunt head injury. *Journal of Neurology, Neurosurgery and Psychiatry*, **46**:1084–1091.

McMillan, T. M., Jongen, E. L. M. M., Greenwood, R. J., and Jackson, H. (1996). Assessment of post traumatic amnesia after severe closed head injury: Retrospective or prospective? *Journal of Neurology, Neurosurgery and Psychiatry*, **60**:422–427.

Merckelbach, H., Hauer, B., and Rassin, E. (2002). Symptom validity testing of feigned dissociative amnesia: A simulation study. *Psychology, Crime and Law*, **8**:311–318.

Miller, J. D. (1993). Head injury. *Journal of Neurology, Neurosurgery and Psychiatry*, **56**:440–447.

Miller, L. J. and Donders, J. (2001). Subjective symptomatology after traumatic head injury. *Brain Injury*, **15**:297–304.

Nelson, H. E. and Willison, J. (1991). *The Revised National Adult Reading Test—Test Manual*. Windsor, UK: NFER Nelson.

Newton, M. R., Greenwood, R. J., Brotton, K. E., et al. (1992). A study comparing SPECT with CT and MRI after closed head injury. *Journal of Neurology, Neurosurgery and Psychiatry*, **55**:92–94.

Norris, G. and Tate, R. L. (2000). The Behavioural Assessment of the Dysexecutive Syndrome (BADS): Ecological, concurrent and construct validity. *Neuropsychological Rehabilitation*, **10**:33–45.

Odhuba, R. A., van den Broek, M. D., and Johns, L. C. (2005). Ecological validity of measures of executive functioning. *British Journal of Clinical Psychology*, **44**:269–278.

Paniak, C., Reynolds, S., Toller-Lobe, G., Melnyk, A., Nagy, J., and Schmidt, D. (2002). A longitudinal study of the relationship between financial compensation and symptoms after treated mild traumatic brain injury. *Journal of Clinical and Experimental Neuropsychology*, **24**:187–193.

Ponsford, J., Willmott, C., Rothwell, A., et al. (2002). Impact of early intervention on outcome following mild head injury in adults. *Journal of Neurology, Neurosurgery and Psychiatry*, **73**:330–332.

Porter, S., Birt, A. R., Yuille, J. C., and Hervé, H. F. (2001). Memory for murder: A psychological perspective on dissociative amnesia in legal contexts. *International Journal of Law and Psychiatry*, **24**:23–42.

Powell, G. E. (2004). Neuropsychology and the law. In: L. H. Goldstein and J. E. Neil (eds), *Clinical Neuropsychology. A Practical Guide to Assessment and Management for Clinicians*, pp. 319–343. Chichester, UK: John Wiley & Sons.

Powell, G. and Wood, R. Ll. (2001). Assessing neurobehavioural disability. In: R. Ll. Wood and T. McMillan (eds), *Neurobehavioural Disability and Social Handicap Following Traumatic Head Injury*, pp. 65–91. London: Psychology Press.

Rapoport, M. J., McCullagh, S., Shammi, P., and Feinstein, A. (2005). Cognitive impairment with major depression following mild and moderate traumatic brain injury. *Journal of Neuropsychiatry Clinical Neuroscience,* **17**:61–65.

Reason, J. T. (1984). Lapses of attention in everyday life. In: R. Parasurman (ed.), *Varieties of Attention,* pp. 103–113. London: Academic Press.

Rogers, R., Harrell, E. H., and Liff, C. D. (1993). Feigning neuropsychological impairment: A critical review of methodological and clinical considerations. *Clinical Psychological Review,* **13**:255–274.

Ruff, R. M., Camenzuli, L., and Mueller, J. (1996). Miserable minority: Emotional risk factors that influence the outcome of a mild traumatic brain injury. *Brain Injury,* **8**:61–65.

Russell, W. R. (1974). *The traumatic amnesias.* London: Oxford University Press.

Russell, W. R. and Nathan, P. W. (1946). Traumatic amnesia. *Brain,* **69**:280–300.

Rutherford, W. H., Merrett, J. D., and McDonald, J. R. (1977). Sequelae of concussion caused by minor head injuries. *Lancet,* **1**:1–4.

Shallice, T. (1982). Specific impairments of planning. *Philosophical Transactions of the Royal Society of London, B,* **298**:199–209.

Shallice, T. and Burgess, P. W. (1991). Deficits in strategy application after frontal lobe damage in man. *Brain,* **114**:727–741.

Shaw, N. A. (2002). The neurophysiology of concussion. *Progress in Neurology,* **67**:281–344.

Stokes, N. and Bajo, A. (2003). The relationship between general intelligence, performance on executive functioning tests and everyday executive function difficulties. *Brain Injury,* **17**:174–175.

Stuss, D. T. and Benson, D. F. (1986). *The Frontal Lobes.* New York: Raven Press.

Sunderland, A., Harris, J., and Baddeley, A. D. (1983). Do laboratory tests predict everyday memory? *Journal of Verbal Learning and Verbal Behaviour,* **122**:341–357.

Teasdale, G. and Jennett, B. (1974). Assessment of coma and impaired consciousness. *Lancet,* **2**:81–84.

Teuber, H. L. (1964). The riddle of frontal lobe functions in man. In: J. M. Warren and K. Akert (eds), *The Frontal Granular Cortex and Behaviour,* pp. 132–143. New York: McGraw Hill.

Thomsen, I. V. (1989). Do young patients have worse outcomes after severe blunt head trauma? *Brain Injury,* **3**:157–162.

Thurman, D. J., Coronado, V., and Selassie, A. (2007) The epidemiology of TBI: Implications for public health. In: N. D. Zasler, D. I. Katz, and R. D. Zafonte (eds), *Brain Injury Medicine,* pp. 45–55. New York: Demos.

Van Zomeren, A. H. and Brouwer, W. H. (1994). *Clinical Neuropsychology of Attention.* New York: Oxford University Press.

Walsh, K. W. (1985). *Understanding Brain Damage: A Primer of Neuropsychological Evaluation.* Edinburgh: Longman Group.

Wechsler, D. (1997a). *The Wechsler Adult Intelligence Scale—Third Edition (WAIS-III).* San Antonio, TX: Psychological Corporation.

Wechsler, D. (1997b). *The Wechsler Memory Scale—Third Edition (WMS-III).* San Antonio, TX: Psychological Corporation.

Wechsler, D. (2001). *The Wechsler Test of Adult Reading (WTAR)*. San Antonio, TX: Psychological Corporation.

Wilson, B. A., Alderman, N., Burgess, P. W., Emslie, H., and Evans, J. J. (1996). *Behavioural Assessment of the Dysexecutive Syndrome.* Bury St Edmunds, UK: Thames Valley Test Company.

Wilson, B. A., Evans, J. J., Emslie, H., Alderman, N., and Burgess, P. (1998). The development of an ecologically valid test for assessing patients with a dysexecutive syndrome. *Neuropsychological Rehabilitation*, **8**:213–228.

Wood, R. Ll. (1987). *Brain injury Rehabilitation: A Neurobehavioural Approach*. London: Croom Helm.

Wood, R. Ll. (2001). Understanding neurobehavioural disability. In: R. Ll. Wood and T. M. McMillan (eds), *Neurobehavioural Disability and Social Handicap Following Traumatic Brain Injury*, pp. 1–28. Hove, UK: Psychology Press.

Wood, R. Ll. (2004). Understanding the miserable minority: A diathesis-stress approach to the post concussional syndrome. *Brain Injury*, **18**:1135–1153.

Wood, R. Ll. (2009). The Science-Practitioner Model: how do advances in clinical and cognitive neuroscience affect neuropsychology in the courtroom? *Journal of Head Trauma Rehabilitation*, **24**:87–98.

Wood, R. Ll. and Liossi, C. (2006). The ecological validity of executive tests in a severely brain injured sample. *Archives of Clinical Neuropsychology*, **21**:429–437.

Wood, R. Ll. and Rutterford, N. A. (2004). Relationships between measured cognitive ability and reported psychosocial activity after bilateral frontal lobe injury: An 18 year follow-up. *Neuropsychological Rehabilitation*, **14**:329–350.

Wood, R. Ll. and Rutterford, N. A. (2006a) Psychosocial adjustment 17 years after severe brain injury. *Journal of Neurology, Neurosurgery and Psychiatry* 77:71–73.

Wood, R. Ll. and Rutterford, N. A. (2006b). The impact of mild developmental learning difficulties on neuropsychological recovery from head trauma. *Brain Injury*. **20**:477–484.

Wood R. Ll. and Williams, C. (2007). Neuropsychological correlates of organic alexithymia. *Journal of the International Neuropsychological Society*, **13**:471–479.

Wood R. Ll. and Williams, C. (2008). Inability to empathize following traumatic brain injury. *Journal of the International Neuropsychological Society*, **14**:289–296.

Worthington, A. D. and Wood R. Ll. (2008). Behaviour problems. In: A. D. Tyerman and N. S. King (eds), *Psychological Approaches To Rehabilitation after Traumatic Brain Injury*, Chapter 10. Oxford: Blackwell.

Chapter 10

The role of the expert witness and acquired brain injury

Graham Powell

This chapter concerns the practical aspects of becoming an expert witness and exercising that role in relation to acquired brain injury. Detailed discussions of legal and academic issues can be found in Larrabee (2005a), Horton & Hartlage (2003), and Powell (2004), and are also covered in Chapter 9 of this volume.

Becoming an expert witness

An expert witness at the most basic level is a person who knows more than the court about some specific field of expertise, in this case acquired brain injury. The expert gives the court an opinion about issues that the court needs to take into account in reaching a judgement. For example, in a criminal setting the neuropsychologist might advise on the relevance of a brain injury to the perpetration of some act (e.g. the ability of the person to form an intent or any history of organic personality change), or on the person's ability to plead guilty or not guilty, or to give evidence, or on aspects of the brain injury that may be considered in a plea of mitigation at the sentencing stage. In a civil court, the neuropsychologist might give evidence about how the brain injury has affected employment potential or how it has created certain treatment needs, which will help the judge to decide quantum, i.e. how much money to award in compensation. Also, in a civil setting, the neuropsychologist might express a view as to whether the person has the capacity to manage their own financial affairs or whether they have the capacity to instruct a lawyer.

Expert witnesses are permitted to give their opinions whereas other witnesses can only give evidence as to facts. The burden of proof is different in civil and criminal courts. In civil cases, a decision is made on the balance of probabilities (i.e. 51:49), but in criminal cases the decision has to be beyond reasonable doubt.

Expert witnesses, including neuropsychologists, have had to become more professional and less ad hoc in their relationship to the legal process and to services provided to lawyers. Increasingly, expert witnesses are expected to have had some training for that function above and beyond their own professional training and are expected to be skilled in presenting evidence (although the court understands that all experts begin less experienced and that every expert has to have their first case). Increasingly, the work of the expert witness is governed by legislation, such as the Civil Procedure Rules (CPR) in England and Wales (Department for Constitutional Affairs, 1998a). These were originally published in 1998 and have been regularly updated; they are currently on the 49th version. The relevant details are to be found in *Part 35 Experts and Assessors* and in *Practice Direction 35* (Department for Constitutional Affairs, 1998b) and this chapter will mention specific CPR rules as appropriate. The expert witness is expected to be familiar with these rules.

The Criminal Procedure Rules (Department for Constitutional Affairs, 2005) do not as yet have a confirmed section on experts, but it is intended that there should be a *Part 33* entitled *Expert Evidence* that parallels *Part 35* of the CPR. A draft of *Part 33* is under discussion and is likely to be very similar to *Part 35*, and so expert skills acquired in regard to working under *Part 35* are likely to be fully transferable to working under *Part 33*.

Work as an expert witness is often initiated by a letter of enquiry from a solicitor to the neuropsychologist as to whether they can assist in a case. The reply to such a letter will typically state the hourly fee rate, how travel will be costed if different, whether a tax is applicable (i.e. VAT in the UK), the average cost of a report, the timescale for seeing the client, the typical length of time to produce the report, and any caveats (e.g. 'depending on the amount and complexity of the material to read'). It will also cover the issue of cancellation fees relating to client non-attendance or to pre-trial settlements or to late vacation of trial dates, i.e. postponement of the trial. It is usual to enclose a CV, which would normally cover in detail qualifications, professional affiliations, employment history, relevant professional activities, academic and research activities, and publications. The CV should also contain an estimate of the percentage of work carried out for the prosecution versus defence in criminal work and for claimant versus defendant versus joint instruction for civil work. This CV could well end up as part of the court papers and the neuropsychologist should be prepared to be cross-examined on it. It is useful for the CV to have an executive summary that can be used as an abstract for appending to their reports. The date of the most recent revision to the CV should be stated, and it should be kept reasonably up to date.

The neuropsychologist actively seeking work as an expert witness may decide to use one of the many expert witness directories. Often the neuropsychologist's own professional body will publish such a directory, such as the British

Psychological Society's Directory of Expert Witnesses (2006a). Directory entries vary in content from directory to directory, but, in addition to qualifications and areas of expertise, they may state languages spoken, number of reports written per year, number of court appearances per year, whether training has been undertaken, whether references have been supplied regarding competence in the witness box, the percentage of work for the various parties, and geographical coverage of the professional service.

In terms of training, there are professional training organizations, and one's own professional body often puts on training events for work as an expert witness or issues written guidance for expert witnesses (British Psychological Society, 2007). In many countries, continuing professional development (CPD) is mandatory or taken as mandatory, and so the CV should indicate that the neuropsychologist meets CPD requirements.

Taking instructions

Having broadly checked expertise, fee levels, and timescale, the solicitor will write a formal letter of instruction. Such letters are for the most part disclosable, i.e. they can be requested by the court, and they will set out the solicitor's perception of the purpose of the assessment and report.

These instructions may be from one party or they may be joint in civil actions, i.e. agreed instructions from both sets of solicitors. The court may instruct solicitors to use only a single joint expert (CPR 35.7(1)).

Sometimes the neuropsychologist will need to seek clarification; for example, the letter might not make it clear whether this is a traumatic brain injury case or not, or might refer to this being a request for a neuropsychiatric report, which may or may not be a typographical error. Also, the letter of instruction may ask questions that are typically outwith the neuropsychologist's competencies, such as issues of life expectancies, risk of post-traumatic epilepsy, or effect on fertility or endocrine function, in which case the neuropsychologist will have to write back and clarify what questions can be addressed and whether the instructions still stand. The instructions might also mention a timescale that is unrealistic, in which case deadlines must be renegotiated, with the solicitor as necessary going back to the court to seek further directions on the timetable for the management of the case. It may also be clear from the letter of instruction that other experts may have to be involved. The neuropsychologist will then have to write back clarifying who else is to be instructed, if only to ensure that the solicitor is not expecting the neuropsychologist to tackle an unrealistic number of issues.

The matter of fees may also be raised again. The solicitor may set an unrealistic 'cap' on fees, in which case this will have to be pointed out and re-negotiated.

The solicitor may also ask for the instructions in civil cases to be accepted on a deferred basis (i.e. fees paid only when the case is over). This is a matter for the individual neuropsychologist, but most neuropsychologists in civil cases do not accept deferred fee terms on the grounds that it may create a pressure on the expert to give opinions more likely to lead to early settlement.

Finally, any conflicts of interest should be considered. For example, the neuropsychologist may know the client or a person close to them, or, if it is a negligence case, may be professionally linked to the defendant or to the defendant's institution. The neuropsychologist is sometimes asked to provide an expert report on one of their own clients, i.e. someone they are seeing for therapeutic purposes. Greenberg & Shuman (1997) have set out the irreconcilable conflict between therapeutic and forensic roles, listing ten differences between the therapeutic and forensic relationship, such as the need for a therapeutic alliance versus the need for evaluative and critical judgement, the issue of whom the therapist's duty is to, the differing cognitive set of supportive versus neutral, and the impact of critical judgement by the expert.

Preparing for the assessment

An initial issue to clarify is whether the assessment is to be in the neuropsychologist's own office, or whether it is to be a domiciliary visit to the client's own home or residential nursing home. Domiciliary visits are often preferred if the client has significant physical difficulties, if they have behavioural difficulties that make them difficult to take out, or if the distance is great and their levels of fatigue are high.

It is usually helpful to invite someone to accompany the client who knows them well, preferably before and after the injury. In the event that a key person cannot attend, such as a partner or parent, then agreement can be sought to speak with that person over the telephone.

In certain cases, primarily the assessment of those in low-awareness states or those that may be 'locked in', it is sometimes helpful to make a video of the session so that it can be replayed and the responses of the person and the scoring double checked. Permission from all parties must be obtained for this, including from the hospital/nursing home if applicable. The unedited tape then becomes part of the report, as well as the neuropsychologist appending a brief log of the tape to the report.

In going through the letter of instruction and initial papers, there will be information that will shape the details of the assessment, such as the age of the client, any physical disabilities that will influence test choice, hints as to the possible nature of continuing deficits, the first language of the client and whether a translator might be needed, and whether there have been or will be any very recent assessments carried out and whether any further neuropsychological assessments are planned after this one.

In the event that there has been or will have been a recent neuropsychological assessment carried out by another psychologist, it is now common practice for the lawyers to agree that the psychologists can cooperate in some way. At the very minimum, the psychologist undertaking the first assessment can be given permission to release the names of the tests given to the second psychologist, but preferably they would be allowed to release not just the test names but also the test results. Even more ideal is if the two neuropsychologists are allowed to discuss the choice of tests and divide the tests between themselves and pool the test results. In order to reduce further the burden on the client, it is sometimes possible for the two neuropsychologists to carry out a joint interview. Typically, the neuropsychologists would only share the test and/or interview data, and would save their actual final opinion for their report.

The assessment

The overall report will be based on (i) test results (ii) interviews (iii) questionnaire responses, and (iv) a perusal of all records, statements, and other reports.

Typically, the assessment session itself will comprise the administration of the tests and the interview. If there is time, any questionnaires can also be completed. If necessary, the client and/or significant others can fill in any questionnaires at a later date, often once they get back home, and return them by post, although this can raise issues as to who completed the questionnaires and how carefully they were completed (see Chapter 12 of this volume). The records (medical, personnel, occupational health, educational, etc.) often come in at different times, sometimes delaying the report until sufficient information has been received for the purpose of an initial report.

It is permitted for the neuropsychologist to arrange for some or all of the test administration to be carried out by another person under their direction, but details of that person need to be given, i.e. their name, qualifications, and exactly what tests they gave (CPR Practice Directions 35 (2.2) (5)). In the UK, it is rare for a neuropsychologist not to give at least some of the tests. Indeed, it can be argued that it is crucial for the neuropsychologist to see for themselves the test-taking attitude and style of the client as there may be abnormalities of test-taking behaviour that are not reflected in the actual test scores and that the neuropsychologist is much better equipped to detect than a less-experienced technician.

The neuropsychologist will be expected to choose tests bearing in mind their scientific status, for example their psychometric qualities such as reliability and validity, their track record of research use, and matters such as cut-off points and decision rules. The neuropsychologist can expect to be cross-examined on their choice of tests.

The psychometric assessment will, of course, cover the main neuropsychological areas as appropriate (see Chapter 9 of this volume), but in the forensic and medico-legal setting, it is becoming increasingly necessary also to use effort tests as measures of symptom validity. This is not being cynical, but reflects the growing awareness that effort accounts for a high proportion in test scores and the fact that significant numbers of those involved in litigation fail effort tests (Larrabee, 2005b; also see Chapter 11 of this volume).

Some of the older effort tests are now considered to have limited value because, although if failed they certainly do indicate poor effort, they are so simple that failures are rare so that passing such an effort test does not by any means guarantee that the person is applying full effort. There is a good discussion, for example, of the Rey 15-Item Test (RMT; Rey, 1964) in Frederick (2002, pp. 18–19). It is concluded that the test '*does not enjoy general acceptance among neuropsychologists or forensic psychologists as a primary detection strategy*', but that '*... Although I do not believe the RMT meets Daubert criteria for acceptability as evidence as a primary detection strategy, I certainly see no problem with including the test as part of an overall strategy ...*'

It is perhaps useful to state the Daubert criteria at this point. Scientific evidence to be admissible must be scientifically valid and relevant to the case. Criteria for scientific validity include (i) a testable and tested methodology, (ii) published peer reviews, (iii) an acceptable error rate, (iv) general acceptance of the methodology, and (v) a technical manual to guide its use (see Melton *et al.*, 1997, for a detailed discussion).

Two more recent effort tests have moved towards achieving Daubert criteria and have gained wide acceptance. The first is the Test of Memory Malingering (Tombaugh, 1996), in which the client is shown 50 line drawings, followed by a two-choice forced-choice recognition trial. This is repeated, and finally there is a 15 minute delayed-recognition trial. The manual gives pass/fail criteria and also some norms for specific groups, such as those asked to simulate memory deficit and people with dementia (who do very well because the test is so easy).

A second, more sensitive test is the Word Memory Test (Green *et al.*, 1999, 2001). Here, a list of 40 words is presented twice (either orally or using the computerized version) followed by a two-choice forced-choice recognition trial and then a 30 minute delayed-recognition trial. Again, pass/caution/fail criteria are given, and also norms for a range of groups, including those with severe brain injuries and those with learning difficulties (who again do very well).

The principle behind both tests is straightforward, i.e. the tests are in fact very easy and those exercising weak effort obtain scores that are too poor to be credible.

Using any forced-choice test, even an ad hoc one, it is possible to detect random responding by using the binomial test:

$$Z = (|(X - NP)| - 0.5)/\sqrt{(NPQ)}.$$

In this formula, Z is the corrected Z score (a Z value of 1.98 is significant at the 0.05 level, two-tailed), X is the obtained score (i.e. the number of correct answers achieved by the client), N is the number of items, and P and Q are the proportion of correct and incorrect options (e.g. both P and Q will be 0.5 in a two-choice forced-choice situation, or 0.25 and 0.75 in a four-choice forced-choice situation), and where the expression $|(X - NP)|$ means the value of $(X - NP)$ regardless of sign, so if $(X - NP)$ were −4, it would be treated as +4.

Case Study

David was a 32-year-old scaffolder who fell 40 feet onto concrete sustaining a depressed fracture of the left occipital skull, his hard hat having been knocked off as he fell. His Glasgow Coma Score was 5/15 at the scene and he remembered nothing for a week, by which time the depressed fracture had been elevated and a subdural haematoma removed. Five months later, he resumed ground work part-time, working for 16 hours a week, and attended for neuropsychological assessment at 9 months. His memory test scores were very poor, but it was noted on the short Camden Test of word and face recognition that he scored only 5/25 and 6/25, respectively, which is below chance levels. The binomial test was applied to the score of 6/35:

$$Z = (|(6 - 25 \times 0.5)| - 0.5)/\sqrt{(25 \times 0.5 \times 0.5)}$$
$$= (|(6 - 12.5)| - 0.5)/\sqrt{6.25}$$
$$= (6.5 - 0.5)/2.5$$
$$= 6/2.5$$
$$= 2.4.$$

A Z score of 2.4 yields a probability of $P<0.05$; therefore his score of 6/25 (and also 5/25) was very unlikely to be due to chance. Following discussion, it turned out that David was scared of returning to work at heights and he thought that if he presented with cognitive problems he would not be expected to return to his previous job. He was too embarrassed to tell people of his fear of heights; even standing on a chair made him feel nauseous and panicky.

This formula is also useful when assessing clients in low-awareness states or clients in whom responses can be obscured by 'noise' in the response system, because if the assessment is framed within a forced-choice paradigm, it can be determined whether the number of correct responses is non-random, non-random responses being indicative of a degree of conscious processing.

As for the questionnaires used, if any, there is a wide range of standardized questionnaires that can be employed in relation to anxiety and depression, but interpretation of scores has to be undertaken carefully as results can be confounded by the direct organic effects of the head injury. For example, not enjoying activities that used to be enjoyed could be due to depression, but could also be due to a residual hemiparesis in a person who is otherwise quite happy in themselves.

Some questionnaires aim at tapping into neurobehavioural problems specifically, and some have ratings of behaviours both before and after the injury, for example the Frontal Systems Behaviour Scale (Grace & Malloy, 2001), which has three subscales: Apathy, Disinhibition, and Executive Dysfunction.

The report

The neuropsychologist should meet any deadlines that have been given by the instructing solicitor or by the court regarding the date by which the report should be submitted. If for some reason it looks as though the deadline may not be achieved, the instructing solicitor should be informed promptly so that the situation can be discussed and a new deadline renegotiated if necessary, which may involve reverting to the court for new directions.

The report should be compliant with current legislation and practice directions. For example, in England and Wales, under CPR the report must be addressed to the court, give details of the expert's qualifications, list material and literature relied upon, contain a statement of the instructions, make it clear which facts are within the expert's domain, say who carried out any tests, summarise the range of opinions and reasons for his or her own opinions, and contain a summary of the conclusion.

Importantly, the expert must also state any qualifications to their opinion and any caveats. For example, the conclusions might be subject to sight of certain specified material, sight of certain test results collected elsewhere, or sight of the case management records.

It is also sometimes the case that it is too soon after the head injury to give a final prognosis regarding recovery, or that it is a time of transition for the client; for example they may be part of the way through a return-to-work rehabilitation programme or may be about to move into their own accommodation for the first time. Under these circumstances, the neuropsychologist can make it clear that (i) they need at the very least to be kept in touch with progress, and (ii) a retest may well be necessary before a firm opinion can be given.

Finally, the report must finish with a statement of compliance of the form:

> I understand my duty as an independent expert witness is to the court. I have complied with that duty. This report includes all matters relevant to the issues on which my expert evidence is given. I have given details in this report of any matters that might affect the validity of this report. I have addressed this report to the court.
>
> Unpublished advice of the British Psychology Society.

The report must also contain a statement of truth of the form:

> I confirm that insofar as the facts stated in my report are within my own knowledge I have made clear which they are and I believe them to be true, and that the opinions I have expressed represent my true and complete professional opinion.

The neuropsychologist is in contempt of court if this turns out to be a false statement.

In criminal cases, there is a similar declaration:

> I am an expert in the field of neuropsychology and I have been requested to provide a statement. I confirm that I have read guidance contained in a booklet known as Disclosure: Experts evidence and unused material which details my role and documents my responsibilities in relation to my role as an expert witness. I have followed the guidance and recognise the continuing nature of my responsibilities of revelation. In accordance with the duties of revelation, as documented in the guidance booklet, I (a) confirm that I have complied with my duties to record, retain and reveal material in accordance with the Criminal Procedure and Investigations Act 1996, as amended, (b) have compiled an Index of all material. I will ensure that the Index is updated in the event I am provided with or generate additional material, and (c) confirm that in the event my opinion changes on any material issue, I will inform the investigating officer, as soon as reasonably practicable and give reasons.

The report should cover all of the main issues within the domain of neuropsychology that are relevant to the instructions. For example, the report will often discuss premorbid status, the nature of mild head injury, confounding factors such as medication and mental health, estimation of post-traumatic amnesia and severity, the capacity to manage their own financial affairs or to instruct a solicitor, and others (see Powell, 2004, for a discussion of report content and report style).

The issue of capacity has been increasingly important over the past few years because of litigation that has sought to overturn previous judgements or settlements on the grounds that the person did not have the capacity to instruct their solicitor or did not have the capacity to manage their financial affairs, including accepting the offer of compensation.

In England and Wales, new Mental Capacity Act 2005 came into effect followed by the Code of Practice in 2007. Essentially, it is a three-way test of capacity: (i) Does the person have a disability of mind? (ii) Is there evidence that the person is incapable of managing and administering their own affairs? (iii) Does this incapacity result from the disability of mind?

The key word in this test is 'evidence' of incapacity. It is not enough for the psychologist just to say that the person has a deficit evident on tests. The psychologist also has to provide evidence that this deficit has in fact led to the client having such a limited understanding of financial matters that these matters will have to be handled by the Court of Protection, who would appoint a Receiver. Capacity and competency are always presumed, so the burden of proof is on the psychologist. Sometimes the client's deficits are so bad, such as those in a low-awareness state or those who are grossly disorientated, that it is self-evident that they simply do not have the processing required to interact with the environment meaningfully or to take any kind of meaningful decision. However, most clients fall in an intermediate grey area, where they have deficits and are at risk, but may have sufficient residual capacity to seek and take advice in a reliable manner, so that they can be supported in making their own decisions without depriving them of their human rights.

Therefore, in those cases where capacity is an issue, part of the assessment and report will touch on how the person seeks support, what sort of support is available, what sort of support might additionally be provided, what they know about their finances, how they use money and how they budget, any history of reckless spending, borrowing or loaning, and so forth. A key feature of the Code of Practice 2007 for the Mental Capacity Act 2005 is that the aim is to maximize autonomy. Guidance on how to assess and report on capacity is often given by the neuropsychologist's own professional organization (e.g. British Psychological Society, 2006b). Capacity has to be considered in all of its aspects as capacity is issue-specific, including, for example, the capacity to manage financial and related affairs, the capacity to conduct litigation, the capacity to consent to medical treatment, the capacity to marry or divorce, the capacity to make a gift, the capacity to vote, and so forth.

Once the report has been completed, it is sent to the instructing solicitor who will make a decision as to whether or not to disclose it. If it is a joint instruction, then the report should be sent to both parties simultaneously.

Further opinions

Once the report has been sent to the instructing solicitor, this is by no means the end of the matter. The solicitor may raise questions to be answered, further records may be received for comment, or further reports or witness statements may emerge. The solicitor will typically ask for comments and ask whether the new information has caused the neuropsychologist to amend their views. Each further opinion should be written as carefully as the original report, because it will be disclosable and is likely to end up as part of the trial papers. The neuropsychologist will charge for each further opinion at the agreed rate.

Each further opinion is liable to develop the neuropsychological understanding of the case. A point may well be reached when the original opinion is somewhat out of date, or when further opinions are beginning to amount to an actual change of opinion. Under such circumstances, the neuropsychologist should discuss with the instructing solicitor whether an actual re-assessment is warranted.

Sometimes the solicitor will point out typographical errors in a report or letter of further opinion such as misspellings or a misdating or the wrong spelling of a name. These should be corrected promptly in case it leads to misunderstanding later on.

Naturally the neuropsychologist would not make any change of detail, content, conclusion, or opinion just because the solicitor sees it as disadvantageous to their case, for example because a matter has been raised that the other side has not thought of and because they do not see it as their role to make the other side's case for them. This is discussed more fully in Chapter 12 of this volume. Under such circumstances, the neuropsychologist is open to allegations of potential misconduct and contempt of court if they make such a change, as they are no longer giving their full opinion and advice to the court, irrespective of who is instructing them.

Once the report and any further opinions have been disclosed, the opposing solicitor has, in England and Wales, 28 days in which to put written questions to that expert. If jointly instructed, both solicitors may put written questions within 28 days once the neuropsychologist submits the report simultaneously to both parties (CPR 35.6). Questions may only be put once, and must be for the purpose of clarification only unless the court gives permission or both parties agree. If the neuropsychologist does not answer the questions, the court may order that neither party may rely on that expert's evidence and that expert's fees are not recoverable from any party other than their instructing solicitor. The fee for answering questions is paid by the solicitors instructing the expert.

Conference with Counsel

There may well be points in the conduct of the case when Counsel decides that a conference with some or all of the experts is appropriate. It will be an opportunity not just to meet with Counsel but also with the solicitors, the other invited experts, and the insurers/re-insurers (if instructed by the defendant).

Prior to such a conference, it is important to prepare thoroughly because Counsel will often use the opportunity effectively to cross-examine the neuropsychologist, i.e. to see how they stand up to firm questioning, how well they can think on their feet and under pressure, and how they come across as a witness.

At the conference, there may well be an agenda drawn up by Counsel of issues that are to be discussed, but the psychologist should not feel bound by it and should add issues as they seem appropriate.

A detailed note of the conference will be kept and often the conference is audiotaped. Sometimes a note of the conference is distributed to all parties, and the neuropsychologist should read it and correct any major errors or misapprehensions.

The conference is a good opportunity for the neuropsychologist to think through their evidence, to clarify in their own mind the main issues and their position regarding those issues, and to suggest any further strategies for collecting evidence that might help resolve outstanding areas of uncertainty, such as obtaining reports from other professions and arranging re-assessments to gauge progress.

Joint statements

In civil cases, as the trial approaches, the two neuropsychologists may be instructed by the judge to discuss the case to produce a joint statement of the issues and the areas of agreement and disagreement, with an explanation of why there is any disagreement (CPR 35.12). The experts are instructed to *'where possible, reach an agreed opinion on those issues'*, but the aim is not agreement at all costs. Sometimes differences in views raise fundamental issues that have divergent implications, and rather than try to paper over the cracks, it is usually best to explain this to the court so that the court itself can take a view and make a judgement accordingly.

Overall, the joint discussions are intended to be private and free-ranging, and to encourage this the court makes it clear that the content of the discussions cannot be referred to at trial unless the parties agree (CPR 35.12 (4)).

As for the content of the discussions, the direction is for the experts to identify the issues, but also *'the court may specify the issues which the experts must discuss'* (CPR 35.12 (2)). The solicitors will therefore often provide the experts with an agreed agenda of points to consider, but the experts are not bound by this agenda; this agenda does have to be covered but the experts can raise any other issues that they wish.

Once the discussions have been held, one psychologist usually takes the responsibility of drawing up the first draft of the joint statement, which will be addressed to the court and will finish with a statement of compliance and truth (changing 'I' to 'we' as appropriate). Once finally agreed, the joint statement is then released simultaneously to both parties.

Occasionally, the solicitors for both parties may decide that the joint statement should be between two experts from different professional backgrounds, such as a neuropsychologist and a clinical psychologist, or a neuropsychologist and a neurologist. Furthermore, more than two persons can join the joint discussions, for example the two neuropsychologists and a psychiatrist. Such variants do not normally give rise to any significant problems as long as everyone remains within their sphere of competence.

The trial

Preparation for the trial will include finding out the estimated length of the trial, the date the trial is to begin, which day the neuropsychologist is to attend and the likely number of days they will have to remain there, what time to arrive, and precisely what court and which court number. Sometimes the neuropsychologist is subpoenaed to attend, in which case some of this information might be given, but often subpoenas are quite non-specific, e.g. 'arrive at court as specified in due course and remain whilst needed'. Once subpoenaed, the psychologist is liable to be fined should they not attend.

Prior to the trial, the neuropsychologist should confirm exactly which parts of their material have been disclosed, and also check which of the other experts' reports have been disclosed. Most solicitors will try to ensure that the neuropsychologist has at least a list of all disclosed material and may send the neuropsychologist a complete trial bundle.

The neuropsychologist in civil cases is often asked to attend on the first day of the trial so that they can advise on last-minute discussions between the barristers, to see if a settlement can be reached. Sometimes this might mean a last-minute joint discussion between the two neuropsychologists on one or more key issues, and a final joint statement in manuscript if there is no facility in the court for typing.

Often, the neuropsychologist will be asked to sit in court to listen to the evidence unfold from lay and expert witnesses. Indeed, in many cases, the judge will have expected the neuropsychologist to listen to the evidence in case there is new material that influences their opinion. By the time the neuropsychologist is to give evidence, there should have been at least a brief meeting with Counsel to clarify whether the neuropsychologist's view has changed at all, and what the current main issues are.

As the trial unfolds and the neuropsychologist listens to the evidence, the neuropsychologist may pass forward to the barrister certain questions to be put to the witnesses. Each question should be clearly written in large letters and there should not be too many of them as it will disturb Counsel's flow. Often questions are forwarded to Junior Counsel first, who will decide whether and when to pass it on to Leading Counsel.

Giving evidence

Anything taken into the witness box is disclosable and so it is best to take nothing at all into the witness box and to rely purely on the court bundle, which will be there; this is the same bundle that the judge and both barristers have. However, it would not be unusual for the neuropsychologist to take into the witness box a file containing the raw data and the interview notes, in case they need to be referred to. Indeed, sometimes the subpoena will state that the neuropsychologist should bring along all relevant material.

The neuropsychologist will be sworn in, either by an oath relating to their religion or by an affirmation. The order of giving evidence is, firstly, the examination in chief by the neuropsychologist's own barrister in which the main conclusions are briefly set out, and in which the neuropsychologist can describe to the court how their views might have changed, if at all, having listened to the previous witnesses. There then follows the cross-examination by the opposing party's barrister, in which the strength of the evidence will be firmly tested. The first barrister is then allowed a re-examination on new points that have emerged from the cross examination. The judge may then put some questions, and both barristers will then be allowed to ask further questions if the judge's questions raise new issues. The neuropsychologist is then allowed by the judge to stand down from the witness box and the judge will normally release them from the court itself.

The neuropsychologist's barrister will then either ask them to remain in court and to continue to advise on subsequent evidence, or the neuropsychologist will be free to leave. In theory, the neuropsychologist may be asked to re-take the stand if new issues emerge later, but this is rare.

When giving evidence, this should be done at a steady pace to allow those in court, including the judge, to take notes, and technical terms should be explained. The neuropsychologist should try to answer each question and should stick to the question. It is not a problem to take a moment to think and it is not a problem to make a quick note of the main bullet points of what is to be the reply. The neuropsychologist should tell the truth and should not stray from the boundaries of their competence. The neuropsychologist should not become defensive or angry, however unjust a question might seem, and politeness should be maintained. The neuropsychologist should, however, be firm in defending and explaining their views, while retaining a flexibility of thought such that, if new material does emerge, then their views can be adjusted appropriately; it does no good to retain a rigid view in the face of evidence that clearly cannot be ignored.

Hartlage (2003, pp. 330–331) gives an interesting A–Z list of points to guide the neuropsychologist as witness. Some of these are:

A	Appearance in court does matter
D	Don't get angry
J	Justice is not your job; your job is to answer questions
L	Legal concepts are different from psychological concepts
N	No aspect of your history is immune
Q	Quarrelling with Counsel is to be avoided
X	Xtra preparation on reliability, validity, and standard error of measurements
Z	Zero deviation from fact; never fill in and if you don't know, say so

The most testing time for the neuropsychologist is, of course, when under cross-examination. The barrister undertaking the cross-examination may well have very considerable experience in such cases, and will be expertly advised by their instructing solicitor's experts. Furthermore, there are journals that set out how to cross-examine witnesses from different professions, including psychologists. For example, the article by McKinzey (1996) sets out how to cross-examine the neuropsychologist regarding the issue of whether there has been any brain damage.

Doerr & Carlin (1991) and Melton *et al.* (1997) give examples of types of questions asked during cross-examination, and how to cope with them. Indeed, for every question in cross-examination there is potentially a wrong and a right answer, where the wrong answer digs a hole for the neuropsychologist and the right one avoids a pitfall. For example, a question might:

- seek to show that the neuropsychologist has a closed mind
  - Sample question: Does your report contain all your opinions in this case?
  - Wrong answer: Yes.
  - Right answer: My report contains all my opinions up to that point and I shall continue to consider further evidence as it is produced and update my opinion accordingly
- seek to get the neuropsychologist to endorse another expert's report
  - Sample question: Do you agree with Dr Jones' report?
  - Wrong answer: Yes.
  - Right answer: I have read the report and there is much to agree with but we do not necessarily agree on each issue; for example we have taken a somewhat different view on premorbid status.

- seek to prove that another expert is more expert
  - Sample question: Is Dr Jones acknowledged as a worldwide expert in this field?
  - Wrong answer: Yes.
  - Right answer: Dr Jones and myself have both worked in this field and have drawn upon our experience in giving the court our opinions in this specific case, and the court will form its own view on those opinions.
- seek to emphasize that the psychologist is fallible
  - Sample question: Have you ever been wrong in a professional opinion?
  - Wrong answer: Yes.
  - Right answer: I make every effort to reach reliable and valid opinions, but of course there have been times when I have not had access to the full information or when information that I understood to be correct turned out not to be correct.
- seek to prove that the expert is ignorant
  - Sample question: Have you read Smith and Jones' research paper in 2006?
  - Wrong answer: No.
  - Right answer: I am familiar with the literature but do not recall seeing that reference. I have borne in mind all of the main papers in this field and if the court considers that this additional paper is crucial, then I would be pleased to read it across a recess.
- seek to invalidate a test result
  - Sample question: Is this test perfectly valid?
  - Wrong answer: No.
  - Right answer: The validity of tests depends upon a range of factors, and in fact there are different types of validity. I have used tests that are of known validity and that are accepted as such in the scientific community, whilst acknowledging that no test is perfect.
- seek to force a simplified 'yes/no' response
  - Sample question: Thank you for that answer on validity but a simple yes/no would suffice, so what is your answer, yes or no?
  - Wrong answer: No.
  - Right answer: I would be misleading the court if I did not make the court aware that validity is a matter of degree and cannot be taken on an all-or-none basis.

- seek to reduce the neuropsychologist's conclusion to a subjective opinion
  - Sample question: That is only your opinion, isn't it?
  - Wrong answer: Yes.
  - Right answer: My opinion is based on consideration of all of the facts and evidence and is therefore scientifically based.
- seek to suggest that the neuropsychologist is evasive
  - Sample question: A while back I asked you to give a simple yes/no opinion on validity and you declined to, didn't you?
  - Wrong answer: Yes.
  - Right answer: My recollection is that I carefully considered your question and explained to the court that validity was dimensional. I would be more than willing to describe the scientific basis of any of the tests I have used if that is what the court wishes.
- seek to suggest that another neuropsychologist's assessment is the standard
  - Sample question: Dr Jones gave the X test in his assessment. This is standard and proper practice, isn't it?
  - Wrong answer: Yes.
  - Right answer: There are a range of good and reliable tests open to use by neuropsychologists, and although tests employed by different psychologists might vary, these will all share certain common features such as having an acceptable scientific basis.

It is, of course, not possible to cover all of the subtleties of cross-examination—there is no substitute for initial training and then direct experience. Normally, simply being a good scientist–practitioner will be sufficient for a solid performance in the witness box, but if the inexperienced neuropsychologist does 'put their foot in it', there is always the opportunity for their barrister to retrieve the situation at re-examination.

Post-trial

It is important for every professional to obtain objective feedback on their performance as an expert witness. It can be useful for the neuropsychologist to talk to their own solicitor or barrister about the adequacy of the evidence given and about its style of presentation.

The best feedback, though, is from the judge. Judges invariably weigh the strength of the witnesses as much as the evidence, and will state quite bluntly why, for example, they preferred one expert's views over another. It is important that the written judgements are obtained, the feedback taken on board, and any relevant training issues tackled within the framework of CPD. (Nowadays, these are available on the internet and so expert witnesses should expect to have been 'googled' by the other side to see whether there have been any adverse comments made about them in the legal or any other context that could be used to undermine credibility.)

Conclusions

This chapter has described the role of an expert witness and has provided, in practical terms, the process that the expert witness will undertake from taking instructions to giving evidence in court. Becoming an 'expert' witness can be a daunting process, and some neuropsychologists give evidence once and never again following a negative, anxiety-provoking experience in court. To become an 'expert', the expert witness must not just be an expert in their field but also become skilled in working within the adversarial framework and in presenting evidence to the highest standards. It is therefore recommended that newly qualified and junior neuropsychologists read and review the literature on expert skills, attend expert witness skills training, and, wherever possible, seek a more experienced mentor to supervise and support them during the learning process.

References

British Psychological Society (2006a). *The Directory of Chartered Psychologists and the Directory of Expert Witnesses, 2006/2007*. Leicester: The British Psychological Society.

British Psychological Society (2006b). *Assessment of Capacity in Adults: Interim Guidance for Psychologists*. Leicester: The British Psychological Society.

British Psychological Society (2007). *Psychologists as Expert Witnesses: Guidelines and Procedures for England and Wales*. Leicester: The British Psychological Society.

Department for Constitutional Affairs (1998a). *Civil Procedure Rules Part 35: Experts and Assessors*. Department for Constitutional Affairs. Available at: http://www.dca.gov.uk/civil/procrules_fin/index.htm [accessed 18 May 2007].

Department for Constitutional Affairs (1998b). *Civil Procedure Rules Part 35 Practice Direction: Experts and Assessors*. Department for Constitutional Affairs. Available at: http://www.dca.gov.uk/civil/procrules_fin/contents/practice_directions/pd_part35.htm [accessed 18 May 2007].

Department for Constitutional Affairs (2005). *Criminal Procedure Rules*. Department for Constitutional Affairs. Available at: http://www.dca.gov.uk/criminal/procrules_fin/rulesmenu.htm [accessed 18 May 2007].

Doerr, H. O. and Carlin, S. A. eds. (1991). *Forensic Neuropsychology: Legal and Scientific Bases*. New York: Guildford Press.

Frederick, R. I. (2002). A review of Rey's strategies for detecting malingered neuropsychological impairment. *Journal of Forensic Neuropsychology*, **2**:1–25.

Grace, J. and Malloy, P. F. (2001). *FrSBe: Frontal Systems Behaviour Scale: Professional Manual*. Lutz, FL: Psychological Assessment Resources.

Green, P., Iverson, G. L., and Allen, L. M. (1999). Detecting malingering in head injury litigation with the Word Memory Test. *Brain Injury*, **13**:813–819.

Green, P., Rohling, M. L., Lees-Haley, P. R., and Allen, L. M. (2001). Effort has a greater effect on test scores than severe brain injury in compensation claims. *Brain Injury*, **15**:1045–1060.

Greenberg, S. A. and Shuman, D. W. (1997). Irreconcilable conflict between therapeutic and forensic roles. *Professional Psychology: Research and Practice*, **28**:50–57.

Hartlage, L. C. (2003). Neuropsychology in the courtroom. In: A. M. Horton and L. C. Hartlage (eds), *Handbook of Forensic Neuropsychology*, pp. 315–333. New York: Springer Publishing Company.

Horton, A. M. and Hartlage, L. C. (eds) (2003). *Handbook of Forensic Neuropsychology*. New York: Springer Publishing Company.

Larrabee, G. J. (ed.), (2005a). *Forensic Neuropsychology: A Scientific Approach*. New York: Oxford University Press.

Larrabee, G. J. (2005b). Assessment of malingering. In: G. J. Larrabee (ed.), *Forensic Neuropsychology: A Scientific Approach*, pp. 115–158. New York: Oxford University Press.

McKinzey, R. K. (1996). The cross-examination of neuropsychologists: countering the claim of brain damage. *Prosecutor's Brief*, **19**:13–20.

Melton, G. B., Petrila, J., Poythress, N. G., and Slobogin, C. (1997). *Psychological Evaluations for the Courts: A Handbook for Mental Health Professionals and Lawyers*. New York: Guildford Press.

Powell, G. E. (2004). Neuropsychology and the Law. In: L. H. Goldstein and J McNeil (eds), *Clinical Neuropsychology: A Practical Guide to Assessment and Management for Clinicians*, pp. 319–342. Chichester : John Wiley & Sons.

Rey, A. (1964). *L'examen clinique en psychologie*. Paris: Presses Universitaires de France.

Tombaugh, T. N. (1996). *TOMM Test of memory malingering*. North Tonawanda, NY: Multi-Health Systems.

Chapter 11

Suboptimal effort and malingering

Gisli Gudjonsson and Susan Young

People undergoing a neuropsychological evaluation may either wittingly or unwittingly, for various reasons, perform below their actual abilities (Rogers, 2008a). Lezak *et al.* (2004) refer to this phenomenon as a 'negative-response bias' and it is often thought to reflect 'incomplete' or 'suboptimal' effort during the neuropsychological evaluation (Green *et al.*, 2001). In this chapter, we use the term 'malingering' to refer to an extreme form of a 'negative-response bias', i.e. intentional faking and exaggeration of symptoms or deficits for instrumental gain.

The purpose of this chapter is to discuss the key conceptual and methodological issues, and to review current strategies relevant to the detection of 'negative-response bias' and incomplete or 'suboptimal' effort. There are a number of excellent texts available for neuropsychologists describing the various tests available (e.g. Faust & Ackley, 1998; Reynolds, 1998; Sweet, 1999; Hom & Denney, 2002; Sweet & King, 2002; Lezak *et al.*, 2004; Larrabee, 2005; Berry & Schipper, 2008). In the present chapter, we build on this existing knowledge and give real-life case illustrations, which will provide practitioners with a tangible understanding of the issues involved in assessing and determining 'malingering' and 'suboptimal' effort.

'Faking good' versus 'faking bad'

'Faking good' and 'faking bad' on psychological tests have important implications for the validity of the test results during a forensic evaluation (Gudjonsson & Haward, 1998; Rogers, 20081a). 'Faking good' means that the persons being assessed are presenting themselves in an unduly positive or favourable light during the forensic evaluation, for example denying undesirable behaviours or genuine symptoms of psychopathology. Many tests have built-in validity scales to measure such test-taking attitude, including the Minnesota Multiphasic Personality Inventory—Second Edition (MMPI-2; Hathaway & McKinley,

1991) and the Millon Clinical Multiaxial Inventory—Third Edition (MCMI-III; Millon, 1997). Specific scales have also been developed to measure 'faking good' responses, including the Paulhus Deception Scales (PDS; Paulhus, 1998). The PDS is a 40-item scale that measures the tendency of the person to present himself or herself to others in a socially desirable way ('impression management') and deceiving oneself ('self-deceptive enhancement). 'Impression management', also known as 'other deception', is more situationally contingent than self-deceptive enhancement (Gudjonsson, 1990).

'Faking bad' performance on psychological tests, which is the primary focus of this chapter, typically occurs in two distinct areas of mental function (Graue et al., 2007). Firstly, the malingering of psychiatric symptoms, including mental illness (Resnick, 1988a; Resnick & Knoll, 2008) and post-traumatic stress disorder (Resnick, 1988b; Resnick et al., 2008). Various tests have been developed to detect the malingering of psychiatric or physical symptoms, including the Structured Interview of Reported Symptoms (SIRS; Rogers et al., 1992; Rogers, 2008b), the Miller Forensic Assessment of Symptoms (Miller, 2001) and the Structured Inventory of Malingered Symptomatology (SIMS; Smith & Burger, 1997; Widows & Smith, 2005). When using these interview methods for detecting malingering, caution must be exercised with regard to persons who are highly acquiescent and may accordingly be misdiagnosed as malingerers (Pollock, 1996).

The second area is the malingering of neurocognitive dysfunction (MND; Slick et al., 1999). Persons with MND are thought to deliberately suppress their performance on standardized neuropsychological tests by using strategies like slow responding, suboptimal effort, and deliberately providing incorrect answers to test items (Graue et al., 2007). Slick et al. (1999) suggest stringent criteria for a diagnosis of MND, which includes evidence of the presence of a substantial external incentive, a 'definitive response bias' (i.e. significantly below-chance performance on at least one forced-choice measure of cognitive function), and behaviours that meet the diagnosis of a definite negative-response bias but cannot be explained by psychiatric, neurological, or developmental factors. In contrast, 'probable negative-response bias' requires, in addition to a substantial external incentive, performance on at least one validated test that is consistent with malingering. Chapter 10 provides guidelines about how to apply a binomial test to the error rate obtained on forced-choice tests.

Various cognitive functions may be subject to malingering, including intellectual, memory, and executive functions, and a large range of tests has been devised to detect malingering of cognitive deficits or dysfunctions (Lezak et al., 2004). Some of these will be described later in this chapter.

Related to the malingering of memory deficits on psychometric tests, in criminal cases (Kopelman, 1987; Christianson et al., 2006; Sweet et al., 2008), and occasionally in civil cases (Guthkelch, 1980), some persons claim amnesia (i.e. pathological forgetting for significant life events) as a way of escaping responsibility for their actions. In cases of homicide, between 25 and 45% of defendants claim amnesia, and malingering of amnesia is common in these cases (Christianson *et al.*, 2006). Various tests can be used in cases of suspected malingering of amnesia; the most promising one appears to be the Symptom Validity Test (SVT; Frederick *et al.*, 1995; Jelicic *et al.*, 2004), which is a forced recognition test originally developed by Pankratz (1979) where validity judgements are based on statistical probability and can be applied to a variety of complaints depending on the individual case (Lezak *et al.*, 2004). The SIMS, which is a self-report measure, is also potentially useful in cases of amnesia (Smith & Burger, 1997; Christianson *et al.*, 2006).

When evaluating the efficacy of the different tests of malingering, a distinction must be made between 'sensitivity' (i.e. the frequency with which the test accurately detects those who are malingering) and 'specificity' (i.e. the accuracy with which the test identifies those who are not malingering). The higher the level of sensitivity and specificity, the better the test is at identifying those who are genuinely malingering and differentiating them from those who are genuinely neuropsychologically impaired. A test that is high in sensitivity has a low rate of false-negative error (i.e. it is good at identifying malingerers), whereas high specificity is associated with a low false-positive error rate (i.e. it is good at identifying non-malingerers).

Conceptual and methodological issues

There are a number of conceptual and methodological issues that need to be considered with regard to 'malingering'. These include the context in which the malingering occurs, whether or not malingering should be viewed as a dichotomous or a dimensional concept, the extent to which one should generalize from one test to other areas of performance or functions, the choice of tests used, issues about cut-off scores, degree of intention, motivation behind the underperformance, the role of moderator variables (e.g. anxiety, depression, poor self-esteem), and the relationship of malingering to the concept of suboptimal effort. There are also important professional issues related to disclosure of confidential test material in reports, books, published articles, and court proceedings, which may undermine the validity of specific tests in future use.

The setting and types of symptoms malingered

The setting in which malingering occurs is important. Malingering occurs in at least three different settings (Slick *et al.*, 1999): (i) in cases of compensation where there is a strong financial incentive to malinger (e.g. disability evaluation, personal injury, medical conditions); (ii) where the person is trying to escape a legally obligated duty (e.g. military, prison, death penalty); and (iii) escaping responsibility for their actions in criminal cases (e.g. fitness to plead and stand trial, avoiding adverse inferences being drawn from the failure to give replies to police, claiming vulnerability during custodial interrogation).

Malingering typically involves fabrication or gross exaggeration of symptoms in relation to medical symptoms, mental illness, and cognitive impairment (e.g. intellectual and memory functions) (Rogers et al., 1998). The feigning of medical or mental illness symptoms involves an exaggeration or fabrication of symptoms, whereas malingering on cognitive tests involves the presentation of an impairment or deficit.

Malingering versus suboptimal effort

The Dictionary of Psychology (Corsini, 1999, p. 565) defines malingering as: '*Deliberate feigning of an illness or disability for financial gain or to escape responsibility, as in faking mental illness as a defense in a trial, faking physical illness to win compensation, or faking a defect to avoid military service. Such a person is called a malingerer.*' This is similar to the description of malingering in the DSM-IV (American Psychological Association, 1994).

This definition of malingering views it as a dichotomous concept (i.e. clients are either malingering or not malingering) and there is a high level of certainty that they are malingering with regard to a particular symptom, illness, or deficit. It involves an exaggeration or fabrication of symptoms or deficits, intentional and goal-oriented behaviour, and usually implies some form of secondary gain (e.g. to obtain financial compensation or the avoidance of responsibility/prison). The consequences of the diagnosis of malingering imply deliberate lying, cheating, or deceit, and if not successfully challenged in court are highly likely to influence the outcome of the case, whether civil or criminal.

There is a reluctance among many psychologists and medical practitioners to use the term malingering in their forensic evaluations. Green et al. (2002, p. 117) stated that malingering '*is such a perjorative and emotionally laden term that most medical practitioners are extremely reluctant to use it*'. Instead, they suggest that poor performance on malingering tests should be described operationally and the examiner should make no inferences in relation to motivation. The term suboptimal effort is sometimes used instead of malingering (Green et al., 2001), although Rogers (2008a) has criticized the use of this term due to its imprecision.

However, there is also a general trend within neuropsychology to view malingering as a dimension rather than as a dichotomous concept (e.g. Sweet, 1999). If viewed dimensionally, we need to be clear what the dimensionality refers to. Does it relate to the motivation, effort, or both? According to Frederick's (1997) conceptual framework of response style during cognitive testing, the dimensionality relates to both motivation and effort. Motivation refers to the intention or goal of the examinee (e.g. doing well versus doing badly, responding correctly or incorrectly to test items). Malingering is associated with the intention to perform poorly. Effort refers to the intensity of the application to produce the intended goal (e.g. to do well or to do poorly).

According to Frederick's (1997, p. 1) framework, '*A valid assessment is possible only when an examinee is motivated to do his best and exerts sufficient effort throughout the assessment.*' A person may be lacking in effort but not 'malingering'. A test taker who is not motivated to malinger but puts in little effort to do his best on the test is unlikely to produce valid results. Therefore, both motivation and lack of effort are needed for optimal performance. Even if these two components are present, the examinee may still underperform due to other factors that adversely affect his performance, such as a disturbed mental state or organic problems. There are many reasons for lack of effort (feeling tired or fed up, being disinterested) and for deliberate underperformance (not wanting to cooperate for some reason, investment in the sick role).

Green *et al.* (2001, p. 1056) showed that suboptimal effort accounted for 53% of the variance in effort test scores and, interestingly, that '*patients with moderate to severe brain injuries or neurological diseases failed effort tests less often than the group composed of people with mild head injuries, major depression, orthopaedic injuries, chronic fatigue syndrome and chronic pain*'. The two Symptom Validity Tests used to detect suboptimal effort were the Computerized Assessment and Response Bias Test (CARB; Allen *et al.*, 1997, cited in Green *et al.*, 2001; Allen *et al.*, 2002) and the Word Memory Test (WMT; Green *et al.*, 1996, cited in Green *et al.*, 2001; Green *et al.*, 2002). Green *et al.* (2001) concluded that it is important to measure and control for suboptimal effort during neuropsychological evaluations, because of its huge impact on test performance, including a range of other neuropsychological tests.

Sweet (1999) made the point that clients may perform well on some neuropsychological measures whilst malingering on others. Similarly, clients may lie about some symptoms and not others. Therefore, good and apparently valid performance on one test does not rule out malingering on another measure and vice versa (i.e. malingering on one measure does not rule out valid deficits on another measure). Clients may also be selective in terms of what they malinger, and may focus on what they see as particularly pertinent to their case. For example, in a criminal case, a client may attempt to explain his failure to recall salient features of the crime to a generally poor memory. In another case, the client may claim he is not fit to plead and stand trial due to depressive symptoms. In addition, an examinee may attribute a genuine pre-existing deficit to a recently acquired head injury.

Bender (2008) provides a number of guidelines for forensic neuropsychologists when assessing cases of traumatic brain injury. This includes being knowledgeable about relevant injury characteristics at the time of the injury and the natural recovery curves for traumatic brain injury, evaluating systematically psychological and litigation factors that may be of relevance, the use of multiple tests of negative-response bias, and evaluating cases with an open mind.

Significant inconsistencies in test data often raise concern about the reliability and validity of neuropsychological test results. Larrabee (2005) identified a number of different kinds of inconsistencies:

- Inconsistencies between neuropsychological domains (e.g. impaired attention, but normal memory)
- Inconsistencies between neuropsychological test scores and the suspected aetiology of the brain dysfunction (e.g. normal IQ and memory scores in alleged hypoxic brain injury)
- Inconsistencies between the neuropsychological test scores and the medically documented evidence concerning the severity of the injury (e.g. low test scores more typically associated with prolonged coma rather than no loss of consciousness)
- Inconsistencies between the neuropsychological test scores and behavioural presentation (e.g. being able to give a clear account of a clinical history and recent events whilst failing on tests of recent and remote memory).

There may also be important inconsistencies in test scores over time (e.g. when clients are tested on more than one occasion) or across similar tests (e.g. logical memory on two similar tests). Here, inconsistencies may be due to practice effect or variable effort and motivation. Consistencies in scores over time and across similar domains add credibility to the findings. Repeat testing may prove highly informative.

The prevalence of malingering in civil and criminal cases

Numerous studies have tried to estimate the prevalence or base rate of malingering in civil and criminal cases. These are typically based on retrospective estimates given by forensic psychology experts who are surveyed about their work. Larrabee (2003) identified 11 studies that were relevant to the base rate of malingering. The mean base rate of suspected malingering was 40% with a range of 15% (Trueblood & Schmidt, 1993) to 64% (Heaton et al., 1978). Larrabee (2003) thought that Trueblood & Schmidt (1993) may have underestimated the prevalence rate due to their strict criterion for classification of malingering (i.e. worse than chance performance), whereas Heaton et al. (1978) may have overestimated prevalence due to a high positive error rate.

The survey conducted by Mittenberg et al. (2002) requires a special mention. They sent a questionnaire on probable symptom exaggeration and malingering to 388 members of the American Board of Clinical Neuropsychology. Out of the 388 questionnaires sent out, 144 (37%) were returned. In 13 cases, the respondent could not estimate the base rate of symptom exaggeration or malingering, which left 131 usable questionnaires. Prevalence estimates for the 131 respondents were based on 33 531 annual cases involving personal injury (6371), disability (3688), criminal (1341), or medical (22 131) matters. The base rate for probable malingering or symptom exaggeration was 29% for personal injury cases, 30% for disability cases, 19% for criminal cases, and 8% for medical cases. Higher rates of probable malingering or symptom exaggeration were reported in cases referred by defence lawyers and insurers in civil cases, and by prosecutors in criminal cases. Mittenberg et al. (2002) discuss a number of possible reasons for this, including selection bias by the referrer, lawyers coaching their clients with regarding to neuropsychological tests prior to the evaluation, and experts being influenced by the side instructing them due to financial considerations. However, Mittenberg et al. (2002) concluded that the source of referral had only minimal effects on the reported base rates (i.e. in the region of 2–4%). Berry & Schipper (2008) discuss the importance of being aware that some clients may look up tests on the Internet or be actively coached by their lawyer.

The respondents were asked about the basis on which they had determined malingering or symptom exaggeration. The results indicated that neuropsychologists typically rely on multiple methods for determining malingering. The most common ones are reported in Table 11.1. These range from the severity of impairment being inconsistent with the condition or complaint (65%) to scores being below chance on forced-choice tests (30%). Mittenberg et al. (2002) argued that using multiple measures or procedures for diagnosing malingering increases the likelihood of a correct diagnosis and is consistent with good practice (Slick et al., 1999). Two important considerations for the diagnosis of malingering discussed by Mittenberg et al. (2002) are the presence of substantial external incentive for malingering, which drastically increases the rate of suspected malingering, and normal performance on psychological tests, which reduces the estimates of malingering. In view of these factors, Mittenberg et al. (2002) speculated that malingering in practice may be higher than their figures suggest.

Table 11.1 Percentage of diagnostic impression in probable malingering or symptom exaggeration cases*

Diagnostic impression	%
Severity of cognitive impairment inconsistent with condition	65
Pattern of cognitive test performance inconsistent with condition	64
Scores below empirical cut-offs on forced-choice tests	57
Discrepancies among records, self-report, and observed behaviour	56
Implausible self-reported symptoms in interview	46
Scores below empirical cut-offs on other malingering tests	46
Implausible changes in test scores across repeated examinations	45
Scores above validity scale cut-offs on objective personality tests	38
Scores below chance on forced-choice tests	30

*Adapted from Mittenberg et al. (2002).

Sullivan et al. (2007) repeated Mittenberg's survey among Australian neuropsychologists and found an overall lower rate of malingering than in the Mittenberg et al. (2002) study. The base rates of symptom exaggeration were 13% for personal injury cases, 13% for disability of workers cases, 17% for criminal cases, and 4% for medical or psychiatric cases. The highest rate of symptom exaggeration (23%) was found in mild head injury cases. It is noteworthy that the number of cases in this study was substantially lower than that in the Mittenberg et al. (2002) study (i.e. 1818 versus 33531 cases).

One further study should also be mentioned. Rogers et al. (1998) carried out a survey of 221 forensic experts, who were almost all doctoral-level psychologists working in clinical forensic, correctional, and medical settings. The estimated prevalence of clients malingering was 17% for forensic assessment cases and 7% for non-forensic cases.

Rogers & Salekin (1998) argued that assumptions of the base rate of malingering, and the application of mathematical principles to the classification of malingering, such as Bayes' theorem, are misleading due to unknown and fluctuating base rates of malingering in cases. They argued that '*malingering is likely to be both situation specific and issue specific*' (Rogers & Salekin, 1998, p. 148). They raised concern about the variation in malingering estimations across experts, and warned against clinicians assigning specific probabilities of malingering with regard to particular scores on psychometric tests.

Rogers (2008a) made the point that some form of deception is common during psychological evaluations and that only 'consequential' deception and distortions should be considered in the context of a negative-response bias.

Motivation for malingering

Until the early 1990s, little attempt had been made to study the motivation behind malingering. The early work of Rogers (1990a, 1990b) specifically focused on the type of person who malingers during a forensic evaluation and on his or her motivation. He introduced three models for explaining the motivation behind the malingering of mental illness. These are referred to as 'pathogenic', 'criminological', and 'adaptational' models. The 'pathogenic' model postulates that mental illness or underlying psychopathology is the main motivational basis for people consciously fabricating symptoms as a way of exercising control over their disorder. The 'criminological' model postulates that people with antisocial personality traits or disorder are less likely than others to cooperate with the forensic evaluation and to malinger when it suits their purpose (similar findings have been reported in relation to police interviewing and false confessions; see Gudjonsson, 2003). The 'adaptational' model postulates that, during a forensic evaluation, clients engage in a cost–benefit analysis of their predicament (i.e. it represents their way of coping with an adversarial environment).

Rogers et al. (1994, 1998) provided empirical support for the three models. The findings in both studies suggested that the 'pathogenic' model is not central to understanding the motivation for malingering. The 'criminological' and 'adaptational' models are more fundamentally important in furthering our understanding of the motivation behind malingering. However, Rogers et al. (1998) recommended that different motivations may prototypically (e.g. 'criminological' versus 'adaptational') relate to such facts as setting, gender, and type of purported impairment. They recognized the limitations of retrospective ratings of the prototype of cases based on one's experience and recommended a prospective study.

External incentives and situational factors are important. For example, Binder & Rohling (1996) carried out a meta-analysis review of 18 studies and a total of 2353 subjects and found that there was a moderate overall effect of financial incentives on disability symptoms, with the greatest effect being found in cases of mild head injury. However, a follow-up study of complainants showed that the majority (75%) did not return to work after the financial settlement (Mendelson, 1995). The findings suggest that factors other than financial gain are responsible for work disability.

Kozaric-Kovacic et al. (2004) recently studied the effects of new legislation in Croatia, which allows veterans with post-traumatic stress disorder symptoms to apply for compensation. The impact was to increase dramatically the number of veterans claiming post-traumatic stress disorder symptoms, which linked the over-reporting of symptoms to compensation-seeking motives. The study showed how external incentives influence the reporting of symptoms.

Graue et al. (2007) argued that the recent US Supreme Court decision in Atkins v Virginia (2002), prohibiting the execution of mentally retarded defendants, is likely to increase the frequency of defendants on death row malingering an intellectual deficit to escape the death penalty.

The consequences of a misdiagnosis

The consequences of the failure to recognize a negative-response bias when it occurs (a false-negative error) or erroneously diagnosing it (a false-positive error) can have serious consequences for the person being assessed and the outcome of his or her criminal/civil case (Gudjonsson, 1993).

Failure to identify malingering can result in unjust compensation or evasion of criminal prosecution and conviction (Golden & Grier, 1998). Conversely, the diagnosis of malingering will usually have serious consequences for the person being evaluated, irrespective of whether or not it is valid (Tombaugh, 1997). For this reason, Berry & Butcher (1998, p. 234) recommended that a diagnosis of malingering '... *should never be reached without careful consideration of available data, the presence of converging evidence from two or more sources, and through evaluation of possible alternative explanations*'. Even in the presence of strong indicators of malingering, clinicians '*should bear in mind that feigning of psychological deficits does not preclude the presence of genuine psychopathology*'. The client may be exaggerating existing neuropsychological problems.

Therefore, correctly identifying negative-response bias when it occurs, and the likely motivation behind it, is important during the neuropsychological evaluation. Indeed, in view of the importance often attached to psychometric test findings in criminal and civil cases, issues regarding possible underperformance, whether due to suboptimal effort or malingering, need to be addressed routinely in the report. The clinician is likely to be cross-examined about possible malingering if the case proceeds to court (Gudjonsson & Haward, 1998). The onus is on the expert witness to demonstrate that the findings obtained on the tests are valid. If malingering is indicated from the test data, this will need to be interpreted in the context of other information that is available in the case. Tombaugh (1997) argues that full confirmation of the diagnosis of malingering is rare unless the client admits to malingering or is caught performing an act incompatible with the reported symptoms. Similarly, Slick et al. (1999) urged that careful consideration is made concerning other possible diagnoses before malingering is diagnosed (i.e. looking for evidence of 'reasonable doubt' concerning malingering).

Lezak *et al.* (2004) pointed out that evaluation of the validity of neuropsychological findings is usually based on four sources of corroboration. Firstly, is there evidence of consistency in the history or examination? This relates to consistency within the examination, consistency in the reporting of symptoms over time, perhaps to different examiners, and consistency with observable facts (e.g. the impact of the symptoms is evident in a real-life setting and can be corroborated from observers or video footage). Secondly, do the symptoms presented, the neuropsychological profile, and the validity measures fit a known disease pattern, i.e. do they make sense clinically or medically? Thirdly, do the findings fit the understanding of the patient's current situation, personal and social history, and emotional predisposition? Lastly, are the emotional reactions to the symptoms consistent with the symptoms?

Confidentiality

In the early 1980s, following a request for detailed disclosure of psychometric tests and scoring in court (Tunstall *et al.*, 1982), the Professional Affairs Board of the British Psychological Society became concerned about the publicizing of confidential test material in open court and the extent to which it might damage the validity of psychometric tests (Newman, 1983). This issue arose out of a fraud case involving a client who had performed poorly on intelligence tests; the prosecution attempted to argue that the client had faked the poor performance (Tunstall *et al.*, 1982). A subsequent survey of members of the British Psychological Society showed that many psychologists had been asked in court to disclose details of tests well beyond the test findings (Gudjonsson, 1985). The current position is that psychologists are commonly asked to disclose details of tests in court and psychologists have a professional duty to disclose it (Gudjonsson, 2008). However, Sweet (1999, p. 255) argued that there is '*a strong need for security regarding the actual decision rules and cutoff scores used to make individual diagnostic decisions*'. He stated that most neuropsychologists have stopped publishing the decision rules and cut-off scores in journal articles and instead require colleagues to contact the authors directly for essential data.

Evidence in court

Mossman (2003) argues that the main role of malingering tests in court cases is to influence the fact finders' decision-making regarding the honesty of the litigant or defendant. In this context, it should be noted that evidence of malingering in court reports or given in oral evidence is likely to be consequential, because it may be viewed an obstruction of justice. For example, in the case of *US v Greer* (158 F.3d 228 (5th Cir. 1998)), the sentence in a kidnapping case was increased by 25 months (from 185 months to 210 months) due to evidence of him having malingered mental illness (Knoll & Resnick, 1999). In spite of this outcome, Knoll & Resnick (1999, p. 625) recommended that *'evaluators should not be discouraged from making a formal diagnosis of malingering if they have sufficient basis for it'*.

Clinical psychologists in the UK commonly conduct neuropsychological evaluations for the purposes of a court report (Gudjonsson, 1996, 2008). In the USA, evidential standards regarding challenges to admissibility of expert witnesses, including neuropsychological evidence, rely on the Daubert standard, which requires four considerations. These are: (i) Has the theory or technique been tested empirically? (ii) Has it been subjected to peer review and publication? (iii) What is the error rate associated with the technique? and (iv) Is there 'general acceptance' of the technique within the scientific community? (Vallabhajosula & van Gorp, 2001; Reitan & Wolfson, 2002; Mossman, 2003). According to Reitan & Wolfson (2002), in neuropsychological practice, concerns have focused primarily on the known error rate and the technique's 'general acceptance' (points iii and iv above).

Vallabhajosula & van Gorp (2001) reviewed, in the context of the Daubert standards for admissibility, the scientific merit of three commonly used malingering tests: the Rey's 15-Item Memory Test (RMT; Rey, 1964), the Test of Memory Malingering (TOMM; Tombaugh, 1996), and the Validity Indicator Profile (VIP; Frederick & Crosby, 2000). Their view, based on certain Bayesian criteria, was that the TOMM met scientific standards for admissibility, the VIP was borderline and should be used cautiously, and the RMT failed to meet the necessary standards for general acceptance. Having reviewed the literature concerning the VIP, we believe that the test should be given more credit. This is the only measure that distinguishes between different reasons for underperformance on cognitive tests, i.e. malingering, and random and careless responding. For readers using the TOMM in Court, Tombaugh (2002) has provided important information and guidelines about how to manage the cross-examination in court with regard to the TOMM in the context of the Daubert guidelines. Frederick (2002a) made the point that, although the RMT should not be used as a 'primary detection strategy', it could be used in the overall evaluation of malingering during a neuropsychological evaluation.

Mossman (2003) reviewed the findings and recommendations of Vallabhajosula & van Gorp (2001) and suggested that their recommendations are not workable in practice due to: (i) malingering tests typically having more than one score and outcome (e.g. possibly containing several error rates); (ii) the authors having ignored ambiguity related to the Bayesian calculations of the likelihood of malingering; and (iii) the fact that most clinicians are unlikely to have the skills to perform complicated statistical operations regarding their test findings. Mossman (2003) suggested that software will be developed in future for clinicians to use in order to create Bayesian interpretations of their diagnostic findings.

Tests of malingering

Potential strategies for detecting malingering

There are a number of different strategies that malingerers can use when attempting to underperform on neuropsychological tests. Rogers *et al.* (1993) identified and discussed six potential strategies for the detection of malingering in a neuropsychological evaluation. These are:

1. Floor effect, i.e. performing at the bottom of a particular test or being unable to provide very basic information (even genuinely severely impaired people may perform above 'floor' level). The Rey's 15-Item Memory Test is one example of this kind of test, and it could occur on a test like the WAIS-III (see Case study 2 below).

2. Symptom validity testing (Pankratz, 1979). The client is presented with forced-choice alternatives, and performance significantly below chance can be monitored (Slick *et al.*, 1999). The most frequently used Symptom Validity Tests are the Word Memory Test (Green *et al.*, 1996, cited in Green *et al.*, 2001), Test of Memory Malingering (Tombaugh, 1996), and the Warrington Recognition Memory Test (Warrington, 1984; Millis, 2002).

3. Performance curve, i.e. malingerers fail to take into consideration differences in item difficulty and fail easy items whilst passing difficult items. According to Rogers *et al.* (1993), Goldstein (1945) was the first scientist to describe a performance-curve strategy. The technique has been used successfully for memory tasks (Graf *et al.*, 1984; Frederick, 2002b) and tests of intelligence (Gudjonsson & Shackleton, 1986; Frederick & Foster, 1991).

4. Magnitude of error, e.g. the qualitative and quantitative features of wrong answers are evaluated for symptom exaggeration or fabricated deficits.

5. Atypical presentation, e.g. performance is inconsistent across similar tests or on the re-administration of the same test over time. Pankratz (1988) warned that inconsistency in presentation is often associated with genuine head injury as well as with malingering and should therefore be used cautiously as an indicator of malingering. Rogers *et al.* (1993) suggested that atypical performance should be followed up with the use of empirically tested strategies for detecting malingering.

6. Psychological sequelae, e.g. malingerers may fake symptoms that are not directly related to their complaint. Rogers *et al.* (1993), whilst suggesting that this is a potentially promising strategy for detecting feigned cognitive deficits, pointed to the absence of systematic research in this area.

The range of tests used to detect malingering

Broadly speaking, cognitive tests that can be used to detect malingering fall into three groups of tests, with the last two being specifically developed to detect malingering. The first group of tests are standard cognitive tests that were not specifically developed for malingering, such as the Wechsler Adult Intelligence Scale—Third Edition (WAIS-III; Wechsler, 1977) and Raven's Standard Progressive Matrices (RSPM; Raven *et al.*, 1998). When impairment is noted on these tests, then a question may arise with regard to possible malingering or poor effort (i.e. the client may be underperforming and the reason for it needs to be addressed).

Larrabee (2003) described the use of atypical performance patterns on a battery of standard neuropsychological tests, which he had been using in clinical practice over many years. He compared the performance of suspected malingerers (i.e. those who had performed worse than chance on the Portland Digit Recognition Test and were involved in litigation but without evidence of brain injury or damage) with moderately/severely impaired head injury patients on a number of neuropsychological tests. The results yielded a sensitivity of 87.8% and a specificity of 94.4% (i.e. a high percentage accurately identifying both malingerers and non-malingerers). The Portland Digit Recognition Test is a forced-choice test that is commonly used by neuropsychologists to measure malingering and suboptimal effort (for a review, see Binder, 2002).

A neuropsychological evaluation typically involves the administration of an IQ test, such as the WAIS-III. It is therefore important to know if there are methods available to guide the examiner in terms of possible malingering on the WAIS-III, which could then be followed up by administering specific malingering tests. There is some evidence that head-injury patients show an IQ subtest pattern that can be discriminated from the profile produced by people malingering an intellectual decline (Mittenberg *et al.*, 2001). There are two methods available to achieve this: one relies on a discriminant function equation and the other on the difference in scores between the Vocabulary and Digit Span subtests. The Vocabulary– Digit Span discrepancy method (i.e. when the Digit Span subtest score is substantially lower than the Vocabulary score) is more practical to clinicians than the discriminant function analysis method. There is no guidance as to how many points should alert clinicians to possible malingering, but the larger the discrepancy, the greater the concern.

Mittenberg *et al.* (2001) recommended that the Vocabulary–Digit Span difference score can function as a useful preliminary screening for possible malingering, but should not be used diagnostically on its own. Greve *et al.* (2003) replicated Mittenberg's approach using the WAIS-Revised (WAIS-R) and WAIS-III and came to similar conclusions about using the method cautiously due to high error rates.

The Raven's Standard Progressive Matrices is another IQ (non-verbal) test that is in common use. It has a built-in formula for assessing the consistency of the individual's score within each set according to a 'normal score composition' that can be used to detect poor effort (Raven *et al.*, 1998). Gudjonsson & Shackleton (1986) advanced this method by applying a statistical formula measuring linear trends (i.e. 'rate of decay' across the five sets of scores). Millis & Volinsky (2001) referred to this method as a 'performance curve analysis' (i.e. performance curves are generated on the basis of items correctly answered across the five sets of scores). The Validity Indicator Profile (Frederick, 1997) is based on a similar performance curve analysis.

The second group of tests are those that appear to measure cognitive ability but are so easy that most people with neuropsychological deficits perform well on them. Rey's 15-Item Memory Test (RMT; Rey, 1964) is an example of this kind of test. The client is instructed to memorize 15 different items, which makes the task sound more difficult than it really is. There are different recommendations for administering the test (Frederick, 2002a) and different cut-off points have been recommended, but it is most commonly 8 or 9 (Lezak *et al.*, 2004). A meta-analysis of the RMT (Vickery *et al.*, 2001) showed that the test is much better at detecting non-malingerers than malingerers and that it compared unfavourably in comparison with forced-choice recognition tests. It should therefore not be used on its own to detect malingering. For readers interested in Rey's work on malingering, Frederick (2002a) provides an excellent review of the RMT and Rey's other malingering tests (Rey's Word Recognition Test (WRT) and Dot Counting Test (DCT)).

The third group of tests are those using forced-choice methodology where it is possible to apply the normal approximation to the binomial distribution (Colby, 2001). Here, clients are considered to be malingering if they perform significantly below chance on the test ($P<0.05$). Typically, there is a two alternative forced-choice recognition format. A test can be specially constructed or an existing measure used that best suits the client concerned (e.g. verbal or visual recognition memory, digit recognition test). Pankratz *et al.* (1975) developed a forced-choice test to measure feigned deafness. Hiscock & Hiscock (1989) developed a special forced-choice method using digits to detect malingering in a man who claimed he could not work due to memory problems related to a head injury he had suffered 7 years previously. Kapur (1994) developed the 'coin-in-the-hand-test', which is a simple and quickly administered test that has been found to be effective in distinguishing patients with amnesia from malingerers (Hanley et al., 1999). The Test of Memory Malingering (Tombaugh, 1996), the Word Memory Test (Green et al., 1996, cited in Green et al., 2001), and the Validity Indicator profile (Frederick, 1997) are all based on a forced-choice format.

Sometimes clients may perform significantly below chance on a forced-choice test, which implies a deliberate effort to perform badly on a test, without an obvious motive for malingering. For example, Gudjonsson & MacKeith (1983) identified a specific recognition deficit in relation to female faces in a man of average intelligence who was convicted of murdering his wife but claimed partial amnesia for his actions. Results from EEG and CT scans and verbal (logical) memory were normal. He was able to recognize all six male faces (100% correct recognition) on the Milner (1968) face recognition test, but only one of the six female faces (17%), which was significantly below chance. There was no clear motive for the specific female deficit, but the authors speculated that the findings demonstrated *'the powerful effects of repressive and/or dissociative mechanism on recognition'* (Gudjonsson & MacKeith, 1983, p. 39), which may have been linked to the murder of his wife.

Examples of tests used in practice to detect possible malingering

There are a large number of tests or methods for detecting suboptimal effort during a cognitive assessment. Many of these tests have already been referred to in this chapter and have been reviewed by Lezak et al. (2004). The purpose of this section is to give examples of a few different tests that are commonly applied in practice. Three of the tests were specifically developed for detecting suboptimal effort, the Test of Memory Malingering (TOMM; Tombaugh, 1996), the Word Memory Test (WMT; Green et al., 1996, cited in Green et al., 2001), and the Validity Indicator Profile (VIP; Frederick, 1997). The TOMM measures recognition memory for pictures, the WMT uses a verbal memory paradigm, and the VIP uses similar tests to those commonly used during a cognitive evaluation (i.e. matching patterns of matrices and word recognition). We will also review the Gudjonsson & Shackleton (1986) formula for detecting deliberate underperformance on Raven's Standard Progressive Matrices (RSPM) as this is a useful indicator of detecting suboptimal effort on a cognitive task (i.e. matching patterns of matrices) associated with intellect.

Ravens Standard Progressive Matrices

The RSMP (Gudjonsson & Shackleton, 1986) is a multiple-choice paper-and-pencil test that consists of a series of visual pattern matching items (Raven et al., 1998). There are 60 items, are grouped into five series (A–E) of 12 items each. The items across the five series become progressively more difficult. Gudjonsson & Shackleton (1986) devised a formula for detecting faking bad performance on the test. It was based on the hypothesis that fakers would show a smaller rate of decay across the five sets on the matrices than non-fakers, because they would be inclined to fake disproportionately on the easy items in the first two series. The linear rate of decay was calculated by the formula (2A+B) – (D+2E) for measuring linear trends across different levels of performance complexity (Snedecor & Cochran, 1967). The 'rate of decay' for each examinee could then be compared with the normative samples of non-fakers to determine whether the score obtained fell below the recommended cut-off for their respective total score.

In the original validation sample, out of a total sample of 81 participants, 29 were instructed to 'fake substantially and convincingly' below their genuine ability on the matrices. Immediately afterwards, they were instructed to complete the test again, but this time they were instructed to do as well as they could. Very large differences were evident between the two sets of scores across sets A–E, demonstrating the participants had indeed followed the 'faking bad' instructions. The rate of decay method for detection of faking bad was superior to Raven's discrepancy method with an 84% rate of sensitivity and a 95% rate of specificity.

McKinzey et al. (1999) pointed out that there are few methods available for detecting faked scores on IQ tests, in contrast to neuropsychological tests, and that the advantage of the Gudjonsson and Shackleton formula is that it can be used on protocols obtained in the past, because it requires no special administration procedures. McKinzey et al. (1999) provided a cross-validation of the formula on 46 'experimental malingers' and 381 normal controls from Raven's standardization sample. The sensitivity and specificity were 74 and 95% respectively. More recently, McKinzey et al. (2003) validated the Gudjonsson and Shackleton rate of decay formula on the RSPM on 44 children and adolescents (aged 7–17 years), producing false-positive and false-negative error rates of 5% after eliminating three extremely simple items suggesting insufficient effort or carelessness.

Wogar et al. (1998) used the formula among 40 healthy adults, 20 of whom were instructed to perform on the test in the way they imagined a person who has sustained a head injury would perform (i.e. they were not specifically instructed to fake bad performance). In this study, only 30% of the 'simulators' were correctly identified, suggesting poor sensitivity. In contrast, there was a high rate of specificity (95% for the healthy adults and 92% for patients with the history of a closed head injury). Wogar *et al.* (1998) attributed the substantially higher false-negative error rate than found in the Gudjonsson & Shackleton (1986) study to the fact that the 'simulators' in their experiment had faked substantially less than the participants in the original study. These findings suggest that both the motivation and the effort put into faking an impaired performance affects the ability of the formula to detect malingering. For example, an examinee who performs suboptimally on the matrices because of low effort with regard to each of the 60 items may not necessarily be motivated to fake poorly on the matrices, in which case it would not be picked up by the Gudjonsson and Shackleton formula.

Lezak *et al.* (2004) argued the formula is likely to have poor sensitivity at a very low level of performance where the false-positive error rate is likely to be higher. In our experience, many people assessed in clinical practice perform poorly on the matrices due not to malingering but because they do not put in sufficient effort and they complete the test in a short time (e.g. often within 10–15 minutes when the test should, according to the manual, take at least 40 minutes). The Gudjonsson and Shackleton formula is only intended to detect poor effort where there is a deliberate attempt to fake poor performance (i.e. the person is responding in favour of giving incorrect answers). It is not intended to detect poor performance due to rushed, careless, or inconsistent responding. The implication is that underperformance on the matrices may be due to a variety of factors without there being a deliberate attempt to perform poorly. It is also possible that, among some malingerers, the formula is insensitive to the strategy they use for malingering. Therefore, when the rate of decay is below the recommended cut-off point, this is a strong indication of malingering.

Test of Memory Malingering

The TOMM (Tombaugh, 1996) is a 50-item recognition test to detect malingering in memory for adults and includes two learning trials and a retention trial. It was developed specifically for detecting malingering (i.e. identifying patients who are intentionally faking or exaggerating memory deficits for personal gain). However, it is important to note that, whilst the TOMM is highly sensitive to malingering, it is insensitive to neurological impairments (i.e. only the most neurologically disabled would not be able to perform well on the test). The TOMM is validated on a normative non-clinical sample, a clinical sample (e.g. cognitively impaired, aphasic, traumatic brain injured and dementia patients), simulated malingerers, and 'at risk' malingerers. Performance on the TOMM is not sensitive to the effect of age or years of education. It is also unaffected by laboratory-induced pain (Etherton *et al.*, 2005) and chronic pain or depression in patients with fibromyalgia (Iverson *et al.*, 2007).

Validation studies given in the test manual show that highly accurate performance, similar to that obtained with non-impaired adults, occurred with a clinical sample of cognitively impaired aphasic and traumatic brain injury patients (exceeding 99% accuracy) and dementia patients (exceeding 92% accuracy).

There are two scoring criteria: a score lower than chance and any score lower than a figure prescribed in the manual on Trial 2 or the Retention Trial raises the possibility of malingering. According to Tombaugh (1997), it is rare for malingerers to fake to the extent that their score falls significantly below chance. Therefore, this second rule has greater practical utility than relying on a score below chance. Tombaugh (1997) makes it clear in the manual that the diagnosis of malingering should never be made exclusively on the basis of the scores on the TOMM. The scores obtained on the TOMM may give a good indication that memory performance on the test is suboptimal (i.e. false or exaggerated), but the intentionality and motivation behind the poor performance must be obtained from other sources.

Tombaugh (2002) lists the essential criteria that need to be met when constructing memory tests of malingering:

1. The test should be sensitive to the feigning of memory deficits.
2. The test should not be sensitive to the type of factors that typically impair scores on neuropsychological tests (e.g. low IQ, socioeconomic background, brain injury, and depression). Sensitivity to these factors would produce a high false-positive error rate.
3. The test should be perceived as being more difficult than it actually is.
4. The test should clearly give the impression that it is a test of memory functions.
5. The test should have universal application.

Tombaugh (2002) provides a review of the experimental validation of the TOMM, discusses important guidelines regarding interpretations of scores, and answers frequently asked questions regarding the test.

Word Memory Test

The WMT (Green *et al.*, 1996, cited in Green *et al.*, 2001) is a test of verbal learning and memory. Its purpose is to detect and measure suboptimal effort with regard to memory as well as actual memory ability. The WMT is a very sensitive measure of suboptimal effort (i.e. it has a very high level of sensitivity) and can be performed adequately by all but the most severely impaired patients (i.e. the false-positive rate is very low and indicates a high level of specificity). The test has been impressively cross-validated against other measures of malingering (Green *et al.*, 2002).

The person completing the test is required to learn a list of 20 word pairs (e.g. pig–bacon, dog–cat), which can be presented either orally or on a computer screen. The person is then shown a new list of 40 words and has to identify words from the original list (e.g. 'dog' from 'dog–rabbit'). The results provide the first measure of effort, referred to as 'immediate recognition trial'. Feedback regarding correct items is then provided, and after a 30 minute delay, a 'delayed recognition trial' is presented, which uses different foil words to the immediate recognition trial (e.g. 'dog–rat'). The purpose is to give motivated people the opportunity to learn the words before later subtests are administered. The different subtests vary widely in their objective difficulty level, a characteristic that the WMT shares with the Validity Indicator Profile (Frederick, 1997).

After the person has completed the main effort measures, four separate measures of memory ability are administered as follows:

1. Multiple choice—the person is shown the first word from each pair of words and asked to choose the word that matches it from eight options.
2. Paired associates—the person is presented with the first word for each pair and asked to recall the second word.
3. Delayed free recall—the person is asked to recall as many of the words from the list in any order.
4. Long-delayed free-recall—the person recalls the words after a 20-minute delay.

The WMT has been very extensively validated in forensic settings and, unlike many other malingering tests, does not rely primarily on simulation research with normal participants but on genuine malingerers (Green *et al.*, 2002). This is a great advantage.

Validity Indicator Profile

The VIP (Frederick, 1997, 2002b) is a forced-choice paper-and-pencil test, which is quick and easy to administer. Like other malingering tests, it is intended to indicate when the results of a standard neuropsychological evaluation may be invalid due to malingering or suboptimal effort. Unlike the TOMM, the VIP is not a memory malingering test; it uses similar test stimuli to those commonly used during a cognitive evaluation (i.e. matching patterns of matrices and word recognition). The VIP comprises two subtests, verbal (VIP-V) and non-verbal (VIP-NV), which can be administered and scored separately. The word-recognition task comprises 78 word-definition problems, whereas the non-verbal test comprises 100 picture matrix problems similar to those found in the RSPM. The items of both tests are presented randomly, but have a hierarchy of difficulty and are reordered by difficulty after scoring and then plotted to generate a performance curve. The performance curve provides details of the person's average performance across item difficulty.

The results provide a fourfold classification of response style or strategies. These are: (i) 'suppression' or 'malingering', where the person is responding in favour of incorrect responding, such as below-chance performance, and there is high effort and motivation to perform poorly; (ii) 'irrelevant' or 'random' responding, where the person is responding at random to test items; (iii) 'inconsistent' or 'careless' responding, where the person is not responding consistently to test items of different difficult, which may be due to incomplete or fluctuating effort due to inattention, distraction, and tiredness, or not caring about the outcome of the assessment; and (iv) 'compliant' responding, a default category that indicates a valid response style, showing that the person exercised high effort and motivation to do well. Failures with regard to the malingering, irrelevant, or inconsistent performance curves provide insight into the type of invalid response in which the examinee is engaged. Frederick & Crosby (2000) and Frederick *et al.* (2000) have provided evidence for the validity of the fourfold classification system.

Decisions regarding valid or invalid performance were established in the development sample (clinical and non-clinical groups) and evaluated in a cross-validation sample (Frederick, 1997). There was an attempt to maximize sensitivity whilst keeping a reasonably high level of specificity (Frederick, 2002b). In the case of the VIP-V, the overall correct classification rate was 75.5%, with 67.3% sensitivity and 83.1% specificity. The corresponding rates for the VIP-NV were 79.8, 73.5, and 85.7%, for overall correct classification, sensitivity, and specificity, respectively.

Frederick (2002b) provided a review of the construction, development, and validation of the VIP. He addressed criticisms that have been made by others of the fourfold classification in favour of a dichotomous classification ('malingering' versus 'non-malingering') and pointed to the disadvantages and dangers of employing a dichotomous classification system of malingering to address complex issues in relation to suboptimal performance.

Cases involving malingering

Case Study 1: Terrorist offences and reliability of replies in police interviews

Mr Tim (a 30-year-old Kurdish man who had come to Britain seeking asylum) was charged, together with two others, with conspiracy to damage property by fire with the intent to endanger life, allegedly launching a firebomb campaign against Turkish targets in Britain. Similar campaigns happened on the same day in several other European countries. Mr Tim was caught carrying petrol in a diesel-driven London cab. During the trial, the defence produced a report from an educational psychologist who had assessed Mr Tim's non-verbal cognitive functions via an interpreter. The psychologist concluded that his non-verbal IQ fell between 60 and 65, that he would have difficulties functioning in a foreign country without a great deal of support, and that he would be unable to hold down any job except an unskilled position. This was apparently going to be used to cast doubt on the reliability of answers he had given during police interviews.

The prosecution instructed their own expert who carried out a psychological evaluation via an interpreter. Mr Tim's solicitor was present during the evaluation. The SPM, two subtests of the WAIS-R (Picture Completion and Object Assembly), and the Warrington Recognition Memory Test (Warrington, 1984) were administered. He performed at the bottom of the WAIS-R and obtained a total score of 10 on the SPM with a rate of decay score of 7. His demeanour during this test was very unusual—he claimed that all of the patterns looked the same, he was reluctant to commit to an answer, and on occasions he talked to himself in Kurdish. He obtained a score of 39 (78%) on the Recognition Memory Test.

Both experts testified. The defence psychologist argued, on the basis of his test findings, that Mr Tim was 'mentally handicapped' and that his cognitive deficits were genuine. The prosecution psychologist argued that, from his evaluation (including the findings from the SPM and Mr Tim's demeanour), there was strong indication that he had attempted to fake an intellectual deficit during the evaluation and that it was unwise to accept the defence psychologist's test scores. The Gudjonsson and Shackleton rate of decay formula and the research behind the study were discussed in court. Mr Tim went into the witness box. He came across as reasonably intellectually able, in great contrast to how he had performed during the psychological evaluation.

Mr Tim and his two co-defendants were convicted of conspiracy to damage property by fire with the intent to endanger life. He received a 15-year prison sentence. This case took place in the early 1990s, when psychologists were beginning to express an interest in malingering, but before tests like the TOMM, VPI, and WMT had been developed and published. It was the prosecution expert's view that Mr Tim had been underperforming during both of the psychology evaluations. Testing clients via interpreters is problematic and only non-verbal skills could be assessed in the case. In another case, the same psychologist had to conduct a psychological evaluation of a Palestinian terrorist suspect via two interpreters simultaneously (Gudjonsson, 2003, Chapter 22).

Attempting to detect malingering in such cases is particularly difficult and this area needs to be researched.

Case Study 2: Fitness to plead and stand trial

Ms Mask (a middle-aged woman of Arab origin who had lived in the UK for 20 years) was charged with fraudulent evasion of duty chargeable on the importation of goods (cigarettes) and dealing with goods chargeable with duty that had not been paid. Ms Mask had made regular trips between London and Dubai returning with cigarettes averaging around 20 000 per trip. She had eight prior warnings that she claimed not to have understood because they were given in English, and previously had 200 000 cigarettes confiscated. On two occasions, Ms Mask had been stopped in a wheelchair holding an oxygen mask that was not connected to anything. It was thought she used the device to hide her face. A defence statement stated that her family funded her trips as she was visiting a relative in a coma, and that the trips were brief because she had to return to care for an elderly relative. Ms Mask subsequently claimed that a man offered to pay for the trips if she imported cigarettes for him. She agreed without realizing it was unlawful. She was referred for psychological assessment by Customs and Excise regarding her fitness to plead and stand trial.

An educational psychologist instructed by the defence assessed Ms Mask via an interpreter as she claimed to speak no English. No test scores or description of her social functioning or mental state were provided to support the conclusion that she suffered mental impairment, although it was reported that she had some unusual difficulties during testing, e.g. she was unable to copy an outline of a house and she constructed a jigsaw of a man (Object Assembly) with his head upside down and with his legs coming out of his trunk. It later emerged that she obtained a score of 1 on each of the WAIS-R subtests, demonstrating a clear 'floor effect', whilst giving a number of bizarre responses to test items. In spite of this, the defence psychologist considered the test findings reliable, stating that Ms Mask was of very low intelligence and depressed.

In the assessment for the prosecution, testing indicated that she was deliberately attempting to fake performance on the SPM (total score of 8, rate of decay score of 5). She stated that she could not do the Rey Memory Test as she had never used a pen and paper; however when shown her own signature, she attempted the test scoring 0 out of 15. She scored below chance on the coin-in-the-hand test (3/10 correct responses). Her social functioning exceeded this; she had lived independently, raised several children, shopped/cooked, cared for an elderly relative, managed her own finances, and travelled unaided locally and internationally. There was no evidence of depression. Inconsistencies in her presentation were noted (e.g. she would clutch her stomach/back as if in pain but would recover quickly with pain appearing to be sporadic). Her demeanour during the assessment also fluctuated. She was able to show assertion and at one point corrected the interpreter after a mistranslation. The psychologist concluded that the test results, her demeanour during the assessment, and her history of successful independent living suggested that she was deliberately underperforming in the evaluation. In this expert's opinion, Ms Mask had the necessary cognitive capacity to plead, stand trial, and give evidence.

At trial, Ms Mask pleaded guilty to the charges at the last opportunity.

In case 2, Ms Mask displayed many of the diagnostic impressions of probable malingering shown in Table 11.1. She performed well below chance on the coin-in-the-hand test, she performed right at the bottom ('floor effect') on the WAIS-R subtests and the Rey's 15-Item Memory Test, and underperformed on the Raven's Standard Progressive Matrices according to the Gudjonsson & Shackleton (1986) rate of decay formula for malingering. In addition, her demeanour and replies during both the defence and the prosecution expert assessments were bizarre, and her performance was in great contrast to her history of social functioning (i.e. she was able to live independently, bring up her children, look after her disabled mother, and travel to England on her own).

Case Study 3: Fitness to plead and stand trial

Mr Smith was indicted with being knowingly concerned in the fraudulent evasion of duty chargeable on the importation of goods. He claimed to have severe memory impairment, and concerns had been raised about his ability to follow the events of a trial and to instruct his legal representatives. He had a history of affective mood disorder and alcohol abuse, but had been abstinent for some months. In the weeks prior to an assessment instructed by the defence, Mr Smith had reported attention and memory problems to the extent that he became acutely disoriented and got lost, even when in familiar places. A review of the medical records had not indicated any reported difficulties with memory that pre-dated him being charged with the offence.

Psychologists instructed by the defence and Customs and Excise administered a battery of assessments including tests of symptom validity and malingering. These indicated variable cognitive ability with IQ scores falling in the low–average range, a premorbid IQ consistent with verbal subtests, average scores on a test of attention, and impaired range on tests of memory and executive functioning. A psychiatric assessment concluded that depression was unlikely to explain his cognitive problems. Both psychologists agreed that Mr Smith's memory problems were unlikely to be due to chronic alcoholism or medication effects. It was concluded that a lack of motivation to do well on tests and deliberate underperformance were the most probable explanations, based on his scores. Further to this, at a follow-up appointment, Mr Smith said he had experienced a significant increase in impairment from the previous level, which is extremely unusual even for people with acquired brain damage, and suggested that Mr Smith was exaggerating his problems. His decline in functioning appeared to coincide with his being formally charged and required to appear in court.

The prosecution expert administered the Raven Standard Progressive Matrices (SPM) and the TOMM to assess possible malingering. On the SPM, Mr Smith obtained a total score of 22 and a rate of decay score of 18 (he completed the test in 8 minutes). The scores obtained on the TOMM were 19, 21, and 23 for Trial 1, Trial 2, and the Retention Trial, respectively. This neuropsychologist concluded that, whilst Mr Smith was genuinely anxious about the forthcoming trial, it was probable that he was underperforming due to insufficient effort.

One of the more interesting aspects of case 3 is the very low score obtained on the SPM, which was substantially lower than the WAIS-III score, and the fact that Gudjonsson and Shackleton's rate of decay score did not suggest deliberate underperformance. The discrepancy demonstrates the important distinction between deliberate underperformance (i.e. malingering) and underperformance due to poor effort, which is so clearly documented by the Frederick *et al.* (2000) fourfold classification of negative-response bias. Mr Smith completed the SPM in 8 minutes, which is remarkably quick and suggests that, even though he was not deliberately failing items, his overall performance was likely to underestimate his true ability and was unreliable due to poor effort.

Case Study 4: Personal injury claim

Mr Magpie was involved in a road traffic accident. Prior to this, he had no history of head injury and was unemployed. On admission to hospital, he was reported to be alert and fully oriented and a brain scan was normal. After discharge, he had numerous referrals for complaints including loss of sense of smell, spelling problems, and word-finding difficulties.

A neuropsychologist concluded that he had suffered no more than a moderate injury from which a complete recovery would be expected in weeks or at worst a few months. The nature and severity of the impairment he presented was inconsistent with the injury, even allowing for minor frontal brain damage. The expert did not specifically test for malingering.

Mr Magpie was further assessed by two neuropsychologists, and some unusual patterns emerged on testing: his performance was inconsistent across tests and time, he failed simple tasks but passed complex ones, he recalled information better after a delay than immediately, and he obtained forced-choice scores at below-chance levels on five separate tests. It was concluded that, although he appeared to be exaggerating, this was not deliberate.

At the request of a psychiatrist, a fourth neuropsychologist tested Mr Magpie's neuropsychological functions, administering tests to detect possible malingering. The test findings were found to be consistent with severe organic damage, but scores on the SPM (total score of 16 and a rate of decay score of 6) and the TOMM (Trial 1 score = 20, Trial 2 score = 26, Retention Trial score = 23) suggested deliberate underperformance.

Mr Magpie reported social functioning at a higher level than that obtained on formal testing (e.g. using the Internet and word-processing programmes when he was apparently unsure of the alphabet). His bizarre general presentation was also strongly consistent with him exaggerating his problems and difficulties. All experts noted his inconsistent presentation. At times, he could not express himself coherently or provide an autobiographical history. He reported distractibility and intolerance to noise, but appeared unaffected by workmen drilling outside the window. During one assessment, he lurched across the table and stared out of the window. When asked what he was looking at, he continued to stare but pointed to the window and said in a loud voice, 'Magpie'. No one else could see it!

In this case, all of the neuropsychologists agreed that Mr Magpie had sustained a mild head injury that was unlikely to have led to any significant brain damage or neuropsychological deficits. They also agreed that his performance on formal cognitive tests was inconsistent with the index head injury. Two experts did not administer any tests specifically to address the possibility of deliberate underperformance, and when these were administered the results indicated that this was a probability. These tests contributed greatly to the assessment as, drawing all of the information together, it was evident that a lack of motivation to do well on tests and malingering (i.e. deliberately underperforming) were the most probable explanations for Mr Magpie's poor test performance. The fourth neuropsychologist concluded that the presentation and test performance of Mr Magpie was a result of deliberate and conscious adoption of disabled behaviour and not due to learned behaviour from his interaction with people with chronic mental health problems or learning disability.

The experts' opinions were discussed at length in a meeting, and after 2 hours the lawyers suggested that the experts observe covert video-surveillance tapes and advise whether these would be of use in court. These tapes clearly showed Mr Magpie as an individual with considerably greater cognitive awareness and social functioning than that expected from his test performance and personal account. He was walking around in a shopping centre and seemed to go about his everyday business and do his shopping without difficulty or constraint. He was careful crossing the road, he queued up patiently at cash registers, he seemed friendly and spontaneous in his interactions with people, he seemed to deal with money adequately, and he walked purposefully and did not appear to lose his way. Everyone agreed that he presented as a completely different person to the one who had walked into their consulting rooms. As the experts observed him window-shopping in a jewellers and then wandering around a furniture store looking at leather settees, one leaned over to another expert and whispered, 'What do you think he is doing?' The expert whispered back, 'Planning how to spend the compensation!'

Conclusions

Clinical psychologists commonly conduct cognitive or neuropsychological assessments in judicial proceedings. When deficits are identified, these may play an important part in the outcome of the case, whether in civil (e.g. compensation) or criminal (e.g. competency issues) cases. It is therefore important that the findings obtained on psychological testing give a valid representation of the client's strengths and deficits. There are a number of factors that can adversely affect the validity of the test results, including a disturbed mental state, fatigue, and poor or suboptimal effort. Suboptimal effort is commonly referred to in recent literature as a negative-response bias.

Over the past two decades, there has been growing interest in negative-response bias. Malingering, which involves deliberate fabrication of symptoms or deficits in cases where there is a strong incentive to deceive, is an extreme form of negative-response bias. There is a general reluctance among clinicians to use the term malingering, because of its pejorative connotation (i.e. it implies deliberate deception and dishonesty) and the dichotomous nature of the concept. A diagnosis of malingering can be consequential in court. For example, in one case it substantially lengthened the sentence the defendant would received if convicted (Knoll & Resnick, 1999). Therefore, the term malingering needs to be used cautiously and with good foundation. A review of the literature suggests that there is a general consensus among practitioners that a diagnosis of malingering should not be made on the basis of a simple test. Test findings need to be interpreted in the context of all other relevant information and factors in the case.

In forensic evaluation, there is often a strong incentive for people to underperform in one or more areas of their cognitive functions. The work of Frederick (1997, 2002b) has been particularly helpful in identifying different factors during a cognitive evaluation that may affect the validity of test findings. The two most important dimensions are effort and motivation along which lie different reasons for suboptimal performance. This raises the question of whether tests of effort should be routinely administered alongside neuropsychological batteries, and, if so, what tests should be used? When considering this question, the tester needs to bear in mind the complexity of the construct relating to suboptimal effort and malingering. A testee may choose to underperform on some cognitive tests but not on others (e.g. verbal memory, non-verbal memory, intellectual function, and executive function).

In the last 10 years, there have been huge advances in the development of specific tests that aim to detect suboptimal effort and malingering. These important tools are at the disposal of practitioners and nowadays should be included in a comprehensive test battery. Of course, if there is no indication that an individual is lacking in effort, then this negates the need for their administration. However, practitioners are not 'mind-readers' and there are undoubtedly many cases involving lack of effort that are unidentified. Therefore, we suggest that there are three 'categories' that should trigger the addition of tests of suboptimal effort in cases where there is a strong incentive to malinger: (i) when testees without a history of learning disability are obtaining scores in a borderline range or lower; (ii) when testees are obtaining lower scores than expected from other sources of information (e.g. social functioning and educational background); and (iii) if the tester suspects that the testee is not putting in full effort (e.g. by their demeanour, completing tasks at a rapid pace, or bizarre responding).

Tests of suboptimal effort and malingering are successful because individuals are naïve as to how they work. However, with ready access to information about test material on the Internet and test procedures being described in court, there is a real risk that individuals may become informed about particular tests and how they operate. In some cases, individuals may even be coached in their use by their legal representatives. This is the greatest challenge that practitioners will face in future and means that the discipline will need to respond by 'reinventing the wheel' with the development of new tests and novel methodologies.

References

Allen, L. M., Iverson, G. L., and Green, P. (2002). Computerized assessment of response bias in forensic neuropsychology. In: J. Hom and R. L. Denney (eds), *Detection of Response Bias in Forensic Neuropsychology*, pp. 205–225. New York: The Haworth Medical Press.

American Psychiatric Association (1994). *Diagnostic and Statistical Manual of Mental Disorders*, 4th edn. Washington, DC: American Psychiatric Association.

Bender, S. D. (2008). Malingered traumatic brain injury. In: R. Rogers (ed.), *Clinical Assessment of Malingering and Deception*, pp. 69–86. New York: The Guilford Press.

Berry, D. T. R. and Butcher, J. N. (1998). Detecting malingering on the Luria–Nebraska neuropsychological battery. In: C. R. Reynolds (ed.), *Detection of Malingering during Head Injury Litigation*, pp. 209–238. New York: Plenum Press.

Berry, D. T. R. and Schipper, L. J. (2008). Assessment of feigned cognitive impairment using standard neuropsychological tests. In: R. Rogers (ed.), *Clinical Assessment of Malingering and Deception*, pp. 237–252. New York: The Guilford Press.

Binder, L. M. (2002). The Portland Digit Recognition Test: A review of validation data and clinical use. In: J. Hom and R. L. Denney (eds), *Detection of Response Bias in Forensic Neuropsychology*, pp. 27–41. New York: The Haworth Medical Press.

Binder, L. M. and Rohling, M. L. (1996). Money matters: A meta-analytic review of the effects of financial incentives on recovery after closed-head injury. *American Journal of Psychiatry*, **153**:7–10.

Christianson, S. A., Marckelbach, H., and Kopelman, M. (2006). Crime-related amnesia. In: A. Heaton-Armstrong, E. Shepherd, G. Gudjonsson, and D. Wolchover (eds), *Witness Testimony. Psychological, Investigative and Evidential Perspectives*, pp. 105–129. Oxford: Oxford University Press.

Colby, F. (2001). Using the binomial distribution to assess effort: Forced-choice testing in neuropsychological settings. *NeuroRehabilitation*, **16**:253–265.

Corsini, R. J. (1999). *The Dictionary of Psychology*. Philadelphia: Brunner/Mazel.

Etherton, J. L., Bianchini, K. J., Greve, K. W., and Ciota, M. A. (2005). Test of Memory Malingering Performance is unaffected by laboratory-induced pain: Implications for clinical use. *Archives of Clinical Neuropsychology*, **20**:375–384.

Faust, D. and Ackley, M. A. (1998). Did you think it was going to be easy? Some methodological suggestions for the investigation and development of malingering detection techniques. In: C. R. Reynolds (ed.), *Detection of Malingering during Head Injury Litigation*, pp. 1–54. New York: Plenum Press.

Frederick, R. I. (1997). *VIP Validity Indicator Manual*. Minneapolis: National Computer Systems.

Frederick, R. I. (2002a). A review of Rey's strategies for detecting malingered neuropsychological impairment. In: J. Hom and R. L. Denney (eds), *Detection of Response Bias in Forensic Neuropsychology*, pp. 1–25. New York: The Haworth Medical Press.

Frederick, R. I. (2002b). Review of the Validity Indicator Profile. In: J. Hom and R. L. Denney (eds), *Detection of Response Bias in Forensic Neuropsychology*, pp. 125–145. New York: The Haworth Medical Press.

Frederick, R. I. and Crosby, R. D. (2000). Development and validation of the Validity Indicator Profile. *Law and Human Behavior*, **24**:59–82.

Frederick, R. I. and Foster, H. G. (1991). Multiple measures of malingering on a forced-choice or cognitive ability test. *Psychological Assessment*, **3**:596–602.

Frederick, R. I., Carter, M., and Powel, J. (1995). Adapting symptom validity testing to evaluate suspicious complaints of amnesia in medicolegal evaluations. *Bulletin of the American Academy of Psychiatry and the Law*, **23**:231–237.

Frederick, R. I., Crosby, R. D., and Wynkoop, T. F. (2000). Performance curve classification of invalid responding on the Validity Indicator Profile. *Archives of General Neuropsychology*, **15**:281–300.

Golden, C. J. and Grier, C. A. (1998). Detecting malingering on the Luria–Nebraska neuropsychological battery. In: C. R. Reynolds (ed.), *Detection of Malingering during Head Injury Litigation*, pp. 133–162. New York: Plenum Press.

Goldstein, H. (1945). A malingering key for mental tests. *Psychological Bulletin*, **42**:104–118.

Graf, P., Square, L. R., and Mandler, G. (1984). The information that amnesics do not forget. *Journal of Experimental Psychology: Learning, Memory, and Cognition*, **10**:164–178.

Graue, L. O., Berry, D. T. R., Clark, J. A., et al. (2007). Identification of feigned mental retardation using the new generation of malingering detection instruments: Preliminary findings. *Clinical Neuropsychologist*, **21**:929–942.

Green, P., Allen, L. M., and Astner, K. (1996). *The Word Memory Test: A user's guide to the oral and computer-administered forms, US version 1.1*. Durham, NC: CogniSyst.

Green, P., Rohling, M. L., Lees-Haley, P. R., and Allen, L. M. (2001). Effort has a greater effect on test scores than severe brain injury in compensation claimants. *Brain Injury*, **15**:1045–1060.

Green, P., Lees-Haley, P. R., and Allen, L. M. (2002). The Word Memory Test and the validity of neuropsychological test scores. In: J. Hom and R. L. Denney (eds), *Detection of Response Bias in Forensic Neuropsychology*, pp. 97–124. New York: The Haworth Medical Press.

Greve, K. W., Bianchini, K. J., Mathias, C. W., Houston, R. J., and Crouch, J. A. (2003). Detecting malingered performance on the Wechsler Adult Intelligence Scale. Validation of Mittenberg's approach in traumatic brain injury. *Archives of Clinical Neuropsychology*, **18**:245–260.

Gudjonsson, G. H. (1985). Psychological evidence in court: Results from the BPS survey. *Bulletin of the British Psychological Society*, **38**:327–330.

Gudjonsson, G. H. (1990). Self-deception and other-deception in forensic assessment. *Personality and Individual Differences*, **11**:219–225.

Gudjonsson, G. H. (1993). The implications of poor psychological evidence in court. *Expert Evidence*, **2**:120–124.

Gudjonsson, G. H. (1996). Psychological evidence in court. Results from the 1995 Survey. *The Psychologist*, **5**:213–217.

Gudjonsson, G. H. (2003). *The Psychology of Interrogations and Confessions. A Handbook.* Chichester, UK: John Wiley & Sons.

Gudjonsson, G. H. (2008). Psychologists as expert witnesses: The 2007 BPS Survey. *Forensic Update*, **92**:23–29.

Gudjonsson, G. H. and Haward, L. R. C. (1998). *Forensic Psychology: A Guide to Practice.* London: Routledge.

Gudjonsson, G. H. and MacKeith, J. A. C. (1983). A specific recognition deficit in a case of homicide. *Medicine, Science and the Law*, **23**:37–40.

Gudjonsson, G. H. and Shackleton, H. (1986). The pattern of scores on Raven's Matrices during 'faking bad' and 'non-faking' performance. *British Journal of Clinical Psychology*, **25**:35–41.

Guthkelch, A. N. (1980). Post-traumatic amnesia, post-concussional symptoms and accident neurosis. *European Neurology*, **19**:91–102.

Hanley, J. R., Baker, G. A., and Ledson, S. (1999). Detecting of faking of amnesia: A comparison of the effectiveness of three different techniques for distinguishing simulators from patients with amnesia. *Journal of Clinical and Experimental Neuropsychology*, **21**:59–69.

Hathaway, S. R. and McKinley, J. C. (1991). *The Minnesota Multiphasic Personality Inventory Manual.* Minneapolis, MN: University of Minnesota Press.

Heaton, R. K., Smith, H. H., Lehman, R. A., and Vogt, A. J. (1978). Prospects of faking believable deficits on neuropsychological testing. *Journal of Consulting and Clinical Psychology*, **46**:892–900.

Hiscock, M. and Hiscock, C. K. (1989). Refining the forced-choice method for the detection of malingering. *Journal of Clinical and Experimental Neuropsychology*, **11**:967–974.

Hom, J. and Denney, R. L. (2002). *Detection of Response Bias in Forensic Neuropsychology.* New York: The Haworth Medical Press.

Iverson, G. L., Le Page, J., Koehler, B. E., Shojania, K., and Badii, M. (2007). Test of Memory Malingering (TOMM) scores are not affected by chronic pain or depression in patients with fibromyalgia. *Clinical Neuropsychologist*, **21**:535–546.

Jelicic, M., Merckelbach, H., and van Bergen, S. (2004). Symptom validity testing of feigned amnesia for a mock crime. *Archives of Clinical Neuropsychology*, **19**:525–531.

Kapur, N. (1994). The coin-in-the-hand test: A new 'bedside' test for the detection of malingering in patients with suspected memory disorder. *Journal of Neurology, Neurosurgery and Psychiatry*, **57**:385–386.

Knoll, J. L. and Resnick, P. J. (1999). US v. Greer: Longer sentences for malingerers. *Journal of the American Academy of Psychiatry and the Law*, **27**:621–625.

Kopelman, M. D. (1987). Crime and amnesia: A review. *Behavioral Science and the Law*, **5**:323–342.

Kozaric-Kovacic, D., Bajs, M., Vidosic, S., Matic, A., Alegic, K. A., and Peraica, T. (2004). Change of diagnosis of posttraumatic stress disorder related to compensation-seeking. *Croatian Medical Journal*, **45**:427–433.

Larrabee, G. J. (2003). Detection of malingering using atypical performance patterns on standard neuropsychological tests. *Clinical Neuropsychologist*, **17**:410–425.

Larrabee, G. J. (2005). Assessment of malingering. In: G. J. Larrabee (ed.), *Forensic Neuropsychology: A Scientific Approach*, pp. 115–158. Oxford: Oxford University Press.

Lezak, M. D., Howieson, D. B., and Loring, D. W. (2004). *Neuropsychological Assessment*. Oxford: Oxford University Press.

McKinzey, R. K., Podd, M. H., Krehbiel, M. A., and Raven, J. (1999). Detection of malingering on Raven's Standard Progressive Matrices: A cross-validation. *British Journal of Clinical Psychology*, **38**:435–439.

McKinzey, R. K., Prieler, J., and Raven, J. (2003). Detection of children's malingering on Raven's Standard Progressive Matrices. *British Journal of Clinical Psychology*, **42**:95–99.

Mendelson, G. (1995). 'Compensation neurosis' revisited: Outcome studies of the effects of litigation. *Journal of Psychosomatic Research*, **39**:695–706.

Miller, H. A. (2001). *Miller-Forensic Assessment of Symptoms Test (M-FAST). Professional Manual*. Odessa, FL: Psychological Assessment Resources.

Millis, S. R. (2002). The Word Memory Test and the validity of neuropsychological test scores. In: J. Hom and R. L. Denney (eds), *Detection of Response Bias in Forensic Neuropsychology*, pp. 147–166. New York: The Haworth Medical Press.

Millis, S. R. and Volinsky, C. T. (2001). Assessment of response bias in mild head injury: Beyond malingering tests. *Journal of Clinical and Experimental Neuropsychology*, **23**:809–828.

Millon, T. (1997). *Millon Clinical Multiaxial Inventory—III*, 2nd edition. Minneapolis, MN: National Computer Systems.

Milner, B. (1968). Visual recognition and recall after right temporal lobe excision in man. *Neuropsychologia*, **6**:191–209.

Mittenberg, W., Theroux, S., and Aguila-Puentes, G. (2001). Identification of malingered head injury on the Wechsler Adult Intelligence Scale—3rd edition. *Clinical Neuropsychologist*, **15**:440–445.

Mittenberg, W., Patton, C., Canyock, E. M., and Condit, D. C. (2002). Base rates of malingering and symptom exaggeration. *Journal of Clinical and Experimental Neuropsychology*, **24**:1094–1102.

Mossman D. (2003). Daubert, cognitive malingering, and test accuracy. *Law and Human Behavior*, **27**:229–249.

Newman, C. (1983). Psychometric tests examined in open court. *Bulletin of the British Psychological Society*, **36**:296.

Pankratz, L. (1979). Symptom validity testing and symptom retraining: Procedures for the assessment and treatment of functional sensory deficits. *Journal of Consulting and Clinical Psychology*, **47**:409–410.

Pankratz, L. (1988). Malingering on intellectual and neuropsychological measures. In: R. Rogers (ed.), *Clinical Assessment of Malingering and Deception*, pp. 169–192. New York: Guilford.

Pankratz, L., Fausti, S. A., and Peed, S. A. (1975). A forced technique to evaluate deafness in a hysterical or malingering patient. *Journal of Consulting and Clinical Psychology*, **43**:421–422.

Paulhus, D. (1998). *Paulhus Deception Scales (PDS): The Balanced Inventory of Desirable Responding—7*. New York: MHS.

Pollock, P. H. (1996). A cautionary note on the determination of malingering in offenders. *Psychology, Crime and Law,* **3**:97–110.

Raven, J., Raven, J. C., and Court, J. H. (1998). *Manual for Raven's Progressive Matrices and Vocabulary Scales.* San Antonio, TX: The Psychological Corporation.

Reitan, R. M. and Wolfson, D. (2002). Detection of malingering and invalid test results using the Halstead–Reitan battery. In: J. Hom and R. L. Denney (eds), *Detection of Response Bias in Forensic Neuropsychology,* pp. 275–314. New York: The Haworth Medical Press.

Resnick, P. J. (1988a). Malingered psychosis. In: Y. S. Ben-Porath, J. R. Graham, G. C. N. Hall, R. D. Hirschman, and M. S. Zaragoza (eds), *Forensic Applications of the MMPI-2,* pp. 34–53. London: Sage Publications.

Resnick, P. J. (1988b). Malingering of posttraumatic disorders. In: Y. S. Ben-Porath, J. R. Graham, G. C. N. Hall, R. D. Hirschman, and M. S. Zaragoza (eds), *Forensic Applications of the MMPI-2,* pp. 84–103. London: Sage Publications.

Resnick, P. J. and Knoll, J. L. (2008). Malingered psychosis. In: R. Rogers (ed.), *Clinical Assessment of Malingering and Deception,* pp. 51–68. New York: The Guilford Press.

Resnick, P. J., West, S., and Payne, J. W. (2008). Malingering of posttraumatic disorders. In: R. Rogers (ed.), *Clinical Assessment of Malingering and Deception,* pp. 109–127. New York: The Guilford Press.

Rey, A. (1964). *L'examen clinique en psychologie* [The clinical examination in psychology]. Paris: Presses Universitaires de France.

Reynolds, C. R. (ed.) (1998). *Detection of Malingering during Head Injury Litigation.* New York: Plenum Press.

Rogers, R. (1990a). Development of a new classification model of malingering. *Bulletin of the American Academy of Psychiatry and Law,* **18**:323–333.

Rogers, R. (1990b). Models of feigned mental illness. *Professional Psychology: Research and Practice,* **21**:182–188.

Rogers, R. (2008a). An introduction to response styles. In: R. Rogers (ed.), *Clinical Assessment of Malingering and Deception,* pp. 3–13. New York: The Guilford Press.

Rogers, R. (2008b). Structured interviews and dissimulation. In: R. Rogers (ed.), *Clinical Assessment of Malingering and Deception,* pp. 301–322. New York: The Guilford Press.

Rogers, R. and Salekin, R. T. (1998). Research report beguiled by Bayes: A re-analysis of Mossman and Hart's estimates of malingering. *Behavioral Sciences and the Law,* **16**:147–153.

Rogers, R., Bagby, R. M., and Dickens, S. E. (1992). *Structured Interview of Reported Symptoms (SIRS) and Professional Manual.* Odessa, FL: Psychological Assessment Resources.

Rogers, R., Harrell, E. H., and Liff, C. D. (1993). Feigning neuropsychological impairment: A critical review of the methodological and clinical considerations. *Clinical Psychology Review,* **13**:255–274.

Rogers, R., Sewell, K. W., and Goldstein, A. M. (1994). Exploratory models of malingering. *Law and Human Behavior,* **18**:543–552.

Rogers, R., Salekin, R. T., Sewell, K. W., Goldstein, A., and Leonard, K. (1998). Exploratory models of malingering. *Law and Human Behavior,* **22**:353–367.

Slick, D. C., Sherman, E. M. S., and Iverson, G. L. (1999). Diagnostic criteria for malingered neurocognitive dysfunction: Proposed standards for clinical practice and research. *Clinical Neuropsychologist*, **13**:545–561.

Smith, G. P. and Burger, G. K. (1997). Detection of malingering: Validation of the Structured Inventory of Malingered Symptomatology (SIMS). *Journal of the Academy of Psychiatry and the Law*, **25**:183–190.

Snedecor, G. W. and Cochran, W. G. (1967). *Statistical Methods*, 6th edn. Ames, IA: Iowa State University Press.

Sullivan, K., Lange, R. T., and Dawnes, S. (2007). Methods of detecting malingering and estimated symptom exaggeration base rates in Australia. *Journal of Forensic Neuropsychology*, **4**:49–70.

Sweet, J. J. (1999). Malingering: Differential diagnosis. In: J. J. Sweet (ed.), *Forensic Neuropsychology: Fundamentals and Practice*, pp. 255–285. Lisse: Swets & Zeitlinger.

Sweet, J. J. and King, J. H. (2002). Category test validity indicators: Overview and practice recommendations. In: J. Hom and R. L. Denney (eds), *Detection of Response Bias in Forensic Neuropsychology*, pp. 241–274. New York: The Hayworth Medical Press.

Sweet, J. J., Condit, D. C., and Nelson, N. W. (2008). Feigned amnesia and memory loss. In: R. Rogers (ed.), *Clinical Assessment of Malingering and Deception*, pp. 218–236. New York: The Guilford Press.

Tombaugh, T. N. (1996). *Test of Memory Malingering (TOMM)*. New York: Multi Health Systems.

Tombaugh, T. N. (1997). The Test of Memory Malingering (TOMM): Normative data from cognitively intact and cognitively impaired individuals. *Psychological Assessment*, **9**:260–268.

Tombaugh, T. N. (2002). The Test of Memory Malingering (TMM) in forensic psychology. In: J. Hom and R. L. Denney (eds), *Detection of Response Bias in Forensic Neuropsychology*, pp. 69–96. New York: The Haworth Medical Press.

Trueblood, W. and Schmidt, M. (1993). Malingering and other validity considerations in the neuropsychological evaluation of mild head injury. *Journal of Clinical and Experimental Neuropsychology*, **15**:578–590.

Tunstall, O., Gudjonsson, G., Eysenck H., and Haward, L. (1982). Professional issues arising from psychological evidence presented in court. *Bulletin of the British Psychological Society*, **35**:329–331.

Vallabhajosula, B. and van Gorp, W. G. (2001). Post-Daubert admissibility of scientific evidence on malingering of cognitive deficits. *Journal of the American Academy of Psychiatry and the Law*, **29**:207–215.

Vickery, C. D., Berry, D. T. R., Inman, T. H., Harris, M. J., and Orey, S. A. (2001). Detection of inadequate effort on neuropsychological testing: A meta-analytic review. *Archives of Clinical Neuropsychology*, **16**:45–73.

Warrington, E. K. (1984). *Recognition Memory Test*. Windsor: NFER Nelson.

Wechsler, D. (1977). *WAIS-III. Administration and Scoring Manual*. San Antonio, TX: Harcourt Brace.

Widows, M. R. and Smith, G. P. (2005). *Structured Inventory of Malingered Symptomatology: Professional Manual*. Odessa, FL: Psychological Assessment Resources.

Wogar, M. A., van den Broek, M. D., Bradshaw, C. M., and Szabadi A. (1998). A new performance-curve method for the detection of simulated cognitive impairment. *British Journal of Clinical Psychology*, **37**:327–339.

Chapter 12

Professional issues

Jacqueline Wheatcroft, Gisli Gudjonsson, and Susan Young

'I'm not asking you, I'm telling you!'

The above quotation was made by a solicitor to place pressure on one of the authors to make changes to a written psychological report prepared for them in a case of a man charged with murder—the expert was asked to delete a reference to a document that the defence had provided but did not want the Crown to see. When the expert refused to delete the reference to the document under the list of documents provided for consideration, the solicitor ordered him to comply with the request. The expert subsequently declined and testified in court without any alterations being made to the report.

Haward (1981, p. 21) defines forensic psychology as '*that branch of applied psychology which is concerned with the collection, examination and presentation of evidence for judicial purposes*'. Within this definition, 'poor' psychological evidence falls into two overlapping categories (Gudjonsson, 1993): (i) evidence that fails to inform, and (ii) evidence that is either misleading or incorrect. In order to avoid these pitfalls, psychologists should at all times act with integrity, objectivity, clarity, and within their areas of competencies.

Professionals engage with sets of rules or principles (normally written codes) that are guides to practice. Codes of practice are important but they do have their limitations. They provide guidelines about the parameters within which professional judgements should be made and do not provide psychologists with answers to every ethical dilemma they may face in their clinical and forensic practice (British Psychological Society, 2006). In addition to general professional/ethical codes for psychologists, special guidelines and procedures have recently been produced for expert witnesses in England and Wales (British Psychological Society, 2007a). Expert witnesses should be familiar with these guidelines. Hall & Smith (1997) set out the various aspects of being a witness and give useful advice to expert witnesses.

Legal work often presents dynamic situations that are not clearly defined, which leave the practitioner with decisions to make that might be based on competing demands or goals. Professional codes of conduct and ethical considerations can sometimes become confused in the sea of complexities that are associated with civil and/or criminal casework. Inevitably, the overlap that exists between codes, ethics, and practice means that clear boundaries for decision-making can, at times, seem difficult to determine.

This chapter aims to provide an overview of some of the practical problems that arise when conducting forensic evaluations in civil and criminal cases, preparing and submitting reports, and testifying in court.

What do surveys of court work tell us?

A number of surveys have been conducted among psychologists about their work as expert witnesses in court (e.g. Gudjonsson, 1985, 1996a, b, 2008; Sigurdsson & Gudjonsson, 2004; Navarro & Gudjonsson, 2008). This has been complemented by surveys among lawyers about the value of expert psychological evidence (Bach & Gudjonsson, 1999; Leslie *et al.*, 2007). We will review much of this work in this chapter.

The Psychologist published the 1995 British Psychological Society survey results derived from 522 psychologists involved in court work (Gudjonsson, 1996a). Eleven years on from a previous survey conducted in 1984 (Gudjonsson, 1985), it was shown that the number of psychologists who had testified in a court or tribunal had grown considerably. This demonstrated an increased willingness by the courts to accept psychological evidence. Moreover, the past couple of decades have seen the legal profession seek experts' opinions more frequently and most commonly, in the form of psychological court reports. A relatively high proportion of experts in criminal cases (about 20%) are required to testify after producing a court report (Gudjonsson, 1996a), and as a result, become increasingly embroiled in legal and courtroom processes. The frequency with which experts have to testify in civil cases is much lower at about 2% (Gudjonsson, 1996a).

In this respect, psychologists can, and do, work in a variety of domains that include clinical, neuropsychological, forensic, educational, and occupational areas. Arguably, the increased demand reflects progressive diversity into specialist areas, and requests for reports are made in a variety of areas such as post-traumatic stress disorder, the psychological effects of head injury, fitness to plead issues, and disputed confessions. Referrals may be made directly by defence lawyers, police, and prosecution, and in the past decade these referrals have increasingly been made independently from medical instructions (Gudjonsson & Haward, 1998; Leslie *et al.*, 2007).

So what did the 1995 survey tell us about psychological evidence in court? The most common categories in which reports were prepared generally fell into three major legal areas: civil proceedings (55%); family, juvenile, or matrimonial proceedings (22%); and criminal proceedings (15%). The greatest source of referral was from solicitors (87%), and it was rare for psychologists to report that their most commonly received referrals came from other source types, such as the police, Crown Prosecution Service, or Probation Service. Over half of the respondents produced reports concerned with post-traumatic stress disorder and other forms of compensation-related issues (i.e. head injury); 47% were related to childcare proceedings with a quarter producing reports for mitigation purposes. A minority of reports were concerned with the reliability of witness or confession statements, diminished responsibility or insanity, and fitness to plead or stand trial. In the 1995 survey, Gudjonsson raised concerns about the extent to which psychologists had been asked to alter the report to make it more favourable to the side instructing them (27% of the participants reported this having happened and, of these, 56% had complied with the request).

The British Psychological Society conducted a further survey of expert witnesses in 2007 (Gudjonsson, 2008), which focused on training needs. Consistent with the previous surveys, most of the reporting psychologists were clinical psychologists and just over half were females. It is evident that the main involvement of these psychologists was in relation to civil litigation and family proceedings (care proceedings), followed by criminal cases and tribunal reports. Out of the 194 respondents who completed the survey and who were all members of the British Psychological Society Directory of Expert Witnesses, 41% stated that they did not feel adequately trained or experienced enough to give oral evidence in court, in contrast to 17.5% in relation to the preparation of court reports. The findings supported arguments for professional accredited training courses and registration.

Arguably, relatively few would dispute that expert opinion can have an important impact in relation to outcome in cases and legal rulings (Gudjonsson, 2003, 2006; Sigurdsson & Gudjonsson, 2004). Indeed, a survey of 79 litigation lawyers (15.4% response rate) found that the majority were satisfied with the quality of psychological and psychiatric reports, although there were some concerns related to the length and lack of clarity of some of the reports (Bach & Gudjonsson, 1999). More recently, a study conducted by Leslie *et al.* (2007) evaluated 62 (42% response rate) criminal barristers' opinions and perceptions of clinical psychologists and psychiatrists as expert witnesses. From the study emerged a number of important findings related to how useful these reports actually are to the legal process. Overall, clarity of language, firm conclusions, impartiality, and consistency were clearly considered important elements of good practice. There are, however, potential conflicts between demand and delivery for practitioners working to provide useful evidence to the court.

The factors that barristers believe are important, as outlined above, can be, and often are, counterintuitive to a professional psychologist's code of conduct, practice, and ways of working. For example, in practice, solicitors tend to want to see firm outcomes, whereas firm conclusions are not always warranted on the basis of a psychological evaluation. Furthermore, the issue of independence is clear to the practitioner, yet, as we will see later in this chapter, illustrative case examples (see section on What actually happens) will highlight the sometimes dichotomous relationship that can exist between what solicitors want, or even demand, and what psychologists can provide in terms of their report and its presented outcomes.

What we are expected to do: Overarching ethical issues and some pitfalls

Under the terms of its Royal Charter, the British Psychological Society is required to maintain a Code of Ethics and Conduct. In 1985, the Society adopted a Code of Conduct, which has been updated regularly. From monitoring complaints and ethical enquiries, the Society's Ethics Committee identified the need for a code that gave more emphasis and support to the process of ethical decision-making (see British Psychological Society, 2006, for details). The aim of the guidelines is to define good psychological practice for all psychologists, to strengthen the identity of psychologists, to benefit the public and its members, and to provide guidance on legal and regulatory issues. Each ethical principle is described in a statement of values that reflects fundamental beliefs that guide ethical reasoning, decision-making, and behaviour. In broad terms, the code sets out minimum standards for professional conduct, which are underpinned by four key ethical principles as outlined below:

1. Respect: *'Psychologists value the dignity and worth of all persons, with sensitivity to the dynamics of perceived authority or influence over clients, and with particular regard to people's rights including those of privacy, consent, confidentiality, and self determination'* (p. 10).
2. Competence: *'Psychologists value the continuing development and maintenance of high standards of competence in their professional work, and the importance of preserving their ability to function optimally within the recognised limits of their knowledge, skill, training, education, and experience'* (p. 14).
3. Responsibility: *'Psychologists value their responsibilities to clients, to the general public, and to the profession and science of psychology, including the*

avoidance of harm and the prevention of misuse or abuse of their contributions to society' (p. 17).

4. Integrity: *'Psychologists value honesty, accuracy, clarity, and fairness in their interactions with all persons, and seek to promote integrity in all facets of their scientific and professional endeavours'* (p. 20).

In addition, each principle is further defined by a set of standards that outlines the ethical conduct that the Society expects of its members. These ethical principles integrate with five core aspects of work: (i) assessment (the identification and analysis of the needs and problems of individuals); (ii) formulation of solutions; (iii) intervention or implementation; (iv) evaluation of outcomes; and (v) clear and effective communication.

In December 2004, the Professional Practice Board of the British Psychological Society commissioned a paper on services for children with acquired brain injury, which included a section on the role of psychologists in preparing medico-legal reports (British Psychological Society, 2004a) and relates to the responsibilities to clients. However, much of what has been written also applies to adult injuries. The paper emphasized the need to take account of pre-injury status and the level of support received following the injury (including educational support, parental expectations, and attitude). Whilst the value of neuropsychological assessments are acknowledged in assessing ability and helping to plan remediation strategies, the paper cautions against the assumption that there is a seamless translation between test scores and everyday 'real-life' skills and/or that long-term predictions can be made from test results. Neuropsychological assessment test results are considered to *'offer only moderate correlations with everyday functioning'* and the paper comments that 'essential' practice is that a broader-based assessment of functioning needs to be obtained before making important statements that may have long-term implications. This includes obtaining ecologically valid information, e.g. by observing functioning in the 'real world' and/or by the use of checklists and rating scales, and assessing family factors such as as stress and maladjusted changes that can follow from a child suffering a traumatic brain injury.

Nevertheless, it is important to take a long-term perspective in drawing conclusions for the court. When assessing youths, this means taking a developmental perspective, as the sequelae of acquired brain injury may not manifest until later in life. *'It is often not until children reach their mid to late teens that the full effects of an injury in early childhood will become evident in their inability to hold down a reasonable job, live independently, handle their financial affairs and form close adult relationships'* (British Psychological Society, 2004b, p. 38). The paper also noted that the pragmatic result of any report is that children will receive a financial settlement to cover both the lifetime costs of their care, the loss of income, and compensation for pain and injury. Any relevant resources, such as those for education and rehabilitation, can be purchased via the court. This is important and can be the most expedient way of obtaining services given that most Statements of Special Educational Need state that children's needs are met within resources available. Whilst this might be satisfactory for some, those children with complex needs (i.e. cognitive and behavioural) may require support or services that are either insufficiently offered or unavailable. Accordingly, where possible, early reports should be made and should include recommendations of most benefit to the child, as these are likely to make a significant difference to outcomes for both child and family.

The legal system considers that experts are more akin to 'quasi-officers of the court' and that the purpose of an expert witness is to inform the court about the questions and issues raised by a commissioning solicitor on knowledge beyond the expertise of the judge (British Psychological Society, 2007a). Furthermore, the overarching duties of an expert are to provide objective assistance to the court that, in essence, override any obligation the witness might have to instructing agents or to those who pay them. Certainly, experts must not be 'hired guns' of the parties. Overall, the main duties and responsibilities of the expert witness (distilled from earlier cases going back to *Whitehouse v Jordan* [1981] 1 WLR 246 include that the expert:

- be an independent and uninfluenced expert
- provides independent assistance to the court with objective unbiased opinion
- never adopts the role of advocate
- states facts or assumptions with regard to basis of opinion
- does not omit relevant facts
- makes clear when issues fall outside of their expertise
- states qualifications and relevant experience
- communicates any material opinion change without delay.

If an expert is uncertain as to the nature of their duties and responsibilities, then they can ask for assistance in writing directly from the court and independently of the retainer involved. There exist a number of possible consequences for experts who fail in their duties, such as contempt of court, perjury, or referral to an appropriate professional body, dependent upon the severity of failure. For example, mistake or error is not usually sufficient, but gross neglect or inaccuracy may fulfil duty failure (*Myers v Elman* [1940] AC 282, 317–319). The concept of witness immunity from suit, based on the premise that a witness needs to give evidence fearlessly, is likely to be deemed as not related to potential liability and subsequent claims for costs from a third party. It is therefore feasible that gross dereliction of duty could result in the court ordering an expert to compensate those who might have suffered as a result. Furthermore, it is generally considered that the signed declaration is warning enough of this potential and that the expert should be aware of their duty to the court given such an endorsement. Such a declaration in the report may include the following:

- 'I have given my opinion as a senior clinical psychologist.'
- 'I understand that my duty as an expert is to the court. I have complied with that duty and will continue to comply with that duty.'
- 'I confirm that insofar as the facts stated in my report are within my own knowledge I have made clear which they are and I believe them to be true, and that the opinions I have expressed represent my true and complete professional opinion.'

Initial terms of engagement in the legal domain can be important. In some circumstances, it might be wise for psychologists to provide clients (e.g. solicitors) with such terms in order to clarify the relationship and to provide safeguards for both parties to the ensuing contractual relationship. This can be particularly important for any legal work to be undertaken, or indeed any work proposed to be undertaken with other organizations. Essentially, the document would include definitions of service provision, fees payment, and psychologist's boundaries in respect of duties, availability, confidentiality, intellectual property rights, and contract termination, and any specific limitations should be made clear from the outset. There can be consequences for those who do not avail themselves of the legal processes and set clear boundaries.

The British Psychological Society Investigatory Committee

In July 2009, psychologists will be regulated by the Health Professionals Council (HPC) and different criteria and processes may apply; for example, the British Psychological Society does not currently suspend psychologists under investigation, but the HPC has the power to do so. The British Psychological Society has an Investigatory Committee that scrutinizes complaints of professional misconduct brought to the Society (Division of Forensic Psychology Report, 2006; Liell, 2006). As such, the Society can investigate complaints that a psychologist has breached the Society's Code of Ethics and Conduct. Naming and shaming can take place, as the Committee provides regular reports of their concerns in *The Psychologist*. Thus, psychologists should be aware that complaints against them could result in a finding of professional misconduct. O'Rourke (2006) has provided advice to psychologists about what to do if they receive a complaint from the British Psychological Society. In such an event, action will be decided on to ensure that any psychologists are not practising when they are not fit to do so. Most detailed codes of conduct present desirable standards of professional conduct from which practitioners tend to fall short. One of the enduring problems with those charged with administering the code is deciding the extent to which the shortfall is morally insignificant, or at which point disciplinary action is justified, and where one draws the line between sanctions that may be imposed. Many of the allegations may be ill-founded or brought by mentally disturbed patients—a common concern among psychiatrists and nurses—or by clients who are unhappy about the conclusions in the report. Where the evidence is sufficient to justify further action, the case is sent to the Disciplinary Committee for a decision. Minor infringements are dismissed with a warning and advice, and the more serious malfeasances are dealt with by suspension of membership for various periods of time, usually 1 or 2 years. The final sanction is to be struck off the membership register, which can lead to termination of a professional career in the public services. In addition to professional misconduct, criminal or civil proceedings against the psychologist may occur, and a number of cases of this type are on record. Among the concerns expressed by the Investigatory Committee arising from formal complaints made against members, are the following (Gudjonsson & Haward, 1998):

1. Practising beyond competence, which may expose the psychologist to legal action.
2. Giving in to pressure by employers to undertake work for which competence, training, or qualifications are inadequate.
3. Failing to provide adequate supervision of junior staff, to the potential detriment of the client and/or public, and putting the employer and junior staff member at risk of civil action by the client or third parties.
4. Using methods or techniques that are out of date. Psychologists need to keep up-to-date with new scientific developments and assessment tools.
5. Failing to obtain explicit consent from the patient or client where necessary.
6. Failing to take appropriate action regarding physical or psychological health problems that could interfere with professional practice.
7. Using inappropriate and potentially offensive language in reports and other communications.

8. Making personal criticisms of colleagues when evaluating their work instead of pointing out factual errors and disagreements where appropriate.
9. Failing to adhere to confidentiality.
10. Failing to comply with instructions for test administration and scoring procedures. The Committee noted that psychological tests are often scored incorrectly. Tests may also be used or interpreted inappropriately (Gudjonsson, 1993).
11. Ignoring evidence from contemporary research that should have influenced advice, disposal, or treatment decisions.
12. Failure to use up-to-date test materials. The Committee draws attention to the need for continuous professional development and the use of up-to-date test material when assessing clients.
13. Inaccurate and misleading information provided to court and tribunals. The Committee sometimes receives complaints about psychologists providing inaccurate, incomplete, or misleading information to the courts.

Any breaches of professional conduct, code, or duty during the course of legal work can also be brought to the court's attention, whereby legal investigation and action/compensation can be taken/awarded against the psychologist concerned if allegations are upheld. For example, in a civil case heard in the Chancery Division of the High Court, estate administrators cited Dr Z as one of a number of respondents. The concern in this case was whether the consultant psychiatrist, Dr Z, had committed breaches of any duty as alleged by the administrators. The issue pertained to mental capacity in that the report concluded that the client was not fit to provide evidence, to go through cross-examination, or to give reliable evidence about past, present, and future events, and additionally, that the client was unable to manage their own affairs, including medical care, and that Court of Protection proceedings should be considered. The key points related to experts' duties. It was claimed that Dr Z had failed to consider all of the relevant materials and further maintain the conclusion in the original report. On judicial instruction, however, Dr Z, following consideration of the full materials, was forced to reconsider and accept that the client was actually able to manage their affairs and that the original reported opinion was not sustainable.

We strongly advise psychologists to ensure that they have satisfactory professional insurance. Complaints and litigation against psychologists are likely to increase and can be costly in terms of time and resources.

What actually happens: Ethical dilemmas, common difficulties, and how to overcome them

The expectations of those instructing us

We already know from the survey of barristers outlined earlier in this chapter that clarity of language, firm conclusions, impartiality, and consistency from psychologists is expected and that these are considered important factors relevant to good practice. These elements are often inherent in initial legal inquiries and with respect to any subsequent instructions. Indeed, expectations can be set in the first communication with a solicitor. It is important, therefore, that practitioners have an awareness of lawyer bias and tactics that can lead to ethical conflicts of interest. To illustrate, one of us was asked by a solicitor to consider civil work in the form of an instruction to produce a report in respect of a single mother. The solicitor intended to defend the client against possession proceedings, already undertaken by the appropriate council, with regard to the client's occupation of property. Initial pressure was applied to the psychologist by the solicitor, asking specifically for a given outcome in the report, which would go some way towards alleviating her client's problems with the council. This was prior to the giving of any preliminary opinion as to relevant issues. It was noted from the outset that the solicitor had intended to obtain an opinion from any psychologist who was able to provide the specific kind of information the solicitor wished to receive (i.e. an insistence on ascertaining the ability of the psychologist to produce a report that would categorically state that her client had suffered sexual abuse as a child) in order that the solicitor could present an arguable defence for the client. When it was explained to the solicitor that one could not simply seek to find evidence that would support her client, although shocked, she continued to attempt to persuade the psychologist otherwise. The instruction was refused. At this stage, rather than solicitors seeking 'independent and uninfluenced' experts, it seems that the ways in which legal teams seek out particular experts related to particular outcomes is counterintuitive to the earlier assertion that experts should be independent and most certainly not 'hired guns'.

Two main types of dilemma relating to 'elements of pressure' and 'assessment procedures' are particularly relevant to forensic psychology. The main concerns with regard to the former is the willingness of some psychologists to provide biased and compromised testimony for the side instructing them, giving in to pressures and inducements from solicitors to present compromised evidence, and presenting opinions that are not based on data or scientific principles. As far as 'assessment procedures' are concerned, dilemmas centre around psychometric tests and computerized interpretations being available to mental health professionals who are inadequately trained in their use, inappropriate use of psychometric tests, psychologists interpreting findings from psychometric tests in isolation to other salient material in the case, and basing conclusions on inadequate data. In addition, experts should not emphasize certain parts of their findings and minimize others in order to favour the side instructing them. However, bias sometimes arises through expert witnesses not having been provided with all of the relevant documentation. When this happens, it is important that they consider 'new' evidence appropriately when it is sent to them or they are faced with it in court.

Being asked to produce a modified report

The 1995 British Psychological Society survey into psychological evidence in court (Gudjonsson, 1996a) showed that many psychologists report being pressured to alter a report in such a way as to make it more favourable to the side instructing them, and the majority went along with it. On the basis of the survey and our extensive forensic experience, it is evident that psychologists, and undoubtedly other expert witnesses as well, are sometimes asked to modify the report. This may include requests for the following:

Improving clarity and consistency and correcting factual errors It is not uncommon for experts to make factual and typographical errors in their reports. If not corrected, these could mislead the court and may cause an embarrassment to the expert if he or she is asked to testify or if an expert from the other side is asked to comment on the report and identifies the errors. It would be quite legitimate for the party who commissioned the report to ask for these to be corrected before the report is served on the other side. Similarly, a lack of clarity is sometimes a major problem in experts' reports. As Lord Chief Justice Taylor pointed out in his 'Lund Lecture' (Taylor of Gosforth, Lord, 1995), expert witnesses must make their specialist evidence comprehensible to the ordinary lay person and they should avoid using scientific jargon. The instructing solicitor may justifiably request that the report be modified to make it more comprehensible. Lastly, experts are sometimes inconsistent in what they say in the report and this may need to be corrected; for example, a psychologist may describe a defendant in one part of a report as 'being suggestible' and in another as 'scoring low on suggestibility'.

Deleting a reference to documents provided When the psychologist is commissioned to prepare a report, the referral agent provides him or her with the relevant documents in the case. These will need to be listed in the report so that the court will know what documents were seen prior to the preparation of the report and what material the expert is relying on. The documents seen will depend on the nature and purpose of the assessment, but they may include such material as the client's 'proof of evidence' and previous psychological or psychiatric reports. Sometimes, solicitors do not want the expert to refer to these documents, because they may then need to be disclosed to the other party, which could be to the client's disadvantage. This may include something that the client told his solicitor that might be construed as unfavourable to his case, such as a confession, or that a previous expert's report contains unfavourable material (Gudjonsson, 1994). The solicitor may ask at the beginning of the assessment that no reference is made in the report to certain documents because they are 'privileged material' and should only be used as 'background material'. Alternatively, the solicitor may ask the psychologist to delete any reference to the documents after the report has been completed.

Whether or not to comply with the solicitor's request raises important ethical considerations. The client's proof of evidence is a privileged document and this is the argument that solicitors typically use when they want experts to delete a reference to the document from their report. However, the legal privilege lies between the client and his or her solicitor. Solicitors may or may not obtain their client's permission before disclosing the proof of evidence to the expert. Once the expert has been provided with the document, it is very difficult for him or her to ignore the fact that they have seen it, particularly when the information obtained from the document is pertinent to the issues being addressed in the report. For example, sometimes the account the client gives the expert of his background and behaviours is in contrast to that given to the solicitors when the proof was taken. This discrepancy may be very important when assessing the client and may influence the opinions given by the expert.

Even when the proof of evidence is provided, it may not be the only proof taken by the solicitors. The following case is an example. In a murder case involving a disputed confession, the proof of evidence, which was undated, showed that the defendant was denying any responsibility for the offence. The implication was that, from the beginning of the solicitor's involvement in the case, his client was denying the offence. During the psychological assessment, the defendant told the psychologist that, for some months after the offence, he admitted the offence and gave the solicitor details of the crime. He then decided to retract the confession and new proof of evidence was taken. The expert contacted the solicitor who freely admitted that a previous proof had been taken but it was not disclosed to the expert because it incriminated his client. It is difficult to avoid the thought that, in this case, the solicitor was trying to mislead the expert into providing a report that was incomplete.

A similar problem may arise in the case of omitting a reference to other experts' reports or findings. For example, omitting a reference to a previous psychological report where extensive psychometric testing was undertaken could be embarrassing to the psychologist if he or she is required to give evidence in court and has to admit that he or she was aware of the previous findings but had failed to acknowledge these in the report because doing so might prove unfavourable to his or her client's case. More importantly, not being able to refer to the previous findings may give a misleading picture of any subsequent test results. For example, in one case, a psychologist was asked to assess a defendant who had been extensively assessed intellectually a few weeks previously, but the client's solicitors did not want the previous report mentioned in the current report due to other test findings, which were not favourable to the defence. During the current assessment, the IQ scores were markedly higher than those obtained previously, particularly on the performance subtests that indicated the likelihood of practice effects. In view of the solicitor's instructions, the psychologist could not mention the likelihood of practice effects in the interpretation of the findings. Therefore, the court might have been left with the impression that the defendant was somewhat brighter than he actually was, which was not in the client's interest.

Our view is that it is very unwise of psychologists to acquiesce in requests to exclude mention of relevant documents that could have a substantial bearing on the expert's interpretations, opinions, and conclusions. Case study 1 below describes a further example.

Case Study 1

The defence commissioned a report for a defendant with a murder indictment. On receipt of the report, the solicitors telephoned the psychologist to thank her for a 'superb' report but asked for the proof of evidence to be removed from the list of documents seen. The psychologist said she could not remove it as it had been sent to her and she had read it. The solicitor asked if the psychologist was relying on it and she confirmed that she had relied on it to provide background information that related to the defendant's social functioning. The following day (a Friday evening), the psychologist received a telephone message asking her to call back the solicitor on the Sunday to discuss the removal of the proof of evidence. The message said that the letter of instruction had said that the proof of evidence was provided 'if required'. The psychologist returned the call but was met with an answer phone. She left a message to say that it had been required and relied upon. The psychologist also stated that, even if not relied upon, it was a document that she had read and had to be listed.

The following day (Monday), the psychologist received two telephone calls from the solicitor that put mounting pressure on her to remove a reference to the proof of evidence. It was 3 weeks prior to the trial start date and the solicitors were being pressured to disclose the report; they would not disclose the report with this document being listed as read. The psychologist refused to remove it. That evening, the QC telephoned the psychologist. He explained that his problem was that the Crown could ask for disclosure of the proof of evidence, as this was a listed document seen. The psychologist still refused. The QC demanded that the psychologist take advice from her professional body. Realizing that the psychologist was not persuaded, he then began to threaten the psychologist saying, 'You realise we are going to have to ask for a stay? We've got to put off the trial to get another expert and start all over again. You have cost the taxpayer £150 000.' This telephone conversation lasted almost 1 hour and, getting somewhat fed up, the psychologist tried to end it by telling the QC that no matter how much he attempted to intimidate her it would not work. The QC denied this and stated that his demeanour was 'a product of his profession—courtroom style'. He then asked for the name of an expert who could be approached to start again. The psychologist did not provide the name of a colleague, but stated that any new expert would need to be informed of the previous report because of practice effects on testing. The QC became very annoyed and said that the Crown already knew about her report because they had warned them it was going to be disclosed that day. The telephone conversation ended. Ten minutes later, the QC telephoned the psychologist again asking her to fax the proof of evidence to him! He said that they wanted to look at the items that had been marked up. The psychologist explained that she was unable to do this immediately, as the psychologist did not have a fax machine at home. He then asked the psychologist to look at the section of the proof of evidence where the defendant had talked about the alleged offence. More pressure followed when the QC talked about his legal dilemma. He said that the solicitor would have to make an emergency visit to see his client in prison the next day to discuss the issue about waiving his rights and privilege, and that there may be a *voir dire* just over this fact, because they did not want to disclose the proof of evidence.

Not mentioning unfavourable test findings There have been a number of cases when some psychometric test findings are favourable to the defence whilst others are unfavourable. There may be a number of reasons for this, including the low correlation commonly found between tests, even when measuring similar constructs, and the complexity of human behaviour. For example, even though persons of low intelligence commonly perform poorly on tests of memory and tend to be more suggestible than their brighter contemporaries, there are some intellectually impaired persons who do not follow this expected pattern. When this happens, solicitors may ask the psychologist to delete any references in the report of the memory and suggestibility tests and then use the low IQ score to imply high suggestibility. Psychologists should not comply with such practice because it can seriously mislead the court and, in addition, undermines the integrity of the psychologist and the profession.

Omitting a reference to a confession made to the expert In cases of disputed confessions, defendants sometimes fully admit the offence when assessed by the defence or the Crown psychologist, even when they have denied it to their solicitor. Gudjonsson (1994) discusses such cases and the ethical issues that may arise as a result. Another growing problem is that defendants are increasingly disputing the reliability of their confession to the police, even when they have never actually retracted or denied it to their solicitor, i.e. the defendant fully accepts that he committed the offence, but the defendant pleads not guilty and the defence want the Crown to prove the case. They then instruct a psychologist to identify whether there is any psychological vulnerability that may render the confession inadmissible, such as significant intellectual impairment or learning disability. In such cases, the solicitor may not provide the psychologist with the defendant's proof of evidence and hope that he or she does not ask the defendant any questions about the offence. In other cases, solicitors have specifically asked psychologists not to ask the defendant any questions about the offence. The more narrowly focused the psychological assessment is, the greater the risk that the psychologist will overlook relevant and salient matters, a consequence that could cause embarrassment to the psychologist if he or she is required to testify in court (Gudjonsson, 1994).

When a psychologist refuses to alter the psychological report, the solicitor may instruct another psychologist to do a more focused assessment, where they focus only on the tests that revealed favourable outcomes in the previous assessment. The solicitor may therefore be able to successfully control the conclusion in the report by giving the expert very specific instructions. Psychologists should avoid colluding with this practice as it can result in serious ethical dilemmas for the psychologist and possibly cause a miscarriage of justice.

Assessment materials, notes, and documents

At all times, psychologists need to be aware of the confidential nature of assessment materials. Many assessment measures are invalidated by prior knowledge of their specific content and objectives. Psychologists who use these materials are required to respect their confidentiality and to avoid their release into the public domain (unless this is explicitly allowed in the nature of the instrument and by the test publisher). Psychologists should, therefore, take reasonable steps to prevent misuse of test data and materials by others. Misuse includes release of such data and materials to unqualified individuals, which may result in harm to the client. Some aspects that pertain to assessments are outlined below.

Disclosure of test material

Following item–item analysis of tests in court in the early 1980s, the British Psychological Society become concerned about the lack of confidentiality of psychologist test material (Tunstall *et al.*, 1982). Lawyers may try to discredit the validity of psychological tests in a number of different ways, including challenging the face validity of the tests and their marginalization of importance and relevance to legal issues. Test forms and manuals may be produced as exhibits in court and circulated among a number of people. As a result, this can undermine the validity of tests in future cases. In some well-publicized court cases in England, judges have been sympathetic to the request of psychologists to protect sensitive test material from being disclosed in open court. Psychologists should be aware of the need to protect test confidentiality and should attempt to minimize any risk of disclosure that may undermine the validity of the tests they are using. Any ethical dilemmas about test disclosure can be discussed with the trial judge and a reasonable compromise can often be reached, for example providing the jury with as much information about the test as is necessary for their deliberation whilst not revealing subtle details that may compromise the test's validity. However, disclosure of confidential test material is mandatory if requested by the court (British Psychological Society, 2007a). When lawyers or prosecutors ask for confidential test material, one way around this is to agree to disclose the test material to a qualified expert instructed by them, rather than forwarding it directly to the lawyers.

Psychologists should be aware that their court reports might also be distributed to a large number of people, both professional and non-professional. Often, the clients themselves are provided with a copy of the report. This can cause difficulties in conducting the forensic assessment. Firstly, once the client has read the expert's report and conclusions, it may prove difficult for the expert for the other side to conduct a neutral assessment. The client may also have discussed the report with a number of people, including his or her solicitor, family and friends, which could influence his or her performance on further testing. Secondly, some psychologists give an unnecessarily detailed description of tests in their report, which may compromise their future validity. For example, some tests are subtle in nature and a client's detailed familiarity with the tests, as well as public knowledge about them, makes it more likely that the answers given are going to be influenced by self-serving factors and deliberate faking. When tests are used in order to detect possible faking, either in terms of clients giving a favourable account of themselves of malingering (e.g. faking intellectual deficits, memory problems, or mental illness), revealing details about these instruments and procedures in court reports or in oral evidence can seriously undermine the validity of these tests for future use. Even if the clients in question know nothing about the tests, lawyers acting for the other party are sometimes quick to use the idea of public knowledge of psychological tests as a way of discrediting the test results in a given case. The issue of test disclosure will become an increasing problem as information becomes easier to access through the Internet; as availability and access to scientific knowledge increases, so does the likelihood of abuse. It is worth remembering that some defendants in criminal cases are highly motivated to seek out information for their defence and they may be surprisingly well informed about certain tests procedures.

General guidance on disclosure of raw test scores to other experts has been published by the British Psychological Society (2007a). When an expert instructed by the 'other side' requests raw test scores, psychologists should note the following. It may be difficult for psychologists to evaluate another psychologist's report without details of the raw scores. Psychologists should disclose raw test scores when appropriate. However, raw scores, like other information from the report, should not be disclosed without the instructing agent's consent. Preferably, this consent should be in writing. The disclosure of the raw test material should not take place unless the report has been properly disclosed to the 'other side' and the instructed psychologist has received a copy of it. Psychologists can refuse to disclose raw test material to experts who they do not believe have the expertise to interpret the scores satisfactorily. For example, one of us refused to disclose the raw scores to a psychiatrist who had been instructed by the opposing side due to his lack of familiarity with the psychometric tests. The opposing lawyers instructed a chartered clinical psychologist to whom the raw scores were disclosed.

In addition, psychologists should keep detailed notes of their assessment and treatment of clients. These, along with test forms and documents in the case, must be stored in a safe and secure place. In hospital settings, these should normally go into the patient's hospital notes. As far as court cases are concerned, some psychologists are in the practice of destroying their notes and test material after a few years. This is very unwise, as cases sometimes reappear several years later and the previous records may be of vital importance at a future date. There have been a number of cases involving miscarriages of justice that went back to the Court of Appeal a decade or more after the original conviction. In one case, detailed notes kept by a psychologist of the assessment were of major importance to the case 20 years after the original assessment.

Problems arise when psychologists retire from practice or die without having made provisions for their confidential case material to be disposed of. In one case, a psychologist instructed by a defence solicitor died in a drowning accident before the case went to court but after he had completed his assessment. The psychologist's father, noting the official witness statements in the case file, unwisely took the case material to the nearest police station, which resulted in the instructing solicitors making a formal complaint about breach of confidentiality (Gudjonsson & Haward, 1998).

Difficulties/conflicts in conducting the assessment

A common problem that can affect the nature and range of tests performed is where assessments are conducted, for example when a client is based in a secure location, such as a prison. It can be extremely difficult to take some tests into prisons, particularly those classified as high security. Consequentially, this limits the assessments that can be conducted if entry for tests is refused; for example computerized continuous performance tests cannot be used, and some tests of effort are computerized. Some other tests recommend that responses are tape-recorded such as the Gudjonsson Suggestibility Scales (GSS) and the Modified Six Elements Test of the Behavioural Assessment of Dysexecutive Syndrome (BADS), or that a tape recorder is required to administer a test, such as the Test of Everyday Attention. Even the conducting of assessments during a trial is possible, e.g. in the cells of the Old Bailey. Special permission may therefore be required to bring in tests or parts of tests, such as those that are computerized, and/or parts of a test (the BADS test equipment includes a metal rod, for example). Furthermore, there are limitations to the amount of time that psychologists have for prison visits, particularly when there is much testing to be done, which can also be time-consuming. As a result, it is possible that short-cuts might be considered or taken (WASI versus a full WAIS-III). It is important that psychologists consider their ethical duties when making decisions that might affect the nature and completeness of tests undertaken.

Obtaining information from third parties

When conducting a forensic assessment, informants, such as relatives, spouse, friends, or colleagues, may need to be consulted. In addition, it may be important to obtain access to medical records, school reports, and other confidential records. This requires the consent of the client being assessed or written permission obtained through the client's solicitor. Psychologists need to be very careful when approaching third parties for information without the client's written consent, as the mere request for information requires some kind of explanation to the third party, which must be handled very delicately. In addition, the information obtained from a third party may well be subject to confidentiality, requiring formal written consent before it can be disclosed.

Confidentiality and disclosure

In clinical and forensic work, confidentiality is one of the most frequently reported ethical dilemmas. Bromley (1981) distinguishes among four different models of confidentiality in clinical settings, which are referred to as: (i) 'absolute confidentiality' (everything communicated by the client is totally confidential); (ii) 'limited confidentiality' (what is disclosed depends on the type of information and to whom it is disclosed); (iii) 'contractual confidentiality' (the clinician and client negotiate any disclosure); and (iv) 'discretionary confidentiality' (the clinician determines the limits of confidentiality).

In forensic work in the UK, 'absolute confidentiality' does not apply and no medical and paramedical professional has a legal privilege that enables him or her to refuse to answer a question as a witness in court or to refuse to disclose clinical notes (Finch, 1984). Psychologists may be served with a subpoena to act as a witness in a civil or criminal case. They may also be subpoenaed to disclose and bring along relevant documents, such as case notes and test forms. If the psychologist perceives ethical problems about handing over records, a consultation with a colleague or lawyer may prove helpful. On occasions, a court order may need to be questioned or challenged. Under such circumstances, judges may be sympathetic to a practitioner who is unwilling to disclose material on grounds of professional conscience. Issues of privilege can pose difficulties as outlined in Case study 2.

Case Study 2

A mother and her partner were charged with the murder of her newborn baby. The mother, who had multiple sclerosis, had limited mobility and was largely dependent on her partner to care for her. Her partner was violent towards her and her children. A psychologist was instructed to conduct a cognitive and personality assessment of the mother and comment on her decision-making capacity in relation to herself, her children, and her partner. A few days after submitting the report, the psychologist received a telephone call from Junior Counsel. This haughty young lawyer was asking the psychologist to remove a substantial part of the interview with the client, which was apparently unfavourable to the defence. The psychologist refused to do this because doing so would have presented a biased perspective of the assessment. The lawyer stated that this should be removed because the psychologist's relationship with the defendant was similar to that of a client/lawyer by being privileged. These requests turned into demands. That day, the psychologist was conducting a series of interviews for a clinical psychology post and her colleagues sat amazed as Junior Counsel continually pestered the psychologist with telephone calls and telephone messages throughout the day and insisted (in a voice that could be heard across the room) that she had not understood that the issue of 'privilege' extended to the psychologist as she was acting on their instructions. On her way home, Leading Counsel telephoned the psychologist and took an altogether more reasoned stance but questioned her carefully and continuously for 1.5 hours to ascertain exactly what the psychologist would say in the witness box in court. It is unknown whether the report was disclosed or not. The psychologist was not called to give evidence.

Case study 2 illustrates one of the potentially problematic aspects of confidentiality that forensic cases can pose. The British Psychological Society has recently published their *Generic Professional Practice Guidelines* (British Psychological Society, 2007b) with regard to applied psychologists, which is also underpinned by the four key ethical principles noted earlier. These guidelines are particularly relevant to forensic psychology, as they deal with possible breaches of confidentiality where public safety is at stake (i.e. disclosure in the public interest). In brief, clients are entitled to expect that the information they give to psychologists about themselves and others will remain confidential. In this respect, psychologists have a duty not to disclose such information. However, clients should be informed of the limits of confidentiality in order that any objection might be stated, particularly where information about them may be shared. Some relevant examples follow

To whom the report should be disclosed

When preparing court reports, only the referral agent and the client are entitled to a copy. The report should not be disclosed to other parties without the consent of the client or lawyer involved. This principle includes colleagues commissioned by the 'other side' who might request a copy of the report. Sometimes, the expert witness is asked to release a report to someone else. For example, we have received requests from the police for a report written for the CPS some years earlier, from newly appointed defence solicitors, from the defendant, and/or from the defendant's medical representatives. An expert witness report is the property of whoever has commissioned it and should be disclosed by them. If this is not possible, then it is important to obtain the client's written consent that he or she is happy for the report to be disclosed to a third party.

Reports prepared for the prosecution

When psychologists conduct assessments for the prosecution, it is very important to explain to defendants that anything they say that is relevant to the assessment will be mentioned in the report and may be used against them in court. The position is different when the defence commissions the report, because if the findings are not favourable then the report need not be disclosed to the prosecution. Solicitors sometimes ask to be present when assessments are conducted on behalf of the prosecution, or request that their defence expert is present. Some psychologists are in the practice of refusing such requests without a satisfactory explanation. Our view is that solicitors, their legal representatives, and defence experts should be allowed to sit in on the assessment if this is requested. There are no reasonable grounds on which such a request can be declined unless that third party interferes inappropriately with the assessment. Indeed, when confessions are made to the expert witness, it is particularly helpful for the defendant's solicitor to be present at the time (Gudjonsson, 1994). However, it is interesting to note here a special presentation paper with regard to third-party observers in neurological assessments (American Academy of Clinical Neuropsychology, 2001), which attempted to clarify aspects of policy in terms of what might be an appropriate response where such a request is made. Two types of observer were noted: 'involved' (those who have a stake in the outcome) and 'uninvolved' (those who have no stake in the outcome). A case study by Binder & Johnson-Greene (1995) illustrated the negative effect that an involved observer can have on performance. The paper related to medico-legal consultations and discussed adverse effects of third-party presence during an examination, which might '*distract the examinee, distort motivation or adversely affect test performance*' (p. 435). The statement made reference to the need for awareness of test material guidelines with regard to administration and noted that simple social facilitation/inhibition effects could impact on outcomes (see Wagstaff *et al.*, 2007). Furthermore, a third party present during test administration may also undermine the security of the test, particularly as those present may be free to take notes and record other test details. It is important, therefore, that practitioners are aware of their ethical responsibilities to minimize and resolve the conflicts, in accordance with ethical codes, that might arise due to third-party observations.

If disclosure of information is deemed necessary, psychologists have a duty to try to obtain specific informed consent from their clients, making the consequences of disclosure as clear and unbiased as possible. There are circumstances where this might not apply; for example, it might emerge that clients may present a risk to others or to themselves, or be at risk from those whom they wish to protect. It is then necessary to discuss the importance of disclosure and to encourage it. In exceptional circumstances, disclosure without consent or against the client's expressed wish could be necessary in situations in which failure to disclose appropriate information would expose the client, or someone else, to risk of serious harm.

Admissions of crime or other sensitive information

Psychologists have an ethical duty not to disclose information about the criminal acts of a patient, although the British Psychological Society certainly recognizes that there are circumstances where there may be an overriding social obligation to disclose it to a third party, such as the social services or the police. However, the Children's Act 1989 (Bridge *et al.*, 1990) and the accompanying guidance for doctors working with child protection agencies make it clear that mental health professionals must not withhold information that may place a child at risk of ill-treatment or neglect. Indeed, knowledge or belief of abuse will usually justify a mental health professional making a disclosure to an appropriate responsible person or officer of a statutory agency. In addition, the deliberate concealment of a crime during an investigation may be interpreted as an unlawful obstruction of an officer in the execution of his duty.

During a forensic assessment clients sometimes request that some of the information provided by them is not disclosed in the expert's report. This may include sensitive material, which is not always relevant to the legal issues of the case, such as a history of having had an abortion or having been the victim of a sexual assault. In many instances, this kind of sensitive information need not be disclosed unless it is directly relevant to the issues being addressed in the report, but it might become important in terms of mitigation in the event of the client being convicted of the offence with which he or she is currently charged.

In recent years, issues of disclosure and confidentiality have become further complicated by multi-agency responsibility for a 'duty to cooperate' in the management of offenders and reducing risk to the public (Young *et al.*, 2005). Multi-Agency Public Protection Panel Arrangements (MAPPA) have a review and monitoring function, which is conducted by an integral group of agencies including police, prison, and probation services; primary care and other NHS trusts and strategic Health Authorities; youth offending teams; local housing authorities; local education authorities; Jobcentre Plus; or electronic monitoring providers, in addition to two lay advisers. The overarching MAPPA duty may conflict with a psychologist's code of conduct and is most likely to arise for recidivist offenders.

Conflict of interest and impartiality

Expert witnesses should not take on a case where there is a conflict of interest. A conflict of interest may arise in many different ways, but the main impact is to compromise the expert's impartiality, or at least the perceived impartiality, of their evidence, even if their evidence is objective and dispassionate.

When working in multi-professional or multi-agency contexts, it is important that experts are impartial in their written and oral evidence. Partiality implies potential bias in the expert witness's evidence, which may seriously mislead the court. Such bias may be unintentional or deliberate. On occasion, it arises out of naivety, as in a case of a psychologist who commented after being criticized by a colleague for producing a biased report, '*I thought if you were instructed by the defence you only included in the report findings that are favourable to the client.*' Thus, psychologists can find themselves in conflict with the approaches to work taken by other individual colleagues or by the multi-professional team or agency.

Psychologists may also be in conflict when clients require support that intertwines with the expert role. Dual-role conflicts raise the possibility of bias, as it is difficult to switch from the role of treatment provider to that of neutral evaluator and expert witness, the latter requiring an independent and objective position irrespective of who instructed the expert. This problem is widely recognized by the professional community (e.g. British Psychological Society, 2007a). Some writers (e.g. Sadoff, 1988; Shuman, 1993) have expressed concern about mental health professionals testifying about a patient that they are currently treating. Seemingly, the disadvantage is that the therapist may be less objective and dispassionate in his or her evidence than a more neutral expert witness. So, should we serve as psychologist and expert witness for patients/clients? This seems to be the question raised by other professionals confronted with similar ethical dilemmas (Strasburger *et al.*, 1997). According to Strasburger *et al.* (1997, p. 448), attempts to treat, support, and evaluate the same person typically creates emergent role conflicts that are largely irreconcilable and leads to problems in '*conceptions of truth and causation, different forms of alliance, different types of assessment, and different ethical guidelines*'. It is crucial to ensure clarity in role definitions, rather than being drawn into legally ambiguous situations that often prevail in this kind of work. However, in rare instances, expert witnesses may be drawn into a therapeutic or supportive role during a court case, which may compromise their position as an expert witness. When this happens, the potential ethical problems it raises need to be discussed with the legal team instructing the expert and appropriate action taken.

Consent and capacity

Fundamental to psychological practice is seeking and receiving the consent of those they work with, given of their own free will, without undue influence, and in accordance with the Code of Ethics and Conduct of the Society (British Psychological Society, 2007b). General good practice suggests that it is important that consent be reviewed, formalized, and recorded, rather than taken for granted. For example, any continued participation from the client cannot be taken as implicit consent. Indeed, for informed consent to be possible, the psychologist needs to provide all necessary and relevant information. It may also be necessary to provide such information in ways that meet specific client needs, such as sensory, cognitive, communication, language, and culture.

Other potential conflicts

According to Brodsky & McKinzey (2002), there are times in the course of clinical and forensic work when serious weaknesses in knowledge, performance, or ethics in other psychologists' work become evident. Gudjonsson (1994, 2003) provides examples of this occurring. For example, a common weakness in cases of disputed confessions is that some psychologists fail to interpret test findings in relation to the broader context of the case (i.e. they interpret test scores in isolation from other factors or material in the case) or act beyond their areas of competence. For example, they find a client suggestible on testing and equate it with him or her having made a false confession, when in fact suggestibility may not be relevant to understanding the confession at all.

Arcaya (1987) discussed the ethical dilemmas of psychologists when they experienced conflicts between their therapeutic role and feelings of repulsion and disgust over the offender's criminal deeds. Many offenders have committed horrific crimes, which can raise intense emotions in the expert witness and result in a bias that is unfavourable to the client. Arcaya suggested that, under those circumstances, clinicians should carefully weigh all of the evidence for and against the client's culpability in their head and provide separate sections in their report for contradictory perspectives on their client. In contrast, Cornell (1987) argues against such a single solution to the problem and emphasizes the importance of considering the context and circumstances in which the report is being prepared.

In many cases, psychologists are asked to prepare reports where the defendant's guilt is being disputed. In such cases, psychologists should avoid forming assumptions about the defendant's guilt or innocence. It is always best to focus on the relevant legal and psychological issues with an open mind. Once the psychologist has formed assumptions of guilt or innocence, it tends to bias the assessment in favour of their assumption. For example, there have been cases of miscarriage of justice where psychiatrists providing psychological explanations for the defendant's denial of guilt proved instrumental in conviction.

Making assumptions about the defendant's guilt and moral culpability raises important ethical problems among expert witnesses about the bias it may cause (Pfeifer & Brigham, 1993). The well-known American academic psychologist Elizabeth Loftus gave an excellent illustration of this type of bias: '*If I believe a defendant is innocent, if I believe in his innocence with all my heart and soul, then I probably can't help but become an advocate of sorts*' (Loftus & Ketcham, 1991, p. 238).

Giving evidence in court

Once a report has been completed and submitted, the expert may be called to give evidence in court. As stated above, the primary duty of the expert is to the court. The evidence presented should be clear, coherent, objective, and dispassionate, and must fall within the expert's scientific knowledge and competence.

Murphy (1994) summarized the general principles relating to testifying in court as follows. In court, every witness called is subject to examination by the party calling him or her, all other parties, and the court. Examinations consist of examination-in-chief, cross-examination, re-examination, and possible examinations by judge and/or bench, usually for clarification purposes. The examination-in-chief is a procedure that rests upon the notion of gaining the trust of the court and jury in the witness. To this end, the witness's own Counsel will encourage their witness to provide a free narrative account of events, and, importantly, leading and suggestive questioning styles are, by the rules of evidence, disallowed. Consequently, the examination-in-chief procedure must be conducted without leading questions.

Cross-examination, however, has a different purpose: to establish the creditworthiness of the witness and the weight that should be given to evidence of that witness. Thus, with regard to cross-examination, DuCann (1964, p. 95) cites Lord Hanworth's, Master of the Rolls, statement that '*Cross examination is a powerful and valuable weapon for the purpose of testing the veracity of a witness and the accuracy and completeness of his story.*'

In this respect, the British Psychological Society 1995 survey (Gudjonsson, 1996a) revealed that 44% of respondents reported that they were usually 'extensively' cross-examined on their evidence. However, interestingly, it was revealed in the British Psychological Society (2007a) survey of psychologists who had given evidence in court that 41% of the respondents stated that they did not feel adequately trained or experienced to give oral evidence in court. It is compelling, therefore, that in testing witness veracity, a witness's knowledge of the facts, impartiality, truthfulness, respect for oath or affirmation, and general demeanour are challenged at this point. Witness character, bias, and unreliability are also open to question. Given that the use of previous inconsistent statements is probably the most effective way of discrediting a witness's account, it is no surprise that cross-examination strategies tend to be built around the development of this consequence (Wheatcroft & Wagstaff, 2003).

Attempts to discredit fall within the general legal rationale for veracity testing of witnesses through cross-examination. However, in addition, techniques to discredit expert witnesses in particular have been highlighted by Leslie *et al.* (2007).

In the survey of barristers' opinions of psychologists reported above, respondents were asked to describe the most useful techniques they have adopted to discredit an expert witness. Responses revealed that 42% of participants believed that the best technique was pointing out weaknesses and omissions in their line of argument.

The overarching legal assumption made in terms of cross-examination therefore is that it is difficult to mislead a witness who is honest in his or her testimony. By implication, a witness who can be misled (i.e. through certain questioning procedures) could be regarded as dishonest, subsequently raising the issue of lying to the court, and ultimately bringing the credibility of any given testimony into question. Indeed, the use of leading and pre-suppositional questioning techniques is often promoted as the way in which the 'truth' can be attained and justice done. Given this, it is clear that there may be implications for forensic practitioners under cross-examination, some of which can be illuminated through the following cautionary advice: (i) beware of leading and pre-suppositional questions (almost any response to the latter can validate the presupposed information contained within); (ii) watch for repeat questioning or other forms of negative feedback; (iii) identify the accusatory context rather than merely providing information for the court to consider (i.e. assume that the search for truth/fact finding is not all that clear but could constitute an attempt to deconstruct the information provided as incorrect, inadequate, or irrelevant); (iv) do not be quick to defend; (v) aim to select propositional statements for challenge (remember one needs to be fairly certain that justification for the challenge made can be reasonably assured). In other words, further questions will ensue and it will be necessary for experts to be confident enough in their own challenges in order to defend them successfully.

The pressure of cross-examination may overwhelm expert witnesses and as a result they may conform to the oppositions' stance, especially if they have limited experience and feel very anxious. The overriding responsibility of the expert is to the court, and he or she must not give a biased opinion (House of Commons and Technology Committee, 2005). However, people instructing them to alter their evidence or to make it more favourable sometimes place expert witnesses under pressure, potentially misleading the court (Gudjonsson, 1994, 1996a). Interestingly, an anonymous survey of 133 expert witnesses conducted in November 2002 by the firm Bond Solon showed that 58% of the expert witnesses did not think that the lawyers instructing them wanted them to be 'truly independent' (House of Commons and Technology Committee, 2005).

Of course, if one assumes that cross-examination of this kind tests the credibility of witnesses to the full (i.e. a witness who rejects all attempts to be led must be accurate in what he or she says), then, from the cross-examiner's point of view, there may be a downside if the witness refuses to be led or comply with the pre-supposition. Accordingly, some legal advisors have openly asserted that asking leading questions in cross-examination can be unwise and may risk losing a case (Evans, 1995). Thus, it is important that experts remember to remain focused on the internal coherence of the evidence and present this objectively, calmly, and with quiet confidence.

Conclusions

This chapter has provided an overview of professional and ethical issues that often arise when conducting forensic evaluations in civil and criminal cases, preparing and submitting reports, and testifying in court. There is increasing reliance upon psychological reports in civil and criminal cases. The key 'take home' message is that all expert witnesses, including psychologists, should at all times act with integrity, objectivity, clarity, and within their areas of competencies. Their role is to inform the judge and jury about matters that are outside their areas of knowledge. Evidence that fails to inform or misleads the court undermines the credibility of the profession and may bring it into disrepute. Our overriding duties and responsibilities are to the courts, not the individual being assessed.

References

American Academy of Clinical Neuropsychology (2001). Special presentation: Policy statement on the presence of third party observers in neuropsychological assessments. *Clinical Neuropsychologist*, **15**:433–439.

Arcaya, J. M. (1987). Role conflicts in coercive assessments: Evaluation and recommendations. *Professional Psychology: Research and Practice*, **18**:422–428.

Bach, L. J. and Gudjonsson, G. H. (1999). Evaluation study of lawyers' satisfaction with expert witness reports. *Expert Evidence*, **6**:261–271.

Binder, L. and Johnson-Greene, D. (1995). Observer effects on neuropsychological performance: A case report. *Clinical Neuropsychologist*, **97**:74–78.

Bridge, J., Bridge, S., and Luke, S. (1990). *Blackstone's Guide to the Children Act 1989*. London: Blackstone Press.

British Psychological Society (2004a). *Commissioning Clinical Neuropsychology Services*. Leicester: British Psychological Society

British Psychological Society (2004b). *Services for Children with Acquired Brain Damage*. A paper commissioned by the Professional Practice Board of the Society. Leicester: British Psychological Society, Division of Neuropsychology.

British Psychological Society (2006). *Codes of Ethics and Conduct*. Leicester: British Psychological Society.

British Psychological Society (2007a). *Psychologists as Expert Witnesses: Guidelines and Procedures for England and Wales*. Leicester: British Psychological Society.

British Psychological Society (2007b) *Generic Professional Practice Guidelines*. Available at: http://www.bps.org.uk/coachingpsy/news/generic-professional-practice-guidelines.cfm

Brodsky, S. L. and McKinzey, R. K. (2002). The ethical confrontation of the unethical forensic colleague. *Professional Psychology: Research and Practice*, **33**:307–309.

Bromley, E. (1981). Confidentiality. *Bulletin of the British Psychological Society*, **344**:468–469.

Cornell, D. G. (1987). Role conflict in forensic clinical psychology: Reply to Arcaya. *Professional Psychology: Research and Practice*, **18**:429–432.

Division of Forensic Psychology Report (2006). The Society complaints-handling process. *Forensic Update*, **86**:5–11.

DuCann, R. (1964). *The Art of the Advocate*. Harmondsworth: Penguin.

Evans, K. (1995). *Advocacy in Court: A Beginner's Guide*, 2nd edn. London: Blackstone Press.

Finch, J. (1984). 'It's great to have someone to talk to': Ethics and politics of interviewing women. In: C. Bell and H. Roberts (eds), *Social Researching: Politics, Problems, Practice*, pp. 70–87. London: Routledge.

Gudjonsson, G. H. (1985). Psychological evidence in court: Results from the BPS survey. *Bulletin of the British Psychological Society*, **383**:327–330.

Gudjonsson, G. H. (1993). The implications of poor psychological evidence in court. *Expert Evidence*, **21**:120–124.

Gudjonsson, G. H. (1994). Confessions made to the expert witness: Some professional issues. *Journal of Forensic Psychiatry*, **5**:237–247.

Gudjonsson, G. H. (1996a). Psychological evidence in court: Results from the 1995 survey. *The Psychologist*, **52**:213–217.

Gudjonsson, G. H. (1996b). Forensic psychology in England: One practitioner's experience and viewpoint. *Journal of Criminological and Legal Psychology*, **11**:131–142.

Gudjonsson, G. H. (2003). *The Psychology of Interrogations and Confessions: A Handbook*. Chichester, UK: John Wiley & Sons.

Gudjonsson, G. H. (2006). Disputed confessions and miscarriages of justice in Britain: Expert psychological and psychiatric evidence in the court of appeal. *Manitoba Law Journal*, **31**:489–521.

Gudjonsson, G. H. (2008). Psychologists as expert witnesses: The 2007 BPS Survey. *Forensic Update*, **92**:23–29.

Gudjonsson, G. H. and Haward, L. R. H. (1998). *Forensic Psychology: A Guide to Practice*. London: Routledge.

Hall, J. G. and Smith, G. D. (1997). *The Expert Witness*. Chichester, UK: Barry Rose.

Haward, L. R. C. (1981). *Forensic Psychology*. London: Batsford.

House of Commons and Technology Committee (2005). Avaliable at: http://www.publications.parliament.uk/pa/cm/cmsctech.htm

Leslie, O., Young, S., Valentine, T., and Gudjonsson, G. (2007). Criminal barristers' opinions and perceptions of mental health experts. *Journal of Forensic Psychiatry and Psychology*, **18**:394–410.

Liell, G. (2006). Ethical enquiries from forensic settings. *Forensic Update*, **86**:24–27.

Murphy, P. (1994). *Evidence and Advocacy*, 4th edn. London: Blackstone Press.

Loftus, E. F. and Ketcham, K. (1991). *Witness for the Defense: The Accused, the Eyewitness and the Expert Who Puts Memory on Trial.* New York: St Martin's Press.

Navarro, J. and Gudjonsson, G. H. (2008). Chilean psychologists as expert witnesses: The challenges of a new criminal justice system. *Journal of Forensic Psychiatry and Psychology,* **19**:249–260.

O'Rourke, C. (2006). What should I do if I receive a complaint from the Society? *Forensic Update,* **86**:12–15.

Pfeifer, J. E. and Brigham, J. C. (1993). Ethical concerns of nonclinical forensic witnesses and consultants. *Ethics and Behavior,* **3**:329–343.

Sadoff, R. L. (1988). Ethical issues in forensic psychiatry. *Psychiatry Annals,* **18**:320–323.

Shuman, D. W. (1993). The use of empathy in forensic examinations. *Ethics and Behavior,* **3**:289–302.

Sigurdsson, J. F. and Gudjonsson, G. H. (2004). Forensic psychology in Iceland: A survey of members of the Icelandic Psychological Society. *Scandinavian Journal of Psychology,* **45**:325–329.

Strasburger, L. H., Gutheil, M. D., and Brodsky, B. A. (1997). On wearing two hats: Role conflict in serving as both psychotherapist and expert witness. *American Journal of Psychiatry,* **154**:448–556.

Taylor of Gosrorth, Lord (1995). The Lund Lecture. *Medicine, Science and the Law,* **35**:3–8.

Tunstall, O., Gudjonsson, G., Eysenck, H., and Haward, L. (1982). Professional issues arising from psychological evidence presented in court. *Bulletin of the British Psychological Society,* **35**:329–331.

Wagstaff, G. F., Wheatcroft, J., Cole, J., Brunas-Wagstaff, J., Blackmore, V., and Pilkington, A. (2007). Some cognitive and neuropsychological aspects of social inhibition and facilitation. *European Journal of Cognitive Psychology,* **20**:828–846.

Wheatcroft, J. M. and Wagstaff, G. F. (2003). The interface between psychology and law in the courtroom: Cross-examination. *Forensic Update,* **75**:8–18.

Young, S. J., Gudjonsson, G. H., and Needham-Bennett, H. (2005). Multi-Agency Public Protection Panels for dangerous offenders: One London forensic team's experience. *Journal of Forensic Psychology and Psychiatry,* **16**:312–327.

Chapter 13

Conclusion: Themes and issues

Michael Kopelman, Susan Young, and Gisli Gudjonsson

As stated at the outset, this book could not possibly cover all of the topics that may arise in a court case involving a forensic neuropsychologist. It should be read alongside standard texts of forensic psychology and neuropsychology. However, we have tried to address many of the most important issues arising in both the criminal and civil courts. In doing this, we have discussed the pertinent background forensic and neuropsychological literature and we have also provided practical advice for carrying out work in the courts.

Previously in this book, the chapter by Bramham and O'Ceallaigh provided a neuroscience and neuropsychological background to our understanding of violent and aggressive behaviour. They highlighted the critical role of pathology in the dorsolateral prefrontal cortex, the orbitofrontal and ventrolateral frontal cortex, and the amygdala in producing violent or aggressive behaviour in some individuals.

Other chapters in this book have highlighted particular conditions, discussing our current neuropsychological understanding of these disorders; for example, Murphy and Clare on intellectual disability, Young on attention-deficit hyperactivity disorder, Clare and Woodbury-Smith on autistic-spectrum disorder, and Bird, Newson, and Dembny on epilepsy. Each of the chapters by Murphy and Clare, Young, and Clare and Woodbury-Smith has drawn attention to the vulnerabilities of people diagnosed with the respective disorders, both in terms of offending behaviour and in terms of the processes of police interview and court hearings. All of these chapters have provided examples of how these vulnerabilities can be mitigated, and, more particularly, have provided advice on the comprehensive neuropsychological assessment and management of such cases.

The chapter by Pyszora, Jaldow, and Kopelman on memory disorders discussed a particular symptom commonly complained of in both criminal and civil cases. The chapter focused mainly on criminal cases. (Wood and Powell in their respective chapters discussed memory disorders in civil cases.)

Whilst memory disorder in itself does not affect criminal responsibility, its genuineness is frequently questioned in the criminal courts. The chapter discussed some of the circumstances in which amnesia may arise and the relevant background literature on this topic. By contrast, amnesia is an important feature of automatism, and automatism does have important medico-legal implications with respect to issues of responsibility, as discussed by Bird, Newson, and Dembny, both in terms of 'sane' ('non-insane') and 'insane' automatism. These authors considered in detail the disorders in which automatism may arise, and the legal rulings that have been made in such cases. Whilst the concept of an epileptic- or somnambulism-induced automatism would be widely accepted, if its occurrence can clearly be demonstrated in court, its hinterlands (as in the case of a very prolonged 'automatism'), and the notion of 'dissociative' automatism, are much more controversial.

Miles and Johns provided a comprehensive review of a specific behaviour—alcohol and substance misuse—which so commonly arises in court hearings, both criminal and civil. As the authors have described, alcohol and/or other substances are often associated with violent crime, acquisitive offences, driving under the influence of alcohol, and family and parenting issues. The authors have reviewed current knowledge of these issues and of psychoactive substances in general, as well as methods and problems of neuropsychological assessment. They have emphasized the importance of the neuropsychological assessment taking place in the context of a wider clinical appraisal.

This is a point also taken up by Wood in his review of traumatic brain injury. Following a discussion of the underlying neurophysiological mechanisms giving rise to cognitive and behavioural change in head injury, Wood has considered the various methods of assessing the severity of head trauma, the place of the clinical interview, neuroimaging, and the methods of neuropsychological assessment. He has also drawn attention to the fact that the Mental Capacity Act 2005 in England and Wales has given neuropsychologists a new and prominent role.

The final three chapters have provided some very practical advice for 'budding' or more experienced forensic neuropsychologists. In particular, Powell has discussed the process of becoming and acting as an expert witness from the initial stages of taking instruction through the whole process of preparing an assessment, conference with Counsel, agreeing and preparing a joint statement with other experts, and giving testimony at a trial. In particular, Powell gives examples of how not to respond to a question during cross-examination (most of these responses were monosyllabic yes/no replies), and how to give more measured responses that are both more accurate and more likely to foil the cross-examination.

Gudjonsson and Young have reviewed important advances in the assessment of suboptimal effort or more frank malingering in forensic or neuropsychological assessments. Some of these methods are essentially clinical, such as examining for inconsistencies, whilst others involve specific tests such as symptom validity testing, the use of Raven's Standard Progressive Matrices with a statistical formula to measure linear trends, the Test of Memory Malingering, and the Word Memory Test. Gudjonsson and Young have also discussed the prevalence of malingering in the civil and criminal courts, the motivation for malingering, the consequences of a misdiagnosis, issues of confidentiality, and the context of such assessments in court.

The chapter by Wheatcroft, Gudjonsson and Young discusses the many ways in which lawyers can put pressure on experts to bias the assessments and opinions that they present to a court. In subtle or more forthright ways, this is a frequent occurrence, potentially compromising the forensic neuropsychologist's role as an independent and uninfluenced expert. The authors have also discussed important issues regarding confidentiality and disclosure, consent, and capacity.

Certain themes have recurred across these various chapters. These include, firstly, the increasing importance of neuropsychological assessments in making decisions about fitness to plead, recommendations regarding diminished responsibility, and assessing mental capacity. Secondly, it is always important to guard against the effects of suboptimal effort, poor motivation, and deliberate malingering. Although no method is foolproof, and a number of detection strategies should be used, the tests available for detecting simulation have much improved during the last 10 years or so. Thirdly, the context in which assessments are carried out is enormously important, and a move towards more naturalistic ('ecologically valid') assessments has been encouraged by some of the authors. Fourthly, the various ways in which lawyers can manipulate experts (not just forensic neuropsychologists) away from unbiased, independent opinions has been highlighted in several chapters. At a time when expert witnesses have been heavily criticized in some cases, allowing one's views to be compromised may not only mean injustice for the client but may have professional repercussions for the expert. Hence, the advice given in several chapters on this issue should be well heeded. In the final analysis, a threat to instructing lawyers that one may take a complaint to their professional body on the grounds of suborning a witness usually produces instantaneously beneficial results, but this will not endear you to your instructing lawyers, and it is a weapon to be used rarely and only in extreme circumstances.

A further issue that several authors have alluded to is the conflict between the black-and-white categories that lawyers employ and the more dimensional or functional approach employed by neuropsychologists and neuropsychiatrists. If anything, this conflict has become worse in the last 15 years by lawyers increasingly adopting the diagnostic criteria of the International Classification of Diseases (ICD) and/or the Diagnostic and Statistical Manual of Mental Disorders (DSM) for discussion and debate in court. Whilst this does represent a move towards the use of more objective and reliable diagnostic criteria, various problems ensue. Firstly, these books are particularly poor in describing neuropsychiatric and neuropsychological disorders (Kopelman & Fleminger, 2002). Secondly, the lawyers may attempt to use these diagnostic criteria in a 'cookbook' fashion, despite the fact that DSM specifically says in its introduction that its criteria are not to be used as diagnostic 'cookbooks' by non-clinical professionals. Lastly, the use of these diagnostic categories, although acceptable and legitimate in many instances, may sometimes discourage the use of a more quantified, dimensional approach. For example, if it is said that a person has 'partial post-traumatic stress disorder' or some post-traumatic symptoms that do not fulfil criteria for a full diagnosis of post-traumatic stress disorder, this will commonly be interpreted as the person not having any symptoms of post-traumatic stress disorder at all.

Finally, the advances in neuroscience, reviewed in Chapter 2 by Bramham and O'Ceallaigh, bear important implications for court procedures and practice. It is sometimes difficult to obtain courtroom agreement about whether a relatively clear-cut medical phenomenon, such as an epileptic automatism, has occurred and whether it has significant bearing on the nature of the alleged offence. Most people would accept that a large glioma in the frontal lobes would provide adequate grounds to argue for an 'abnormality of mind' giving rise to 'diminished responsibility', but the burgeoning literature on relatively subtle neuropsychological and/or neuroimaging anomalies in offenders, or in those diagnosed as having behavioural or personality problems, calls into question how severe such anomalies should be before they have bearing upon issues of responsibility, mitigation, or fitness to plead. Many of the findings of forensic neuroscience to date have been relatively subtle, but there can be no doubt that, as forensic neuroscience advances, such debate will arise with increasing frequency in court.

References

Kopelman, M. D. and Fleminger, S. (2002). Experience and perspectives on the classification of organic mental disorders. *Psychopathology*, **35**:76–81.

Index

abnormality of mind 35
absentmindedness 88
acquiescence 55, 60, 71
acquired brain injury 12–14
   expert witnesses in 247–65
acquired sociopathy 15
acquisitive crime and substance misuse 195
actus reus 1, 68, 146, 165–6, 180, 181
Adaptive Behavior Scale–Residential and Community Version 71
adaptive functioning 71
Addiction Severity Index 212
ADHD *see* attention-deficit hyperactivity disorder
admissions of crime 321–2
Adult Eyes Test 119
Adults with Incapacity (Scotland) Act 2000 112
affective lability 13
aggression and violence 7–51
alcohol-associated 194–5
   disorders associated with 8–21
      acquired brain injury 12–14
      antisocial personality disorder 10–11
      conduct disorder 9–10
      dementia 17–18
      epilepsy 18–19
      learning disability 16–17
      prefrontal cortex damage 14–16
      psychopathy 11–12
      schizophrenia 19–20
      substance misuse 20–1
   epileptic automatism 168–9
   forensic neuropsychology 34–7
   instrumental 7
   neural circuitry 21–2
   neuroimaging 22–5
      functional 24–5
      structural 23–4
   neuropsychological explanations 25–34
      instrumental aggression 31–4
      reactive aggression 26–31
   postictal 18, 169
   psychosocial factors 7–8
   reactive 7
   risk of 7
   substance misuse 194–5
agitation 13
agnosia 204
alcohol 20–1, 198–204
      binge drinking 199
      intoxication 138, 198–9

      and sleepwalking 176
      Wernicke-Korsakoff syndrome 201–3
   alcohol hallucinosis 199
   alcohol misuse *see* substance misuse
   Alcohol Use Disorders Identification Test (AUDIT) 193, 211
   alcoholic blackouts 137, 138, 144–5, 199
   alcoholic dementia 203–4
alexithymia 225
amnesia 135–63
   alcohol-induced 200–1
   associations 135–6
   in criminal cases 135
   defendants 152–7
      anxiety and depression 156
      general intellectual function 154
      memory 154–5
      motivation 156–7
      naming 156
      perception 156
      planning and organization 155–6
   dissociative 141
   legal aspects 146–52
      criminal responsibility 148–51
      fitness to plead 146–8
      malingering 151–2
   length and nature of 145
   malingering 151–2, 269
   mechanisms underlying 136–45
      medical causes 137–40
      psychological factors 140–5
   post-traumatic 226–8
   recovery of memory 145–6
   retrograde 227–8
   substance misuse 197
   Wernicke-Korsakoff syndrome 203
amphetamines 20, 196
amygdala
   aggression and violence 21–2
   damage to 22, 37
   dysfunction 34
anabolic steroids 20
antisocial personality disorder 2, 10–11, 136
anxiety in amnesic subjects 156
anxiolytics 204–5
aphasia 204
appropriate adult 64–5, 86
apraxia 204
Arrow-Dot Test 141
Asperger's syndrome 110

assessment
  ADHD 91–104
  difficulties and conflicts 318
  expert witnesses 251–4
  preparation for 250–1
  suspects/defendants 70–3
  witnesses 60–1
  see also tests
Assessment of Capacity in Adults: Interim Guidance for Psychologists 237
Atkins v Virginia [2002] 276
attention 233
attention-deficit hyperactivity disorder 27, 81–107
  assessment 91–104
    classification of symptoms 91–5
    cognitive/neuropsychological assessment 100–1
    consistency across different sources 102–3
    consistency across tests 102
    consistency across time 103
    developmental history and interview 97
    differential diagnosis vs comorbid issues 103–4
    effort 101
    information from records 98
    interviews with others 97–8
    medication status 99
    mental state 101–2
    presentation and behaviour 98–9
    presentation to court 96
    rating scales 99–100
    recommendations 104
  and conduct disorder 9–10
  criminal responsibility 87–9
  developmental course 81–4
    compliant personality 83
    confrontational interpersonal style 83–4
    inattention 83
    labile temperament 83–4
    lack of internal controls 82–3
    sensation-seeking behaviour/recklessness 82
  fitness to plead 86–7
  mitigation of sentence 89–91
  police interview 84–6
    appropriate adult 86
    attentional problems 85
    interrogative suggestibility 85
    maladaptive coping strategies 84–5
    memory problems 85–6
    need for immediate gratification 85
    vulnerability 84
attention-deficit hyperactivity disorder (ADHD) 2
attentional deficit 85

Autism Diagnostic Interview–Revised 114, 121
Autism Diagnostic Observation Scale–Generic (ADOS-G) 115, 123, 125
Autism Quotient 114
autistic spectrum disorders 54, 109–33
  behaviour, interests and activities 119–22
  central coherence 118–19
  diagnosis 113–15
    confusing issues 115–17
    good practice 114–15
    personal interaction 113–14
  emotional understanding and empathy 120
  executive functioning 118
  forensic assessments 122–7
  high functioning 110, 115
  interview analysis 121–2
  range of 109–12
  referral 112–13
  social cognition 117–18
  Theory of Mind tests 119
  triad of impairments 109
Autobiographical Memory Interview 155
automatism 137, 138–9, 150, 165–91
  and epilepsy 167–74
    aggression and violence 168–9
    classification and description 168
    and criminal behaviour 170–3
    factors influencing 169–70
    practical advice 173–4
  general defences 182
  insane 151, 166–7, 183–7, 332
  legal perspective 178–80
    Fitness to Plead and Insanity Act 1991 179
    use of automatism defence 179–80
  psychogenic 151
  sane 151, 166, 332
  and sleepwalking 174–7
  specific defences 182–8
    diminished responsibility 182–3
    insanity 183–7
    legal reforms 187–8

Barkley Symptom Scales 100
Beck Anxiety Inventory 156, 213
Beck Depression Inventory 156, 157, 213
Behavioural Assessment of Dysexecutive Syndrome (BADS) 125, 155, 235–6, 318
behavioural observation, ADHD 98–9
benzodiazepines 20, 204–5
binge drinking 199
binomial test 253
blackouts 136, 137
Block Design Test 118
borderline disorder 2
Boston Naming Test 156

brain injury
    acquired 12–14
    expert witnesses 247–65
    traumatic *see* traumatic brain injury
Bratty v Attorney General for Northern Ireland [1963] 179, 185, 187
British Picture Vocabulary Scale II 60
British Psychological Society
    Code of Ethics and Conduct 304–7
    Generic Professional Practice Guidelines 320
    Investigatory Committee 307–9
    survey of court work 302–4
Brixton Spatial Anticipation Test 155, 157
Brown Attention Deficit Disorder Scales (BADDS) 100
bullying 54
Butler Report 187
Byrne [1960] 182

CAGE 212
Cambridge University Obsessions Questionnaire 121
Camden Test 253
cannabis 20, 196, 205–6
capacity 54, 58, 256, 323
    traumatic brain injury 237–8
cautioning 62, 63
    understanding of 71
central coherence 118–19
challenging behaviours 16
Change Readiness & Treatment Eagerness Scale (SOCRATES) 212
charging, safeguards following 65
children
    age of criminal responsibility 68
    aggression in 9
    conduct disorder 10
    traumatic brain injury 305
Children's Act 1989 321
circumscribed interests 120
Civil Procedure Rules 223, 248
clarity of reports 311
clinical interview
    ADHD 97
    autistic spectrum disorders 121–2
    traumatic brain injury 229–31
clinical neuropsychology 1
cocaine 20, 195, 207–8
codeine 208
cognitive assessment
    traumatic brain injury 231–7
    attention and information processing 233
    executive ability 234–7
    intelligence 231–2
    memory 233–4
cognitive deficit 10
cognitive empathy 32–3

cognitive skills 60
Coin-in-Hand Test 156
Competence Assessment for Standing Trial for Defendants with Mental Retardation (CAST-MR) 67
competence of psychologists 304
competency 2, 147
complex partial seizures 167
compliant personality
    ADHD 83
    intellectual disability 60, 71
computed tomography, aggression and violence 23–4
Computerized Assessment and Response Bias Test (CARB) 271
conduct disorder 9–10
    children 10
    see also antisocial personality disorder 10
confabulation 55, 56, 60
    Wernicke-Korsakoff syndrome 203
confessions to experts, omitting reference to 314–15
confidentiality 318–20
    absolute 319
    contractual 319
    discretionary 319
    limited 319
    malingering 277
conflict of interest 322–3
confrontational style 83–4
Conners' Child and Adult Rating Scales 100
consent 323
consistency of reports 311
continuing professional development 249
Continuous Performance Test 102
coping strategies, maladaptive 84–5
Court of Protection 256
court work, surveys of 302–4
crack 20, 196, 207
crimes
    acquisitive 195
    admissions of 321–2
    against people with intellectual disability 53–4
    hate 53
    of passion 136, 142
criminal behaviour
    epileptic automatism 170–3
    substance misuse
        acquisitive offending 195
        violent offences 194–5
Criminal Procedure (Insanity Act) 1964 66
Criminal Procedure (Insanity Act) 1991 66
Criminal Procedure (Insanity and Unfitness to Plead) Act 1991 150

children (*cont.*)
  Criminal Procedure Rules 248
  criminal responsibility
    ADHD 87–9
    age of 68
    amnesia 148–51
    intellectual disability 68–9
    and substance misuse 196–7
curriculum vitae 248

Daubert criteria 252, 278
deaffectualization 141
defendants
  amnesia 152–7
    anxiety and depression 156
    general intellectual function 154
    memory 154–5
    motivation 156–7
    naming 156
    perception 156
    planning and organization 155–6
  assessment 70–3
  intellectual disability 61–4
    likelihood 61–2
    vulnerability 62–3
definitive response bias 268
delirium tremens 199
Delis Kaplan Executive Function System (DKEFS) 156
dementia 252
  aggression in 17–18
  alcoholic 203–4
depersonalization 141
depression in amnesic subjects 156
detention, fitness for 64
Diagnostic Interview for Social and Communication Disorders (DISCO) 114
Diagnostic and Statistical Manual of Mental Disorders see DSM-IV
Digit Span tests 280
diminished responsibility 88, 166
  automatism 182–3
  substance misuse 197
disclosure 318–20
disinhibition 12
dissociative amnesia 141, 144
dissociative identity disorder 141
dissociative states 166, 177–8
  see also automatism
distraction 83
Domestic Violence, Crime and Victims Act 2004 66, 69, 150
Doors and People Memory Test 155, 157
Dot Counting Test 281
DPP v Majewski [1976] 149
drug intoxication 139
drug misuse *see* substance misuse
drug offences 195–6

DSM-IV
  acquired brain injury 12
  ADHD 81, 92, 93–5
  antisocial personality disorder 11
  autism 115
  conduct disorders 9
DuPaul ADHD Rating Scale 100
duping delight 152
duress 88, 181
Dusky v United States [1960] 147
Dutch courage 197
Dysexecutive Questionnaire (DEX) 235–6

ecstasy 139, 195, 206–7
electrodermal studies 120
Embedded Figures Test 118
emotion recognition
  labelling tasks 120
  matching task 120
  sorting task 120
emotional lability 83, 86
emotional understanding, tests of 120
empathy
  cognitive 32–3
  impaired 32–3
  loss of 225
  tests of 120
England and Wales Mental Capacity Act 2005 237
epilepsy 54, 137, 167–74
  and aggression 18–19
  and automatism 167–74
    aggression and violence 168–9
    classification and description 168
    and criminal behaviour 170–3
    factors influencing 169–70
    practical advice 173–4
  complex partial seizures 167
ethical dilemmas 310–18
  assessment materials, notes and documents 315–18
  expectations of solicitors 310–11
  modified reports 311–15
ethical issues 304–7
executive deficit 9, 118, 154, 225
  amnesic subjects 155–6
  post-head trauma 234–7
expert witness 247–65
  assessment 251–4
    preparing for 250–1
  becoming 247–9
  conference with Counsel 257–8
  confessions to, omitting reference 314–15
  further opinions 256–7
  giving evidence 260–3
  joint statements 258–9
  post-trial 263–4
  report 254–6

taking instructions 249–50
  trial 259–60
eyewitness identification 54–5
Eysenck Personality Questionnaire 212

facial expressions 27–8
factual errors in reports 311
Fake Bad Scale 240
'faking bad' 267–8
'faking good' 267–8
falls 224
Faux Pas Test 119, 123, 125
FEEST 123, 125
Fitness Interview Test–Revised (FIT-R)
  67, 126
fitness to be detained 64
fitness to plead, criteria for 67
  ADHD 86–7
  amnesia 146–8
  intellectual disability 66–8
Fitness to Plead and Insanity Act 1991 179
flunitrazepam 139
forensic neuropsychology
  definition 1
  psychologists' roles 1
forensic psychiatry 2
forgetfulness 88, 234
  see also amnesia
frontal lobe paradox 232
Frontal Systems Behaviour Scale 254
fugue states 178
functional abilities 2

$GABA_B$ 139
GABA receptors 204
Gage, Phineas 15
gamma-hydroxybutyrate 196
giving evidence 325–7
  expert witnesses 260–3
  on malingering 277–9
Glasgow Coma Score 153, 157
  traumatic brain injury 226
Graded Naming test 156
Gudjonsson Compliance Scale (GCS)
  60, 71, 213
Gudjonsson Suggestibility Scale (GSS) 55, 58,
  71, 126, 213, 318

Hamilton Depression Scale 122, 123
hate crimes 53
Hayling and Brixton test 236
Hayling Sentence Completion Test
  155, 157
head injury 137
heroin 195, 208
Homicide Act 1957 149, 182, 197
hyperkinetic syndrome 92
hypoglycaemic attacks 137

hysterical personality 136
  amnesia 140

ICD-10
  ADHD 91–2
  autism 115
Ice Cream Van Test 119
ictal aggression 18
ictus 167
illusion of transparency 63
imaging see neuroimaging
immediate gratification 85
impartiality 322–3
impression management 268
impulsivity 2, 26, 82–3
inattention 83
incompetence 66
information processing 233
inhibitory control 26–7
  loss of 225
insane automatism 151, 166–7, 183–7
insane in bar of trial 66
insanity 197
instrumental aggression 7, 31–4
  impaired empathy 32–3
  insensitivity to punishment 31–2
  integrated emotions systems model 33–4
integrated emotions systems model 33–4
integrity 305
intellectual ability 71
  amnesic subjects 154
intellectual disability 53–79
  acting as suspect/defendant 61–4
    assessment 70–3
    likelihood 61–2
    vulnerability in police station/court 62–3
  acting as witness 53–61
    assessment of ability 60–1
    likelihood 53–4
    special measures 59–60
    support 57–60
    vulnerability 54–7
  crimes against people with 53–4
  criminal responsibility 68–9
  fitness to plead 66–8
  safeguards 64–5
    following charging 65
    police station 64–5
  verbal understanding 56–7
  vulnerability 53
intelligence 231–2
intent 2
  and voluntary intoxication 196–7
  see also mens rea
internal control, lack of 82–3
International Classification of Diseases and
  Related Health Problems 10th
  revision see ICD-10

interrogative suggestibility 85
intimidation of witnesses 58
Iowa gambling task 30
IQ 232
    understanding of court proceedings 58

Jackson v Indiana [1972] 67
joint statements 258–9

ketamine 139, 196
Key Search test 236
Korsakoff's syndrome 201

lability 83
    affective 13
    emotional 83, 86
language skills 60
learning disability and aggression 16–17
legal language, comprehension of 56–7
legal rights 63
Letter Cancellation Test 102
Lishman's Organic Psychiatry 2
literacy 71
Liverpool Model of Witness Support, Preparation and Profiling 59
Loftus, Elizabeth 324
LSD 195

MacArthur Competence Assessment Tool–Criminal Adjudication (MacCAT-CA) 67
MacArthur Law and Neuroscience Project 69
McNaughton Rules 149, 182, 186, 198
magnetic resonance imaging
    aggression and violence 23–4
    traumatic brain injury 229
Majewski lack of intent defence 145, 149
maladaptive coping strategies 84–5
malingering 267–99
    adaptational model 275
    amnesia 151–2, 269
    case studies 288–92
    confidentiality 277
    criminological model 275
    definition 270
    diagnostic impression 274
    evidence in court 277–9
    failure to identify 276–7
    faking good vs faking bad 267–9
    motivation for 275–6
    neurocognitive dysfunction 268
    pathogenic model 275
    prevalence 272–4
    setting and types of symptoms 269–70
    tests of 279–87
        Raven's Standard Progressive Matrices 283–4
        Test of Memory Malingering 284–5
        Validity Indicator Profile 286–7
        Word Memory Test 285–6
    vs suboptimal effort 270–2
manslaughter 35
Maudsley Addiction Profile (MAP) 212
MDMA *see* ecstasy
mechanical forces in head trauma 224–5
memory
    in ADHD 85–6
    amnesic subjects *see* amnesia
    post-head trauma 233–4
    recovery of 145–6
    repression 140–1
    semantic 55–6
memory functioning 60
memory loss *see* amnesia
mens rea 1, 2, 68, 87, 146, 165–6, 180, 181
mental age 68
Mental Capacity Act (England and Wales) 2005 112, 237, 255
Mental Control Test 156–7
Mental Health Act 1983 65, 69
methadone 208
3,4-methylenedioxymethamphetamine *see* ecstasy
methylphenidate 196
Miller Forensic Assessment of Symptoms 268
Millon Clinical Multiaxial Inventory III 101, 212, 268
Minnesota Multiphasic Personality Inventory (MMPI-2) 212, 240, 267
Miranda v Arizona [1966] 63
Misuse of Drugs Act 1971 195
mitigation of sentence 89–91
modified reports 311–15
    clarity and consistency 311
    deletion of reference to documents provided 311–14
    factual errors 311
    omissions
        confessions 314–15
        unfavourable test findings 314
Modified Six Elements Test 318
moral/conventional distinction 120
morphine 208
motivation in amnesic subjects 156–7
Multi-Agency Public Protection Panel Arrangements 322
Multiple Errands Test (MET) 235
multiple personality disorder 178
Myers v Elman [1940] 306

naming ability in amnesic subjects 156
National Adult Reading Test–Restandardised (NART-R) 232
National Adult Reading Test–Second Edition 154, 157
National Appropriate Adult Network 65

negative-response bias 267
  failure to identify 276–7
neurobehavioural disability 225
neuroimaging
  aggression and violence 22–5
    functional 24–5
    structural 23–4
  traumatic brain injury 228–9
  see also individual techniques
neuropsychiatry 2
neuropsychological assessment
  substance misuse 209–14
  traumatic brain injury 229–37
    clinical interview 229–31
    cognitive abilities 231–7
nicotine 204

Offences Against the Person Act 1861 181, 185
opiates 208–9
  withdrawal syndrome 208
orbitofrontal cortex 21
  damage to 15, 28, 37
other deception 268
OWLS 125

Paulhus Deception Scales 268
perception in amnesic subjects 156
performance tests 154
personality disorder 225
phencyclidine 139
Pictorial Recognition Memory Test 156, 157
pitfalls 304–7
planning and organization in amnesic subjects 155–6
police caution 62
Police and Criminal Evidence Act 1984 64, 65
police interview
  ADHD 84–6
    appropriate adult 86
    attentional problems 85
    interrogative suggestibility 85
    maladaptive coping strategies 84–5
    memory problems 85–6
    need for immediate gratification 85
  intellectual disability 62
police station
  safeguards at 64–5
  vulnerabilities in 62–4
Porteus Mazes Test 11
Portland Digit Recognition Test 280
positron emission tomography
  aggression and violence 24–5
  traumatic brain injury 229
post hoc ergo propter hoc 225
post-concussional syndrome 238–41
post-traumatic amnesia 226–8
postictal aggression 18, 169

prefrontal cortex
  in aggression 22
  damage to 14–16, 37
privileged material 312–14
Probation Orders 65, 70
professional issues 301–29
  assessment materials, notes and documents 315–18
  British Psychological Society Investigatory Committee 307–9
  confidentiality and disclosure 318–22
  conflict of interest and impartiality 322–3
  consent and capacity 323
  ethical dilemmas and difficulties 310–18
  ethical issues and pitfalls 304–7
  expectations of solicitors 310–11
  giving evidence 325–7
  modified reports 311–15
  surveys of court work 302–4
provocation 35
pseudopsychopathy 15
psychoactive substances
  illegal 205–9
  legal 198–205
    alcohol 198–204
    anxiolytics 204–5
    nicotine 204
psychogenic automatism 151
psychopathy 11–12, 111
Psychopathy Checklist–Revised 11
punishment, insensitivity to 31–2

R v Ante and Bailey [1983] 186
R v Antoine [2000] 184
R v Billy Joe Friend [2004] 86–7
R v Burgess [1991] 176, 178, 185
R v Cash [2004] 69
R v Charlson [1955] 179
R v David Blackender [2001] 89–90
R v Falconer [1990] 178
R v Hardie [1984] 185
R v Hennessy [1989] 186
R v Issitt [1978] 151
R v James [2006] 149
R v Karimi [2006] 149
R v Kemp [1957] 179, 184
R v Kingston [1994] 150
R v Lippman [1970] 186
R v M'Naghten [1843] 68
R v Parks [1992] 176
R v Pritchard [1836] 86
R v Quick [1973] 150, 178, 186
R v Robertson [1968] 66
R v Smith (Morgan) [2001] 149
R v Sullivan [1983] 180, 184, 185
rating scales, ADHD 99–100
Raven's Standard Progressive Matrices 101, 280, 281, 283–4

Re C [1994] 112
reactive aggression 7, 26–31
  inhibitory control theories 26–7
  reversal learning theories 27–9
  somatic marker hypothesis 29–31
recklessness 82
red-outs 136, 142, 143
reliability of witnesses 54
'REM sleep behaviour disorder' 177
reports
  disclosure 320
  expert witness 254–5
  modifications to 311–15
    clarity and consistency 311
    deletion of reference to documents provided 311–14
    factual errors 311
    omitting reference to confessions 314–15
    omitting unfavourable test findings 314
  for prosecution 320–1
  self-report 120
respect 304
responsibility 304–5
  criminal
    ADHD 87–9
    age of 68
    amnesia 148–51
    intellectual disability 68–9
    and substance misuse 196–7
  diminished 88, 166
    automatism 182–3
    substance misuse 197
retrograde amnesia 227–8
reversal learning 27–9
Rey 15-Item Test 252, 279, 281
Rey's Word Recognition Test 281
risk assessment
  aggression and violence 7
  substance misuse 214
Ritalin 196
Rivermead Behavioural Memory Test–Third Edition 60
road traffic accidents 224
Rohypnol 139

safeguards in criminal justice system 64–5
  after charging 65
  at police station 64–5
sane automatism 151, 166–7
schizophrenia and aggression 19–20
Schonell Graded Word Reading Test 71
self-deceptive enhancement 268
self-report 120
semantic memory 55–6
Sensation Seeking Scale 212
sensation-seeking behaviour 82
Severity of Dependence Scale 212
Sex-Ken ID 125

Sexual Offences Act 2003 112
Significant Others Scale 123
single proton emission computed tomography *see* SPECT
sleep drunkenness 175
sleepwalking 166, 167
  and automatism 174–7
social cognition 117–18
social communication, deficits in 10
Social Communication Questionnaire 114
Social Network Map 125
solicitors, expectations of 310–11
somatic marker hypothesis 29–31
somnambulism *see* sleepwalking
SPECT
  aggression and violence 24–5
  traumatic brain injury 229
startle response 21–2
Statements of Special Educational Need 306
stimulus-punishment 32
stimulus-reward 32
Strange Stories 119
Stroop interference test 11
Structured Interview of Reported Symptoms (SIR) 268
Structured Inventory of Malingered Symptomatology (SIMS) 268
suboptimal effort 267–99
  vs malingering 270–2
substance misuse 193–221
  and aggression 20–1
  amnesia 197
  criminal behaviour 194–6
    acquisitive offending 195
    violent offences 194–5
  and criminal responsibility 196–7
  diminished responsibility 197
  neuropsychological assessment 209–14
  and neuropsychological functioning 197–209
  and parenting 196
  psychoactive substances
    illegal 205–9
    legal 198–205
  risk assessment 214
suggestibility
  ADHD 85
  assessment 71
  intellectual disability 55, 58, 60
supervision order 69
suspects
  intellectual disability 61–4
    likelihood 61–2
    vulnerabilities in police station/court 62–4
Symptom Checklist-90-R 101
symptom validity testing 228, 279
Symptom Validity Tests 269, 271, 279

taking instructions 249–50
Test of Everyday Attention 318
Test of Memory Malingering 101, 156, 158, 252, 278, 279, 282, 284–5
tests
  consistency across 102
  disclosure of material 315–17
  emotional understanding 120
  empathy 120
  malingering 279–87
  performance 154
  theory-of-mind 119
  unfavourable findings, requests for omission 314
  see also individual tests
tetrahydrocannabinol *see* cannabis
Theft Act 1968 180
theory-of-mind 117–18
  deficit 10
  tests of 119
third parties, obtaining information from 318
Tourette syndrome 104
Trail-Making Test 11
trance states 141
transient global amnesia syndrome 137
traumatic brain injury 223–46
  and aggression 13–14
  capacity 237–8
  children 305
  mechanical forces involved 224–5
  neuropsychological assessment 229–37
    clinical interview 229–31
    cognitive abilities 231–7
  post-concussional syndrome 238–41
  severity 225–9
    Glasgow Coma Score 226
    neuroimaging 228–9
    post-traumatic amnesia 226–8
trial of facts 66

unconscious defence 188
unfit to plead 66
US v Greer [1998] 277

Validity Indicator Profile 278, 281, 282, 286–7
verbal abilities, deficit in 9

verisimilitude 235
vigilance 233
violence *see* aggression and violence
violence inhibition mechanism model 33
Visual Object and Space Perception Battery 156
vulnerable witnesses
  ADHD 54–7, 84
  intellectual disability 62–4
  special measures 59

Warrington's Recognition Memory Tests 155, 157, 279
Wechsler Adult Intelligence Scale–Third Edition (WAIS-III) 60, 71, 125, 154, 231, 280
Wechsler Memory Scale–Third Edition (WMS-III) 155, 233
Wechsler Test of Adult Reading (WTAR) 154, 232
Wender Utah Rating Scale 100, 102
Wernicke-Korsakoff syndrome 201–3
whiplash injury 224, 239
Whitehouse v Jordan [1981] 306
Wilson v United States [1968] 148
Wisconsin Card Sorting Test 11, 19, 155, 157
witness
  ability to act as 60–1
  compliant 55
  intellectual disability 53–61
  intimidation 58
  likelihood of acting as 53–4
  reliability 54
  semantic memory 55–6
  suggestibility 55, 58, 60
  support for 57–60
  vulnerable
    ADHD 54–7, 84
    intellectual disability 62–4
    special measures 59
  see also giving evidence
Word Memory Test 252, 271, 279, 282, 285–6

Youth Justice and Criminal Evidence Act 1999 54, 58

Zoo Map test 236